NEVADA'S TURBULENT YESTERDAY

WESTERNLORE GHOST TOWN SERIES I

Nevada's Turbulent Yesterday

...a Study in Ghost Towns

by

Don Ashbaugh

WESTERNLORE PRESS ... 1980

Library of Congress Catalog No. 63-13925
ISBN 0-87026-024-3

First Printing February 1963
Second Printing August 1963
Third Printing March 1964
Fourth Printing February 1967
Fifth Printing September 1980

PRINTED IN THE UNITED STATES OF AMERICA BY WESTERNLORE PRESS

FOR MY WIFE, ALICE . . .

Who has been the inspiration for this book
since long before it was written.*

---

*Alice died a week after her husband's burial.

"Thanks an Awful Lot"

IN RESEARCHING FOR SUCH A BOOK AS THIS it is necessary to consult every source which might yield a tiny tidbit of interesting (or pertinent) material. Looking back through the years it seems that I have pored through vast piles of brittle old newspapers, read many bundles of treasured old letters and studied scores of books. Oddly, not many volumes on Nevada history are available, except the many written about Virginia City and the Comstock Lode. For that reason this author has been surprised numerous times to stumble across old Nevada information where it might never be expected. An example is the fine early Pioche material which was found in a book titled *A Yankee Trader in the Gold Rush*. Certainly, that title wouldn't indicate a source of Nevada historical lore.

This writer is so deeply indebted to so many persons that it would be impossible to list them all, although I really appreciate the aid all have given me.

I must express my deep appreciation to A. E. Cahlan, long-time general manager, and John F. Cahlan, former managing editor, of the *Las Vegas Review-Journal* for their assistance and support through the years. Most of the incidents related in this book previously have been printed in that newspaper as a weekly Sunday feature series titled "Ghost Towns of Nevada." This series, which has appeared regularly since January 1956, was presented the 1959 Award of Merit by the American Association for State and Local History and has won other honors during the years since it started.

I cannot fail to express my sincere thanks to Clara Beatty, director of the Nevada State Historical Association, and her associates, who went far beyond their regular duties to assist me at all times. Too, Nell Murburger, that fine contemporary author of the Great Basin scene, and my good friend, E. W. "Shorty" Darrah of Winnemucca, who has visited and photographed more of Nevada's ghost towns than any other man, have voluntarily aided this writer a great deal through the years.

It would take pages to list all of the newspapermen in Nevada, the various libraries in the western states, and elsewhere, who have given of their time and help, and the scores of publishers, authors and heirs of authors who have granted me permission to use material from various publications.

To them I say with all of the appreciation in my heart, "Thanks an awful lot." Without the co-operation of all, this volume could not have been written. I am very grateful.

DON ASHBAUGH.

Las Vegas, Nevada, July, 1960

PUBLISHER'S NOTE

BECAUSE of the untimely death of Don Ashbaugh, and his wife
Alice, the publishers have been denied the usual close cooperation and help of the author in bringing a work of this magnitude
to press. It has been most necessary for us to lean heavily on the
surviving members of his family, and his friends. For their great
patience and help we are deeply grateful.

To Robert L. Brown, editor, and his staff at the *Las Vegas
Review-Journal*, Clara S. Beatty and her staff at the Nevada State
Historical Society, to David F. Myrick, E. W. Darrah, Theron
Fox, and the many others who have assisted in the almost impossible task of sorting out and properly crediting the photographic
material accompanying the book, we acknowledge this help
with deepest thanks and appreciation. You have been the vital
assistance in making the book possible.

Without the usual close liaison between author and publisher
in an historical work, there is always the possibility of the sins of
omission and oversight. If such be the case, please forgive us as
publishers, for we have striven valiantly. And, please know, that
if Don Ashbaugh could have lived to see his work through to
fruition, no friend of his, nor assistee in this task, would ever
have been neglected, or missed in the final count.

THE PUBLISHERS.

Contents

Illustrations

Just So You'll Know . . .

THIS IS A STORY ABOUT NEVADA'S GHOSTS, tales of long-gone towns and the rugged individuals who built them . . .

Of men with hope in their eyes who braved the unknown, laughed at hardships and death, lived and loved violently, drank prodigiously, and never gave up their search for the beckoning bonanza at the rainbow's end . . .

Of women who followed them, fought with and for them, loved them and in a great many cases buried them.

It is a story of the hundreds of Nevada towns which boomed, bloomed and withered during the last 100 years. Some have returned entirely to their original dust and desert brush. Others have as the only reminders of their heyday a few heaps of rubble, rock piles of mine dumps and forlorn, forgotten graveyards. The remnants of many consist of a few shacks of sun-bleached rough lumber, the grain of the boards sandblasted into sharp relief by years of unhindered winds, the dripping rust from nail-heads staining brownish teardrops down their length. Yet there are quite a number of brave, never-say-die wraiths of once-bustling, busy and populous bonanza cities clinging tenaciously to life in the quiet, diminished tempo of shriveling old age.

These are Nevada's ghost towns—more than 1300 of them.

To Genoa and Gold Hill in the West, Pioche and Osceola on the eastern border, to frozen Charleston and Mountain City in the extreme north, and to the riverports, Eldorado and Callville, in the sunny southern tip and to everywhere in between, the miners and the Mormons, the gamblers and the saloonkeepers, the mistresses and the ministers—and all the others of every ilk and type—found their way and created the now dead or dormant communities.

They all flourished for various lengths of time and then languished or died as reports came in of richer strikes on the other side of the hill someplace. They ranged in size from not less than twenty-five inhabitants and at least one saloon, to "modern" cities with populations in the thousands.

Their existence left a jumble of heterogeneous names on the maps and in the histories of Nevada. Since nearly all of them were the result of the wide hunt for precious metals, many bear titles from the mineral lexicon. Strangely for a southwestern state, there are relatively few Spanish names. There are quite a few towns which were christened for personages who achieved more or less fame. Two were labeled for the automobiles driven by the twentieth-century prospectors who located them—a National and a Packard. Important Tuscarora was named for a civil war gunboat. Some town baptizers either were very literal or had twisted senses of humor—they bear such labels as Pizen Switch, Lousetown, Mazuma and

Pronto. The syllable "pah" means "water" in Paiute and there are a number of Indian names throughout the state in which it appears, such as Tonopah, Weepah, Pahranagat and Pahrump. Hiko also is Indian, meaning "white man." Its twin, Elko, means "white woman." Together they symbolize the female strength in survival, Hiko today being very much a ghost while Elko is a major community and an important county seat.

You should know a few facts about Nevada to enjoy the full flavor of these tales. Since Alaska's admission to the Union, it is now the seventh largest state in area, its 110,000 square miles of mountains and deserts stretching north and south from the thirty-fifth meridian at its southern point to the forty-second on the Idaho-Oregon border, and east and west from the 114th degree of longitude at the Utah border to the 120th on the California line.

This is more understandable in road map terms. The two shortest highways from the southern to northern borders, U. S. 93 and U. S. 95, are 583 and 616 miles in length. Across the state, east and west, the shortest route is U. S. 50, the old Pony Express and Overland Stage track, which is 403 miles, while its busier twin, U. S. 40, the original Humboldt Trail, stretches 419 miles between Utah and California.

In this mammoth area of magnificent distances are "no less than sixty-five groups and chains of mountains," noted the naturalist, John Muir, in 1878, "which rise to a height of about 8,000 to 13,000 feet above the level of the sea" and "every one of these is planted, to some extent, with coniferous trees, though it is only on the highest that we find anything that fairly may be called a forest."

But tree-clad mountains are spread all over Nevada, one of them, 11,910-foot Mt. Charleston, is only a forty-minute drive from sun-drenched Las Vegas.

And less than an hour's drive from Las Vegas will put one at the state's lowest point, on the Colorado River just below Davis Dam, where the elevation is 450 feet, which still is further above sea level than the mean elevation of several states. The state's high point, Boundary Peak near the California border, rises 13,145 feet in elevation. Clear across the state on the Utah border is Mt. Wheeler, second highest at 13,061 feet, which mothers a living glacier.

If the above doesn't completely dispel the idea that Nevada is a copy of the dreaded Sahara, sitting in the bottom of a dry, desolate sun-scorched bowl, consider the further startling fact that the state's overall mean elevation is 5,500 feet above sea level, according to the National Geographic Society. This makes it the fifth highest state in the nation.

Since World War II, millions of tourists have "discovered" Nevada, but very few realize that it was actually the last segment of the United States to be explored by white men. The Spaniards had wandered all over the southwest for 300 years without straying into any of its vast area. The fur hunters, too, had gone around it in their searches for virgin trapping grounds, simply because Nevada's rivers practically all flow into desert sinks and didn't offer a water roadway for the trappers.

Actually, only four streams arising within the state ever reach the Pacific. This lonesome quartet is the Muddy, which flows into the Colorado in the South, the Owyhee, Bruneau and Salmon, which rise in the mountains just below the northern border and reach the Snake, thence the Columbia. The Owyhee's name is not an Indian title. Originally, it was dubbed the "Sandwich Island River" in honor of a couple of Polynesian sailors who were killed along its banks by Indians while with a Hudson's Bay Company trapping expedition. When later the name of the islands was changed to "Hawaii," it seemed fitting to somebody to make the river's name conform to the new designation. Whoever he was, he spelled it phonetically, hence, "Owyhee."

It apparently seemed logical to the early day trappers that the melting deep snows on the west side of the Continental Divide had to reach the Pacific some way. The legend became wide-spread that across Nevada a wide stream flowed to the Pacific. It was given a name, the Santa Buenaventura, and was shown on early maps long before any white man ever dared to wander out across the Great Basin.

Spanish fathers in Santa Fe, then a venerable city nearly three hundred years old, decided in 1776 to seek a shorter route to California than the way across Arizona. Father Francisco Silvestre Velez de Escalante started out to find such a course. He went north, then west and reached western Utah, where he turned south and was within a few miles of what is now the eastern Nevada border when he veered eastward on his return trek to New Mexico. If he had ventured just a few miles farther west he would have moved the "discovery" of Nevada ahead exactly fifty years.

It was that much longer before three well-known Rocky Mountain trappers, Smith, Sublette and Jackson purchased the Ashley and Henry fur trapping business at the annual rendezvous near Salt Lake City and decided that Jedediah Smith should explore westward, scouting for new trapping grounds.

Smith left Salt Lake Valley on August 22, 1826, "with a party of 15 men for the purpose of exploring the country S.W. which was entirely unknown to me." His entry into what now is Nevada a week or so later is the earliest recorded visit to the area by any white man. He apparently entered what is now the southeastern corner of the State, near the present towns of Caliente and Panaca, and followed the route of the present Union Pacific railroad's main line through Meadow Valley Wash, "which I called the Adams River in compliment to our President." He went on to the Muddy River, so titled by Smith's clerk, Harrison G. Rogers in his daily journal and visited the Indian rock salt mines, near the confluence with the Virgin, which he named for a member of the party, Thomas Virgin. He trekked down to the Colorado, across it and southwest to the

Mojave villages north of Needles, thence across the desert through Cajon Pass to Southern California. Smith made a second trip the following year, this time following down the Virgin from southern Utah to the Colorado and then over his previous route.

Three years behind him came rugged men from Santa Fe looking for the shorter path to California which Escalante had failed to find.

José Antonio Armijo led a party which established trade between California and New Mexico over what became known as the Spanish Trail across southern Nevada. He left for the westward trek on November 7, 1829, and camped Christmas Day near present Littlefield, Arizona, a few miles east of the Nevada border on the Virgin River. Rafael Rivera, a daring scout, pushed forward on an exploration trip. Armijo's party followed down the Virgin and then along the Colorado westward through rugged Boulder Canyon and camped near the mouth of what since has been named Vegas Wash, the drainage stream from the Las Vegas Springs. History does not record whether it was this party or some later Spanish Trail group that named the now-lusty resort area "Las Vegas," which means "The Meadows." River turned up to rejoin Armijo and the party at Vegas Wash on January 7, 1830. He reported having reached the Mojave River and told of finding an Indian village on the Amargosa River at the south end of what is well known as Death Valley.

Rafael Rivera probably was the lone trail blazer of the route which became the busy Spanish Trail, later the Mormon Trail. At any rate, he guided the Armijo party generally southwestward from Vegas Wash and into Southern California, the first recorded party of whites to see Las Vegas Valley.

In 1828, Peter Skene Ogden, trapping for the Hudson's Bay Company, came southward up the Owyhee and trapped down the Humboldt.

In 1833 Captain Benjamin Eulalie de Bonneville sent Joseph R. Walker from the Green River rendezvous with a party to explore the Great Salt Lake and the "unknown country" to the west in search of beaver.

Walker, a veteran trapper, was so curious that he went all the way to the coast. His name remains in the Walker River and its sink, Walker Lake, in Nevada and Walker Pass in the Sierra.

General John C. Frémont, then a lieutenant, with his guide, Kit Carson, and a party, came south from the Columbia River through western Nevada searching for the fabled Buenaventura River in the winter of 1843-44. They didn't find it and Frémont gave Carson's name to one of Nevada's rivers and valleys.

After this, traffic across Nevada became continuously heavier, hardly a year passing without parties traversing the long desert and mountain trails.

When the Mormons reached the Salt Lake Valley in 1847, parties headed by such doughty lads as Jefferson Hunt, Howard Egan and Porter Rockwell were sent on frequent trips to the coast for needed supplies and stock. It was Egan who blazed the mid-state route, shorter than the Humboldt way. The famed Pony Express, Overland Stage and transcontinental telegraph lines later followed the Egan trail.

Identity of the first discoverer of gold or silver in Nevada is a secret kept by the shadowy inhabitants of the ethereal world. No two historians seem to agree on the matter.

Who was first to lift the lid from Nevada's great trove of minerals? Hunt, Bigler, Prouse, or Orr? Does it make any great difference? Not any more than the solution of that other problem some historians worry about, "Did old 'Pancakes' Comstock sleep with his whiskers under the covers or outside them?"

Whoever it was, apparently it was a Mormon—and they really weren't hunting mineral riches because Brigham didn't want his flock chasing after Mammon.

The discovery of gold in California brought a continuing and rapidly growing parade of wealth seekers across Nevada and some stayed and settled in small clusters of habitations. As more and more mineral was found, prospectors spread in all directions over the huge unpopulated area, tapping the hiding places of subsequent millions of dollars' worth of Nature's hoard.

Nevada's first great boom burst wildly and richly in 1860, multiplied madly in every direction, and then faded and became dormant as the century warned. It awoke again in 1900 when Jim Butler's burro went wandering and the lazy old Belmont farmer sat down beneath a mesquite to rest and knocked off a chunk of rock which led to the great Tonopah strike. It started a chain reaction which brought about discovery of Goldfield, Rhyolite, Rawhide, Fairview, Wonder, Seven Troughs, Jarbidge and the rollicking other rich diggings of the first decade of the Twentieth Century.

A great many of the tales of the raw, rich, riotous, early-day towns haven't been told. These stories are among those related in this book, some old, some new, and some "blue."

Of course Virginia City, with its fabulous Comstock Lode which purportedly "paid for the Civil War," was the largest and most fabulous of all Nevada's early communities. Naturally, practically all authors who have since written about the early Nevada scene have concentrated on the Queen City and its doings to the exclusion of the others, which also deserve a share of the glory. It is these others which take the spotlight in this narrative. So let's travel the Bonanza Trail of the nineteenth century and bring back to life the long dehydrated doings of those days and the memories of the men and women who made history—but, forgot to write it.

—Don Ashbaugh

PART ONE

'Way Down South

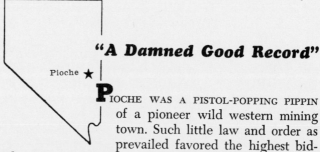

"A Damned Good Record"

Pioche ★

PIOCHE WAS A PISTOL-POPPING PIPPIN of a pioneer wild western mining town. Such little law and order as prevailed favored the highest bidder—the sheriff's job at a reputed $4,000 annually; mighty potent pay for those days, and a richer golconda than most of the holes in the hills above town.

Nobody is certain just how many graves crowded the boothill cemeteries—somewhere in excess of two hundred of them. Records generally agree that the first seventy-five or seventy-six deaths occurred violently before anybody turned up his toes from natural causes. The only thing Pioche ever lacked to make it as famous a kill-'em-quick place as Dodge City, Deadwood or Tombstone was a paucity of press agentry. You can be certain that if there are any dull moments in that spectral world where the ghosts of the wild west gather, it is only because Pioche's quick-triggered specters are taking a siesta.

Probably another reason Pioche is so little known to the reading public is because it was so far from everywhere else in the raw, raucous early days. The movies and TV have glorified the gun-shooting episodes of many other towns, but as far as can be learned they've never even heard of Pioche. In fact, most Americans and a great many Nevadans don't know anything about Pioche. They should, it was in a class by itself.

The first recorded killing occurred March 29, 1868, just as the town was getting started. Frank P. Pitt, a saloon keeper, sampled his own stock so plentifully that he picked a fight with a gent named Jacob Colburn, who promptly ended Frank's spree with a well-placed shot. History records that "nothing was done with Colburn."

That set the pattern. Thompson and West's *History of Nevada, 1881* lists 36 of the subsequent "important" killings through the years—too many to note the details of each, but enough to prove that Pioche was no place for the faint of heart or slow of draw during its swaggering days.

Probably one of the finest on-the-spot descriptions of this early town was written by Franklin A. Buck, a college-educated gentleman who was one of Pioche's first merchants. It was in a letter to his sister in Maine dated November 3, 1870, appearing in *A Yankee Trader in the Gold Rush.*

He portrayed early Pioche this way—"You are right in thinking that we live here just as we please. If we want a hot whisky toddy we have it. If we choose to lie abed late, we do so. We come and go and nobody wonders and no Mrs. Grundy talks about it. We are free from all fashions and conventionalities of Society, so called with you. I like this.

"About one half of the community are thieves, scoundrels and murderers and then we have some of the best folks in the world and I don't know but what our lives and property are as safe as with you. You can go up town and get drunk and get shot very easily if you choose or you can live peaceably. I will send you the paper with an account of the last fight . . . I was in hopes eight or ten would have been killed at least, as these fighting men are a pest in the community.

"In Pioche we have two courts, any number of sheriffs and police officers and a jail to force people to do what is right. There is a fight every day and a man killed about every week. About half the town is whisky shops and houses of ill fame."

Even Virginia City, which likes to take credit for everything of note that ever occurred in Nevada, recognized early Pioche's superiority in the field of mortal mayhem. The *Territorial Enterprise* in 1872 complained, "Pioche is overrun with as desperate a class of scoundrels as probably ever afflicted any mining town and the law is virtually a dead letter . . . It is high time that something should be done, for as matters now stand, the name of Pioche has become a byword of reproach and a synonym for lawlessness throughout the state."

The U. S. government also took cognizance of the situation in a publication, *Mineral Resources West of the Rocky Mountains*, 1873, noting that ". . . two classes of persons reap a rich harvest, lawyers and 'roughs.' The former are paid to maintain titles and the latter to hold the ground. Pioche has been a bloody camp; but it is to be hoped that the days of violence are passing away . . ."

Undoubtedly, the Meadow Valley Wash Indians were the first Nevada natives ever to gaze upon a white man. He was Jedediah Smith, the earliest known explorer of the Great Basin, who passed through the area about the first of September, 1826, on his initial trip into "the unknown." Heavy travel westward in subsequent years went farther south along the Virgin River on the old Spanish Trail, later the Mormon Trail, but occasionally wanderers veered away from the main line and followed Smith's route. In later years it became a sort of shortcut alternate of the Mormon Trail, travelers leaving the regular route near Mountain Meadows, coming through Clover Valley, thence to Bennett's Wells—a few miles southwest of present Pioche—to Crystal Springs, and across the desert to Pahrump Valley where they re-joined the main route.

Most notable of these detouring parties was the group that since has become known as the ill-fated Death Valley Forty-Niners. This company split from the leadership of Captain Jefferson Hunt (noted veteran of the Mormon Battalion who had earlier made the overland trip) at Mountain Meadows to follow an abortive map. It showed a purported "Walker Cutoff" and led the party to Death Valley, after untold privations and misery, second only to the Donner Party.

The next exploring party of any note to visit the area was a group called the "White Mountain Boys" from Parowan, Utah, who had been sent out in 1858 on a scouting expedition by Mormon church authorities, seeking possible new areas for settlement, in case an exodus from Utah became necessary during the nationwide furor aroused by the Mountain Meadows massacre. Some histories report that this group broke ground in Meadow Valley, near present Panaca, planted several acres of grain and built irrigation ditches. Subsequently, when the popular clamor subsided, they left these plantings to the Indians and returned home. However, in 1863 and 1864 small colonies were sent out from St. George to occupy Clover and Meadow Valleys, as well as Eagle and Spring Valleys further north, between Pioche and the present Utah state line.

Discovery of the heavy ores in the Highland Hills of Pioche definitely must be credited to the Paiutes. Undoubtedly, the Indian grapevine had made the crazy greed of Americans for "heavy rock" a subject of frequent gossip around the campfires of all Nevada Indians. Then, too, the Indians had witnessed the "foolish" hauling of lead ore from the old Potosi to the Las Vegas Springs in 1856 where the Mormons smelted it into brittle silver-studded lead. Through this episode, the Paiutes, although unaware of the value of the base metals, had learned that fire would melt down the stuff in the rocks so that it could be moulded into bullets. Hence, the long standing legend of the "silver bullets" made by Nevada Indians.

So, it was the Meadow Valley Indians, facing a long, tough winter, who divulged the location of the Pioche mines to Jacob Hamblin, "friend of the Indians," who lived in the Santa Clara Valley, west of St. George. The "discovery," some 450 miles southeast of Virginia City, was to produce about $100,000,000 worth of bullion.

Actions of the squirrels and other animals had indicated to the Paiutes that a hard winter was coming. As the rough weather closed in during the fall of 1863, they decided to trade secret Indian information for food. A delegation made the long trip to Hamblin's home and told him they knew of a rich ledge of "panaker," or "panacre," their word for silver, in the mountains to the west. They took Hamblin back and showed him. He put up a large stake near the spring at Panaca, claiming all the land in an area covering sixty square miles, which took in the entire Pioche district.

A short time later he returned with John Vandermark and Stephen Sherwood, who understood mining laws and knew a little about ore. They located a number of claims and took samples from the Panacker, Vermillion and Creole locations,—all of which subsequently became rich producers—and crudely processed some of the ore. One source says they managed to melt out 1400 pounds of metal. This amount is questioned by those who know the difficulty of smelting some of this state's complex formations.

When the group returned to Santa Clara Valley the men formally organized the Meadow Valley Mining District. The samples were taken to Salt Lake City by Vandermark and Sherwood and shown to Brigham Young and General P. E. Connor, then commanding U. S. Troops at Fort Douglas. Young was little interested in the silver, holding to his plan of expanding the Mormon economy through agriculture, but the reaction of General Connor was very different. He sent the samples to San Francisco and Denver and the assay report showed values of more than $300 per ton. A company was organized to develop the new fields early in 1864.

Indian trouble was encountered immediately. The Paiutes claimed the whites were poaching on their spring, and demanded they leave. Gifts of cash, food and trinkets appeased the group and the Indians departed. The miners immediately discovered they had merely started a chain-reaction blackmail parade, as different bands of aboriginal racketeers continued to arrive daily to make identical claims to the spring.

Eventually the miners ran out of white man's wampum and were forced to leave. Vandermark went to New York to raise funds and thought he had succeeded when he returned to the mines in 1865. But the eastern capitalists backed out when widespread Indian hostilities erupted throughout the west, and failed to come through with the needed cash. General Connor sent troops to subdue the Pioche Paiutes, but they might as well have stayed in Salt Lake City. The Indians merely faded into the brush when the soldiers arrived and reappeared with their demands the minute the troops trotted off.

As it always happened, the rumor of the rich Pioche ore spread with the speed of light through the western camps, and shortly prospectors began heading for the faraway new district. Sherwood, as recorder for the mining district, went to Salt Lake to obtain a book to list the claims.

While he was gone newcomers located on top of older claims. These secondary locations sowed the seeds of future armed guard warfare over Pioche's buried riches, caused many boothill killings and led to a multitude of lawsuits which dragged through the courts for years afterward.

The Pioche claims were located in a box canyon, a poor place to defend, and the Indians became so unruly that the miners spent most of their time at Panaca, twelve miles south, where a Mormon agricultural colony had been established. Overlapping location squabbles and Indian trouble caused Sherwood to sell his interests to newcomers and disappear from the scene. History of activities for the next two years is practically non-existent.

Many Nevadans believe that the name of this great eastern Nevada mining center is an Indian title. It isn't.

The fame of the rich Panacker ore had reached San Francisco. A French capitalist named F. L. A. Pioche in 1867 sent one of his men, Charles E. Hoffman, to acquire some of the rich holdings. It was this group which built the first small smelter. Fire bricks and castings had been shipped around the Horn, thence to the end of the Central Pacific's then-building line, probably Palisade. From there they were carried by muleback over the hundreds of miles to the mines. Bullion was transported back over the same route by the returning pack trains.

It was then natural that the initial operation should be known as "Pioche's" and, when the post office was established August 17, 1870, Uncle Sam dubbed it "Pioche," which it still is. Incidentally, that post office has never closed.

Actually, except for an odd twist of fate, it might have been named Ely—the title borne now by its lusty neighboring county seat, one-hundred miles northward. John H. Ely had found good prospects at Logan City in 1865 and with William H. Raymond, an investor from the east, built the mill at Hiko to handle the Irish mountain ore. The Pahranagat operations had declined badly by 1869 so Ely and Raymond went in the search for something better. They found it at Pioche and acquired some locations.

They dickered with Panaca Mormon farmers and, by promising to locate the plant at Panaca and pay for the hauling job with proceeds from its operation, they managed to make the move on credit.

First, the two operators brought ten tons of ore from their new Pioche mine the sixty miles across the desert to Hiko, treated it in their plant, and produced a nice bar of bullion. This chunk of silver was the final clincher in the deal to get the mill moved to Meadow Valley.

Bullionville, which helped considerably "to make" Pioche, resulted.

Ask any number of Nevadans what and where Bullionville was and maybe one of them might be able to give you a vague answer. Even then it would be a ten to one bet he'd be from Lincoln County. True, it didn't rank with the great towns of the bonanza days, but neither was it inconsequential among the state's more than thirteen hundred ghost towns. In the early seventies, when Virginia City, Austin, Eureka, Belmont and Pioche were Nevada's major cities, Bullionville certainly ranked among the first twenty in importance. It was a vital factor in Pioche development and, was the location of the initial successful mill operation that proved the richness of the Pioche ores after efforts to retrieve the values through crude smelters failed.

Then, too, it was the terminal of Nevada's third railroad, the narrow-gauge Pioche & Bullionville, which was completed in 1873, two years after the Virginia & Truckee began chuffing up Gold Canyon to the Mt. Davidson treasure trove and four years after the Central Pacific was built.

There are several versions of the manner in which John Ely and W. H. Raymond, after failing to produce a profit from the Irish mountain ores in their little five-stamp mill at Hiko, founded their fabulous fortunes at Pioche.

Of all the stories, I choose to put reliance in the memoirs written in 1908 by Charles Gracey for the Nevada State Historical Society. He had moved from the White Pine diggings to the Highland Mountain strike in 1868. During his first year at Pioche he had joined with some others, including Charley Meyers, a friend who knew the process, in burning charcoal and selling it to the Meadow Valley mine group headed by Monsieur Pioche.

"In November, 1869," he wrote, "I went over to where the Raymond and Ely people were at work and found Tom Greaves trying in vain to put steel into a pick. Here was my opportunity. I was a blacksmith by trade. I put the steel in and became great in an hour. John Ely was informed of the circumstance. He came to me and said, 'Gracey, you are just the man for whom we are looking; you stay here and do our work and you can board at our camp.'

"Board looked good to me and I stayed. They were building a furnace and had a threshing machine horsepower to run the blower. A German named Shuner was employed as the furnace expert. After some time of experimenting the furnace was declared a failure.

"While working at odd jobs I had by this time shown I understood machinery. Mr. Raymond came to me and said, 'Mr. C. P. Hall tells me that you are a machinist as well as a blacksmith.' I replied that I was.

"Said he, 'I never expected this furnace to work, but I wanted my partner Mr. Ely to be satisfied, which I think he now is. I have a silver mill in Pahranagat Valley. If you think that you could take it down and put it up again in good shape, I would have it brought over . . . and set up, I think that this ore can be worked by the same process.'

"I assured him that I could do any kind of machine work, having erected two sawmills in California . . . 'But,' we have no money. If we can take it out in the mine, we will pay you, and it also will make your mines more valuable.'

"I agreed that I would work without pay if he would furnish the grub. He replied that he could not even do that, but that John Ely, his partner, was acquainted with the Mormons in Panaca and could get grub from them. Moreover, he did not even own the mines as yet, but if I would promise to stay with him and build the mill he would buy the mine.

"That night around the camp fire were Pony Duncan, Bob Winans, the Burke brothers (Ed and Pat), myself and several others. All were very glum. The smelter was a failure. No one had any means and it was on the whole a rather dull outlook.

"After a while Mr. Raymond spoke and said to Mr. Burke (called 'Pat Maloy') 'This furnace is a failure. I have a proposition to make to you boys that own the Burke mine. I have a five stamp mill in Pahranagat Valley. I am willing to pay you $35,000 for the mine, provided you will wait for your money until I get the mill here and take out the ore.'

"All were very quiet for a time. Then Pony Duncan spoke up and said, 'I am willing to agree to that,' Bob Winans also agreed to it. The Burke brothers, who owned one half of the mine, said nothing . . . then Pat Burke asked, 'Where will we get anything to eat while we are doing all this?'

"Raymond replied that John Ely would see to getting grub. Then said Burke, 'It is all right,' and Mr. Raymond handed him his silver watch and turning to me, said 'Charlie, you are a witness that I have bought this mine and I give him this watch to bind the bargain. Boys, you are all witnesses. This watch is worth $60. Charlie, we will start for Pahranagat at once."

The group departed right away and went the eleven miles to a site near Panaca where they camped, first getting a "loaf of bread and a large piece of boiled beef" from Withe Walker, who was left to tend the camp at the mine.

The party then traveled the sixty miles to Hiko and "We took down the mill and made arrangements with residents of Meadow Valley to have it loaded on teams as they came in."

John Ely had arranged with the Panaca Mormons to haul the mill to the proposed site by promising to pay them after it was in operation and by promising them exclusive hauling rights to bring the ore from the Pioche mines to the mill.

The miners returned to the site selected, a mile northwest of the Panaca settlement, where they graded the mill site and built the road to the Pioche mines. Timbers were brought in for the new structure from the Clover Valley mills operated by Woods, Edwards, Roeder and John M. Pulsipher. The construction went along slowly, Gracey related, but in January, 1870, he felt he had the plant ready and tried out the five stamps on ore which already had been hauled from the mines.

"Mr. Raymond had gathered around him men who had some knowledge of working ore. The head man was L. B. Sever, an assayer and a good man," he wrote. "There also was a carpenter named Mortimer Fuller, afterwards District Judge. I had considerable trouble with the mill but finally got it started. The first night I stayed up all night. We drew off the charge from the pans into the settler and then drew off the quicksilver from the settler and strained it through a sack. In the morning I had the sack full of amalgam. Mr. Raymond came down about four in the morning and asked me how things were. I showed him the sack of amalgam. He pinched it and said, 'This is good, it squeaks. Gold and silver amalgam is the only one that will squeak.'

"Well, it was a success. The ore was worth $300 a ton and we were working seventy-eight percent. There was plenty of ore and in sixty days Raymond and Ely had paid every cent they owed and were rich men. We had shot off a gun that sounded around the world, but were not aware of it, at least I was not."

How right he was—that first squeak of amalgam between Raymond's thumb and finger brought the Pioche rush which boomed it to a community of ten thousand within a couple of years.

"When with our five stamp mill we proved how easily money could be taken out, that was the making of Pioche," Gracey wrote.

He continued, "I was chief engineer of the Raymond and Ely for seven years and had sixty stamps running the last five years. In that time the Raymond and Ely company produced seventeen millions. The Meadow Valley company did not produce as much. But that mine was also a good one and produced many millions."

The town which grew up around the mill originally was called Ely City, but because of the constant stream of bullion pouring from it as new stamps and Stetefeldt furnaces were installed to give up a larger percentage of the ore's gold and silver content, it became known to everybody as Bullionville. The name of Ely for a community had to wait a few years until the copper strikes in White Pine County gave the name permanently to its present county seat.

The Panaca Mormons, keeping a constant stream of wagons on the road, were well repaid for their original trust in Raymond, getting $5 a ton for hauling the ore from mine to mill. Reliable memoirs of pioneers claim as high as one-hundred-twenty teams daily were engaged in hauling Raymond and Ely ore to the mill prior to the advent of the railroad.

The Raymond and Ely Mining Co., incorporated in 1871, began to acquire a large number of claims and installed G. W. Lightner as superintendent. He sank a vertical shaft, a departure from the common method of descending on a forty-five degree angle, and at one-hundred feet struck one of the richest ore bodies ever found in the United States.

Raymond and Ely stock became the hottest thing on the San Francisco exchange. In August 1871 Meadow Valley stock was selling at $22, R. and E. was a dollar less at $21. In less than a year, Meadow Valley had dropped to $17.50 while Raymond and Ely had soared to $145 a share.

New strikes were reported daily. New companies popped up like toadstools after a rain. Operations were zooming. Hired gunmen protected the better diggings and some even erected stone forts.

Although gunfire was the accepted means of settling almost any dispute, even those of minor consequence, the battles over the rich mining locations were the principal causes of most of the killings. Overlapping claims were the subject of constant dispute and, while many of them were taken to court, more were settled by hired gunmen.

Competition was keen for iron-nerved pistoleers with reputations, and Pioche became the habitat of some of the greatest thugs of the period.

At the same time, the various litigants, who had hired the finest legal talent obtainable, were as greatly concerned about "fixing" the judges as they were in having the sheriff "in their pocket." From competition for his favor came the story, probably true, that the job of Lincoln County sheriff was "worth $40,000 a year," regardless of the salary received. Likewise, jury duty, in mining cases, was a highly lucrative "civic duty" and those favored for selection were said to have fattened the sheriff's boodle. It is a common story that the jury never retired to deliberate, but only to drop a boot on a rope from the courthouse window to pull up the pay-off, the most generous litigant gaining the decision.

Probably the most notable mining case in Pioche history was the Raymond and Ely suit against Hermes. Both companies claimed contiguous ground which was said to be the richest in the area. Each side believed it controlled the sheriff.

During the trial, saloonkeeper Mike McClosky, who ran one of the biggest bistros in town, was allegedly the go-between on the high-priced bribery which existed. He conveniently was stricken with an attack of gout, which supposedly kept him in his bed.

The story, as related by W. A. Chalfant, that fine historian of the early-day camps, relates that one morning a friend rushed to Mike's house and informed him that the saloon safe had been robbed.

Mike, showing great excitement, hobbled to the bar, which like all others stayed open day and night, and verified the fact that the safe was empty. Turning to his bartender, he asked, "Was anybody near this safe during the night?"

The liquor dispenser, innocent of what was occurring, replied, "Not a soul has been near it since you took the little box out of there at 3 A.M."

McClosky, immediately on the defensive, drew his pistol and declared, "I can make as good use of that cash as the sheriff."

He disappeared that day. Legend says he was later operating one of the "swellest" saloons in Brooklyn, probably purchased with the $30,000 in bribe money both sides had paid to buy off the sheriff.

When the verdict in the case was found for Hermes, members of the jury hired guards to escort them safely away from Pioche. Their payoffs made it worthwhile to leave.

The next real battle of note was over the Washington & Creole, also owned by Ely and Raymond. Tom and Frank Newland, brothers, located adjoining this property, on the upper side, and received permission to tunnel the Ely-Raymond claim to reach their own. In driving the shaft they encountered a bonanza vein in the Washington & Creole property. They obtained a thirty-day lease to work the vein, but when the time expired temptation proved too strong, they hired themselves an "army" of shoot-'em-quick lads and built fortifications at the mouth of the mine.

When Ely and Raymond failed to regain their property through the offices of the sheriff, they hired an "army" of their own. Heading it was Morgan Courtney, the "dandy" of the desperadoes. He always was dressed in the height of fashion, wore spotless white linen and kept his fingernails manicured, which certainly was unusual in Pioche. He had arrived with three pieces of luggage—a satchel, a Henry rifle and a six-

shooter with a handle well notched, He added three other fast-draw lads
to his troop, Michael Casey, Barney Flood and William Bethards.

The quartet offered to drive off the Newland gunmen in return for a
written promise to be allowed to work the mine for thirty days. The mine
owners accepted the offer.

Courtney, using guile instead of foolish bravado, sent a couple of cases
of whiskey to the hired defenders, the messenger informing them that it
came from the Newland brothers. Then, Courtney and his men waited until singing and shouting indicated the defenders were sufficiently soused,
and attacked. The fight was short and sweet. One of the defenders,
named Snell, was killed. Courtney and his men took possession. It was re-
liably reported that they netted $60,000 from their thirty days' working of
the mine.

Shortly afterwards a desperado named George McKinney, who had
killed three Italian woodchoppers near Elko, found it expedient to leave
that area, and arrived in Pioche. When he met Courtney, who was rumored to have killed a friend of McKinney's in Montana, they agreed the
town wasn't big enough for both of them. They decided to "come shootin'"
and did, with McKinney firing first from his half-hidden place of ambush.
Courtney was disabled by a bullet in the shoulder and when he fell
McKinney emptied his gun into the dapper former "chief." That ended
Courtney's career. The record says "McKinney was acquitted." The date
was August 1, 1873.

The life of Michael Casey, Courtney's partner, ended the same way.
He was depositing his $15,000 net from the Washington mine deal in a
bank when Thomas Gorson accosted him and asked for return of a $100
loan he had made the gunman. In the dispute Casey killed Gorson. Later
he heard that Jim Levy, a pistoleer with a high reputation from Deadwood, S. D., had said Casey fired without giving Gorson a chance. Casey
went gunning for Levy. The latter proved that his reputation had some
basis of fact, and blasted away. Mr. Casey's hopes of enjoying his hard
earned $15,000 ended with a swift, well placed shot.

The old files of the *Pioche Record* are filled with reports of other violent affairs. This for instance: "It is rumored that last night a man who
attempted to set fire to the gas house near Charleston bridge was seized
by the infuriated crowd and unceremoniously hanged to a lamp post."
That's all, period.

But times were changing and more and more solid citizens were arriving to gain a balance of community power—although it was wielded somewhat confusedly. The *Record* reported: "Woe unto the poor unfortunate
devils who steal a bottle of whiskey and a couple of boxes of musty cigars.
They must suffer for their crime. But a band of murderers shoot a man
in the back and then are permitted to roam unpunished. Lincoln County
is surely in need of a vigilance committee."

But with all of the criminals about, making it unsafe for women and children to walk the Main street, Pioche folks occasionally got a chuckle.

One of the incidents which amused them greatly was the exploit of Jack Harris, a notorious Nevada bandit whose favorite sport was robbing Wells Fargo stages—which carried boxes filled with minted coins to meet mine payrolls.

The Pioche stage agent devised a "sure-fire plan" to halt the depredations. He convinced his superiors in San Francisco it would save them a great deal to hire Harris and keep him on duty around the office when a stage was due. The bandit readily agreed to the proposition—but the robberies continued, even though Harris always could be found sitting on the Wells Fargo porch whenever a stage pulled up and the driver reported a robbery.

It took some time before the station agent realized that although Harris kept his part of the bargain by always being at the station ahead of the stage arrival, he had been waylaying the Concords several miles out of town and then racing over a shortcut to arrive at his post long before the harassed driver could get there around the looping mountain road. Harris lost his "job" with the stage company.

On September 15, 1871, as if daily shootings weren't enough violence, one of Pioche's greatest calamities occurred. A fire, started in a restaurant in the heart of the business section, was whipped to adjoining buildings by a brisk breeze. Scarcity of water would have made the job of controlling it difficult even had there been any fire-fighting organization.

A large number of the business houses were saloons. As the fire approached, owners merely rolled kegs of liquor into the street and invited the awe-struck throng to help themselves. And, as Pioche burned, its residents reveled in an orgy of free whiskey. It was only when a large supply of powder stored in the "fireproof" cellar of the Phillip Felsenthal's store exploded, throwing flaming boards in every direction and shaking the town, that a sober cessation was brought to the carnival. The explosion blew thirteen of the revelers to shreds and injured forty-seven others. Between 1500 and 2000 were made homeless. Damages totalled more than half a million dollars, and there was little insurance.

The town was rebuilt after the holocaust, but without benefit of city planning. It remained a misshapen town, in a crooked little canyon—on the east flank of the Highland range of mountains. Main street writhed in pretzel turns along the floor of the canyon. Twisting trails and roads sprouted from it and ran up the hills in all directions to a cluttered profusion of rock-and-board shacks and unpainted houses, which 8,000 or more citizens called "home."

Thirty days elapsed before arrival of the first shipment replacing the burned-out supplies, equipment and materials—a delay that was disturbing proof of Pioche's remoteness from the centers of civilization, with neither the lifeline of railroad or telegraph.

There were other fires, and there were floods, but Pioche always bounced back. The discovery of new lodes assuaged her wounds, and flocks of newcomers, pulled as by a magnet to her silver treasure, enlivened flagging spirits.

The continued growth in population and the increased activity in the mines and at the expanding Raymond and Ely mill at Bullionville pointed up the need for a railroad; and a permit to construct a line was granted by the State legislature. General A. L. Page was the principal promoter and president of the narrow-gauge company receiving the franchise.

The *Pioche Record* of October 4, 1872, furnishes us with an actual starting date of construction. The first message sent over the new telegraph line to Pioche on that date, was from General Page to James Gamble, superintendent of the Western Union Telegraph Co. at San Francisco. It read: "Accept my hearty congratulations for the never tiring energy you have displayed in connecting Pioche by magnetic wire with the civilized world. Ground will be broken tomorrow for the Pioche and Bullionville Railroad. I bespeak a bright future for eastern Nevada."

A few days previously, on September 25, the *Record* had reported that the rails and other materials had been shipped from Salt Lake City. The paper predicted, "This road will prove of great advantage to this camp ot once, and in the not remote future it will unite with the Utah Southern and so place our city in railroad communication with all parts of the country east and west."

It was an editor's hopeful dream never to be realized. The railroad was routed in a roundabout way to avoid grades and traveled over about twenty miles of rail. It went through Dry Valley, ten miles north of Pioche where a twenty-stamp mill had been built, and through Candos Canyon, five miles north of the county seat, where there was a fifteen-stamp mill, serving these as well as the big mill at Bullionville.

As more and more solid citizens arrived, life in the town settled down to a normal pace. In December, 1873, the *Pioche Record* gloated, "The people of Pioche have been on their good behaviour these many weeks. There has not been a homicide or serious altercation for nearly two months, and we begin to think that a healthier state of morals pervades the community. We believe the improved condition due to the rigor with which the law was enforced against its violators during the session of the District Court preceding the present session."

By the following year, when the peaceful spell was broken by the hurdy-house murder of James King by Jim Gleason, Pioche had grown to one of the principal "cities" of the State. Giving reckless credence to the inflated population estimates of the day, it ranked second to the bustling Virginia City.

That is not to say, however, that the town enjoyed the amenities of sophisticated living. Quite the opposite; cattle, pigs, chickens and sundry other animals roamed the streets at will, rudely insulting the public rights of way and offending sensitive noses. The *Record* editorially blasted at the repulsive scene, reserving its sharpest condemnation for the practice of allowing dead dogs to lie in the streets. And it seditor sarcastically vented his distaste of the sanitary condition of the local court room. "Visitors," he declaimed, "are compelled to wade through two inches of muck which has accumulated on the floor, made up of tobacco juice . . . and influenza ejections. This is as it should be. There is nothing in the law to prevent spitting."

The new business buildings which had arisen from the ashes of the 1871 fire evidenced a faith in the continued richness of the mines. Most of the new structures were built of stone for permanency. The wild-eyed mining camp was attempting to be a city.

Although wagers were still laid on the outcome of local shooting affrays, the community had hearkened to a call for the redemption of its wayward soul. The Rev. Ozi William Whittaker, the famous Nevada Episcopal Bishop, had made the long trip from Virginia City and on September 13, 1870, held the first church service in Pioche's history.

The indomitable dominie, whose Nevada diocese in 1869 consisted of three churches, one rector, one-hundred communicants and thirty children, noted in his report that the Pioche service was held in a saloon, with the congregation being composed of "150 rough miners."

The town's leading gun slinger, Morgan Courtney, reportedly passed the hat and the collection was pleasingly large to the Bishop. The owner of the bistro, in keeping with the occasion, covered the saloon art with blankets.

This first service led to a general co-operative effort to provide regular homes for both the Episcopalians and the Catholics.

Bishop Whittaker sent the Rev. Henry L. Badger to Pioche as vicar. He arrived on September 19, 1871, four days after the big fire, and the townsfolk tendered him a warm welcome. Within a short time nearly everybody in town was helping build a frame church and rectory, there having been collected some $2000 along Main Street. "We have a Mason & Hamlin organ and several organists but few singers . . . business generally stops Sunday afternoon," Buck wrote his sister.

The church cost $3764. The committee had $13 left when it was completed. Bishop Whitaker again made the long trip from Carson City to consecrate it on July 21, 1872.

It was shortly after that event when Buck wrote another letter to his sister, telling how the better elements of the Pioche citizens celebrated the yuletide: "This is the last day of the holidays and the town will probably get sober today and Monday things will go on as usual. We have so many Irish, Cornish and Germans among us that we keep the Christmas holidays for a week. The Catholic church keep a religious holiday Christmas, have a high Mass at 12:00 o'clock and keep it up all night. The Episcopal church have a service on Christmas Day. The ladies spent three evenings decorating the church with evergreens and fixing the tree.

"We all went on Christmas Eve. Everything went off splendidly . . . the church was crowded, the children sang very prettily. There are one hundred and thirty children in the Sabbath School but our minister, Badger's successor, is a failure. He has no faculty for talking. Is even a poor reader. He gave a kind of sales account of what the presents cost. How much candy he bought. How much trouble he had to dress the tree and not a word about Christ or Christmas. Everybody was disgusted . . . this man has mistaken his calling."

Buck concluded this letter—"New Year's night the Young Men's Social Club gave a ball and invited the guests, and the ladies overhauled their trunks and came out in full feather. We had a nice time and a pleasant supper . . . Everybody was polite and on their best behavior . . . We have the most cosmopolitan society. I could see in the hall ladies and gentlemen from nearly all the principal cities in the Union, besides English, French and German . . . I had no idea we had so much musical talent. We had a little Glee Club of five Cornish men who sang first rate; a pianist; three lady singers; a comic singer; a jig dancer and a Negro performer. Everybody got more than their money's worth and all the ladies had a chance to air their fine clothes."

But lest it be surmised from Buck's homey reminiscences that all of Pioche had succumbed to the ameliorating influence of religion, observe what happened on the arrival of an eastern bride who had come to join her young lawyer husband. She had braved the long, tedious journey across the plains to Salt Lake City, and then had choked in the swirling clouds of alkali dust that her stage had stirred up along the three hundred and fifty mile trip to Pioche. As the Concord's sweaty team of four were braked to a halt in front of the hotel, she was thoroughly disillusioned with the primitive West.

At the moment that her waiting bridegroom handed her down from the coach, a deputy sheriff nearby espied three rough characters across the street for whom he had been gunning.

Before the wearied bride could reach the hotel door, the deputy had dropped the trio with a fast fusilade from his forty-five and the victims were rolling and screaming in the dust. The shooting caused no uncommon excitement among onlookers; gunplay was a way of life. A short time previously, the *Record* reported, there had been a battle in which eleven gunmen bit the dust.

But the frightened bride wasn't having any of it. She flounced her fancy furbelows right back into her still-warm coach seat and headed straight home to Mother.

When Pioche's citizens managed to wrest the county seat from almost-abandoned Hiko in 1871 the stage was set for one of the weirdest political fiascoes in all western history . . . the famous "million dollar Lincoln County courthouse" tangle.

This was a classic combination of corruption and compound interest, the consequences of which kept the county deeply in debt from 1871 to 1937—sixty-six years.

It started, after the county seat was moved from Hiko, when the commisioners decided to build a courthouse and jail. Contracts totaling $26,400 were awarded. It was planned to pay off the indebtedness with revenues from bullion taxes, licenses and other tax incomes which naturally were expected to keep increasing. This seemed logical at the time and probably would have worked out except for some fancy financial finagling by the contractors, the tumbling of silver values, collapsing of the mining boom and a continuation of the disastrous fires throughout the town. When taxes nose-dived, graft multiplied.

For reasons known only by those involved, the original building contract for the two-story courthouse, about fifty by one hundred feet, was voided and the original contractors were allowed to continue construction on a piecework basis. This move provided a grab bag for the greedy, the contractors collecting several hundred dollars for rude stone steps, $45 for lamps worth a fifth that amount, as much as $8000 for a water closet with every other detail being paid for at the same ratio.

A Salt Lake newspaper reported that when it was finished in 1872 the cost had zoomed to $88,000, more than three-hundred percent of the original contract. In those days you could build a palatial business block for that amount. But Pioche courthouse neither was very large nor very palatial.

As county revenues diminished, most of what cash remained in the treasury was diverted to crooked sources and there was nothing left with which to retire the courthouse bonds. Interest kept compounding year after year. The value of the scrip fell to 30 cents on the dollar. New bonds totaling $181,000 were issued to meet the sky-rocketing interest on the original issue.

By 1907, the still-unpaid debt on the old, badly cracked, almost unusable building had reached $670,000.

The bondholders, realizing there wasn't a chance of squeezing that amount from such an impoverished county, agreed to accept half the amount in full payment of the long standing debt. By this time Senator William Clark had built his San Pedro, Los Angeles and Salt Lake Railroad and constructed a spur to Pioche, giving the community its first rail connection with the outside world. The railroad company agreed to pay off the old bonds and accept new ones.

County officials saw this as a way out, expecting a revived prosperity to result from the coming of the railroad. The new bonds were issued, the old ones paid off. U. S. Judge William E. Orr, only lately retired from the United States Appellate Court, was Lincoln County Clerk at the time. "It was my job to sign those new bonds so I had a small part in that historical Lincoln courhouse matter," he remarked recently.

The load fell on Clark County, too. When that county was established during the first decade of the century, it was stipulated that Clark would help assume burdens under which Lincoln County had been staggering for so many years. Consequently the larger share of the new bonds bought by the railroad was paid off by Las Vegas taxes.

Finally, in 1937, the bonds were retired. At long last Lincoln County, at a cost of around one million dollars to the taxpayers, owned their old courthouse which was to cost originally $26,400.

The most recent episode in the fiduciary follies occurred in the late autumn of 1958. The Lincoln County Board of Commissioners, still suffering from a pecuniary pinch, decided to do something about the eighty-seven-year-old "white elephant" courthouse which had been condemned for twenty years. The long abandoned structure was advertised for sale to the highest bidder—with the stipulation that the building never be removed from the site, be restored "as reasonably as possible to its original state," and that it be used only for "legal purposes."

There was only one bidder, Robert S. "Doby Doc" Caudhill, long-time Elko and Las Vegas gambling figure, who has made a vocation of collecting and storing a vast trove of Nevada historical objects, including whole railroad trains, Chinese joss houses, and nobody knows, including Caudhill, what else. He bought the building and the four lots upon which it stands for $150.

Altruistically, he announced that he intends to refurnish the building and install a museum, saying "Nevada's heritage should be saved and if I can help in this manner I want to do it." Time will tell.

To be sure, somebody should save the memory of mercurial, erratic, eccentric Pioche. Her citizens repeatedly fought their way back to normalcy from calamities, fires and cloudbursts. The price of silver all but ruined the economy, and when her mines were flooded in 'Seventy-Six they drowned out the roar of the Bullionville mill's sixty stamps— a roar never again heard at full crescendo.

The discovery of Delmar led to a great exodus in the 1890's, with buildings as well as people moving to the new Lincoln County golconda. When that boom withered the railroad came and Pioche bustled again with new facilities to profit from lower grade ores.

Again in the 1930's when Hoover Dam was built, Lincolnites banded together and brought a power line 250 miles across the desert to provide a new shot in the arm—cheap power to run the pumps and the mills. But recently the government cut off the subsidy on tungsten and other ores and once more headlines proclaimed "Pioche to Become Ghost."

Don't believe it—Pioche is too hardy a perennial ever to pass away completely. During its lusty life it has gone through many crises and always came back. It always will.

Tough? Of course Pioche was tough. Charitably, however, her pioneer residents are to be remembered as distantly isolated, far removed from the mores and niceties of civilization. Understandably, they developed a liberal tolerance for morality.

A good illustration was Virginia Marlotte. She was a rare girl for an isolated mining town—a happy-go-lucky, good-hearted orphan. When anybody took sick Virginia was right on the job to lend a hand. No beggar ever went hungry when she knew about it. Virginia, was, in fact, fondly known as the town's "do-gooder."

In the elastic morals of the time, no one in Pioche thought of branding her with a scarlet letter when an ardent youth did her wrong. Nor were many duly concerned when Virginia accepted a bit of largess for generously dispensing her feminine favors. That was, the townspeople figured, her own business.

When she caught pneumonia and died the whole town mourned the lovable, generous strumpet. Her funeral, it was unanimously decided, would be the biggest ever to be held in Pioche. Committees were appointed to take care of the details.

One group was delegated the task of composing a suitable epitaph. Its effort has been rewarded by a timeless notoriety:

> Here lies the body of Virginia Marlotte,
> She was born a virgin and died a harlot.
> For eighteen years she preserved her virginity—
> That's a damned good record for this vicinity.

Early Day Pioche

—Las Vegas Review-Journal Photo.

Pioche's Old
Silver Bell

—*Las Vegas Review-Journal Photo.*

"Million Dollar" Lincoln
County Court House,
at Pioche

—*Las Vegas Review-Journal Photo.*

Potosi was First

BELIEVERS OF FAIRY TALES AND LEGENDS have a field day with southern Nevada history. Many improbable, even impossible incidents, cut from the fabric of fantasy, embroidered and embellished by repeated word of mouth, have devoted groups of supporters.

There are some who insist that Alarcon sailed his Spanish ships up the shallow, muddy Colorado four centuries ago practically all the way to within a few miles of Las Vegas. They like to delude themselves with the idea of armored Spanish soldiers stomping around the area where scantily-clad chorines prance in resort hotel shows these days.

Alarcon's own record answers that one—he only reached a point near present Yuma, more than three hundred miles from Nevada's southernmost tip.

Even more commonly believed is the claim that Francisco Garces, the famed exploring Arizona priest, was the first white man to visit the southern Nevada area in the 1770's. Las Vegans accepted this as fact to such a degree that it named a downtown street after him—and the Daughters of the American Revolution titled the local group, "Garces Chapter." Certainly the desert trail-blazing Padre richly deserves such posthumous honors—but, his own journals in the New Mexico State Library disclose that he never got within a hundred miles of the Las Vegas valley and most certainly didn't name the famous Nevada resort town.

Neither did his opposite number, Father Francisco Silvestre Velez de Escalante, who opened the eastern half of the Spanish Trail in 1776. He failed to reach any part of Nevada—especially what is now Clark County. The western limit of his jaunt came within about twenty miles of the present eastern Nevada border when he turned south through the Santa Clara Valley, just west of St. George, Utah, reached the Virgin River and then went back east through the Zion Park and Kanab country, fording the Colorado at the Crossing of the Fathers, near the site of massive Glen Canyon dam.

Nor did General John Frémont name Las Vegas, as another coterie of legend believers contend—although he was a prolific bestower of names on natural wonders wherever he seemed to travel. He merely camped at the Vegas spring just one night, in 1844, long after the Spaniards had been making this a favorite stopping place.

"Las Vegas" just came naturally from the fact that vast acres of wild hay grew upon the plains from the overflow of gushing artesian springs which provided a happy oasis for the early New Mexico trading caravans between Santa Fe and Los Angeles from 1830 to 1846. Las Vegas means "The Meadows" in Spanish.

Another romantic tale relates that a group of Spanish explorers found gold in Eldorado Canyon in the 1700's—and that a century later a group came back seeking the mine, bearing a parchment map supposedly marking the spot. This incident has been retold in several books—but nobody can find the slightest record of the event. A devoted researcher, the late Fred Wilson of Las Vegas, hunted through old records in Santa Fe, Mexico City and Madrid seeking some inkling of evidence that would establish white men in the area before 1826. He was never able to discover a single reference to such happenings.

Probably more fanciful tales have been perpetrated in print through the years regarding the origin of the old Potosi mine, and the derivation of its name, than any other mining camp in all Nevada history. It is a large mountain of lead, silver and zinc ore some thirty miles southwest of Las Vegas, and was the first lode ever worked in the state.

One supposedly highly authoritative source declares that the Indians knew about the Potosi lead and made bullets from it for their guns "long before white men came to the area." This is quite interesting but it makes one wonder where they obtained the guns and powder to use such bullets.

Then there is the legend that the deposit was named by members of the Mormon Battalion returning from California in 1847, and several histories add the informative fillip that the location was shown them by a Paiute named "Potosi." The apocryphal tale stirs the ire of students of Indian lore who can't imagine the rather dull-witted southern tribes picking such a Spanish name for a papoose.

Potosi is just as distinctly Spanish as "Sierra." It means "Great wealth, gold mine; source of great wealth" in the Castilian language.

If the Mormons did bestow the name it was because one of them possibly knew of the Potosi silver mine in Bolivia, the richest ever discovered in the world at that time, or some other mine named for it. It seems much more likely that New Mexican traders, traveling the trail right past this mountain of ore, must have discovered and christened it either after the Bolivian mine or the much older one of the same name in the Pyrenees of northern Spain. It certainly seems logical that they would know about such mines in other Spanish speaking countries.

There are many lesser legends, some quite recent and probably dreamed up in some bar, which are delightfully titillating to the imagination. Such as the "Lost Diamond" mine, somewhere just north of Lake Mead. This story keeps cropping up, although the Nevada Bureau of Mines insists that not one diamond has ever been found in the state. Crystals of volcanic glass abound in spots; amateurs who find them may believe they have discovered diamonds until they try to sell some of them.

Jedediah Smith was the first white man to wander into what is now Nevada in September, 1826, leading an exploring party down Meadow Valley Wash to the Muddy River where it joined the Virgin, in a search for new trapping grounds.

He followed this stream to the Colorado, crossed it and went south through what is today known as Detrital Wash, passed near present Davis Dam to the Mojave villages north of Needles and then traveled west over the Mojave Desert to California. (The Indians and a large county in Arizona spell Mohave with an "H" while in California the Spanish "J" is used.)

The earliest record of a Spanish trading party to cross southern Nevada, instead of taking the established Arizona route between Santa Fe and Los Angeles, was led by José Antonio Armijo. He left the New Mexico capital in the autumn of 1829 and followed Escalante's route to Utah. His chief scout was a lad named Rafael Rivera, who separated from the main party on the Virgin River and traveled alone all the way to the sink of the Mojave River, south of present day Baker, California. He retraced his path and rejoined Armijo's party in the first week of January 1830, at the mouth of Vegas Wash, on the banks of the Colorado—a spot some two dozen miles east of Las Vegas, now under some 300 feet of water in Lake Mead. Rivera led them westward across Las Vegas Valley and over the Spring mountains on the pass along the north flank of Mt. Potosi.

It appears very probable that Rivera discovered the shorter fifty-mile waterless route from the Muddy River to Vegas Spring on his scouting trip—and very certainly Armijo's party was the first group, which left any sort of record, to cross Las Vegas Valley. It established the shorter, more popular Spanish Trail between the coast and Santa Fe, over which a constant string of trading caravans continually passed until the United States obtained all the southwestern area from Mexico.

Nowhere is there better proof that Americans are prone to honor legendary historical characters rather than the real ones. Many Las Vegas streets and schools are named for early trappers and explorers who never came within hundreds of miles of southern Nevada. But, there isn't a single thing in all southern Nevada bearing the names of Jedediah Smith, José Antonio Armijo or Rafael Rivera—although Smith did name the Virgin River after his chief scout on his second expedition.

Further, few southern Nevadans ever heard of William Bringhurst or Nathaniel V. Jones, and it's a pity. The former actually was the founder of Las Vegas and the latter was the "father" of Nevada's lode mining, which grew into magnificent proportions a few years later. Bringhurst arrived in Las Vegas Valley on June 14, 1855, with thirty men, including Oscar Hamblin, brother of the famed Mormon Indian missionary, with orders to establish a mission of the Latter-day Saints Church. A year later, Nathaniel V. Jones, assigned by Brigham Young to the mission, arrived on May 16, 1856, to "explore for minerals" in this region.

Naturally, the Las Vegas Valley Indians knew about the "heavy rock" at Potosi and they told the Mormons at Bringhurst's Mission.

So, Jones was a little flabbergasted when Bringhurst informed him that he already had sent out an exploring party to investigate a report by Indians that there was a huge mountain of lead southwest of Las Vegas. This party had reported they "had found the lead in large quantities. They brought 180 pounds with them."

·Jones immediately visited the spot, verified the deposits and headed back to Salt Lake City in a hurry to report to Governor Young that there "was a great quantity of lead about thirty-five miles southwest of Las Vegas." In the meantime President Bringhurst had hurried speedily to Salt Lake City, also to report to Brigham—which indicates that the two gentlemen were not above seeking a bit of personal glory and credit with the heads of the Church.

Bringhurst came back in July to run his mission colony, and it is interesting to note from the mission records that he took his flock to task by severely scolding them at meeting for the "prevailing spirit of grumbling, fault-finding, laziness and cussing."

The President of the Mission, with orders from Brigham Young to start mining operations, didn't waste any time. He organized a mining company to work the lead ore on July 23, with Almon J. Fuller as president of the group and fifteen men assigned to assist in the operation.

This pioneer Nevada mining party had been gone from the mission five days when, on August 8, Nathaniel Jones arrived again with orders "for the commencing of operations in the lead mine."

Further, Jones' orders instructed him to "take those brethren who were called on their missions at the April conference, and proceed immediately to working out the lead; that some teams were coming in a few weeks with flour from Cedar City for the use of the mining company; that his mission was a separate and distinct concern from the Las Vegas settlement . . ."

Such a muddle was bound to arouse ill feelings, even in such a rigidly administered organization as the Mormon Church. It did.

Bringhurst refused to release men or supplies to Jones "until the proper documents were produced by him or further written instructions were received from President Young." Accordingly, in a truce, a joint letter written by the pair and sent off to Young—Bringhurst agreeing to lend "men and wheat" for the mining operations until clarifying orders were received.

Before a reply could be had, Bringhurst received orders from Brigham Young on August 19 which undoubtedly upset him:

"We have appointed Nathaniel V. Jones of this city to take charge of this business [the lead mining] and superintend the whole matter, so whatever is done we wish to have it done under his direction. At the same time we wish to have you render him all the assistance in team work and manual labor that you can and he can employ to advantage."

That settled the argument.

Jones drew heavily on the men, stock and supplies at the mission but Bringhurst refused to allow him to take along the one blacksmith in the colony, Edward Cuthbert. This added to problems at the mine, as dull and broken tools had to be sent to Las Vegas for repairs.

Plenty of water was needed to smelt the ore, so it was decided to erect a fireplace furnace near the Las Vegas Spring, which was to be operated by Isaac Grundy and Dudley Leavitt of Santa Clara. The ore was hauled the more than thirty miles across the desert by ox-wagons.

Long afterward the big spring was absorbed in a huge city reservoir, but a few years ago Lister Leavitt, son of pioneer Dudley, pointed out a small depression in the ground on the banks of the now-dry creek as the exact site of the old furnace. There seems to be no dispute that this 1856 Mormon fireplace smelter was the first ever built and operated in Nevada.

The operation was simple—the complex, heavy ore was melted in the fireplaces and poured into limelined Dutch ovens. In this manner the lead shelled out in hunks. Altogether, according to the records, some nine thousand pounds were smelted in this crude manner, but it proved disappointing since Potosi ores are notoriously complex and contain sulphur and other ingredients which burned in the process.

The "lead" was sold at Mormon settlements all the way to Salt Lake City, but proved brittle and "shiny". It soon was found that the shine came from silver content and assays showed the product contained more silver than lead, which was the cause of slugs from the product ruining the rifling of the guns in which it was used. This was five years before the Gold Canyon miners learned that the "blue stuff" clogging their gold riffles was silver.

The curious Paiutes undoubtedly watched the smelting operations and copied them to make bullets for their few guns. This seems to be a logical background for the oft-repeated story that Nevada Indians used "silver bullets" to bring down game and white invaders.

Food and other supplies were scarce at isolated Potosi. In addition, Indians caused repeated trouble, so in January, 1857, Jones gave up the mining operation. The nearest water was at Mountain Spring, which the Indians defended. He reported to church authorities that his reasons for abandoning the operation were the low grade of ore, lack of water and other problems which made "mining impracticable."

Thus, the first lode mine in Nevada was abandoned and Potosi became the state's initial ghost town.

However, word of the high silver content in the Potosi mountains prompted a group of miners in Eldorado Canyon to form the Colorado Mining Company and resume operations.

A graphic incident of those days is included in the report of the U. S. Boundary Commission, which was engaged in the survey of the California-Nevada line during the early 1860's. Arthur Woodward, author of *Feud On The Colorado*, furnished pertinent portions of the report for this writer's use from articles printed in the Sacramento *Union* in 1861.

Lt. Beale's camels, used in earlier surveys, had been brought from Fort Tejon to Los Angeles. A party composed of fourteen men, three horses, twenty-two mules and three camels left there in the winter of 1860 and camped near the Mojave Villages north of present Needles, California. It was planned to make a reconnaissance of the border area to locate camps for the future survey parties. Guided by a man named Brooks, with a former soldier named Fritz as camel driver, the group on February 16, 1861, moved northwest, roughly along the present state boundary. Four days later, Woodward quotes the report, "We had the choice of three springs known to Fritz—the Kingston Springs, some twenty miles to the southwest on the Salt Lake Road; the Mountain Spring about the same distance on the same road to the northeast; the Stump Spring, towards the northwest, whose distance he could not exactly tell. [This location would put the party in the extreme south end of Pahrump Valley, about a dozen miles straight west of Goodsprings.]

"As we neared the point of the hill we descried two other wagons driving to the northeast, and when we overtook them they proved to belong to the Colorado Mining Company, hauling supplies to the Potosi Mines, which they told us were only twelve miles off, where some water and grass could be obtained. So we concluded to follow them. Bending our course around the Point, more to the east, we arrived at 2 p.m., considerably fagged out."

The same report furnishes a rather good picture of the reborn little community as it existed in February, 1861, saying, "the mines are situated near the head of a ravine three miles in length, which is entered from the south . . . the Mormons, who worked them for the lead the ore principally contains . . . several years ago, dug a well, furnishing the only water, and constructed a cabin of stone, which is still the best building in the settlement. Besides this, Potosi consists of some half-dozen log cabins of cedar and pinyon, and a tent or two, which shelter about forty men attached to the mines."

Two years later the Colorado Mining Company gave up its attempts to solve the puzzle of the complex Potosi ore, and once more the camp returned to the spectral world—just about the time the Comstock towns were roaring their loudest.

When the San Pedro, Los Angeles and Salt Lake Railway was built in 1905, affording a rail outlet at Jean for the products of the Spring Mountain area, Potosi again was opened up. It was found that the ore also was rich in zinc, which was in heavy demand. A hundred ton reduction mill was built at Goodsprings and Potosi became the major zinc producer of the district.

All this must have popped the eyes of the ghost of Nathaniel Jones, especially the fact that Potosi had a nearby railroad to haul the ore rather than oxen.

In 1913, Potosi was purchased by the Empire Zinc Co. and turned out much of the zinc needed in World War I. It was leased to A. J. and A. R. Robbins in 1919, and the Las Vegas *Review-Journal* said in 1926 that it had produced 31,000 tons, valued at $42,000, during the previous year.

That healthy production led the International Smelting Co. to send engineers to inspect the property in July 1926. Frank Cameron, company mining engineer, took out a ton of samples and made 300 assays which showed the ore contained 21.7 percent zinc, four percent lead, and four ounces of silver to the ton. International leased the operation for two years.

But as with other operators before, the ore proved economically unfeasible to reduce and the firm soon ceased operations.

Several other operators tried to take the measure of Potosi but all have been defeated by the problems first encountered by the Mormons in the 1850's.

While its production was only a drop in the Nevada mineral pool, 8500-foot Mt. Potosi has watched a great horde of southwestern history makers parade in her august shadow since Raphael Rivera blazed that first trail in the winter of 1829.

The venerable mountain—mother of the first lode mine in the State—which gave Nevada its first smelter and in her vanquishing ways the first ghost town, shares with some but concedes to none the glory of the pioneering past.

On the Way to the Potosi.

—Las Vegas Review-Journal Photo.

Colorado River Scene (in Clark County)

46

Last steamboat on the Colorado—91 feet long, 18 feet wide,
lost in break-through of levee in 1906

Steamboats in the Sagebrush

Eldorado

ELDORADO CANYON MAY BE THE MOST oddly christened place in Nevada. American usage has compressed the original Spanish form of El "Dorado," into the compound word. This, of course, was an imaginary region in the heart of South America which was supposed to surpass all others in the richness of its gold, gems, etc.

As noted previously, legends persist that early Spanish explorers, de Alarcon, Cardenas, Ulloa, Garces or others unnamed, found the ore of Nevada's Eldorado and bestowed the legendary Peruvian name upon the place.

Who, then, christened Eldorado Canyon?

A piece was added to the puzzle a few years ago when Dr. Arthur Woodward, dedicated researcher of Colorado River doings, printed the journal of Captain George Alonzo Johnson, who piloted the first steamboat up the shallow, muddy, sandbar-gridded stream from Yuma in the winter of 1857-58.

In his *Feud On The Colorado*, Woodward quotes Captain Johnson as recording, "We left Fort Yuma December 20, 1857 . . . We reached a point which I named El Dorado Canyon, and which was determined to be the head of navigation, it being seventy-four miles above Fort Mohave, the point where Lieutenant Beale crossed the Colorado."

Queried recently, Dr. Woodward wrote, "I don't believe anyone beat Captain Johnson to Eldorado Canyon unless it was some of those unknown, valorous but locoed trappers who went down the Colorado in the 1830's and may have passed Eldorado."

Offhand that might seem to settle the matter—Johnson's record is authentic, Woodward is devoted to facts.

At any rate, Johnson's trip opened the Colorado to navigation and led to establishing Eldorado as the busiest river port in all the vast desert regions of Nevada—an incongruous, but actual fact.

Realizing that all this happened some five-hundred roadless, unexplored miles from the excitement in Gold Canyon, which later led to the Comstock boom, it's to be expected that much of the history of this isolated area in the southern triangle of Nevada is missing and muddled.

Most sources agree that the first ore was found by a group of soldiers from Fort Mohave camping in Eldorado Canyon in 1859. These chunks of rock were brought to Las Vegas where some of the residents, having been through the Potosi experience, recognized them as ore containing both silver and gold. This resulted, according to Elbert Edwards, longtime Boulder City school superintendent and one of the most reliable of southern Nevada history authorities, in a group going from Las Vegas and staking out claims. These became known as the Honest Miner claims.

In the spring of 1861 Joseph Good, a resident of North San Juan, California, learned from an Indian about a canyon "where gold glittered all over." Good and a group of friends made the long trek across the desert to Eldorado to investigate. They found the ground glittering—but not with gold, only iron pyrites.

They prospected around and located some claims—the Techatticup, January, Morning Star, Wall Street and others.

No record appears showing what these second-wave discoverers did with their claims. Joseph Good next appears in 1868 when he camped with a group of prospectors at a spring on the southern slopes of the Spring Mountains, east of the old Potosi. The place was named for him—Goodsprings, and later became a famed Nevada mining town.

Good's Techatticup claim turned out to be Eldorado's richest producer. Its unusual name is interesting. Supposedly, the Indian who led Good to the canyon asked for food, using the Paiute word for hungry, "Tecahenga," and "to-sup," meaning flour or bread. His gutteral pronunciation apparently was corrupted by the prospectors into Techatticup—although one historian declares that a mining engineer insisted the proper spelling was "Thatticup" and that the name was carried that way on the company books.

Word of these new discoveries traveled on the wings of wind and in a very short time Captain Johnson's Colorado Steam Navigation Company's stern wheelers were churning their way back and forth between Yuma and Eldorado on an ever-increasing schedule.

A vignette on early-day Eldorado life is given by that eminent desert historian, Dix Van Dyke, in a *Barstow Printer* article in May 1941. It quoted letters written by James M. Sanford from Eldorado to John Brown in San Bernardino. The latter was the owner of ferries across the Colorado which he had established to transport travelers on the old Government road.

Sanford wrote from Eldorado on December 20, 1862, "I have deserted Fort Mohave and fixed my quarters at the silver mines. Silver has already been obtained from ten or twelve leads. The work on Mr. Vinyard's mill is going on—a capitalist from San Francisco [George Hearst] has been here and purchased stock and we expect brisk times here as soon as steamboats can reach here from San Francisco. [This was the low-water period of the year.] We have petitioned for soldiers to be stationed here to protect the miners."

Hearst seemingly missed no bets on Nevada's mid-century booms, regardless of how isolated they were. He acquired the Queen City, next to the Techatticup, and in his ownership there occurred a few years later, one of the major hair-raising shooting scrapes of southern Nevada history.

On April 12, 1863, Sanford again wrote, "I have built a cabin and am as near comfortable and happy as may be expected for one in a forest of meskee [*sic*] surrounded by howling wolves, starving Mohaves and thieving Paiutes. The gold region I discovered is now attracting great attention. Strain every nerve to get this place garrisoned by a few soldiers."

A month later, on May 17, 1863, he wrote, "Your ferry boat has been doing a good business for the last two months. If the soldiers come here by land come with them if convenient. There are only thirty soldiers at the post now. They came with the steamer to guard the supplies she brought a month ago."

Most of the habitations which sprang up as the population multiplied (one estimate puts 1500 residents there by 1863) were made of stone. Lumber was very scarce, what little there was being hauled almost one hundred miles from the Spring Mountains, west of Las Vegas. Freight from San Francisco cost $150 a ton.

The little wood-burning steamers performed prodigious miracles in making the trip upriver from Yuma. The shallow Colorado, always a silt-laden, muddy stream, was a constantly-shifting gridiron of sand bars which blocked the way. Most of these could be broken open by ramming, but occasionally the captains encountered one which was too thick to butt through. The astute river skippers quickly devised a way to surmount this problem—they merely turned their boats around and backed into the sandbars. The whipping blades churned a passage right through the barriers, whereupon the skippers would turn around and go steaming merrily ahead.

When word of the start of the Civil War filtered through from the outside it immediately caused trouble. There were desertions of southerners from the Army contingents stationed at Fort Mohave and Eldorado. Too, there was an infiltration of rough characters from both the North and the South who were seeking a safe place to avoid the dangers of war or the horrors of conscription.

The two factions, still loyal to their sections, divided into different camps under their respective flags. The Unionists dug in at Buster Falls, the Rebs at Lucky Jim Camp a mile down the canyon. From behind the walls of their stone shelters they carried on a continuous warfare, albeit mostly verbal. It was about as near as the war ever came to Nevada, although it was several months after Appomattox before the "battle" of Eldorado came to an end—with no fatalities reported.

Throughout the war the only powder burned at Eldorado was for about 4500 feet of tunneling—mostly in the Techatticup. The Gettysburg, which cut across it, later became part of the mine, as did Hearst's Queen City, later to be called the Savage.

The first mill, a ten-stamper finished in 1863, obviated some of the ore shipping on the long voyage down the length of the Gulf of California, around Cape San Lucas and up the coast to San Francisco.

After the war, new operators began to appear and the camp started to step up its tempo. There is no record of random killings during this

period since the place was so far from civilization, but frequent later discoveries of unidentified graves indicate that numerous shootings occurred.

The best-known affray occurred in 1873. One John Nash had moved
in, acquired several properties in one way or another and organized the
Eldorado Company. George Hearst had done little with his Queen City,
being elsewhere with his varied mining promotions on the Comstock, at
Star City, Cortez and other western strikes.

Nash decided to acquire the Queen City by jumping the claim. He
didn't have to hunt far to find men willing to do the job. He picked James
Harrington, reputedly already the killer of three men; William Piette, a
part Indian who thirsted for a reputation as a "bad man;" and Jim Jones,
a half-breed Cherokee who arrived at Eldorado on the run to avoid being
hanged for horse stealing. Nash agreed to pay them $500 apiece to do the
job, but failed to produce the cash and offered his notes. Jones refused to
accept the paper—feeling that Nash would fail to honor it. The mine
operator induced Piette to kill Jones.

Jones was washing his face one morning in a keeler—half a powder
keg—when Piette shot him in the back but failed to drop him. Instead, the
intended victim knocked down his assailant and ran into the cabin to get
his gun. As he fell over his bunk he turned, shot and wounded Piette, who
had followed, intent on finishing the job he had bobbled. The latter ran.
Jones, wounded, hastened to his attacker's cabin, but there was nobody
there except the latter's squaw. Jones grabbed the rifle which Nash had
given Piette, and ran up the hill.

By this time Nash's hired gunman had aroused others in the camp
saying Jones had attacked and shot him. Jones could hear shouts of "Kill
him" from below.

He took cover in a shallow prospect hole. Three men came over the
crest—Tom King in the lead, followed by men named Tuttle and Johnson.
Jones leveled his gun and killed King. The others ran. Jones grabbed the
opportunity to get King's gun and add it to his arsenal.

Shortly he was surrounded by the mob, but held his fort, the attackers
warily keeping out of his range. The sun poured down on his unprotected
hole and the injured Jones grew weaker by the hour. He held out through
two days and a night until the second evening, when he raised his handkerchief fastened to a gun in sign of surrender.

One of the original trio, Johnson, assured by the wounded man through
parched lips that he would not shoot, approached the hole, a pistol hidden in his pocket. Jones begged for a drink. Johnson said he would give
him one, but instead pulled his pistol and shot the beaten man through
the head. His body was covered and the men took time enough to put
King's corpse into another prospect hole and cover it.

Nash jumped the Queen City, and Eldorado's uninhibited citizens returned to their potent libations to celebrate the successful ending of the
gun fight which had enlivened their lives for a couple of days.

Johnson, who betrayed Jones after he'd surrendered, was haunted by his conscience and died a miserable death a short time later. Tuttle, the other ringleader in the attack, was shot for horse stealing in Utah.

Piette? He continued his desire for fame as a killer and reportedly murdered three more men, but met his match and ran like the coward he had shown himself to be with Jones—escaped to Mexico, and is said to have died there from natural causes, which is some sort of travesty on justice.

Eldorado, besides being Nevada's largest river port in history, could claim several other unique distinctions. Outstanding among these were two of the worst Indian renegades in western history, Avote and Queho; the first dredges ever used in Nevada to obtain gold; and the state's first use of a steam tractor to replace mules in hauling ore from the mines.

The most romantic tale is the oft-repeated story of the "Spanish Cavalcade." Nearly every history of Nevada has related this story as a factual occurrence.

It is supposed to have happened in the mid-seventies—shortly after the fight over John Nash's jumping of Hearst's Queen City—when citizens of Eldorado were startled into open-mouthed wonder by the arrival of a group of Mexicans from across the river, their gaily-colored caballero costumes covered with dust.

The party conferred briefly over a piece of faded parchment, and then without saying as much as *buenos dias* to the surprised miners, started plodding up the canyon. Some of the curious followed. After occasional stops to confer, they marched straight to the location of the Wall Street Mine. John Powers, the owner, walked out of his cabin to learn what the excitement was about.

The Mexicans showed him a stained, yellowed map and explained that it had been found in an old church in Mexico and that they had come to locate the mine. The map unmistakably indicated the site of the Wall Street, one of the first staked in the canyon by white men. According to the various versions, the Mexican group accepted a meal from Powers, and then realizing that Americans had beaten them to the treasure trove, disappointedly returned the way they had come.

Nothing further, apparently, ever was heard from the Mexican treasure hunters. Neither has later search ever turned up any actual verification of the yarn. If it is true—and C. M. Alvord, an old timer in Eldorado Canyon, included it in the Eldorado material he wrote for the Nevada State Historical Society—it means that Spaniards actually found mineral in Eldorado Canyon a century before white men discovered it.

Ike Allcock, Eldorado Canyon pioneer, told this writer before his death just a few years ago, that he had heard the tale frequently in his early days there, but that it had happened sometime before he arrived. It is probable that Alvord also heard it secondhand.

During the 'Seventies Nash and his El Dorado Mining Company just about controlled activities in the Canyon. His associates included "Old Man" Davis, a title which differentiated him from his son, Percy W., who also was a member of the firm, and J. Fuller.

The company built a new mill, replacing the original little ten-stamper, and things began to hum again.

Croffut's Pacific Coast Guide, published in 1879, showed that Eldorado still depended on steamboats. It announced that "Steamers leave Yuma, Arizona, for Fort Mohave every fifth Wednesday, commencing about the middle of January. These steamers run to El Dorado from May 1 to the last of October (stage of water permitting). In season of high water the river is navigable to Callville. Distance from Yuma to El Dorado 365 miles, fare $45.

In the summer of 1880, Andy Fife, ex-sheriff of Lincoln County (remember, that was a lucrative job) and George M. Goodhue built a new mill and organized the Lincoln Mining Co. They sold out a year later to Wooley, Lund & Judd, who subsequently disposed of their holdings seven years later to the Barker Brothers of Philadelphia. The latter organized the South West Mining Co. and soon controlled all the proven mines. They continued its operations and dominated the community for a long time.

The Barkers were absentee owners and their managers at Eldorado were the "kings" of the canyon. One of the best known and liked of them was Charles Gracey, that early Pioche pioneer who had built and operated the Ely and Raymond mill at Bullionville. After Pioche folded, Gracey drifted to Eldorado, following his old trade of blacksmith and machinist. His reputation and experience made him a natural for the job of operating the South West mill and mines.

Gracey, always a man of piety, had no love for renegades and he deplored the morals of isolated Eldorado. According to one old timer who was there, he insisted on a divided cemetery—one side for Christians, who had some chance of getting to Heaven, and the other for renegades who were headed in the other direction. Only two of those who died during the period were deemed worthy of places in the Heaven-bound side while the other section was well patronized.

If the tale of the old timer is true, it serves well to illustrate the general cussedness of Eldorado's populace, even though no record tells how many lads succumbed to lead poisoning. There were only three decipherable markers on the graves when the U. S. Bureau of Reclamation moved the thirteen remaining ones to higher ground in 1950—Cornelius Conover, who died May 26, 1888; R. E. Andrews, who succumbed August 25, 1881, and Lars Frandsen who departed May 12, 1897.

Frandsen's death is the only one upon which information is available. It inaugurated the Saga of Avote, first of Eldorado's historic Paiute terrorists. Avote was one of the ever-present Paiutes who hung around the camps, looking for something to steal or beg. He was known to be extremely jealous of his good-looking young squaw—and probably had reason to be, since women of any sort were scarce in the area. Whether his suspicions of Frandsen were justified is unknown, but Avote probably believed they were as he had been heard muttering threats against the man.

He lay in wait behind a rock above Huess Spring, about a mile down the canyon, on May 12, 1897. Frandsen and a helper, hauling ore to the mill at Eldorado, stopped to water their teams and Avote blazed away. When the two men didn't appear at the mill, searchers went up the canyon hunting them and found Frandsen dead and the other man badly wounded.

Avote couldn't be found—but knew he was a hunted man and apparently decided to wipe out the entire white population and give the canyon back to the Indians.

He next sneaked up on Charlie Nelson, a miner for whom the newer settlement at the head of the canyon was named, and killed him. A little later he hid in the cabin of Charlie Monohan, partner in a mining operation, and shot him dead. The morning following this slaying, "Judge" Morton saw Avote coming over the hill as he prepared his breakfast. Hoping to protect himself, Morton dished out a plate of beans for the Indian. The latter sat down, ate the food, and then blasted Morton into eternity.

These killings roused the entire canyon. Some of the wiser heads realized it would do no good to hunt Avote in the wild desert hills he knew so well, so they resorted to the strategy of telling his brothers and the rest of the Paiutes that they would be wiped out unless they brought in the killer, dead or alive.

By this time Avote's clan members were pretty mad about the trouble he had caused. They weren't getting any further handouts from the white miners. The Paiutes went after him, found him alive on Cottonwood Island, a few miles down the river, and ended his career—bringing his head back in a burlap sack to prove they had finished him.

The turn of the century created many changes in the district. The big Searchlight boom, twenty miles south, brought civilization closer. The town of Nelson burgeoned at the head of the canyon.

At about the same time, the second generation Barkers became involved in a South American mining promotion and mortgaged their Eldorado properties to finance it. It proved a bust and the South West Mining Company was picked up by Joseph Wharton, a wealthy Quaker and a steel and iron tycoon from Philadelphia.

He kept Gracey in charge of operations—he was the last postmaster at Eldorado, closing the office August 31, 1907, the mail being transferred to Nelson. But this didn't end the didoes in Eldorado by a long, long way.

The saga of Eldorado can't be told without including some of the activities of its best-known long-time resident, Isaac William Allcock. He arrived there in 1878 when he was twenty-two years of age. In 1880 he cast his first vote for president—for Garfield. He never missed a subsequent election, supporting every Republican candidate from Garfield to Eisenhower, and held the distinction of being the oldest registered voter in Clark County when he died in a Las Vegas hospital on September 30, 1955, just 34 days before his 100th birthday.

Right up to the end Ike's mind and memory were sharp and clear. Although deaf in later years, he kept his own teeth and read newspapers without glasses. He was one old-timer whose stories were easy to believe —he related facts as they happened and didn't attempt to garnish them with added flourishes.

It's too bad somebody didn't record all of them for posterity. One was about the three California tenderfeet who located a claim near Ike's place and made a habit of "borrowing" water from him without ever returning it. Since Ike had to haul it in barrels for several miles he became tired of being an involuntary philanthropist.

The next time one of the men appeared with a bucket Ike suggested he strain the water through a piece of dirty rag he handed him.

The man asked if it had bugs in it. Ike grinned. "I told him no, but that a stray jackass had fallen into the waterhole a few weeks ago and that the hair was just startin' to slip. You know, they never borrowed no more water from me."

Another of Ike's favorite memories was the time an eastern outfit prospected the river bed near the old steamboat landing, found good showings of loose gold and silver, and decided the river bottom must be rich from the tons of ore spilled overboard during the years of loading barges.

When they had assembled a large dredge, shipped in at great expense, they sought somebody willing to don a diver's suit and go under water to keep the opening of the suction pipe clear of trash, boulders, driftwood and other debris. Nothing ever stumped Ike Allcock, he'd try anything once. He took the job.

"Easiest danged job I ever had," Ike grinned, "I just sat there, all dressed in that big monkey suit, and watched the mud go up that pipe."

But it didn't last long. "They didn't know how the Colorado could go up and down," Ike explained. "Water fell one night and the next morning there was the dredge balanced high and dry on a reef. Danged thing was so heavy it broke in two when the water dropped a little more. They gave up and I didn't have no more underwater job."

Then there was the time the mining operators decided they could use one of the old steam tractors "Borax" Smith had built a few years back to to haul borax from Death Valley to the railroad at Ivanpah. This attempt had flopped when the tractors didn't have power enough to climb grades pulling a load, and one of them blew up.

Since the haul from the mines to the mill at Eldorado was downhill the operators figured the steam contraption would work on the haul from the Techatticup—it wouldn't have a load to pull back uphill. The tractor, with two huge ribbed steel wheels behind and one smaller one in front, was shipped into Searchlight by rail and sat disconsolately in the yards for awhile—nobody was willing to chauffeur it until somebody thought of asking Ike. "Sure, I'll give 'er a go," he replied.

The tall vertical boiler was fired up and Ike began to fiddle with levers and wheels until he got the hang of it. Then he went snorting out of Searchlight and made the trip safely.

The arrival of the tractor in Nelson was for years one of Eldorado's most oft related bits of folklore.

"Injuns went high tailing for the brush and the eyes of the folks just popped out as we came roarin' and rattling down the canyon like a bat out of hell." Ike said. "Well, anyway, at least three miles an hour."

But, even with such an indomitable operator as Ike, the tractor didn't work any better for the mining company than it did for "Borax" Smith. It went downhill all right, but it wouldn't go back up. It sat for nearly half a century, abandoned just above Murl Emery's fishing camp at the mouth of the canyon. Then, when Lake Mohave was forming, "Pop" Simon, the last owner of the Techatticup, derricked it aboard a truck and hauled it to his resort at Jean, thirty miles south of Las Vegas on the Los Angeles highway. Few of the thousands of passing autoists who ever glance at it have any idea it had its brief place in the heritage of both Death Valley and Eldorado Canyon.

Probably Eldorado's most notorious figure was another Paiute, the famed Queho, whose story has been written more than any other Nevadan's by every sort of author from school children to imaginative sensationalists. Several years ago this writer decided to sift some of the facts from all the fiction which has been printed about Queho. The actual story is good enough to rate a high place in history since there is no doubt he was Nevada's No. 1 public enemy. The best way to get the real story was to dig through the files of the southern Nevada newspapers, which were close to the actual scenes during the period.

He first was recorded as the suspect in the death of another Paiute during a tribal fight, probably fanned into fireworks by white man's whiskey, on the reservation at Las Vegas. (Incidentally, this small reservation still exists beside the railroad tracks in the heart of Las Vegas, commercial district.)

A few days later Queho was reported to have attacked one Hi Bohn in Las Vegas, breaking both his arms with a club, and then fleeing "southward into the mountains."

On December 3, 1910, the Clark County *Review* told of the return of a posse after an unsuccessful chase through the desert mountains for Queho who had departed swiftly "after having killed two men in the El

Dorado district." Queho had one leg shorter than the other and made a distinctive track so the posse had been able to follow him to the Gold Bug mill on the Arizona side of the river where they found the slain body of the watchman, his next victim.

Nevada State Police Sergeant P. M. Newgard was detailed to run down the murdering Paiute. He organized a posse including Eldorado old-timers Ike Allcock and J. E. Babcock, and a group of Paiute trailers. Anent this, the Las Vegas *Age* declared on December 31, 1910, "Queho's chances of living a long and happy life are slim."

The posse found no trace of him. "Long-haired Tom," Queho's closest pal, told the posse he was dead. He wasn't!

Early in January of 1919, John F. Perkins, of St. Thomas, sent word to the sheriff's office that he had found the murdered bodies of two Moapa Valley men, Eather Taylor and William Hancock. Perkins noted that "signs indicate two men did the murdering." Investigation showed both victims had been shot in the back near prospecting holes and their shoes stolen.

Deputies found one set of limping footprints at the scene which immediately stirred another Queho scare. It was justified.

Nelson residents were horrified on the night of January 21 when Mrs. Maude Douglas, wife of Arvin Douglas, was shot and killed in their cabin at the Techatticup mine by a "mysterious assassin." The next morning Ike Allcock identified tracks leading toward the river as those of Queho— the Paiute terror really was back in the news. Posses combed the country, spurred by $2500 in rewards offered by the State of Nevada and relatives of the slain victims. The trackers found still-warm fires where Queho had camped, and located a cave in Black Canyon which showed evidences of somebody having lived there.

But they didn't find Queho. However, the Las Vegas *Review* reported on November 25, 1927, that the body of "Long-haired Tom," Queho's partner, "had been found lying along the Colorado River near Cottonwood. It was Tom who guarded the hiding place of Queho back in 1910 and 1911 . . . carried provisions to his pal. Tom was an old man and may have died a natural death. But it is the theory of Deputy Sheriff I. W. Allcock of Nelson" . . . that Tom was bitten by a snake and died as a result of the rattler's poison."

In 1940, two explorers on the Colorado River found the mummified remains of a dead Indian in a cave high on the side of Black Canyon, a few miles south of Hoover Dam. Frank Wait, who as a deputy sheriff had trailed Queho in the 1919 hunts, immediately went to the cave and identified the corpse by the difference in the length of his legs. This started a strange legal battle for possession of the mummy. It finally ended up in the possession of the Las Vegas Elks lodge and was displayed for years at the annual Helldorado celebration in the county seat town.

Eldorado's day now is long past—steamboat whistles no longer echo up the canyon and claim jumpers are only a rare subject for discussion in

Nelson's one remaining bar. It caters mostly to the constant stream of fishermen who zip up and down the canyon on the paved highway to seek the wily bass of Lake Mohave and the big trout in Black Canyon. A few Sunday prospectors with modern metal detectors still seek gold in Eldorado's sun-scorched hills.

L. W. Mescher, at the ruins of old Fort Call
Walter R. Averett photo, courtesy of Las Vegas Review-Journal.

St. Thomas home, already partially under water from Lake Mead.
Photo taken June 11, 1938.

—*Las Vegas Review-Journal Photos.*

St. Thomas as it was being covered with water from Lake Mead.

Three Wet Mormon Communities

THREE OF SOUTHERN NEVADA'S EARLIEST Mormon settlements, Fort Callville, Rioville and St. Thomas are the wettest wraiths in all Nevada ghost-town-dom. Only the fishes visit the former two, both lying more than a hundred feet beneath the low water surface of Lake Mead, the huge man-made reservoir backed up behind Hoover (Boulder) Dam. St. Thomas was dubbed "Atlantis-on-the-Muddy" by Maureen Whipple, historical writer, in an article she wrote a few years ago for the old *Collier's* magazine. The southern Nevada Mormon agricultural community has had more lives than a cat and now its mud-covered, water-soaked remains periodically pop up, Phoenix-like, from the floor of Lake Mead after long periods of drought in the Rockies. Callville and Rioville were steamship river ports, which enjoyed only a fraction of the traffic of Eldorado. Both were above Black Canyon and its roaring rapids, which roiled mightily during flood stages, leaving a maze of sharp rocks across the channel when the Colorado was docile.

Old-time river men, in their ingenuity, solved a way to transit the dangerous gorge when need for upstream travel developed, not long after Eldorado started to boom. Salt was needed for milling at the mining town and so was hay and feed for the animals used to haul the ore.

There was plenty of both in Moapa Valley, a few miles up the Virgin from its junction with the Colorado. By road this was a hard, rocky haul of more than one hundred and fifty miles, mostly without water. The river route, only a third the distance, was far more feasible even if Black Canyon's dozen-mile funnel of rapids did present a despairing hurdle. It was the decision of the heirarchy of the Mormon Church in 1864 to build Fort Call—later called Callville—that actually brought about the solution to the problem of transiting the canyon.

Continued trouble with the Federal government and threatened Army attacks caused the church to seek a safer route over which to bring its constantly growing stream of converts from Europe to its colony of Deseret, hard by the Great Salt Lake. Logically, it figured that a back-door route was preferable to the dangerous overland trek across half of the hostile nation. The church charted a route which would take the faithful converts to Vera Cruz or Panama, thence overland to the Pacific where they were to be trans-shipped up the Gulf of California and the Colorado to Callville, and beyond by land some five hundred miles to Salt Lake City.

The Mormon officials had considerable knowledge about the lower Colorado from the reports of scouting parties which had made reconnaissance trips down the river as far as Fort Yuma. They could see another possibility in the plan. The Mormon colonists of southern Nevada sought a safer, easier and more economical way to obtain needed articles—and steamboat freight would provide it. Too, such a transportation facility would afford an outlet for surplus Mormon products, especially those of an agricultural nature.

Elder Anson Call was delegated to take a party and find a suitable port site, erect the necessary buildings and wharves and clear a road to connect with the Mormon Trail. At the same time he was to survey the Muddy (Moapa) Valley for possible agricultural use.

Church records show that Call came down the Muddy and continued down the Virgin about twelve miles below the junction of the two streams. Here he turned westerly up what now is known as Echo Wash. His detour from the Armijo route through Boulder Canyon was taken because this gorge was too precipitous for a road. Some twelve miles up Echo Canyon the party swung southwest to the banks of the river. A site was picked about three miles upstream from the mouth of Vegas Wash.

McClintock, writing in church history, declared that Call started the the settlement "as agent for the Trustee in Trust (the President) of the Church in December, 1864, according to a plan which was conceived to bring church immigration . . . up the river to this landing." He also noted that a company of Salt Lake City merchants had been formed to co-operate in the plan and to build warehouses at the landing "with a view to bringing goods up the river." Call also was delegated to function as agent for this company at the river port.

According to one historian, Call laid off forty lots, each one-hundred feet square, and marked out a site for the warehouse which was the first structure to be built. The same writer reported that Call left Thomas Davids and Lyman Hamblin to dig the foundation trenches while the rest of the party returned to Salt Lake to report their findings and bring back tools and equipment to construct the riverside community. They returned early in the spring of 1865 to complete the job.

One of the members of the original party, named Mack, was quoted by Rulon Beus in a 1927 issue of the Church's magazine, *Improvement Era,* as saying, "the men gathered rocks, made our own lime, cut and hauled the lumber for the roof, and after considerable hard labor and time, completed the building." This must be considered a modest statement—limestone had to be hauled for several miles and the nearest timber from which to saw lumber was on the Charleston or Sheep Mountains, seventy or eighty miles away.

However, the men built well—many of the walls of those buildings stood solidly right up to the day they were submerged, some seventy years later.

In the meantime, Brigham Young had contracted with a trader in San Francisco to put boats on the Colorado and ship plows, machinery, wagons and tools up the river, hauling back hides, wheat, potatoes and cotton on the return trips.

Nobody ever recorded, as far as this writer can determine, who the genius was that conceived the method of traversing the rapids of Black Canyon, but the solution was comparatively simple. Heavy iron rings were imbedded into the rock walls of Black Canyon at strategic points, the most important being at the head of the worst stretch of water which soon became known as Ringbolt Rapids. When the steamer *Esmeralda*, first of the craft bound for Callville, came up-river, it had been equipped with a steam winch. Its sister ship, the *Niña Tilden*, was similarly fitted.

A cable attached to the ringbolts was picked up by the crew and fastened to the winch. On the upstream haul, the winding capstan assisted the paddlewheel to get the craft through the rapids—on the down trip the process was reversed, with the cable let out slowly and serving as snubber to prevent the boat from going out of control. After the *Esmeralda* and *Nina Tilden* showed the way, many of the other river boats added equipment and extended their service upriver, even to the mouth of the Virgin.

Tons of hay, grain and other produce, as well as the badly needed salt from the vast mountain of it near the new Mormon town of St. Thomas, were hauled down the river to supply growing Eldorado and the other communities as far as Yuma.

But even with the ringbolts, Black Canyon remained a tumultuous passage for the little steamboats and schedules could never be depended upon because of the violent vagaries which resulted from concentrating the flow of the nation's second largest river system into one narrow chasm. Heavy downpours anywhere in the entire Rocky Mountains range southward from Yellowstone could send a flood soaring seaward only to have water so low the following day that sandbars created traffic hazards.

However, the *Esmeralda* and *Nina Tilden* soon were making reasonably regular trips between Callville and the mouth of the river—and sometimes to Mazatlan to pick up loads of converts, according to reports. Other boats, too, began hauling freight up river to Callville during its busiest period. A constant stream of wagon trains carried away the freight across the long, rugged road to the Mormon settlements and Salt Lake City.

When Arizona became a territory the present southern Nevada triangle was part of it. The area north of the thirty-sixth degree of latitude, which cut right through the Roaring Rapids, was designated Pahute County by the Arizona Territorial legislature. Callville was made its county seat.

The community's most disputed event occurred September 8, 1867, when a raft of three cottonwood logs, lashed together, drifted ashore bearing the emaciated, delirious body of a man named James White.

When he recovered he told a yarn about being attacked by Indians near the mouth of the San Juan River, north of Grand Canyon, where, with two companions who were killed, he was prospecting. He built the raft, lashed himself to it without food, and floated downstream to escape.

As near as he could recall, that had been sixteen days back and he had traversed the entire Grand Canyon with its hundreds of wild rapids. The only food he had eaten, he declared, was the hind-quarters of a dog, for which he had traded his gun to a friendly Indian.

White, a blacksmith, returned to his small Colorado home town and lived out a long life there, insisting to the end that his tale was true. His neighbors considered him a paragon of probity. But, probably based on the hardships suffered two years later by Major Powell's expedition through Grand Canyon, a large clan of doubters grew up. Since then dozens of researchers into river lore have written violent words on both sides of the question.

The first rosy dreams for Callville never did quite pan out, the long rough road overland to Salt Lake City made freight charges so high that profits were small for the backers of the mercantile phase.

As the Central Pacific tracks grew closer to the westward-building Union Pacific, church leaders realized that within a short time they would have rail transportation from both coasts, and decided to abandon the river route. Traffic to Callville diminished, and died.

A thrilling little finale to the old port's history was reported in a June 1869 Salt Lake *Desert News*, which quoted a St. George mail carrier as saying that three desperately fleeing horse thieves, closely pursued by an irate posse, had found Callville deserted. Trapped, the river blocking one escape route and rugged Boulder Canyon the other, with hanging their certain fate if caught, they pried the huge doors off the warehouse, launched them as a raft, and set sail down the Colorado. No trace of them or the doors ever was found.

When Hoover (Boulder) Dam was built in the 1930s and Lake Mead slowly commenced to back up behind it, the water daily creeped toward Callville. Frank Crowe, superintendent of construction on the dam, for Six Companies, and Charles P. Squires, pioneer Las Vegas newspaperman, made a sentimental farewell voyage to the site in a power boat.

They stood on the threshold of the seventy-year old warehouse until the water came up and lapped over their shoes, and then they climbed into their boat and bade a final farewell to romantic and historic old Callville. Today the big-mouthed Lake Mead bass are its only visitors.

In the early sixties the Civil War had brought many shortages to the Deseret Mormons, one of the most desperate being cotton. Reports of the balmy weather of southern Utah and Nevada brought back by those Saints who had been traveling through that area for a decade, caused Brigham Young to consider the section as an ideal place to raise cotton.

So, concurrently with the delegation of Anson Call to find a suitable place and build the river port, which became Callville, the 1864 conference of the church also instructed that a colony be started along the Muddy.

Thomas S. Smith, of Davis County, Utah, was named by Brigham to head the Muddy mission. The conference called one hundred and eighty-three members to the "Cotton Mission." All readily answered the "call," although it entailed great personal hardship. They had to abandon half-built homes and leave growing crops and their young orchards which were just starting to bear fruit.

A greater portion of those called headed for the St. George country in southwestern Utah. [This area is still commonly known as "Dixie" throughout Utah and Nevada.] Only eleven men and three women were able to answer the Muddy colony call immediately, having sold their property or given it away and bartered their little wealth "for ploughs and flour and ammunition and seed wheat and cottonseed and wagons."

Then, uncomplaining because the Lord's will came first, "and Brigham's will was the Lord's will," the small band of colonists set out on "another trial-by-heart and by bunion" on the five hundred mile trek to a swampy outpost, which they all understood at the start might starve them out in the end.

Southwestward the little party plodded across deserts and mountains, and on January 8, 1865, the group reached the Muddy and camped. This small party was described in old diaries with a phrase which aptly described their determination and invincibility—"hard-gutted." They had to be—and they had to do things as a unit. They "slogged together, suffered together, played together and prayed together." That's how they conquered the desert, the swamps and the isolation. Any who proved "clogs to the wheel soon got a passport home!"

They laid out a town near the junction of the Virgin and the Muddy and named it St. Thomas for their leader, Thomas Smith. [Remember, all Mormons are "Saints."] A town of eighty-five lots, each an acre in area, and about the same number of vineyard plots half as large, and a similar number of five-acre farm plots were laid out amid the cats-claw bushes.

The little group found the new life far from a picnic—the swamps bred mosquitoes and brought chills and fevers which sucked energy from the colonists. There were light-fingered Paiutes, not unfriendly at first, who helped themselves to anything they wanted. And there were grasshopper hordes, drouths and flash floods which ripped out irrigation canals dug with back-breaking labor. Worst of all, there was the summer heat which sizzled above the hundred degree mark for weeks.

It took plenty of "hard-guttedness" by those first Mormon settlers to make a go of it. They could laugh at their woes, too. Miss Whipple quoted a song they chanted which illustrated their indomitable spirit . . .

The wind like fury here does blow
That when we plant or sow, Sir
We place one foot upon the seed
And hold it till it grows, Sir.

In April, thirty-five more men arrived for the Muddy mission—six of the original group had returned to their families or to settle unfinished business in Utah. The latter were to bring back flour since the first year's crop would be small. As soon as the initial grain crop was harvested that first June, the settlers replanted the land to cotton, the weather in the region being so temperate that two crops could be raised annually.

President Erastus Snow of the southern mission at St. George visited in April and looked over the valley to learn its agricultural possibilities. He reported a fine meadow two miles above St. Thomas "very promising" as the grass there was then ready to cut. Two miles farther north he found another meadow, and located several others upon which he recommended the establishment of colonies.

Since the original site had many disadvantages it was decided to move to the new large meadow site, two miles north, in December 1865. Streets and lots again were laid out and St. Thomas, which was to become famous in southern Nevada history and to father many of its leading citizens, was reborn there.

The settlers erected solid houses, mostly of adobe bricks and dirt floors "bottomed so hard they could be scrubbed every morning." Those pioneers had come to stay and the streets were lined with shoots of mock orange trees, which for years spread their lacy shade over the thoroughfares. Their stark trunks and branches are still there, and their skeletons stand out starkly when the lake waters sink and uncover the old community.

By May many of those called the previous autumn had arrived and brought the colony added strength. President Snow picked a spot six miles north of St. Thomas as the site for a new settlement, and Joseph Warren Foote was appointed to head the group there. This became the first St. Joseph (probably name for Foote)—about one and one-half miles north of present Overton and on a sandy beach where James Leithead later erected a grist mill. When old St. Joe was abandoned it became known as Mill Point, and today is another of Nevada's myriad of little ghosts.

More and more settlers came, and cotton prospered. Although a cotton factory was being built at St. George, the Moapa Valley product had to be ginned locally.

The Moapa Stake records definitely show that southern Nevada's first cotton mill was operated here in 1866. It was located at Simondsville (another of Moapa Valley's smaller specters) "six miles above St. Thomas and two miles below St. Joseph," according to a letter, written February 11, 1866 by John Perkins, which was published in the *Deseret News*. He

determining whether Moapa was in Utah or Nevada. In the meantime, Nevada officials posted tax notices on every tree and post in the valley. These continued to flap in the breeze long after all had departed.

The boundary survey was completed December 15, 1870. Moapa was in Nevada!

Once more guidance was asked from high church officials.

In answer to the frantic colonists, Brigham sent a letter addressed to "Brother James Leithead and the Brethren and Sisters residing on the Muddy." In it he pointed out that "Your isolation from market, the high rates property is assessed in Nevada with the unscrupulous character of many of the officers . . . all combine to render your continuance in developing the resources of the Muddy a matter of grave consideration."

Then, according to James G. Black's history of St. George Stake, permission for the colonists to abandon their homes and return to Utah was given. This fateful message was signed by Young, George A. Smith and Erastus Snow.

The Moapans hadn't taken the situation without a squawk, writing to Congress and Nevada officials, declaring ". . . this region was a vast alkaline desert, destitute of timber and grass. Our object in coming here was the production of cotton for the clothing of ourselves . . . and the toiling brethren of Utah . . . we have expended at least one-hundred-thousand dollars in labor constructing dams and irrigation canals . . . one hundred-fifty dwellings, orchards, vineyards, and about five hundred acres of cotton fields . . . We have been compelled to feed an Indian population out-numbering our own, and that, too, without the aid of a single dollar from the government . . . it is impossible for us to convert our produce to cash . . . we shall be compelled to abandon this valley . . . throwing away the toil and energies of seven years."

The Muddy colonists met on December 20, 1870, and decided once more to pull up stakes—leave everything they had gained by hard labor—and move again. Some of them had been doing it for thirty years. Only one family voted against leaving, although others were opposed in their hearts. Daniel Bonelli and his wife stood firmly against giving up everything and plodding back over their old tracks.

The population of the valley at the time, according to old records, was St. Joe, 193; St. Thomas, 150; West Point, 138; and Overton, 119.

On February 20, 1871, Bishop Leithead led the caravan of colonists out Main Street and up onto Mormon Mesa for the trek back to Utah, every wagon loaded with all the personal goods it could hold. The hard-won, well-built homes, with cradles and other furniture standing in front rooms for the pack rats to play upon, the mock orange trees, the orchards and vineyards, all were left alone without human company except for Bonelli, whose sturdy Swiss frame watched unmoved as the last wagon disappeared over the mesa rim. That morning his wife had borne the Bonelli's fourth child, Benjamin Franklin Bonelli.

Later Bonelli declared, "I didn't leave the church, it left me."

Maybe the departing settlers made an agreement with two non-Mormons named Paddock and Hennings, who lived in the valley, to pay them for the grain crop when it was harvested and sold. The Mormons, who settled near Kanab, later learned that the men had disposed of the six thousand to eight thousand bushels of grain at the new mining town of Pioche for six cents a pound. Word also reached them that the two men had removed the lumber from the St. Thomas homes, hauled it to Pioche, and sold it there for ten cents a foot. But the former valley residents never received a cent of this money.

By 1880 the mines in southern Nevada and Utah offered a market for agricultural products and some of the valley's old-timers, who couldn't forget their Muddy mission, voluntarily decided to come back. There were three families in the van of this second migration, Moses and Lizzie Gibson, Harry and Ellen Gentry, and Ed and Eleanor Syphus. There to happily meet them were Daniel and Jane Bonelli, who had driven up from their busy place downriver at Rioville.

There was plenty of enthusiasm, although they found many changes. The major one was that outsiders had acquired title on, or squatted on, what had been lush Mormon farms. Wooley, Lund and Judd, of St. George, had obtained title to all the land held by the non-Mormon Jennings, which included the entire St. Thomas townsite. Through an agreement, the returning settlers were allowed to occupy this land, which was repurchased in 1892 by the Gentrys, the Syphuses, Fanny Byers and Daniel Bonelli.

St. Joseph, at the time of the exodus the largest town in the valley, had been appropriated by a Civil War veteran named Logan. He changed the name to Logandale—which it continues to be called.

More and more Mormons migrated to the Muddy, and it expanded into a lush agricultural oasis. Its cantaloupes, asparagus and other products became widely known for their quality. The coming of the Clark railroad across the north end of the valley in 1905 made a vast difference —shipping could be done by carload lots and there not only was the produce to be marketed, but there was an abundance of borax, rock salt and other materials which could be exported easily and cheaply. There was enough business to warrant the railroad building a branch line into the valley in 1912, adding to the importance of St. Thomas, which long had been the distributing center for mail for the mines of southern Nevada and northwestern Arizona.

But before this St. Thomas had gained fame afar—it was the half-way point stopping place on the old Arrowhead Trail, the predecessor of today's U. S. 91, which generally is the route of the new national cross-country freeway. After five hundred miles of desert, mountains and sand, those early-day, hard-tire motorists greeted the trees of St. Thomas and the cool shaded lawns at the Gentry Hotel as a sort of Elysia. The meals were excellent, the Howell and Syphus boys who ran the garage knew all there was to know about how to make an ailing tin-lizzie purr peacefully, and the citizens were friendly.

This sort of thing made St. Thomas southern Nevada's first widely publicized automobile tourist Arcadia, even if Ross Whitmore and Little Harry Gentry did develop a regular income from pulling them through the Virgin, above St. Thomas, at two dollars a car after the bridge was burned.

Everybody was welcome in St. Thomas—Miss Whipple recounts how John Abbott and his new bride served sixteen astonished outlaws breakfast when they stopped at his place.

However, all wasn't entirely peaceful—every once in a while a posse of St. Thomas men organized to go after some criminal. They always prayed before going, and one old timer said their prayer was, "if you want to avoid bloodshed, Lord, you'd better keep them varmints out of our way."

Even after autos and trucks had changed the life in Moapa Valley, St. Thomas still clung to its happy ways—its hayrack rides, groups of girls and boys, hand-in-hand, walking along the roads singing in the moonlight. The farmers always expected to lose half their melons to the "kid gangs," and did little to stop the swiping.

When they re-routed U. S. 91 several miles north of St. Thomas, the economy of the pioneer town suffered. During the depression of the 1930s another blow hit when the Grand Gulch copper mine, just over the Arizona line in the mountains to the east, ceased operations because copper and gold weren't worth digging any more.

But nothing could ever quite defeat these Moapa Mormons. John Perkins discovered a deposit of widely-desired silica sand, used in glass making. This resulted in the location of a sand mill above St. Thomas. Silica sand is still a valley industry.

About the same time a national firm announced that it was establishing an operation to mine the salt from the mountain which had attracted travelers since the earliest Indian migrants.

It was during this period that John and Fay Perkins, digging around in valley deposits, stumbled upon the Lost City of the "Old Ones" who had lived many centuries before Christ was born. This brought archeologists swarming in to find, preserved in fine state, untold and unbelievable numbers of Indian artifacts—stone hammers, atlatls, flexed mummies, rabbit fur robes, and a vast variety of other articles which were saved for posterity.

But a dark cloud loomed over the future—the United States Government was building a dam downriver at Black Canyon. Nobody in Moapa could conceive of the water backing up this far—more than thirty miles. Then came the government appraisers—a professor, and a politician. Levi Syphus represented the people. Their work was convincing evidence either that government was crazy, or that the water actually would get that far.

So, for five years, with evacuation notices tacked to trees, posts and buildings, the occupants, doubting and wondering, continued to live at St. Thomas with the government's permission.

The dam, 726 feet high, was completed in 1935, and the water began covering the desert land behind. Then the wagers started on how long it would take to reach St. Thomas. One day the first blue finger of water was spotted down the Virgin canyon. Then they believed! The government had bought everything—but they had sold buildings at auction for the materials to be removed. They paid the Gentrys $18,000 for the hotel and Rox Whitmore bought it for $285. He hauled the bricks to Overton, where he built his new home. Others removed lumber and stones and carted them away. A contract was let by the government for removal of the graves in the cemetery to higher land, which would be safe from the highest waters.

Day by day the St. Thomas citizens bade farewell, one after another, and departed for new homes elsewhere. The exodus continued through 1935, '36 and '37, families moving to Overton, Las Vegas, Pahranagat, even to Idaho, Oregon, and of course, to Utah.

The fateful day finally arrived, June 11, 1938—when the waters began to lap closer and closer to St. Thomas homes and buildings. Rox Whitmore and his son, Postmaster Leland, raced frantically against time cancelling thousands of "last day" envelopes which had been sent to St. Thomas by philatelists from all over the world. The idea of a town "being drowned" was something new for the stamp and cover-collecting clan.

They finished the job and got out with their heavy load of mail just before the waters would have forced them to halt. As a gesture of finality, Whitmore threw the St. Thomas cancellation stamp far out into the waters of the rising man-made lake.

Hugh Lord, St. Thomas garageman, generally is given credit for being the last to leave. He had vowed he would be. He waited until waters lapped around his bedstead, then he set fire to the Lord home and splashed out of the water to follow the others to higher ground.

That was the last seen of St. Thomas alive—but in 1946, eight years later, a series of dry winters in the Rockies depleted the Lake Mead water supply to such an extent that the lake dropped low enough for the skeletal remains of St. Thomas—the concrete walls of the school house, the bare, dead branches of the mock oranges and cottonwoods, the frames of old wagons and automobiles and other such machines— to rise slowly from the receding waters. Gone were most of the homes and other buildings whose adobe walls had melted away.

Similar protracted dry spells have exposed the old town several times since—St. Thomas just doesn't seem to want to stay down.

Rioville, the other drowned river port lying beneath the waters of Lake Mead, at the former confluence of the Colorado and Virgin, may mark the spot where the first migrants arrived on what now is Nevada soil. The waters of the Colorado here find their first place to spread out and rest after their wild plunge through the narrow gorge of Grand Canyon. As a result, the river often was so shallow that it was easy to ford the stream.

The initial travelers to pass that way probably were those red-skinned "old ones" who colonized near the junction of the Muddy and Virgin sometime between 8000 and 18,000 B. C. Then other Indians began traveling that way from Arizona right after the start of the Christian era, and either subjugated or mixed with the earlier residents. The great attraction to the site where Lost City was built was the huge mountain of salt in the neighborhood—a necessity through the ages to man and beast.

Actually, Lost City is Nevada's oldest "Ghost Town"—by several centuries.

The trail along the Virgin was the route of Jedediah Smith, Armijo, and other early explorers, and it also was the busy path followed by horse thieves from the north, prospectors, soldiers and the Mormons. Actually it was the only north-south trail through southern Nevada for many years.

Sometime prior to 1869 the Church authorities had directed that land be staked and settled at the junction of the Colorado and Virgin, some ten miles south of St. Thomas. The *Deseret News* printed a letter from Joseph W. Young in its January 8,1869, issue which established the beginning of Rioville as a settlement. It read, "I got your letter just as I was leaving St. Joseph today, in company with some eleven brethren enroute for the Colorado where we go to make a beginning on our claims at Junction City [the first name for Rioville]. We take a boat and seine, and tools, for making water ditches and building cabins. We shall also sow a little wheat on the bottom as an experiment."

According to Moapa Stake history some land was cultivated "and a few houses built" but the project wasn't prosperous. The next year those called to develop Rioville asked to be allowed to abandon it because of constant Indian harassment. But church heads telegraphed to St. George, from whence the message was forwarded to the valley, "Leithead's letter received. Tell him to hold Junction until President Young comes in March."

It is probable that when the rest drove off and left the Bonellis on that February morning in 1871, Daniel Bonelli already had realized some of the potentialities of the river junction development—the southern mines needed salt and agricultural products. Also, there were many long periods of high water when the Colorado could not be forded and was too wide for stock to swim.

The nearest settlement was St. George, ninety miles over desert and mountains. The Indians were not exactly friendly, although Dan Bonelli

had gained their grudging respect through honest and fair dealings.

Bonelli visualized the possibilities of a ferry across the Colorado on the busy north and south thoroughfare. Eldorado's diggings were booming. Pioche was booming, too. There was continual traffic up and down the valley road, and the river crossing was difficult at times.

Bonelli retained his St. Thomas holdings—and probably took over some of the better abandoned farms—but decided to move his major operations down the river. He cleared a homesite on the mesa on the east bank of the Virgin and above the Colorado. His first home was constructed of driftwood logs salvaged from the big river's flood stage. Later, he replaced it with the nine-room structure built of stone, with walls two feet thick. The house had a large patio in the rear. Some of the lumber used was salvaged from the river, but most of it was brought from Mt. Trumbull, high on the Shivwits plateau south of St. George, one hundred and fifty miles away, at a cost of $150 per thousand feet. Across the Virgin, on the west bank, he cleared one hundred acres, which were planted in various crops.

Bonelli changed the name of the place from Junction City to Rioville—but in later years it was generally known by all as Bonelli's Ferry. He succeeded in raising hay, which, together with vegetables from his St. Thomas fields and meat from his herds, supplied the mining camps at Eldorado and other newly booming northern Arizona towns.

He had filed on the various salt locations, which were abundant, and one of his major sources of income was from furnishing this much-needed chemical to the mines.

Rioville became an important place in the mining economy of the area, and river steamboat captains brought more and more paddle wheelers through Boulder Canyon to haul back supplies and rock salt.

The Bonelli establishment expanded, and as more and more cattle and agricultural production was developed, more hands were needed. Bonelli hired out-of-work travelers, and a great many Indians. It had the only store for many miles and was a Pony Express station for mail riders traveling from Kingman and the southern mining centers to Pioche, and other northern places. It remained an important spot in southern Nevada activities right up to the turn of the century. Its official postoffice was opened November 2, 1881, and continued until June 30, 1906.

But successive problems began to confront Bonelli. The constantly growing agricultural development of upper Moapa Valley increasingly used the water from the Virgin and Muddy, and many times the stream went dry before it reached Rioville. Bonelli's large fields withered and died. He leased the ferry and farm, but his successor pulled out in a year,

 A ghostly reminder of St. Thomas, the drowned Mormon community.

—Las Vegas Review-Journal Photo.

as the new railroad across southern Nevada slashed travel and shipping on the ferry to a trickle.

Late in 1904 Bonelli leased the place again and made a trip to the county seat at Pioche to settle title and right to the salt mines. He was on his way home when he suffered a stroke which resulted in loss of memory and partial paralysis. He never recovered. He was buried on the mesa overlooking the river and the farm he had carved from the wilderness and developed into such an important place in Nevada's history.

After the second lessee had pulled out, the farm returned to its native mesquite and desert brush. Rioville, like the sturdy old Swiss pioneer who had built it, had served its purpose and died.

Then came Boulder Dam and Lake Mead. The waters of the reservoir backed up and covered Callville, Rioville and St. Thomas. Daniel Bonelli's body was removed ahead of the flood and taken to Kingman to lie beside that of his faithful wife.

Up river a short distance, rearing high above the waters of the lake, stands the 720-foot-high conglomerated mass of limestone which Bonelli had named "The Mormon Temple" many years before. Today fishermen and lake visitors refer to it simply as "The temple."

It really is a natural monument to the memory of that intrepid old wilderness-breaker from Switzerland, Daniel Bonelli, who had refused to give up when all the others left him and his family alone on the Muddy, on that February 1, 1871.

Daniel Bonelli

—*Las Vegas Review-Journal Photo.*

Pahranagat's Stones Stand Still

Pahranagat

PAHRANAGAT IS A PAIUTE NAME. YOU can take your choice of the "authentic" definitions given it by the Indian experts. One group says it means "Valley of the Watermelons," the other "Valley of Many Waters." Since it is doubtful that any Paiute ever saw anything nearer a watermelon than some sort of squash or pumpkin until the whites came along, the latter sounds more logical.

It makes good sense too, for it is a "Valley of Many Waters," an agricultural oasis nearly thirty miles wide located in the midst of Nevada's southeastern desert country. Travelers along U.S. Highway 93—the Canada to Mexico road—always get a pleasant surprise when they strike Pahranagat with its lakes, wide fields and groves of green trees.

The approaches to it for many miles offer such dull scenery that a service station operator with a sense of humor erected a sign along the most boring portion reading "Monotonous, isn't it?"

Pahranagat's lakes are filled and its fields irrigated by three ever-gushing springs, Hiko, the most northern; Crystal; and Ash, the southernmost. They pour water from what seems an inexhaustible underground river at the rate of thousands of gallons an hour.

Naturally such a place was bound to be discovered early in Nevada's settlement.

Crystal Springs was the original and major settlement in Pahranagat Valley in the very early days when horse and cattle thieves brought their stolen critters from the north down the White River Valley and turned them loose to fatten in the valley's lush grasses. The rustlers, and others skipping from the law, gravitated toward the plentiful water supply at Crystal and built stone and brush cabins around its clear pools.

And probably the most real-gone county seat ghost town of Nevada's whole collection of communities which once flourished is Crystal Springs. Under the cottonwoods around the pools formed by the gushing springs, which pour more than five thousand gallons of water a minute right out of the middle of the desert, the only signs of humans are scattered empty beer cans and picnic refuse. There isn't a stick or stone left from the buildings which clustered there nearly a century ago.

Today the heavy flow of traffic on U.S. 93 whizzes past a mile east, and even those who swing off on the Hiko or Tempiute roads zip past Crystal unaware of the vacant site. In fact, you have to ask an old-timer to make certain this is the place of Lincoln County's first seat in 1865, for there isn't even a sign designating it as Crystal Springs.

That's too bad—for it is loaded with early southern Nevada history.

There is little doubt but that the ill-starred and famed Death Valley Forty-Niners watered there before going over the pass and down into

Emigrant Valley across what was to become the atomic bombing range country. The log of Sheldon Young, a member of the Jayhawker party, now in the Huntington Library at San Marino, California, as quoted by Dr. Margaret Young in her excellently researched book on the Forty-Niners, *Shadow of the Arrow*, has these notes:

> "(Nov.) 19 (1849) — This day went five miles. Came to plenty of grass and water . . . no timber, had the best grass since we left the Platte.

> "(Nov.) 20th (1849) — This day we left Ward's Muddy and bore off on a southwest course. Went sixteen miles . . . dry camp. Not much grass."

Since the map they followed, made by a fellow named Barney Ward, designated the Pahranagat stream as the west branch of the Muddy, this seems definitely to put the Forty-Niners there. One thing is quite certain, those misguided folk who left Capt. Jefferson Hunt's train near today's Enterprise, Utah, and struck off west by themselves most certainly crossed Pahranagat, and if they didn't camp at Crystal Springs they did at its neighbor Hiko Spring—five miles north.

History records the next white visitors at Crystal Springs in 1858 when the "White Mountain Boys," a group from Parowan, Utah, scouted out possible areas for settlement in anticipation of a new exodus of the Mormons if the troubles between the church and government could not be settled. They camped at Crystal Springs while surveying the thirty-mile length of Pahranagat Valley.

Just when the first horse thief discovered the area is unrecorded but by the early 'sixties it rapidly was becoming a rendezvous. Then came other new settlers, men who had traveled back to Nevada with the furor over the Comstock and Austin discoveries and were looking for some place to take up their former occupations as farmers.

Among the early arrivals was A. W. Gear. While he lived, he always insisted that early Pahranagat was "The toughest place I ever saw." He'd been to the California gold fields, Virginia City and elsewhere—so it must have been really tough. One observer claimed to have counted three hundred and fifty different brands on grazing horses.

It was in 1862 that Dan DeQuille, the famed writing partner of Mark Twain on the *Territorial Enterprise*, dreamed up what became one of his most famous "quaints" about "The Rolling Stones of Pahranagat" and made the isolated spot known throughout the world. It was the habit of the two reporters to attempt to outdo each other with hoax tales when news was dull. Virginia City readers could recognize these yarns for what they were—many others swallowed them whole.

DeQuille had a brilliant engineering mind, and his mining articles were accepted as factual. So when he wrote his story about some mysterious power in Pahranagat, isolated five hundred miles from Virginia City, which pulled the stones in the valley to a magnetic center and then repulsed them and sent them rolling back to their original places, he did it in an erudite manner. Dan's theory of magnetic propulsion and repulsion was so vividly "scientific" and convincing that other papers throughout the nation picked it up.

The story reached Europe. German scientists had been making a concentrated study of electromagnetic currents, and the tale created a sensation among them. They wrote to Dan and demanded further details. His reply that the story was just a hoax aroused their anger—they charged that he was attempting to withhold scientific facts from them. They were certain he had made a startling discovery about the laws of nature.

The affair threatened to become an international incident as Germany wrote United States officials demanding details about the discovery, "first observed and recorded by Herr Dan De Quille, the eminent physicist of Virginiastadt, Nevada."

The topper of this tale was an offer by Phineas T. Barnum. He would put up $10,000 if Dan would make the Pahranagat stones perform for his audiences.

The rocks around Crystal Springs don't roll—they sit mighty still in their same old spots. In fact, one has sat so solidly for so long on the hill west of the springs that the U. S. Geodetic Survey picked it as the place to mount one of its brass survey base markers.

Logan City had blossomed into the area's first mining town after an inquisitive group of prospectors had heard rumors of a silver mountain near the Colorado. The party had searched along the river in the Muddy Mountain section west of the Virgin and, finding nothing, was on the way back to the Panaca district, then in Utah territory. The group picked up some rich looking float ore. In the party were John H. Ely, T. C. W. Sayles, David Sanderson, Samuel F. Strutt, William McClusky and Ira Hatch, an Indian interpreter. An old Indian in the Pahranagat Valley said he knew where there was a great deal of the same kind of rock. He led them to what became the "Ely and Sanderson lode," in the Irish Mountains, on March 17, 1865.

The discovery marked the real opening of future Lincoln County and the beginning of the saga of John Ely, who was later to become one of the big men of eastern Nevada mining in Pioche.

The party staked out a number of locations, and returned to Panaca for supplies. In June a group went back to the spot and started to work. Only nine were left in July when Indians attacked and chased them away. By October, however, a permanent camp was established and Logan City came into being, and the start of 1866, had a population of approximately two hundred, according to the State Mineralogist's report. Among the newcomers was William H. Raymond, who bought a number of the claims.

He and Ely gravitated toward each other. When they realized that the Irish Mountain ore was going to net little unless they could mill it on the spot, Raymond went to New York to raise funds for such a project. He returned early in 'sixty-six, and the partners picked a site at Hiko Spring for the five-stamp mill. The location provided a plentiful water supply, and a downhill haul. This marked the start of the town of Hiko.

When the first Nevada State legislature, in 1865, established Lincoln County in the far southeast corner of the State, Crystal Springs was designated as the provisional county seat—probably because it was the only place in the area they'd ever heard about in Carson City.

Gov. H. G. Blasdel, and a party from Carson, decided to make an investigation trip to the new district. That ill-fated journey took them through Death Valley, where they ran out of food in the Amargosa desert. The Governor and a companion made the long trip across country—through what is now the atomic range—to Logan City, and obtained food and aid. When the rescue party got back to Ash Meadows they found one member of the party had died.

They buried him and returned to Pahranagat, where they discovered there weren't enough voters in the designated area to establish a full-fledged county. At that time the state line extended north and south about fifteen miles east of Pahranagat. Later in the same year the United States Congress gave Nevada another degree of longitude eastward, where the present boundary still is, adding Panaca and Cherry Valley to Nevada's territory.

This provided the area with enough citizenry for the formal establishment of the county and, in 1866, this step was accomplished. In the meantime, Ely and his partner, Raymond, had built a mill at Hiko to handle the Logan ore.

It was natural for a town to grow up near the mill, and by 1867 Hiko had become the largest community in Lincoln County, and the logical site for the county seat until 1871, when Pioche popped into prominence and stole it away.

Pahranagat abounds in thrilling incidents, such as the time a group of irate Utah farmers rode into the valley on the trail of a horse thief. Honest citizens joined the Utahans in a posse and captured the alleged rustler, assembled immediately and conducted a midnight trial. The culprit, as usual, was quickly convicted and sentenced to hang. The rope had been tossed over a rafter for the execution when activities were halted sharply by a stern voice from the darkness. It ordered release of the thief. The farmers could do little as the voice was backed up by a shotgun, while the barrels of several others gleamed in the light. The other horse thieves had come to the rescue of their comrade. Instead of hanging, the culprit rode off with his friends.

Nell Murbarger tells of another incident in her *Ghosts of the Glory Trail* in which Hiko's 601 vigilantes had a leading part. This time Tempiute Bill and a sullen character remembered only as Moquitch, were suspected of killing a harmless old duffer at Crescént, near Logan. Hearing they were suspected, the two departed for the desert mountain ranges of Nye County. Officers followed and picked them up. Deputy Sheriff J. A. Bidwell was bringing them back to Pahranagat when a determined delegation waylaid him and took away the prisoners, who admitted other murders and implicated a companion named "Johnny." The vigilantes recessed the trial long enough to go after Johnny, who elected to shoot it out. This suited the 601 posse members fine. When the smoke cleared Johnny and several of his companions would never need a trial. The vigilantes returned to Moquitch and Tempiute Bill at Hiko.

The *Pioche Record* reported the conclusion in this succinct and graphic manner: "Moquitch and Tempiute Bill were placed on a wagon, with ropes around their necks, and taken to a two-story building, and from an upper window a plank was run out and the ropes attached. The horses, it is supposed, took fright at something and dragged off the wagon, leaving the two hanging by the neck, and as no one relieved them, they soon died."

Quite naturally, the Indians didn't like the idea of the whites moving in on their fertile oasis. There were recurring troubles with the redskins until the whites subdued them in a bloody, but determined manner.

Three young easterners, walking to California along the Emigrant Road, were accosted by Indians about six miles east of Hiko. The Indians attacked, killed two of the men and shot the third through the shoulder with an arrow. It failed to halt his flight, instead apparently adding speed to his fleeting feet as he outran the irate red men all the way to Hiko.

News of the killing aroused the whites. They immediately organized an Indian hunt. The two Indians responsible for the attack were caught and hanged.

The rest of the Paiutes swore revenge— but had no opportunity even to gather for a war dance as the whites took immediate stringent action. They attacked two of the main Indian camps in daybreak raids. At the largest, on the site of Pahranagat's present community center, Alamo, seventeen Indians were killed. About the same number were slaughtered at another camp further up, probably around Crystal Springs. For a long time afterwards any Indian attempting to make peace was shot or chased off. When the strife finally ended, it was for good. The red men had had "enough."

Hiko's most frequently reported trial was that of Frank Vale in the late 'sixties. It was as fine an example of efficient dispensation of frontier justice as you'll find.

Vale, known as an avid collector of horses belonging to others, appeared in Hiko with a stranger. They rode on south through the valley. A few days later Vale came riding back through Hiko alone with an extra horse.

Nobody thought much about this until a squaw noted Indian dogs digging in the remains of the fire where Vale and his partner had camped in a meadow at the lower end of the valley. She investigated, discovered the dogs had uncovered a buried saddle and reported the incident. A group of settlers dug up the site and came upon the remains of Vale's partner.

A posse was formed and trailed Vale three-hundred miles to Austin where he was caught. He was returned to Hiko and in the words of Justice Clapp, who presided, "given a fair trial." Twelve residents had been called to sit on the jury. At the same time two others were delegated to go into the next room and build a coffin.

While the trial proceeded, the din of hammering and sawing was plainly heard by everybody in the courtroom including the defendant. Vale quickly was found guilty by the jury, hanged and buried that afternoon.

The Irish Mountain mines, like many others, were proving pretty ephemeral as far as worthwhile ore was concerned. By 1869 the Hiko Silver Mining Company, as the Raymond and Ely combine was known, had just about played out its limit in the venture. The pair nosed around the newly-found Pioche district and bought a location. This turned into the famous Raymond and Ely mine and it brought down the curtain on Logan City's heyday. In 1869 the mill was moved to Bullionville, two miles northwest of Panaca. With it went most of the Logan City and Hiko population, only farming families remaining in Pahranagat.

Pahranagat's mining epitaph was written in a periodical of the time: "No company ever organized to operate mines on the Pacific Coast spent so much money and kept at it so long without results as this company."

Hiko's prosperity finally hit bottom in 1871 when Pioche mustered enough votes to snatch away the county seat. However, the post office, which was established June 24, 1867, after being known at first on the records as "Pah Ranagat" from March 25, 1867, served the entire valley until Alamo, in the central position was given an office on May 12, 1905.

It was the building of U. S. highway 93 a few years ago, which almost wrote "finis" to the Hiko story—its route went four miles south of the pioneer county seat. What little business was left moved down to Alamo. The post office remained, though, and so did the ancient bubbling springs and some of the oldtime farm residents.

They are the ones who keep Hiko peacefully and quietly alive today, just a little way off the busy highway on State Route 38, which goes northward up the valley toward Hamilton—on the old horse thief trail.

PART TWO

The Colossal Comstock

"Nevada also was Born at Genoa"

THE GENESIS OF ANY CHRONICLE OF NE-
vada's early-day settlements has to be
Genoa. It was first. The name is fitting—as Columbus was born in the
Italian Genoa, Nevada's civilization was spawned in its namesake. Both
went on to greater glories.

Originally dubbed Mormon Station by early travelers across the Great
Basin on the Emigrant Trail, its site was dictated by geographical and
economic factors.

Located right at the foot of the Sierra, it was the gateway to California and situated at the northern end of Carson Valley, whose broad
acres grew lush with feed for stock jaded from the 500-mile-long alkali-
dusty trail from Salt Lake City. It was the principal stopover for the
constant stream of gold-seeking argonauts, of the early 1850s.

Actually, Genoa may not seem to belong in a series about ghost towns
because it is still a fairly busy place—especially during the tourist season
when dozens of cars daily detour from the present-day main routes to
see its old buildings and visit its curio stores, "oldest" saloons, etc. The
rich farms around it have been purchased in recent years by plush Gold
Coast society folk, who maintain legal residences there as an aid to
saving something from the annual feast of the tax ogre.

Yet, because it was the base from which all of Nevada's later white
settlements and subsequent mineral discoveries developed, it is the dow-
ager queen of the State's spectral world. Its own phantom population in-
cludes a large host of wraiths who were major characters in Nevada's
history. Among them are such legendary western pioneers as John Reese,
"Hank" Monk, "Snowshoe" Thompson, Abe Curry, "Lucky Bill" Thorrington, Isaac Roop and a host of others equally as famous in Nevada's
pioneer days.

It was a most important spot in western development for several
years, during which it hosted thousands of hopeful gold seekers, silver
chasers, emigrants, authors, actors, stage robbers, politicians, promoters
and a constant stream of curious travelers such as Horace Greeley, Artemus Ward, Richard Burton, the British author of *Arabian Nights* fame;
John Muir, the noted naturalist, and many, many others equally as well
known.

History gives Joseph Walker, early-day Rocky Mountain trapper and
explorer, credit for being the first white man to intrude on these happy
hunting grounds of the Washoe Indians. He camped in Carson Valley in
1833 "until he could find a pass over the Sierras."

Many mistakenly believe that General John Frémont and his noted
pioneer guide, Kit Carson, were among Genoa's early visitors. But this

is one historic honor for upper Carson Valley, (named for "Kit", as is the Carson River and the State capital) that doesn't appear to be borne out by the record. History indicates that on their exploration from Oregon down through western Nevada in February, 1843, they struck the Carson River fifty or sixty miles eastward, where Carson climbed a tall hill, saw the meadows along the Walker River and followed this route further south. The river led them to the foot of the Sierra range and they made their fabulous winter crossing by following up Markleville Creek.

Even before the Frémont exploration, earlier westbound California argonauts had ventured away from the Oregon Trail, hunting a shortcut to the Coast and had passed this way seeking a road over the Sierra.

An unusual sequence of incidents led to the founding of Genoa.

When members of the Mormon Battalion were discharged in California in 1847, they began their long treks toward Salt Lake City. Many traveled the Old Spanish Trail from Los Angeles across what is now southern Nevada. Others went northward, planning to cross the mountains and thus reach the new land of Mormonism. It was late in the year and heavy snows halted them on the California side. They sought employment until spring arrived and the mountains became passable.

Several obtained jobs helping to build a sawmill for John Sutter at a place called Coloma on the south fork of the American River. One of them was W. Bigler and he was working with James Marshall when the latter found gold in his millrace on January 24, 1848, the incident which triggered the great mid-century westward gold rush.

Later, when warming spring weather cleared the passes, the Mormons continued their journey to their new homes. They came down the eastern side of the mountains and turned north, parallelling the river through Carson Valley. One of the men, H. S. Beattie noted that it might be a logical place to establish a trading post. In 1850, he, with six companions, brought a considerable number of supplies and erected a building. This marked the actual birth of Mormon Station, although hardly anything is recorded about the incident in western history.

Travel had increased heavily as the rush to the California gold fields brought a never-ending parade across the desert. Beattie quickly disposed of his small stock of supplies at Genoa, including the cattle he had brought, which were butchered and eagerly bought by the emigrants at the unbelievable price for those days of 75 cents a pound. He sold the post to a man named Moore and returned to Salt Lake City.

There he obtained a job with the Reese brothers, who had recently transported a wagon train of goods across the prairie from their family store in Brooklyn, N.Y., and opened a branch mercantile establishment among their Mormon brethren. When Beattie related his Mormon Station experience to John Reese, the merchant could visualize an opportunity for excellent profit in a well stocked trading post, beyond the desert, and on the doorstep of the mountains.

His brother agreed to operate the Salt Lake store while John gave the plan a trial. He loaded thirteen wagons with eggs, bacon, flour, grain and feeds of all kinds, and headed west across the Humboldt Trail. His drivers, including Stephen A. Kinsey, who was to become a prominent Nevada pioneer, were the only other persons in the party. The group arrived at Mormon Station on June 1, 1851.

The first thing the newcomers did was to erect a building. "It was a kind of hotel and store," Reese wrote in later years. "I had a store in it and also a dining room. It was built of logs, two stories high and about 50 by 130 feet." It was the first house built in what now is Nevada.

Reese ploughed 30 acres and "put in wheat, barley, grain and watermelon on one side and mixed things all around." Turnips were a best seller. He later recalled, "I never saw such things to make money on. I could get one dollar for a bunch which only cost ten cents in Salt Lake."

Reese's autobiography notes that "not a single white man was there" when he arrived. "The nearest white man was in Gold Canyon," he wrote. "He had . . . wintered there in kind of a small dugout . . . he was nicknamed 'Virginia'."

This was James "Virginia" Finney or Fennemore—nobody seems to be certain which—who later "discovered" the Comstock Lode and gave his nickname to the fabulous silver metropolis in one of Nevada's most amusing legendary tales. Reese's statement seems to correct some of the historians who say that "Old Virginny" was one of the trader's wagon drivers. It appears that Finney's Nevada arrival preceded Reese's.

The building of the trading post soon attracted others who settled nearby on the rich valley lands. The first were John and Rufus Thomas and a man named J. Brown. William Thorrington came along and started a ranch. A man named Job opened a store about ten miles west of Genoa. Henry Van Syckle and his brother built a blacksmith shop south of Reese's store at the foot of the Kingsbury grade.

The first woman resident of Carson Valley was Mrs. Israel Mott, who arrived with her husband in the summer of 1852 with a wagon train bound for California. The Motts liked the looks of the place and located four miles along the trail up the canyon over the mountains. Their first house was built from lumber in the wagon beds, Mott hand-carved a window sash, and according to Thompson and West's *History of Nevada,* "paid 75 cents a light for seven-by-nine inch glass to put in it."

In December Reese and Mott obtained a toll road grant over the Carson River and up the canyon road from the Utah territorial government. They were to repair the road up the mountain and were allowed to charge toll of $1 per wagon, 25 cents a head for horses and mules, 10 cents a head for horned cattle and two and a half cents apiece for sheep.

During 1852 many others took up ranches as civilization moved in. Miners from California were flocking to Gold Canyon to pan out the gold while they could as the creek "dried up in the summer time."

The primary objective of Reese was to sell goods at a profit, mostly to travelers on the California trail. When "Ben Holladay came out in 1852 with a train of horses, flour, ham, bacon, etc. I bought him out," he wrote.

That puts Holladay into the Nevada scene, where he became a very important figure. After selling to Reese he went into partnership with George Chorpenning, who had the contract to carry the mail from Salt Lake City to Genoa and thence to California. Holladay later bought out Chorpenning and in 1862, when the Pony Express failed, he purchased it at auction, foreseeing that while the overland telegraph doomed the fast horse-carried mail, a speedy overland stage line would be a profit-making necessity in the expanding western territory. He was the one who was to organize the future overland stage operation.

The discovery of gold and the western migration of Mormons to the agricultural lands, quickly brought about the establishment of other communities. Johntown was the mining settlement at the mouth of Gold Canyon, not far from where Dayton now stands. In November 1851, a party of Californians finding all the land in Carson Valley taken up by Mormons, settled on the Eagle Ranch, in Eagle Valley, twelve miles away. Today that is the site of the State capital, Carson City.

Population was increasing, but the residents found themselves far removed from any sort of government or law and order. Utah had become a territory in the fall of 1850 and the Nevada area was known as "Western Utah Territory." Lines more than four hundred miles long extended across the map from the western tier of Utah counties all the way to the then unsurveyed California line, marking narrow strips of land. These meant nothing as far as any legal processes were concerned in the far western sections of the various counties.

Confronted with the need of some readily applicable rules regarding property rights and human actions, the citizens, both Mormons and Gentiles gathered in occasional "citizens' meetings," the first being held in November, 1851. The initial action of this squatter government was the appointment of a surveyor and recorder to establish property limits and claims. Later steps provided a system of judicial procedure and provided for a sheriff and a tribunal of justices.

Appeal from a decision of this court went to a "Court of Twelve Citizens" which had absolute power. Nobody ever thought about asking Governor Brigham Young's sanction. In fact, the Genoans later ignored the Mormon leader and petitioned Congress to make Western Utah a separate territory.

Young, however, had taken cognizance of their actions and in January, 1854, the Utah Territorial Legislature passed a bill establishing "Carson County," which took in all territory in "Carson and adjoining valleys."

Governor Young appointed a leading Mormon, Orson Hyde, as probate judge of the new county. Coincidentally, Federal Judge George

P. Styles was named to preside over a "third district," which included Carson County. Hyde, Styles and a federal marshal arrived in Genoa on June 15, 1855, with an escort of thirty-five men, and formally organized the county.

Hyde changed the name of Mormon Station to Genoa and designated it the County seat, an honor it was to retain until 1915.

Two actions of the pioneer merchant Reese, in 1854, left their imprint on Nevada history. The first was construction of a saw and grist mill at Genoa. "Flour was worth $75 a hundred pounds," he wrote, "but after my mill was built it came down to $6." The machine age had reached Nevada!

The second event occurred when Reese accompanied an exploring party on its way to Salt Lake. It proposed going straight east from the Carson sink, in the hopes of finding a shorter route, instead of turning northeast and following the Humboldt around its long loop. Near the center of what is now the state, the party came to a small stream running northward.

Reese decided to follow it and determine if it ran into the Humboldt. It did. The party named it Reese River, and as such it was to shine brightly on the pages of Nevada history ever after.

This exploring party reported that it thought it had found a shorter route, and the following year Howard Egan, one of the great trail blazers of Mormon history, established the way which became known as Egan's Trail.

He had such faith that it was shorter and better than the Humboldt route that he wagered he could ride a mule from Salt Lake City to Sacramento in ten days. He won his bet, causing a national sensation at the time. As far as anybody knows, nobody ever has beaten that time horseback without relief or changes of mounts.

On the record-breaking trip Egan passed through Genoa around seven in the evening on September 28, 1855, his diary noted, reached Hangtown (Placerville) at five the next morning and completed the marathon at Sacramento at six that evening. The Egan Trail later became the route of the Pony Express, the Overland telegraph, the Overland Stage line and presently is generally followed by U. S. 50, the Lincoln Highway.

The rich lands at the foot of the Sierra soon were filled with Mormon immigrants. Following the program set by the church leaders, they built communities, tilled the ground and worked hard to make a new stronghold of their faith in western Nevada. The mixture of devoted, agricultural Mormons and rugged gold-hunting miners was antagonistic. Strife was constant, and many early land titles were determined by gunfire.

Wherever humans cluster in habitations, one of their first needs is communication. Genoa was on the main route, and messages could be sent back and forth at first with travelers. Then, as the volume grew, a postoffice became a necessity. Since Genoa was in Utah Territory, Governor Brigham Young, attended to the details and the "Carson Valley" office was opened on September 30, 1853, with C. L. Barnard as postmaster. He was succeeded in 1855 by J. C. Fain, and on September 30, 1857—four years after it opened—Stephen A. Kinsey, one of Reese's original teamsters, took charge. The mail continued to be cancelled "Carson Valley" when Nevada became a territory in 1861, not being changed to Genoa until 1863.

The Carson Valley's green fields were ripening, livestock was fat and the young orchards were just coming into fruit in the summer of 1857, when three tired and worn horseback messengers rode up to Bishop Hyde's place at Franktown, in Washoe Valley north of Carson City. They carried orders for all of the Mormons in Nevada to return to Salt Lake City and help defend their capital from the United States Army. Practically all made immediate plans to comply. A few were able to sell, others gave away their belongings, the rest just walked off and abandoned their hard-won fields, orchards and homes.

A train of 150 wagons and a 1,000 of these rugged pioneers gathered along the Carson River and marched eastward on the long trek, retracing their original migration, and reached Salt Lake City, November 1, 1857. Three died on the return trip, but six newborn Mormons increased the ranks.

With the departure of the Mormons, Gentiles moved in, settled on the abandoned farms and purloined buildings and equipment. "Lucky Bill" Thorrington hauled the school house from Franktown to his Genoa farm as soon as the Mormons departed, and used it for a barn.

Some had agreed to pay Orson Hyde for his properties. When they didn't he sent back a letter to the "people of Washoe and Carson Valleys" demanding $20,000 for his sawmill and land holdings. He quoted numerous scriptural references and declared that if the claim was ignored they would be "visited with thunder and with earthquake, and with floods, with pestilence and with famine until your names are not known among men."

Intervention by the Army in Mormon affairs also afforded the Gentile citizens of western Utah an excellent opportunity to raise the question of establishing a separate territory. Their efforts a year previously, to have the Nevada area annexed to California, had failed in Congress.

A number of the Mormons refused to follow Brigham Young's order to return to Salt Lake. One of them was John Reese. So, when a group of citizens assembled at Genoa in August, 1857, "Colonel" Reese served as chairman. History has bestowed the military title upon the founder of Genoa for no explained reason. Among those present at this meeting was William B. "Lucky Bill" Thorrington, one of the valley's early pioneers.

A little later "Lucky Bill" either was struck by Orson Hyde's curse, or was the victim of his own folly. He became one of Nevada's legendary characters as a result. He had achieved his nickname because of his seeming ability always to win at gambling. Bill was a huge, jovial fellow, who assertedly had left a family in Michigan and ran off with a young girl, who lived with him as his wife and raised their children at Genoa. One of his well known characteristics was his friendship with a number of suspected men whose activities were outside what little law existed. One of these was a fellow named Edwards.

Evidence became strong that Thorrington had connived with him in the killing of a Frenchman who was driving a herd of cattle through the Truckee Valley near the present site of Reno. Some of the stolen cattle were reported to have been seen on the Thorrington ranch. Citizens formed a vigilante group and hauled Thorrington into a rump court before a jury of eighteen men. Lucky Bill was found guilty by his neighbors and sentenced to be hanged as an accessory to the murder.

The citizens still sought Edwards. They convinced Thorrington's son, Bill, that they might go easier on his father if he'd help them nab Edwards. The youth went to the latter's hideout and induced him to come to the Thorrington house that night by telling him his father wanted to see him. When Edwards walked into the trap he was grabbed by hidden vigilantes and received a similar sentence. A delegation from Honey Lake was present and had positive evidence Edwards had killed another citizen there, so he was turned over to the Californians for execution.

Thorrington was hauled to a nearby cottonwood tree, where he stood up in a wagon, a noose adjusted around his neck and fastened to a limb. Always a gay, devil-may-care sort, he loudly sang his favorite song, *The Last Rose of Summer,* until the wagon was driven from beneath him, strangling the final phrase. Lucky Bill's luck finally had run out. The date was June 18, 1858.

Another phase of civilization made its debut in Nevada on December 18, 1858, when the *Territorial Enterprise,* later to become famous as the birthplace of Mark Twain as an author, published its first issue at Genoa. Previously Nevada's only periodicals had been handwritten sheets, one at Genoa, the other in Gold Canyon. The first was *The Scorpion,* issued in 1854 by Stephen A. Kinsey for a few issues, the latter the *Gold Canyon Switch,* the brainchild of Joe Webb. These were the forerunners of more than 100 different Nevada newspapers which were to pop up within the next two decades, most of them to disappear almost as rapidly, as only thirty still survived in 1880.

The new, shorter Egan Trail brought increased travel and freight intercourse with Salt Lake City, but Nevadans still had no intention of being governed by the Mormons. On June 11, 1859, a day or two before the discovery of the Comstock Lode, citizens of growing Gold Hill held a meeting and decreed "the isolated position we occupy, far from all legal tribunals . . . renders it necessary that we organize in a body politic, for our mutual protection against the lawless, and for meeting out justice between man and man."

Similar meetings were held elsewhere in the district and on July 18, 1859, delegates gathered at Genoa and adopted a "Declaration of Independence," reproaching the Mormons for abuses against the residents of the western end of the territory, and drafting a form of government. Provisional officials were elected. Isaac Roop, a delegate from Susanville, which then was believed to be in Nevada, but proved later to be part of California when the survey was made, was elected "Governor."

Genoa was designated the Provisional Territorial Capital. The "legislature" met at Genoa on December 15, 1859, organized and passed a memorial to Congress in behalf of a separate territory. Everything was highly informal, but the provisional government did provide a cloak for a semblance of enforcement of law and order.

Genoa, during these years, was the major community in the entire district. "Hank" Monk was one of the stage driver heroes of the line which had been established to Placerville. He leaped into national fame when Artemus Ward made him the hero of a hoax story built around Horace Greeley's ride over the mountains in 1859.

Greeley was anxious to run for U.S. President and the humorist opposed him. The tale gained nationwide prominence and belief. Monk ever after was considered by the general public as the kingpin of the stage drivers. Mark Twain wrote his version of the famed Greeley ride, further greatly twisted from the real facts, in *Roughing It*. But whether Hank was a better driver than some of his contemporaries such as "Charlie" Parkhurst, "Uncle Jim" Miller, "Dutch John" and "Curly Jerry" Robbins, is a matter of opinion. However, he gets credit for discovering one thing still much in vogue—copper rivets on the pockets of "Levi's."

Wells Drury, noted early-day Comstock editor, later related that "Hank, when on the road . . . was wont to mend his clothing with copper harness rivets in lieu of buttons." Drury asserted that a San Francisco clothing manufacturer, Levi Strauss, learned of the success of Hank's ingenious method during a trip with him. Anyway, Strauss made a fortune from his denim work clothes, which had (and still have) copper-riveted pockets.

Carson Valley also was the birthplace of another idea which two-score years later developed into a piece of machinery known today throughout the world by practically every man, woman and child, the Ferris Wheel.

While everybody is familiar with this common amusement device, it is doubtful if many know that it is as American as Bull Durham cigarettes or that the idea for it undoubtedly germinated in the fertile mind of a pioneer youngster in early-day western Nevada.

The various encyclopedias note that George Washington Gale Ferris Jr., an American engineer who was graduated from Rensselaer Polytechnic Institute in 1881, invented the 1000-passenger revolving wheel which became a sensation at the World Columbian Exposition in Chicago in 1893 and fathered all the Ferris wheels since then. But they don't tell the story behind that invention.

Young Ferris came across the plains at the age of five in 1864 with his family, which settled near Genoa. Nearby, William Cradlebaugh had erected a toll bridge across the Carson River on the Overland Trail. Cradlebaugh had built an undershot water-wheel to lift a plentiful supply of water from the river for the trail-weary travelers and their stock and to irrigate his hay fields during dry periods.

Young Ferris never wearied of lying in the grass beside the river and watching the wheel perpetually performing its task. It held a magnetic attraction for him. So, it seems entirely logical that the ideas, which ran through the youngster's mind during those days must have planted the seed from which the huge 250-foot Chicago Fair wheel was conceived and built in 1892.

Genoa had its share of stage robbers, bandits and rough characters in the early lawless days. One legendary tale was about the $20,000 in kegs which was lifted from the Placerville stage in 1860.

No trace of the robbers ever was found until twenty years later, when an old man, dying in prison in another state, admitted he was one of the holdup men. His intimate knowledge of the crime gave credence to his tale. He said that he and his partners took only $2,000 of the gold, all they could carry comfortably, and buried the rest "under a pine tree near Genoa."

He insisted that it had never been dug up, since he was the only survivor and the only one who knew where it was located. When his story was printed there was a "gold rush" to Genoa.

Frantic folk dug around practically every pine tree on the slopes and in the valley. They never found the treasure. If the old man's story was true, it's still there. All anybody has to do to get the remaining $18,000 is to locate the right pine tree and dig.

Then, too, Genoa was the eastern terminus for the astounding "Snowshoe" Thompson, who carried the mail over the Sierra in dead of winter, without extra food or bedding. This husky Norseman probably was America's first skier on his cumbersome, hand-carved heavy runners. There are enough tales about him to fill a book. They can be found in almost every one ever written about the Comstock times.

The Indian war, the finding of the Comstock with its fabulous riches, and the imminent possibility of Civil War all had their influence on Congress, which organized Nevada Territory early in 1861. James W. Nye, a New York politician, was appointed Governor. He arrived in Carson City, on July 11, 1861, and proclaimed organization of the terri-

torial government. Six days later Carson City was designated as the
territorial capital and Genoa's reign of glory was over.

The census ordered by Governor Nye and reported on the following
August 5 showed 3,284 in Virginia City; 2,076 in the Carson City area;
1,297 at Gold Hill, with another 1,022 at Silver City, just down the
canyon; while Carson Valley, including all the area south of Clear Creek,
tallied only 1,057.

Genoa had been passed by in the rush to the Comstock. However,
in November, when the Territorial legislature set up the nine original
counties, Genoa received a slight sop to its wounded feelings over losing
the Capital. It was designated as the seat of Douglas County, named in
honor of Stephen A. Douglas, President Lincoln's long-time opponent.
The first County commission rented quarters for official offices and used
part of John Reese's old mill for a jail. A year later the Catholic church
was purchased for $75 and transformed into a courthouse. Then in 1865,
the county finally moved into permanent quarters in a new $18,000
building equipped with iron doors and shutters.

But even with the coming of official law and order at last, Genoa's
strong-minded pioneers still believed in direct action when necessary. A
fellow named Sam Brown took a couple of shots at Henry Van Syckle, one
of the town's earliest citizens who chased him down and returned the
fire with much deadlier aim. A coroner's jury brought in a verdict which
epitomized the general attitude toward those who were too free on the
trigger. The jury found that Brown had come to his death "from a just
dispensation of justice." Freely translated, this could mean "It served
him right!"

Genoa's economic and political importance lasted only a decade.
But, historically it rates first place in Nevada's history; it was the birthplace of that fabulous State's civilization. Loyal Nevadans regard it as
the Plymouth Rock or Williamsburg of the Sagebrush State; never sensational, but the matriarch of the family.

Genoa as it is Today

—*Las Vegas Review-Journal Photo.*

"Gold Flakes and Dime Drinks"

★ Gold Hill

WITHOUT GOLD CANYON THERE IS NO TELL-
ing how long Nevada might have remained largely unexplored and unknown. Certainly the State's mineral
riches which brought the great rush of the mid-nineteenth century
might have lain undiscovered for many years. Yet this fabulous treasure
place has scarcely been noticed by historical authors who have written
reams of copy about its world-famed offspring, Virginia City.

Gold Canyon was the spark that lit the fuse which boomed Nevada's
population from nothing in 1850 to 6857 in 1860, and 42,491 in the succeeding decade.

The identity of Gold Canyon's "James Marshall" is entangled in one of
those incidents upon which historians probably never will reach an agreement—various "discoverers" have their staunch supporters.

There is the written claim that John Bigler and the returning Mormon
battalioneers, who had been at Coloma with Marshall, panned the sands
of Gold Creek and retrieved a pinch of dust which he took back to Salt
Lake City. On the other hand, that astute historian, Eliot Lord, whose
Comstock Mining and Miners is so accurate it is almost presumptuous
for anybody to dispute, gives the credit to William Prouse, a young Mormon member of a party being led to California by Thomas Orr. He was
among a group of men who had gone ahead of the main party to re-
connoiter a route over the mountains. This group made a noon halt on
May 15, 1849, where a creek ran into the Carson River and Prouse, according to Lord, took a milk pan and washed some of the surface gravel
in the creek water, finding gold flakes. Lord quoted the date and result of
the discovery from Prouse's diary, the latter being still alive at the time
(1881) and living in Millard County, Utah.

Prouse's 1849 "discovery," however, was a year later than the reported finding by the Mormon Battalion group. It is a little baffling to
understand why Lord gave it so much credence when he has a footnote
on the same page quoting a letter which said, "William Prouse declares
that he made a still earlier discovery of gold dust in the same creek bed,
in the autumn of 1848, on his return to Salt Lake from the South Fork of
the American River. He lingered behind his party in order to prospect,
and on coming up with the train again told its members, Joseph Bates,
Frank Weaver and Rufus Stoddard, that he would 'show them a place,
if they ever traveled that way again, where they could find gold'."

If this be true, it is evident that Prouse's milk-pan discovery was the
result of his find of the previous fall. Why, then, didn't Lord make that the
discovery date?

Whoever actually found the first fine flakes, the fact remains that there certainly was gold in that creek and the Orr party is given credit for so naming it, calling the ravine Gold Canyon. Other westbound pioneers later found showings, and carried the word over the mountains.

Soon miners, always ready to hurry to a new source of mineral wealth, began crossing the Sierra eastward and commenced working their way up the canyon. They came in the spring, stayed as long as water flowed in the creek and then returned to California for the winter.

John Reese, who established the first trading post in Nevada at Genoa in 1851, later wrote in his memoirs that when he arrived he found "Old Virginia" Finney living in a dugout at Gold Canyon. By the middle of that summer a rush was on, with an influx, in addition to prospectors, of grog-shop owners, merchants, farmers, herders, teamsters, and blacksmiths. Communities began to appear—Chinatown, at the mouth of the canyon, later to become Dayton; Silver City, a little way up the ravine, and further up, Gold Hill situated on a red mound at the head of the canyon.

Just over the divide, above Gold Hill, a few miners built their shacks and dugouts. This spot had several different names—Pleasant Hill, Mount Pleasant Point, Ophir and Ophir Diggings, but the one that stuck was Virginia Town, later changed by circumstances to Virginia City.

There is a legendary tale about how the famous town got its name. "Virginia" Finney was a lad who liked his "Forty-rod" whiskey. Purportedly a real pioneer could stagger forty rods without falling down after drinking some of it. One night he was stumbling to his hut on the high side of the divide when he fell and broke the bottle he was carrying.

Finney decided that some use should be made of the spilled hooch and mumbled "I baptize ye Virginny Town." He later told the story, and the name stuck. This yarn has been subjected to varied literary license by every subsequent writer of the Comstock story.

The next noted Nevada historical personage to arrive was Allison "Eilley" Orrum Hunter Cowan—a Scotch convert to Mormonism, who divorced her Bishop husband at Nauvoo when she found he had some other wives. Eilley had then married Alexander Cowan and they had come to Nevada in the Mormon migration of 1855. She shed him, too, when he obeyed Brigham Young's call to return to Salt Lake in 1857. Eilley then started a boarding house in Johntown, the settlement at the mouth of the canyon.

"Virginia" Finney decided to pan a little of the red dirt at Gold Hill which others had ignored. It proved to be rich in precious metal. Prospectors rushed to stake claims. Among them was Lemuel S. "Sandy" Bowers, one of Eilley's boarders. Another boarder staked the adjacent claim and when he failed to pay his board bill, Eilley jumped it.

Business moved up the canyon. Nicholas "Dutch Nick" Ambrosia dragged his eating house and bar from Johntown. Eilley quickly followed, hauling her log boarding house up the ravine and locating it next to "Dutch Nick." They were the first two business houses in Gold Hill. The third was a sixteen-foot-square frame shack built by Solomon Wiehl for his grocery store. Other log and board buildings soon rose.

Meanwhile the miners were plagued continually by thick, heavy bluish-grey material which clogged their pans and rockers.

It is recorded that a Mexican called "Old Frank" kept telling them that it was "mucha plata." None of them knew that this was Spanish for "much silver" nor anything about assaying. Anyway they were not interested in anything but gold until a couple of young brothers, Ethan Allen and Hosea Ballou Grosch, came along from Pennsylvania.

Studying their metallurgical books, they made tests on the "blue stuff." Their investigation convinced them they had a silver fortune in their hands. With the Mexican guide, they discovered and located the silver lodes running across Sun Mountain. Their assays showed ore values as high as $3500 in silver to the ton. Then tragedy struck—Hosea hit his foot with a pick and died of blood poisoning on September 2, 1857. Allen, mourning his brother's loss, set out over the Sierra to close up their affairs. He was trapped in a winter storm and died December 19, 1857.

He had left Henry "Pancake" Comstock, a shiftless, lazy hanger-on in the camp, to live in his cabin and watch over his property. When he learned of Allen's death, Comstock claimed the Grosch properties. He never quite explained how he obtained them and, although others questioned his rights, his claims to virtually the entire district led the miners to start calling it "Comstock's lode." This stuck, too, like Finney's nickname for the town on top of the hill.

But it wasn't until July 1, 1859, when Augustus Harrison, a worker at the Stone and Gates Truckee River ranch, visited the diggings of Pat McLaughlin and Pete O'Reilley on the other side of the mountain in Six Mile Canyon, that the silver "discovery" really was made. Harrison took some samples of the discarded blue stuff and sent them to Grass Valley assayers. They could hardly believe it when their tests indicated that the ore ran better than $3000 to the ton, mostly silver.

The famous Washoe rush quickly got under way. Virginia City became the focal hub of that famous Golconda. Its "C" Street was the main highway of America's new-found wealth—it extended right on over the divide, wound around the bottom of "Slippery Gulch," Gold Hill's main drag, on down the canyon through Silver City and out to Dayton on the main east-west road.

The early locators sold their claims to the newcomers. Comstock was cockily pleased over a deal in which he turned over future untold millions, plus his claimed water rights, on a contract which brought him "$10 in cash and $10,990 in promissory notes."

Practically all of the first locators sold out except Eilley Orrum and her new husband, "Sandy" Bowers. She wouldn't allow him to accept any of the offers for their Gold Hill claims. These became their world-famous Imperial mine which produced millions.

"Old Virginia," that original first resident whose spilled forty-rod hooch christened one of the most famous mining towns in the world, didn't live to see the unbelievable aftermath. He reportedly fell from a horse at Dayton during one of his frequent drinking spells and died of injuries.

Virginia rapidly grew into a big city on a hillside. Gold Hill and Silver City mushroomed into towns of a few thousand inhabitants each. The *Territorial Enterprise,* now at Carson City, made its third move—to Virginia City. But Gold Hill was soon to have a newspaper of its own, one which holds a high place in the brilliant journalistic history of Nevada.

Alf Doten, one of the State's great early newsmen, who came to nearby Como in 'Sixty-two, started the *Gold Hill Daily News* on October 12, 1863. Its files are a treasure trove of history, although it is not as well known as the garrulous *Enterprise.* Doten and his editors refused to take a back seat to Joe Goodman, Dan DeQuille and Mark Twain, the *Enterprise* aces.

Gold Hill and Silver City made Virginians ashamed of themselves on the famous Gridley Sanitary sack of flour charity affair by subscribing more than their larger neighbor on the first sale. Virginia City was forced immediately to repair this damage by holding another sale and contributing more generously to the Sanitary Fund. You'll find the story of this interesting event in the later chapter about Austin.

The Gold Hill folks always were patriotic and generous. On April 24, 1864, the ladies of that town conducted a benefit—"In addition to dancing, there was a concert and an elaborate supper, all for five dollars a person." The *Gold Hills News* reported that $3080 had been raised for the Sanitary fund at the event—which was a very nice little take for a charity benefit affair in those early days—or even today in any place of similar size.

The Sanitary Fund led to a bitter duel of words between Twain and the opposition paper in Virginia City, and the subsequent departure of the author from Nevada. Twain accused the staff of the other Virginia City paper of failing to support the fund. During the journalistic sniping the *Gold Hill News* took due sideline cognizance of the affair with a story twitting Twain. It was headlined "Hoity Toity!"

The Gold Hill paper noted Twain's departure a short time later from the Nevada scene in this way—"An Exile——Among the few immortals who have departed . . . yesterday morning on the California stage, we notice that of Mark Twain. We don't wonder . . . Giving away to the idiosyncratic eccentricities of an erratic mind, Mark has engaged in the game infernal. In short, 'Played Hell'."

However, when the former *Enterprise* reporter, already gaining literary fame, came back to the Comstock on April 24, 1868, the Gold

Hill paper joined in the widespread welcome, announcing, "The remarkable Mark, who has been cruising among the far-off Turks, Piutes, Arabs and outlandish ruins and queer cities of the 'Holy Land' and now returns perfectly saturated with interesting information and funny stories relative to his journey . . . will 'harikari' his immense fund of collected information of a highly pleasing, varied, and interesting nature to crowded audiences at Piper's Opera House."

The "Queen City of the Comstock" is still one of the best known and most widely publicized "ghost towns" in the country. Far from being a specter, it has several hundred residents, is still the seat of Storey County, and attracts thousands of tourists annually.

One writer who recognized Gold Hill's right to its own place in the sun during the boom period was John J. Powell. He wrote in his *Nevada —The Land of Silver*, published in 1876, that "Gold Hill has now within its municipal limits one-half of the great Comstock Lode, and the canyon contains the works of some of the most noted silver mines in the world. Among those located in Gold Hill may be mentioned the Alpha, Bullion, Belcher, Empire, Imperial, Yellow Jacket, Crown Point, Overman etc. . . . Three churches, four public schools, and some excellent private educational establishements to the solid attractions of the city, which has, also, Masonic and Odd Fellows' lodges in active operation."

Gold Hill was incorporated by an act of the territorial legislature on December 17, 1862, "Bounded on the north by the southern line of Virginia City; on the east and south by the boundary line between Storey and Lyon; on the west by the boundary line between Storey and Washoe." This took in quite a chunk of Sun Mountain's south slopes.

It is possible that Gold Hill wouldn't have bothered to incorporate as a town except for the greediness of some of the Virginia City politicians, who were prone to grab at any opportunity to increase ways and sources to add to their loot. In this case, the Virginia City boys introduced a bill in the legislature to consolidate all of the Storey County towns—the only others of real importance being Gold Hill and its adjacent neighbor, American Flat—into one municipal government.

The residents of the upper end of the canyon rebelled en masse and descended on the legislature like mad hornets. It was bad enough, they claimed, to have to pay taxes to support county officers who strutted around Virginia City and forgot the other towns, and Gold Hill wanted no part of paying for "the fancy sidewalks, gas street lights, sewers, already big municipal debts and other political rascalities of the cocky Comstock county seat."

Gold Hill's opposition was so hot that the legislators dropped the consolidation bill and substituted the incorporation measure for the canyon town, which included American Flat. This brought on another battle. American Flat residents arose in violent protest against having

A view of Gold Hill about 1870

—*Courtesy Nevada State Historical Society.*

Gold Hill as it looked in 1878

—*Courtesy Nevada State Historical Society.*

to pay taxes "to support in lazy dignity the Gold Hill swells." So the bill was amended to leave out American Flat.

Having enjoyed the sweet taste of political victory, the Gold Hill folk decided to go farther. They had a bill introduced in the first session of the newly admitted State's legislature in 1864 to create a new county with Gold Hill as its seat. This was slapping Virginia City right where it hurt and a new battle raged. The *Territorial Enterprise* led the fight against the plan editorially, claiming that Storey County, without Gold Hill and American Flat, "wouldn't be worth a damn for officers."

Alf Doten and his *Gold Hill News* punched back with the claim that the county was being run by Virginia sports and gamblers "who were plunging everything into ruin and piling up a huge debt for Gold Hill to pay."

After a while the battle simmered down, the proposed county division act got "lost" in a committee, and Storey County politics continued in the same old sweet way—sweet for the office holders.

But the boys on the Comstock had not finished reaching for other political prizes. This time American Flat had its inning. The Storey county politicos decided to bring the State Capital up on the hill and started a campaign to have it located at American Flat, offering $50,000 for buildings.

This flurry had resulted from the high rent Carson City owners were gouging out of the embryo State government. Gold Hillers pulled together with the Virginia City folk on this one, but Armsby residents met the challenge by forcing rent reductions on the State buildings and the capital stayed at Carson City.

Since there was little to do besides work, drink, fight, and sleep, the first municipal election in Gold Hill on June 6, 1864 stirred up a large amount of intramural dog fighting. When twenty-one double votes were found in the ballot box, charges flew thickly. One side claimed fraud, the other claimed a "triumph of law and order." In the end, the Citizen's ticket was declared elected and the first city board of trustees was seated, composed of C. S. Coover, S. H. Robinson, H. C. Blanchard, Moses Korn and G. W. Aylsworth. The citizens erected a town hall costing $15,000.

The rise and decline of the Comstock mines affected the economy and prosperity of Gold Hill just as much as Virginia City—maybe in some ways more, since the Crown Point, Belcher and Yellow Jacket were among the big mines of the district. It was the new rich strikes in the Belcher and Crown Point, followed closely upon completion of the Virginia & Truckee Railroad up the canyon through Gold Hill, which brought the resurgence of the early '70's to the district. The Yellow Jacket also brought another distinction to Gold Hill—the largest single one-piece casting ever turned out up to 1880 on the Pacific Coast, was the 44,500 pound flywheel made at John McCone's Fulton Foundry on the Divide, just above the canyon, for the Yellow Jacket hoisting works.

The early miners knew that the Gold Hill portion of the Lode differed in composition from the Virginia City district—the ore below the divide was in continuous sheets, above it in compact bodies. It took thorough geological study to determine the reasons and explain why there was a barren period between where several millions were said to have gone down the holes of the Alpha, Bullion, Exchequer and others, without paying dividends. The major Gold Hill operations made up for these, though. The 1880 figures show that the Yellow Jacket produced $14,372,172 during its first twenty years. The Crown Point paid $11,-898,000 in dividends during this period, with the Belcher, next to it, turning out $15,397,200 in dividends. These two adjoining mines produced an aggregate of $58,110,240 during the first two decades. Others in the Gold Hill city limits produced in smaller totals of millions.

Yes, Gold Hill really had a big part in the fabulous story of the Comstock—being a major factor in all phases of the legend, bonanza and borrasca, stock ascensions and falls, prosperity and panic, successes and tragedies.

Among the latter was the great Yellow Jacket fire on April 7, 1869—the blackest day in all Gold Hill history. It started at the eight hundred foot level about seven in the morning. Part of the day shift had been lowered into the Yellow Jacket and the adjoining Crown Point and Kentuck mines before the flames burst out.

Fire companies from Gold Hill and Virginia City could do nothing to stay the flames which swept through the underground tunnels. Practically everybody in both communities gathered at the scene but little could be done. The sulphurous vapors generated by the hot flames against the rocks filled the lower levels. Wives who had husbands below screamed and had to be restrained from jumping into the inferno.

Thirty-six persons perished, twenty-seven bodies being recovered and identified. The fires burned in some portions of the vast underground workings for the next three years, before being finally extinguished. Another fire in the same mine on September 19, 1873, killed four and injured a dozen more. On both occasions damage was suffered in the workings of the Kentuck, Crown Point and Belcher, all connected with the Yellow Jacket tunnels.

Gold Hill had its share of listed killings, too, but not as many as Virginia City. The first, recorded in the Thompson and West 1881 *History of Nevada*, occurred on April 29, 1859, when one Jessup, alias "Pike," was stabbed and killed by William Sides "over a game of cards." Then on October 26, Yuk Lee was "shot and killed by another Chinaman four miles out on the Ophir Road." James Todd was shot and killed by Daniel Farney in a Gold Hill saloon because of a dog fight on November 11, 1863. "The jury disagreed." A jury finally convicted one killer, Louis Seldt, and later one William Janes won himself a life ticket to the

State prison by shooting and killing P. H. Dowd in the Gem Saloon in a "quarrel about business." And on and on. Life was cheap then, and the law was lax.

Although its once lush boom days ended decades ago, Gold Hill clung tenaciously to a shred of life until World War II. It retained enough citizens to keep the post office in business until February 27, 1943. Then after all the years of hearing the V & T locomotives chugging up and down the hill, the railroad ceased operation and they tore up the rails. The new highway was built around the flank of the hill and left the canyon towns on a side road. Snow demolished the fire hall in 1951.

There are extensive ruins, a few old buildings and maybe an old prospector or two living in them. But, Gold Hill really "died" when the great lodes dwindled and disappeared, long, long ago.

In those "good old days" saloons were a main gauge of a town. "Good towns" were those where drinks cost twenty-five cents. Communities where the price was a dime weren't of much importance. Wells Drury, one of the great Comstock editors, left this story about his old boss, Alf Doten. It makes a typical final curtain scene for the Comstock. For his nightly drink Doten had gone to his favorite saloon—only a few were around. He read a sign which hung over the cash register, announcing that at midnight the price of drinks in Gold Hill would be reduced to a dime.

"Thus passeth the glory of the world," exclaimed Doten. "It doesn't seem to me that I can endure this humiliation."

The clock showed 11:55 p.m.—in five minutes Gold Hill's brag that it could still support one first class bistro would be gone.

"I want to have the honor of buying the last two-bit drink in the old town," Doten insisted.

Then he drank to "the departure of Gold Hill's glory and pride" and sighed, "not much use in trying to run a nonpareil paper in a long-primer town. I was willing to stick it out as long as there was a living chance, but now that there is nothing but ten cent shebangs, the old *News* might as well suspend."

It did—the next day.

Hooligan Hill in Rawhide, about 1907

—*Las Vegas Review-Journal Photo.*

★ Dayton

"Chinatown to Pizen Switch"

Located right at the mouth of Gold Canyon—and probably the camping place of those first discoveries of gold in Nevada—Dayton also rates more recognition than it has received. It ranks very closely behind Genoa as one of the first settlements in Nevada, predating nearby Carson City. All through the Comstock rush Dayton was a busy shipping point for the roaring Gold Canyon and Virginia City mines. Today it's still a lively little place through which speeding tourists rush on U. S. 50 without a sideward glance. That's the way things have been most of its life, crowds hurrying past and just taking Dayton for granted.

Dayton was located where a crossing of the Carson was made on the immigrant trail. The place acquired an informal name, Ponderer's Rest, probably resulting from weary California-bound travelers, pondering whether to give up and remain along the Carson or continue and make the difficult climb over the high mountains rearing skyward to the west.

In 1851, shortly after Col. John Reese settled at Mormon Station, a man named Spofford Hall halted at the spot and set up a station on the west side of the river. Hall built the first house and it became known as Hall's Station until he sold out in 1854 to James McMartin. Then it was called McMartin's. Sometime before 1860 Major William M. Ormsby, of Carson City and later Indian war fame, acquired the McMartin holdings and owned the property when he was killed by the Paiutes at Pyramid Lake.

It was during this period that the name changed again. Large numbers of Chinese had been brought in by John Reese to dig a water ditch to the placer mines in Gold Canyon and, much to the disgust of white settlers in the district, it became known generally as "Chinatown."

The argument over the name was continued when a meeting was held by the folk living around the Carson crossing to pick a satisfactory name. Such appellations as Nevada City, Mineral Rapids and Mormon Crossing had supporters, but when the smoke cleared the majority had voted for Dayton, honoring a leading resident, John Day, who later became the first county surveyor.

As the Comstock rush grew, Dayton soon became a busy place, the focal point for mining and agricultural communities in the area. Freight arriving there from the east was transshipped to the Comstock and all the other districts. Active business induced Dayton merchants to stock a wide variety of items. Several mills soon were built. It is where Adolph Sutro, of later Sutro tunnel fame, got his start with a small quartz mill.

As it happened in all the rough early towns, the Lord's standard bearers were quickly on the scene. The Rev. Cyrus Willis Rees arrived in 1861 to establish a Baptist congregation. The others followed swiftly. First among the social organizations were lodges of Masons, Odd Fellows and Druids. The hall of the latter still stands in good condition.

The Territorial legislature picked Dayton as the seat for Lyon, one of the nine counties designated at its initial session. Proud of its honor, Dayton citizens soon erected a suitable courthouse, which also handled most of the administrative business for Churchill County until its seat was moved from Bucklands to La Plata in 1864. The town served as the seat of Lyon County government for more than half a century until 1909. when fire gutted it and furnished fast-growing Yerington, in Mason Valley, with a sound and winning argument for moving the county seat.

The courthouse, rebuilt after the fire, became a high school which has been used regularly through the years. Near it also stands a little brown stone school house which was built by the civic minded early Dayton citizens in 1865.

The Greuber House, now called the Union Hotel, boasted the first piano in Nevada. The instrument was hauled across the plains in an ox-wagon. There are other early-day buildings of various sorts still standing and in use at Dayton. Actually, the friendly little town, now virtually by-passed by recently rebuilt U. S. Highway 50, is still one of the best preserved of Nevada's early communities.

In its heyday Dayton was a railroad center. Its first road was a narrow gauge line connecting the Douglas and Rock Point mills with a large tailing pond east of town. A little later a short line was built from Dayton to Sutro, at the mouth of the famous tunnel a few miles east. Subsequently, the Carson and Colorado, the Darius Ogden Mills road down the Walker River to Candeleria and into Owens Valley, was constructed. Terminus of this road, and its shops and roundhouse, was at Mound House, between Dayton and Carson City.

The record indicates that violence wasn't the common thing in Dayton. John Doyle was stabbed to death by James Linn. The record reports that "Linn was hanged by the citizens at 3 a.m." four days later. Not much foolishness about that one.

Thomas Riley shot and killed Sheriff Tim G. Smith of Ormsby County near Carson City and escaped toward Dayton in June 1868. He was spotted there by Asa L. Kenyon, who raised a posse and gave chase. Riley fired upon the fast advancing posse, wounding one member, H. A. Comins. After a gun fight, as the slayer neared the end of his ammunition, he killed himself.

Today Dayton drowses quietly, a pleasant suburb of fast-growing Carson City, where some of the finest of Nevada's leading citizens of the past were born or lived. It always is worth a detour from the rushing main highway for a few minutes of quietly re-living the glorious past of a once-bustling town.

Dayton's early-day mountain suburb, Como, is almost impossible to reach without a jeep. The rough old road which climbs the Pine Nut Mountain, fifteen miles southeast, has been rutted and washed badly through the years and is no thoroughfare for a low-slung modern car.

Only piles of tailings, mine dumps and ruins of old buildings mark the site of Como, which flourished with a population of 700 during the Civil War. But it bequeathed two amusing incidents to the lore of the old west.

The "Piñon Pine Nut War" is one of them. There was a large tribe of Indians living on the slopes of the Pine Nuts, in which 9000-foot Mt. Como is the highest peak. They objected strenuously to the wholesale destruction of the trees for mine timbers, since the nuts were a major source of their food supply. Friendly Chief Numaga, known as young Winnemucca, called upon the mine owners, and asked them to quit destroying the trees.

They disregarded his plea and soon tension increased as the rumor spread that the Indians "were mad and preparing to make trouble."

A group of miners and loggers noticed a party of redskins watching them from behind trees. They fled up the road, carrying word that the Paiutes were on the warpath. A hurried message to Fort Churchill, a few miles eastward on the Carson River, brought troops. A camp password was arranged with orders to shoot any person at night who failed to answer with it.

Unacquainted with this turn of events, two Como residents, who had been "outside" to Dayton on a little celebration, were returning late at night and failed to answer the command for the password. They were fired upon. Immediately all Como residents piled out of bed to join in defense of their homes. One over-anxious citizen tripped on his gun and discharged it. This unintentionally served as a signal for others who thought the Indians were shooting, and they immediately began firing down the canyon, the only way from which the Paiutes could attack. The two surprised and cowering miners huddled in safety behind a boulder, fearing for their lives. The shooting kept up all night.

When dawn arrived the defenders found that their ammunition was nearly exhausted, but apparently the Indians had withdrawn—neither had there been any return fire nor could the scared Comoites spot any dead or wounded braves.

While they were wondering what had happened, Chief Numaga came sauntering into the camp wanting to know what all the shooting was about. He said his village had been very disturbed and his warriors were caused no end of worry by all the noise. Como's citizens felt pretty sheepish when they learned that a couple of inebriated homebound miners had caused the one-sided "war."

The Como *Sentinel* related the story of the first death, an unusual event since "Como was a healthy place." It was a common phrase that

Fort Churchill from contemporary sketch. Photo Nevada Historical Society.

Fort Churchill, from a contemporary sketch

—*Photo courtesy of Theron Fox and Nevada State Historical Society.*

Dayton, looking down Pike Street

—*Courtesy Nevada State Historical Society.*

a person would "have to move away from here to die." Although the deceased had taken his own life, his fellow citizens decided he must have a decent burial. Sawed lumber was a luxury, but there was an old wagon bed being used as a shelter for a hog.

Alf Doten, a California newspaperman, who had arrived in 1862 and was working in Como as a carpenter while also doing a little writing for the *Sentinel*, built a coffin from the material in the wagon bed, turning the pig out into the cold.

There was no paint in town so a mixture of blood, pine pitch and other materials furnished a stain for the box, the friends of the deceased polishing it with cloth. The whole funeral cost forty dollars, the miners feeling it was no more than right to contribute generously toward "doing the first funeral up first rate."

Like many others, Como's first promises didn't prove out and by 1864 it was found that the ore was too skimpy to warrant the high cost of milling and shipping over the rough road. Gradually population drifted down the hill and soon all were gone.

Judge G. W. Walton, never despairing in the comeback of Como, stayed on alone. Tragedy finally took him and Como was deserted. Friends, wondering why they hadn't seen the Judge lately found him burned to death in his cabin in 1874.

Early westbound Argonauts first struck the Carson River some 30 miles east of Carson City. Here the Samuel Sanford Buckland family had come from California and settled in 1858. They erected a large ranch house and catered to ox-team caravans with a trading post, stage station, tavern and hotel. The Bucklands raised stock and cattle and employed a crew of workers.

When Paiutes burned Williams Station, just a few miles east of Buckland's in May, 1860, and killed all the white men there, a hurried call was sent over the territory for leading citizens to gather at Buckland's and plan steps to halt the Indians. The 105 men who answered the call decided to divide into four companies of volunteer militia with the intent of pursuing the Indians to their Pyramid Lake camp and subduing them. William Ormsby, prominent Carson City leader, was Major in command of the Carson City Company.

This abortive and disorganized little volunteer army rode determinedly into battle on the home grounds of the Indians and promptly suffered one of the most devastating defeats ever dealt to a volunteer American military force. Fewer than half of the volunteers returned. Among the first slain was Major Ormsby, who bravely—but rather foolishly—led his small company into an ambush of a vastly superior force of Indians hidden behind rocks and sagebrush. When the territory's original counties were designated, the one in which Carson City is located was named for the Pyramid Lake "hero."

The Pyramid Lake outbreak caused U. S. Army officials to order the regulars to establish a post to keep the Indians subdued. The site

selected was about halfway between the Pyramid and Walker Lake
Indian camps and a mile from Buckland's ranch. It soon grew into
Fort Churchill, Nevada's first regular military establishment and head-
quarters for the Army in the rapidly expanding area.

The fort became a recruiting center for Union troops and the seat
of all Federal authority in the state throughout the Civil War.

Fortunately Col. Charles McDermitt was in command during this
period and he was well liked by the Indians. He treated them fairly,
going so far as to take prisoners alive in any skirmishes, bringing them
to the fort and feeding them while they were in custody. This was a
new approach to the Indian problem and seemingly worked, although
some of the whites objected because he was "too lenient with the
savages." Ironically McDermitt met death from an Indian ambush.

Fort Churchill, as a military post, ended its career in 1871, just eleven
years after it was built. Subsequently, it became an Indian school and
reservation. When this activity was moved to Wabuska and Schurz, the
fort was sold at auction and everything of value removed. Most of the
timber used in the forts roofs, gates and doors was used later to build the
Towle house on the Fernley-Yerington road.

During the last couple of years, the Nevada State Park Commission,
has taken over the ruins of Fort Churchill in a laudable effort to save
what is left of this historic spot for posterity.

About the time Fort Churchill was passing from the scene the town
of Sutro, five miles northeast of Dayton, on the south flank of the Comstock uprising, was born through the stubbornness of "Crazy" Adolph
Sutro, who had one time conducted a cigar store in Virginia City. It was
located at the adit of Sutro's proposed tunnel into the heart of Mt. Davidson with which he hoped to drain the water which was drowning the
rich mines.

His difficulties many times appeared insurmountable but the former
cigar clerk with the wild dream continued to battle for more financing
and dig. Finally the miners, clawing through the last 100 feet by hand
while working in almost unendurable heat and hot mud from the
sulphuric mineral springs, broke through into the Savage mine on July
8, 1878, 18 years after Sutro first had his dream. They had driven
20,000 feet straight as an arrow into the mountain and hit the target right
on the bullseye.

Today the tunnel entrance is barred—the town where the *Sutro
Independent* clarioned the exciting stories of the diggings is overgrown
with sagebrush again. Only a few weatherbeaten buildings recall the
scene of one of the most stupendous projects in a state where colos-
sal undertakings are commonplace.

It was natural that prospectors would range farther southward from
Buckland's and Fort Churchill along the trail followed by Frémont and
Carson through the Walker River Valley. This became a busy route and

one of the main roads to Aurora when that town began to boom in 1861.

In keeping with the early-day economic pattern, an enterprising dispenser of forty-rod whiskey set up business in a willow-thatched hut a score of miles south of Buckland's where the trail branched toward Walker Lake, Dead Horse Wells and Austin.

The spot became known to all as the "Switch." The merchant's stock ran so low and he bolstered it by adding a few gallons of water, flavored with whatever was handy—particularly a few plugs of tobacco and cayenne pepper. Thirsty travelers drank the concoction but agreed that it didn't deserve to be called whiskey, and in the vernacular of the day it was quickly dubbed "Pizen."

Far and wide the place quickly became known as "Pizen Switch"—challenging Lousetown for the distinction of bearing Nevada's most unusual early day name.

Disappointed immigrants of an agricultural bent, who had failed to find riches in the mines, quickly settled on farms in the valley. They objected to the name. Legend says that they organized a committee for the avowed purpose of scalping anyone uttering "Pizen Switch" when referring to the town.

Within a year it became known bucolically as Greenfield. By the 'eighties it had a Methodist church, a school, Wells-Fargo office, three hotels, stores, saloons and restaurants.

Then, as an inducement to attract the extension of the Virginia and Truckee to the agricultural valley the citizens re-named it again, this time in honor of H. M. Yerington, boss of the railroad. It didn't get a railroad though until several years later but the title remained and since 1909 it has been the Lyon County seat and is one of Nevada's most prosperous towns.

Argenta, 1869

—Courtesy of E. W. Darrah.

Eilley and Sandy Bowers' Mansion at Franktown
—Courtesy Nevada State Historical Society.

Theodore Winter's House, Washoe City
—Courtesy Nevada State Historical Society.

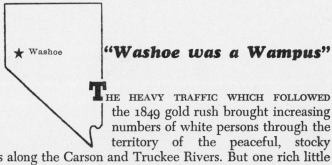

"Washoe was a Wampus"

THE HEAVY TRAFFIC WHICH FOLLOWED the 1849 gold rush brought increasing numbers of white persons through the territory of the peaceful, stocky Washoe Indians along the Carson and Truckee Rivers. But one rich little ten-mile-long valley, lying between those two routes and the Sierra and Sun Mountain was not molested until Bishop Orson Hyde arrived on May 17, 1855 to set up Utah's Carson County.

Bishop Hyde picked out a delightful spot near the south end of the valley's rich stream-fed meadow lands as the site for his personal kingdom and the location of his far western church headquarters. It was called Franktown, and Apostle Hyde immediately set about establishing a community in the pattern prescribed by the order's leaders.

It was laid out with wide, regular streets, along both sides of which ran ditches carrying water from Franktown Creek to the homes and gardens of the settlers. Each of the Mormons was allotted a home and farm site. They first built a church, then their own log cabins, roofed with shakes split from the plentiful trees on the edge of the meadows. One of the very first community projects was a sawmill and next a school.

The Saints and their families were happy and contented in their little paradise, located away from the busily traveled east-west pioneer roads. Then came that fateful order from Brigham Young in the summer of 1857, ordering the return to Salt Lake of all members of the church to defend the citadel of Deseret against the threatened attack of the United States Army. When the Mormons left, disobedient church members and Gentiles flocked into Washoe Valley and settled on the rich lands.

Among them were Eilley, of Gold Hill boarding house fame, and her latest husband, Sandy Bowers. When the Mormons departed, Eilley obtained a 120-acre land claim about a mile from Orson Hyde's Franktown site. It particularly took her fancy because it was similar to her native Scotch highland and lake country.

As the money poured in from their mining claims, Eilley decided to build herself a mansion which would surpass those of the Lords of her native land. She also planned to make a trip to Europe so she could display her wealth before the relatives who had argued against her coming to America as the child bride of a Mormon missionary Bishop.

The story is recounted in detail in many books—how she and Sandy cut a wide swath through Europe. Before going, plans for the mansion had been completed and approved. Competent stone cutters shaped the granite blocks so truly that very little mortar was necessary. The fine job of craftsmanship still is apparent in the manner in which this century old structure has defied the elements.

The couple bought, and shipped around the Horn furniture, marble mantles and a great collection of household odds and ends for which they willingly paid outrageous prices. It proved a vain splurge.

Social leaders of the Comstock failed to flock to the mansion as Eilley had expected. Sandy was more at home with his cronies in the Gold Hill and Virginia City saloons than in the fancy big house. He liked to boast that he "had money to throw to the birds." He died suddenly in 1868, at the age of 35. He had asked that members of the Miner's Union accompany his body "as far as they could."

The Gold Hill Masonic lodge conducted the services after his body had lain in state all morning. More than 100 carriages and as many more on horseback made up the funeral procession down the Ophir road and across the bridge all the way to Franktown, where his grave, back of the mansion, still is visited annually by hundreds of tourists.

Immediately Eilley was engulfed in litigation. Her former Scotch thrift seemed to have deserted her. Soon she was destitute. The mansion quickly became heavily mortgaged. She tried to operate it as a resort without success. Finally, she turned to her crystal ball in which she had great faith—claiming it had foretold her rise to wealth. She tried to rebuild her income by holding readings for fees.

When she died, a lonely, fantastic old Scotch woman, she was laid in a grave beside Sandy and their adopted daughter, Persia.

In 1873 the State of Nevada seriously contemplated purchasing the mansion for an insane asylum. The lengthy report of an Assembly committee recommending such action gives a fine picture of the establishment. The State could have acquired the mansion and its 120 acres for $20,000, the report noted—a bargain, even for those days.

Today, the proud old mansion is operated as a county park, swimming pool and picnic grounds, with a refreshment stand, and juke box music blaring over outdoor loud speakers, helping to create a modern bedlam in this former playground of the Washoes. Admission is charged for touring the mansion—but it's worth it, and helps preserve the famous landmark.

Franktown never was a rooting, tooting wild west town. In fact, Isaac Mathews, one of Nevada's most noted pioneers of the State, wrote in his later years, "I lived through the 'Sixties in one of the liveliest mining periods of the west. I saw very little gun toting. Life and property were far safer then than they are today. I never heard of a woman or child being molested. The men and women pioneers were a splendid type of citizens."

From the outset, developers of the Comstock faced a major problem. Everything had to be hauled. Roads were constructed up the mountainside from the North, South and West. Especially acute was the lack of lumber to fuel ore mills and shore up mine drifts and shafts. The nearest forests were across Washoe Valley, in the Sierra.

An economical solution was the construction of both ore and lumber mills in the valley. Bulky loads of silver-laden rock from the mines, and wagon loads of logs from the Sierra, both would have a downhill pull; and wagons from the Comstock, instead of returning empty would carry back timber.

Washoe City was one of several municipal children begotten by the ore and lumber trade. In 1861 the town was designated the county seat, which brought an influx of lawyers, doctors, businessmen and journalists. The newcomers joined the saloon keepers, mill men, lumberjacks and bullwhackers already resident. Population zoomed. Churches, a hospital and a school were erected, as were fraternal halls and—in 1862—the inevitable brick courthouse and jail.

From inferences found in historical archives, it is apparent that fistic and gun battles were common. The lumberjacks and log-wagon bullwhackers from Galena, four miles up Galena Canyon, had no love for the muckers and teamsters from the mines.

Burning lead more frequently settled disagreements than legal actions—in fact, the first county officers appointed by the Territorial legislature apparently were satisfied to accept their political largess and let law enforcement take its course.

Probably the most famous Washoe killing was that of George W. Derickson, editor of the *Washoe City Times*, on January 23, 1863, by a subscriber, H. F. Swayze. Swayze submitted a humorous skit to the paper as his own work. Derickson, according to Nell Murbarger in her *Ghosts of the Glory Trail*, recognized it as a plagiarized version of something previously run in his paper. The editor printed a sarcastically worded editorial, which among other things referred to Swayze as a "tall, gawky greenhorn dressed in a buckskin suit." These were fighting words to the latter, who called the editor a "goddam liar" and drew his gun. Details vary regarding exactly what happened, but apparently both men shot simultaneously and well.

The editor died instantly, Swayze was hit in the chin by a bullet which broke his jaw and knocked out a mouthful of teeth. Swayze faced trial before a jury, which found him guilty of manslaughter. He served three years in the Carson City penitentiary—and didn't get his article published.

Three years later, on February 6, 1866, Washoe City was the scene of another fatal affair which deserves note because of the weapons used. One Dodge, first name unnoted by Washoe City papers, entered a gambling joint operated by "Doc" Kimball. Dodge reportedly drew a "slung shot" and struck Kimball over the eye. Although it was an effort worthy of a David, it didn't fell Kimball, who stabbed Dodge with his Bowie knife. Kimball was not held.

Even the peaceful south end of the valley contributed at least one holiday "honor killing." During the 1864 Fourth of July ball at Ophir, another ore mill town, Charles H. Plum was stabbed to death by the brother of a girl "he kissed in a sportive manner when dancing with her." In those days, nobody allowed the slightest trifling with a good girl's honor or reputation.

Those rugged pioneer individualists who made the tough trip across the plains included many colorful characters. Jim Mathews was one of them. Jim was a bullwhacker dragging the huge log shores for the mines down the rough road from Galena to Washoe City.

He had a speech impediment, except when he was cursing his oxen. He was a recognized master of lurid language, which seemed to be an occupational requisite in handling slow teams on rough mountain roads. His yokes developed the troublesome habit of balking in the middle of creek crossings and refusing to pull together. Upon such occasions Jim became furious and would mount a stump and call upon all the Apostles to come down "and help me cuss these cattle." His blasphemous plaints or shouts always worked, and soon Jim and his wagon would roll into Washoe City, where he was acclaimed for bringing in larger loads than any of the other drivers.

The great demands of the roaring Comstock for timber and fuel soon denuded the lower foothills. A disastrous fire in 1865 burned the eleven Galena mills. The town rebuilt, to be burned out again in 1867—but by this time it was necessary to go higher and higher on the Sierra for trees.

This resulted in the unbelievable flumes, which were engineering masterpieces, built down the mountainsides to float the logs to the valley. They were the initial step toward the decline of Washoe City. The flumes filled the Carson River with log jams and brought the timber closer to Virginia City at the southern entrance to the Sun Mountain activities.

The next "villain" on the scene was the "notorious" William Sharon, who had moved in as major domo of the Virginia City mines. He wanted a railroad from Virginia City to connect with the Central Pacific, which Charlie Crocker was pushing through the Sierras. This, he declared, would solve all of Virginia City's shipping problems. The clever Sharon wasn't above playing politics. He campaigned, pointing out that such a railroad would bring enormous advantages to property owners along its route through increased trade, commerce and industry.

When the legislature met in January, 1869, apparently with votes judiciously primed by Sharon, it authorized the County Commissions of Lyon, Ormsby and Storey counties to issue bonds which would be turned over to the railroad company when the track was completed between certain points in the counties. This allowed the citizens to pay for the mine company's railroad. One can't help but note that Sharon didn't include Washoe County, indicating that some of the smarter citizens of that county seat weren't blinded to his actual purpose and weren't having any of his railroad financing shenanigans.

Construction work started on February 18, 1869, and by the end of the year the track was finished between Virginia City and Carson City.

It foretold the end of Washoe City. In the following year the Ormsby County assessor estimated for tax purposes that this twenty-five mile link of railroad had hauled 50,000 cords of wood, 10,000,000 feet of lumber and seventy-five tons of ore. The wood and lumber came down Clear Creek and the Carson River. Mills were built at Virginia City, and ore and timber wagons were no longer needed to roll down the mountains to Washoe Valley.

It remained for Crocker with his Central Pacific, and W. C. Lake, who had bought the toll bridge in Truckee Meadows, to administer another blow to Washoe City.

Lake, with a bright promotional idea, deeded Crocker forty acres surrounding his hotel, with the stipulation that a townsite be laid out and a station built. This was done. The new town was named for a Civil War general named Jesse Reno. The Central Pacific tracks reached Reno on May 4, 1869; lots were sold on May 9, and a month later the first train from Sacramento pulled in. Washoe citizens were among those who bought Reno lots and moved to the new town.

The first business institution to desert the waning county seat was the newspaper, *The Eastern Slope*. In 1868 it moved to the new community, to become Reno's initial periodical, *The Evening Crescent*.

As Reno grew rapidly and began to feel its oats, it decided it should be the county seat. Maybe fuel was added to this desire when Washoe County officials decided to levy an assessment on Reno's beloved Central Pacific. The rail tycoons refused to pay, but lost a suit in the county court at Washoe City. Deputy Sheriff Jim Kinkead was ordered to go to Reno to collect the assessment. Jim, giving the matter deep thought, came up with a solution. He waited at the Reno station until the first train pulled in. Then he promptly chained the driving wheel to a rail, and leaned back against the cowcatcher to await developments.

An uproar ensued—frantic messages clacked back and forth over the telegraph wires to Sacramento headquarters. Kinkead calmly whittled on a stick. Another train arrived. Jim chained it to the track, too. Still the railroad tycoons were adamant in their refusal to pay the tax.

A third arriving train received the same treatment before the railroad officials conceded defeat. The Bank of California wired that the assessment funds had been deposited to the account of Washoe County. Only then did Jim turn loose the trains.

A special election was held June 14, 1870, to settle the issue of moving the county seat. Reno mustered 544 votes. Washoe City could round up only 362, and the latter's only remaining reason for existence ended.

It was the death blow—more and more stores closed, population dwindled and soon Washoe City was on its way to becoming one of Nevada's first major ghost towns.

Reno even compounded the felony of municipicide. The fine eight-year-old Washoe City courthouse was torn down and the bricks were hauled to the new seat to build a jail.

Only a few residents remained—mostly those who had ranches in the area. The richest and most important of these was Theodore Winters, who was an early arrival on the Ophir strike. He had purchased the home of William Jennings, a Mormon, who had built it in 1862, hauling the framing and interior woodwork and hardware over the mountains from Sacramento.

Winters made the Washoe City place his home for forty-three years and died there at 83 on August 3, 1906. During that period he became one of Nevada's most important citizens, serving many terms in the legislature and once getting the Democratic nomination for Governor.

He was the principal stockholder in the Mexico mine on the Comstock, and as his wealth increased he added to his Washoe Valley land holdings until they embraced 6000 acres. Early during his residence there he started raising and breeding fine horses, and many of them won races on the old Lousetown track.

The coming of the railroad down the valley and up the hill to Virginia City also ended the busy times in Franktown and Ophir City. Hilarious Comstock sports no longer raced down the Ophir toll road, the hoofs of their horses clattering a wild tattoo on the wooden bridge the company had built across the lower end of the lake.

Time and the elements gradually disintegrated the early buildings of the Washoe Valley town. Today it takes diligent searching to find their remnants—the Bowers Mansion at Franktown being by far the outstanding relic. A few pieces of heavy machinery and scattered foundation stones spot the location of Ophir.

For years, three nearly a century-old buildings along the highway at the north end of Washoe Lake afforded a romantic idea of the manner in which the brief-lived county seat had been built by its optimistic founders. Now there is only one—a stone building. The other two, ravaged during the years by vandals stealing old bricks, fell victims of a gale-like Washoe wind on the morning of March 30, 1959, and tumbled in a mass of bricks, timbers and mortar. The Winters residence, built in 1862, remains proudly among the modern architectural mansions of the wealthy dude ranches which now fill the valley.

One final little requiem for the early day area came on July 15, 1959, when the Washoe County school board announced that the pioneer school building at Galena, the old lumbering town, would not open for the fall term. Modern transportation makes it more economical to haul students from that area by bus to Reno.

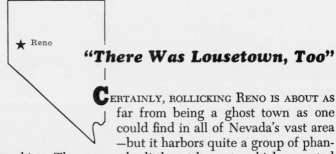

"There Was Lousetown, Too"

CERTAINLY, ROLLICKING RENO IS ABOUT AS far from being a ghost town as one could find in all of Nevada's vast area —but it harbors quite a group of phantoms beneath its skirts. They were the little settlements which sprouted when the huge wave of excitement spread in all directions from the discovery of the rich Comstock.

In addition to major communities, such as Washoe City, Franktown, Carson City and Dayton, which flourished around the edges of Sun Mountain, Virginia City was the mother hen for a flock of smaller settlements. Among them, in addition to mining communities, were stopping places for the constant stream of supply wagons and stages and agricultural centers which grew up to supply the voracious appetite of the thousands who flocked to the fabulous Comstock.

The "Biggest Little City in the World," Reno, actually got its start a decade before the Central Pacific was built. Since the first early rush of the Forty-Niners, the route up the Truckee and over the summit, at what was to be known as Donner Pass, was favored by many. Grass grew lushly through the length of the Truckee Meadows to supply ample stock feed.

In 1859 W. C. Fuller came down from Susanville and established a makeshift ferry across the Truckee. This was followed by a rickety wooden toll bridge. He also built a few small buildings where the Riverside Hotel now stands to serve as an inn and store for travelers. The spot became known as "Fuller's Crossing." If Fuller could have foreseen just a couple of years into the future he probably wouldn't have sold when floods took out his bridge in the spring of 1862.

The purchaser was W. C. Lake, another erstwhile resident of the Susanville area. He was energetic and quickly rebuilt the bridge, added a larger stock to the store and erected a tavern. Far and wide the place became known as "Lake's Crossing."

Virginia City was demanding food supplies and Lake soon had a small bonanza of his own from the tolls collected on the large herds of cattle, strings of freight wagons and ore seekers headed for the Comstock bonanza.

His bridges washed out twice, in 1863 and 1867, and both times he replaced them with better structures. The coming of the railroad induced him to build the first hotel in the Truckee Meadows, the Lake House, which opened on New Year's eve, 1870, where the Riverside Hotel stands now. Then Lake persuaded the railroad to put its station across the river and donated the townsite which became the heart of today's Reno.

Some of the early-day femmes who followed mine strikes and railroad construction were tough enough to take care of themselves. Mollie

Forshay was one of them—she took no pushing around. Thomas Kelley, a cook in an early-day Reno hash house attempted to put Mollie out of his place for disorderly conduct on December 8, 1871. Mollie stabbed him fatally. No record is found reporting she ever paid any penalty for her lethal carving. Women, regardless of the kind, were more or less exempt from what law existed in those days.

Seven miles down the Virginia Road was Huffaker's station, established in 1859 by G. W. Huffaker and L. W. Drexler, the first travel stop south of the river. It was important and catered to the public with a large store. The place grew into a busy little trading and ranching spot and got a post office of its own on September 22, 1862. It was designated "Truckee Meadows," a fact which causes no end of bafflement among amateur philatelists who think a post office with such a name must have been right along the river. Huffaker was the postmaster. Langton's Pioneer Express had an office there, later taken over by Wells Fargo. The Bonanza V flume terminated at Huffakers, the lumber was shipped via the V & T from there to Virginia City.

Hunter's Bridge, another river crossing midway between Reno and Verdi, with a hotel, store and post office, formed the nucleus of a settlement starting around 1867. Its post office was in business from March 19, 1867 to January 31, 1870. Fire wiped out most of the village, and when the railroad brought boom days to Reno it never regained importance. Auburn, another hamlet laid out in 1865, is practically unknown to anybody now, and long ago was absorbed by the burgeoning metropolis.

The steam jets rising in the air from a myriad of hot springs caused early travelers to name the section five miles south of Huffakers, Steamboat Springs. One portion of the springs was located in 1860 by a Frenchman named Felix Monet and another section by a man named Cameron. The latter neglected to perfect the title and a Dr. Ellis took it over in 1861, building a hospital accommodating 34 patients, with six bath-houses. It was a favorite place of Comstockers to cure hangovers.

Then Charles W. Cullins bought out Cameron's claim and instituted suit to gain possession of the springs. In 1867 the courts finally gave possession to Cullins. Oddly, and many felt suspiciously, before Cullins could dispossess Dr. Ellis, the place burned down.

During the years the resort had become another oasis for Virginia City-Truckee Meadows traffic so the new owner immediately built a depot and various other buildings for the accommodation of guests. The Virginia & Truckee completed its rails from Reno to Steamboat Springs in 1871, and for the next year the resort served as the terminus for the railroad, and a substantial community sprung up. An immense freighting business briefly gave it a busy life.

Those who believe in retribution probably will think it nothing less than justice that Cullins, the dispossessor of Dr. Ellis, fell into one of the hot springs in 1873 and scalded himself so badly that he died from the effects. M. and J. Rapp bought the property in 1874 and erected a hotel, which became a favorite resort place for Reno, Carson City and Virginia City sports. Steamboat obtained its own post office on February 12, 1880, with J. Rapp as postmaster. This office still is open and serves folk at the resort and from nearby farms in Steamboat and northern Washoe valleys.

Probably the most important of these several Truckee Meadow ghosts which sooner or later crawled under the cloak of spreading Reno was Glendale, southeast of Lake's Crossing a few miles. In the spring of 1857 John F. Stone and Charles C. Gates established a trading post and built there the "Farmer's Hotel," previously known as Jameson's Crossing. In 1860 they constructed a bridge across the Truckee.

A few settlers, former farmers, soon followed and broke open the fertile meadows. An important agricultural area developed when the Comstock boomed a couple of years later and Stone and Gates Crossing became well known throughout the entire district.

Renamed Glendale when the post office was established on October 4, 1867, stores, saloons and other businesses clustered around the hotel and bridgehead. Since it was a farming settlement population didn't entirely fade out when silver mining declined—the census count in the mid-'Seventies showed a total of 130 and Reno's outskirts had almost reached it. A toll road was built from Virginia City down the north side of the mountain to Glendale in 1860.

About halfway along this road, at the foot of the mountain, was located another small settlement whose name ranks as one of the most unusual in the entire list of Nevada towns.

It was Lousetown. The settlement consisted of a few buildings which furnished lodging, meals and liquor to weary freight drivers. A number of habitations clustered about the place. Teamsters rested their animals, preparatory to the climb up the mountain, and repaired equipment here.

A few years later, when Virginia City attained its famed high-rolling free-spending standard, Lousetown was the location of the race track, where wagering ran into high figures at the week-end meetings of blooded runners, pacers and trotters. All that remains of it today is the rubble of some of the buildings.

It was mineral most of the searchers wanted—and some found it. One of the better strikes was nine miles northeast of Reno on the high slopes of Mt. Peavine. The town which grew up first was called Peavine, later was known as Poe City and Poeville and by some referred to as Podunk, believe it or not.

It was discovered in the early 'Sixties, boomed rapidly and hit a peak population of 1500 persons living in both brick and log houses, served by a variety of stores, bistros and bawdy houses. It had rich ore but it gained its little place in fame's spotlight by furnishing the ore comprising the first westbound rail shipment on the newly built C. P. tracks. The cars of ore were hauled to a smelter in Sacramento. Through the years Peavine, or Poe City, has made an occasional quiver in an effort to revive, but never has. About all that remains are some mine dumps.

Crystal Peak was laid out in 1864 on a grassy nook along the Truckee, in the rising foothills of the Sierra. It missed a questionable spot in historical glory when the Central Pacific Railroad built its tracks two miles south and named the new station Verdi. Crystal Peak was a lusty lumber and mining mill town in 1868 when the railroad, for which its mills supplied a great deal of lumber and ties, did it wrong. Verdi even moved the Crystal Peak post office, established July 25, 1864 and changed its name on March 30, 1869—after the railroad was built that far. In a way the old town got even when Verdi received all the headlines as the scene of the west's first railroad express robbery, giving birth to a criminal pattern which was to supply authors and motion picture writers with a continuous stream of holdup plots in the succeeding years.

The story about this granddaddy of all the western shoot-'em-up TV and movie train robberies is one of the most colorful of early-Nevada's historical occurrences.

It begins on the Virginia City stagecoach run, where robberies became commonplace. Since money was plentiful in early Virginia City and a majority of the populace was not suffering from any moral inhibitions, the crime of relieving Wells Fargo's carriers of bullion wasn't considered highly heinous. In fact, some of the known stage robbers were accepted by most citizens as "good fellows."

Then, too, it was quite a temptation, not only to the highwaymen but even to some of the shippers, to relieve the express tycoons of their cash. The company always made good all losses, and it was not unknown for a shipper, for a cut of the swag, to tip off a hold-up man when a shipment was leaving.

Wells Fargo naturally didn't appreciate this situation and took steps to eliminate temptation by putting guards, armed with shotguns, aboard the stages. When a single guard proved inadequate, a second was added and in some cases, extra armed men rode horseback escort to heavily laden coaches.

Later when the Verdi bandits were captured, Big Jack Davis, who had been an unsuspected Virginia City businessman until he admitted being the ringleader of the train holdup, declared that it was one of the "unfair tactics" of the company in adding extra guards to the stages that had forced the bandits into robbing the train.

Wells, Fargo and Company's "Robber's Record" credits Davis—along with two of his train robbery cohorts, John Squires and a lad named Tilton B. Cockrill—with at least three holdups of Virginia stages on the Geiger grade.

It probably was one of these events, or another Wells Fargo hadn't managed to tag on Davis, that brought Big Jack his reputation for being "a gentleman." It seems that upon one occasion the down-bound stage was halted on the grade by Davis and his pals. When the bandit discovered two feminine passengers aboard, he proved gallant to the extreme. While his confederates held the driver and others at bay, Davis spread a blanket beside the road for the women to sit upon while the business of the robbery was completed. When Big Jack discovered a case of champagne in the cargo he opened a bottle and served the feminine "guests," telling them they "must be thirsty after their long, dusty trip."

So with stages becoming rolling arsenals, Davis, Squires, Cockrill, and five others, J. E. Chapman, R. A. Jones, James Gilchrist, J. C. Roberts, and E. B. Parsons, a well known Virginia City gambler, planned and executed the daring and sensational train holdup.

Chapman went to San Francisco to inform the others by telegraph when a large shipment of treasure was being made. The fateful coded message which he sent November 4, 1870 read, "Send me sixty dollars, and charge my account.—J. Enrique." Nobody could suspect it, but it told the group a rich shipment was on train No. 1.

That night, when the train slowed down for a switch at Verdi, the seven of Chapman's confederates clambered aboard. Two found the conductor and induced him to sit down quietly inside one of the cars. The others went forward, forced the engine crew to stop and disconnect the express car and pull it ahead half a mile.

At that point the highwaymen quickly impressed the fact upon the express messenger that it would be healthier for him to remain quiet too. The treasure chests were broken open and the bandits carefully selected their loot, taking only gold coins and gold bars. They passed up the heavy bar silver and bank currency notes. The latter had little value in the hard-money West. Then the seven slipped away into the night to split their $41,000 plunder.

It was a smart deputy sheriff, Jim Kinkead, who found the prints of a pair of distinctive high-heeled boots at the scene. These were the clue which led to the subsequent roundup of the entire gang, and furnished Nevada with its most sensational trial of the period. All were convicted.

Davis arrived in the Nevada State Prison at Carson City on Christmas Day, 1870—less than two months after the holdup—to serve ten years. Because of his cooperation with the authorities at the trial he was pardoned just a little more than four years later, on February 16, 1875, and was killed a short time after when he attempted to hold up the stage en route from Eureka to Tybo.

Today, the slot machines set a din along Reno's Virginia Street where the old-timers plodded through the mud to Lake's ferry nearly 100 years ago. Reno and its family of phantoms have seen a large chunk of Nevada history made since then.

The Exchange Hotel at Aurora

—From an old etching in Thompson and West, "History of Nevada."

Came the Dawn!

AURORA WAS THE FIRST, AND ONE OF THE finest real ghost towns that I ever visited. On a long-ago summer day I herded my steaming flivver around and through the sagebrush and weeds which had grown up in its streets. More than one hundred of its solid masonry buildings still stood at the time.

Many of them still were filled with fixtures and furnishings, much as they had been left many years before. But now Aurora is gone, hardly anything is left but the cemetery. The post-war craving for used bricks in Beverly Hills and Malibu was the cause of the desecration. If every fireplace built from these bricks smokes, it is just the ghosts of those old Aurorans getting even for the despoilment of their beloved town.

My curiosity had been aroused by articles written by W. A. Chalfant in his *Inyo Register* at Bishop, California. Chalfant's father, a Forty-Niner, had come to Nevada in the early Washoe rush and was among the first to settle in Owens Valley. The younger Chalfant published the paper there until his death a few years ago and frequently wrote about the old-timers he had met and known and the early days of the West. It was his delightful and factually correct articles which stirred my first interest in the historic early days and its town. Many of these stories have been published since in *Gold, Guns and Ghost Towns* and other books.

Aurora, a contemporary of Virginia City, had a gay and glorious existence during the 'Sixties. Although it never equalled the Comstock center in silver, sin or society, it did have one distinction that no other community could claim—it was simultaneously the county seat of Mono County, California, and Esmeralda County, Nevada.

Nobody knew where the state line was located until the survey was completed in the fall of 1863, and Aurora was determined to be just inside Nevada.

When its rich surface minerals were discovered in August 1860, the area was in the western part of Utah territory. Its ore was found by J. M. Corey, James N. Braley and E. R. Hicks, three fortune-hunters who had failed to locate anything on the Comstock. Corey and Braley had come over the Sierra from San Jose, California. Hicks was a part Cherokee whom they had met around Virginia City. The trio ranged southward, in search of minerals, and one day they camped where there was water and good grass.

Hicks, hunting for game, broke off some pieces from quartz outcroppings on August 25. This became the old Winnemucca lode, near the western crest of what was named Esmeralda Hill. On the same afternoon Corey located the Esmeralda lode, which they considered the best prospect for a mine. The party posted notices on four claims, including the above two, the Cape and the Plata.

Corey apparently was well educated and quite a reader. He suggested the name, Aurora, the "Goddess of Dawn," for the area. It was appropriate since the location was 7400 feet high. An unencumbered eastern horizon permitted each day to break in a full array of color. Corey also christened the mining district which the group formed. The name he proposed lives on permanently in Nevada. It was "Esmeralda," meaning "emerald," one of the comparatively few Spanish names in the State. He had admired the title when he read it in Victor Hugo's *Notre Dame de Paris*.

From the start, prospectors rushed to Aurora and during the first two months 357 mining locations were made. Corey and Braley sold out for $30,000 apiece and returned to California where they settled on orchards near Santa Clara. Hicks departed from Aurora for Arkansas with $10,000.

The trail to Aurora on my first visit was rough. It made me appreciate more fully the determination and enthusiasm of those old-time pioneers who had to haul in every pound of food, supplies and building equipment over even worse roads. They had to travel 90 miles to Carson City and 130 more across the rugged Sierra to Sacramento, the main supply point for the new Nevada towns. Prices, naturally, were very high.

Strangely, meals were reasonable, averaging 75 cents apiece or $10 a week. Actually, humans could live cheaper than horses and mules. It cost about $3 a day to feed an animal. Freight costs on hay and grain amounted to much more than for beans and bacon.

Winter comes early there, and by the first thaw there was a sizeable population living in dugouts and shacks. Chalfant quoted a letter, dated February 1861, listing more than one hundred "places of abode" and "quite a catalog of places of business." The first commercial structure in the camp was Pat Hickey's place, which, he noted was constructed of "sticks, stones, shakes, canvas and mud."

An on-the-spot record of life in Aurora that first winter came to light in 1959 when Ethel Zimmer, one of Nevada's most devoted researchers, completed the work of deciphering the faded, scrawled occasional diary of Samuel Youngs, one of Aurora's founders and leading early citizens, and published the result in the Nevada Historical Society Quarterly. Young's journal had been found face down in a stable at Carson City.

A pioneer of the California gold rush and an educated man, Youngs, disappointed at his failure to stake a good claim at Virginia City, decided the new Esmeralda boom held commercial possibilities. He left Virginia City November 19, 1860, "with fifteen hundred pounds of provisions, blankets, etc." and arrived at the Aurora diggings six days later.

The crudity of living on that snow-swept mountain top in those earliest days is easily visualized from his brief reports—"December 5, A light snow—very cold for two days and nights freezing water in the pail solid.

Sleeping on ground and cooking outdoors. Read by fire evenings. One side burns and the other side cold enough to freeze . . . Sunday, January 13, 1861, An intensely cold day, Snow . . . deep. Fine sleighing but only 2 or 3 sleds here for hauling wood and lumber . . . We are living in a canvas tent, sleeping on the ground. I get up by daylight. Intensely cold and I make a fire. We having no table and chairs, set our dishes on the ground which is our table and gather around. Lumber sells for 200 dollars 1000 ft. Flour 21 dollars. 100 lbs. Fresh beef 20c."

On February 20 they "Put a canvas roof on our stone house" and on March 8 they were beginning to acquire "conveniences." Youngs noted, "Put green hides in bottom of bunks." Just a week later he could report happily, "Slept first night in berths covered with raw hides. Have been sleeping on ground since Nov. last."

No mining could be done while the snow was deep on the hills and the population had to seek other pursuits. Chalfant wrote that Braley reported a "constant buying and selling of lots, ranches and other properties of questionable value and dubious ownership." Braley also wrote that one of the favorite sports consisted of target shooting across the town's main street, which he regarded as "a diversion not eminently calculated to soothe the nerves of one having occasion to cross the line of fire."

It was during the first winter that citizens of the fledgling town, only half a year old, decided to petition the California legislature for a new county to bring about a semblance of law and order, and also to avoid "being subjected to the hated and oppressive laws of Utah."

The California legislators were agreeable to the plan, although there was a spirited dispute over what to name the county. The Senate voted for "Esmeralda," opposing "Mono," the name the assembly had approved, mostly because one legislator insisted the latter meant "monkey" in Spanish. The argument waxed, another claimed it was Latin for "alone" while a third argued that its definition was "good looking." However, "Mono" prevailed and the bill was passed April 24, 1861, with Aurora designated the county seat.

With the coming of spring a new flood of citizens arrived. Population had reached 1400 in June and was increasing daily. Lots were selling for as much as $1500. Four brickyards had been started and masonry buildings began to replace the stick-stone-canvas shelters. Citizens erected a brick school house for the eighty children in camp.

The weather was pleasant and life began to take on a semblance of civilization during that first spring and summer. Young's diary furnishes us with some previously unpublished tidbits which brighten the picture of activities in the burgeoning mining town.

In such isolation entertainment was practically non-existent. On April 7, 1861, he deemed it noteworthy enough to record, "Saw an Indian feast dance in Town to amuse the citizens who gave them a few shillings . . .

20 or 30 Indians form a circle, commence singing and humming a nasal tune, stamp first one foot and then the other, shaking their arms, painted on faces, backs & bodies, naked except cloth around their loins."

And on April 15 Aurora's first stage arrived from Carson City at midnight . . . "Left Carson in morning at 5 A.M. Left here next morning at 5 A.M. Passengers came with it. Fare 20 dollars."

May brought Aurorans an almost-forgotten dietetic treat, eggs. It was unusual enough for Young's to record, "Get Gulls eggs from Mono Lake. Pay 75c doz. About the size of a turkey's egg and very dark speckled."

Early milling was done in five arrastres—the Mexican method of crushing ore in a pit by dragging heavy stones through and over it—but during that first June a new amalgamating mill was being built. It was the first of eighteen which were in full operation by 1864.

Amos Green and his son, George Augustus, had come over the mountains from California and set up sawmills at nearby Sweetwater and Bridgeport. Their lumber was freighted to the booming town and its new neighbor, Bodie, a few miles to the West, and the price of this greatly needed product dropped to $100 per thousand feet.

Aurorans weren't certain whether they were within California's Mono County or still part of Utah Territory. The rabid Unionists, who considered California a hotbed of secessionism, insisted on the latter and were highly pleased when Nevada was made a territory in 1861.

Youngs was so devotedly pro-Union, having been a city and state legislator in New York, that he sent for an American flag, since there was none in Aurora. His diary records that on June 4, 1861, he "Hoisted American flag with 'Stars & Stripes' over our cabin in Aurora, Mono County, Cal." Three weeks later the record shows that he became even more active when he noted on June 23 that he "Wrote notices & put them up for meeting to form Union Club."

Two days later the Unionists held a meeting with Youngs as chairman. He notes that he "Wrote preamble & Resolutions, Constitution" and that it was a "large enthusiastic meeting, Songs, etc."

Youngs was elected president of the Club which became an important adjunct of local social and civic life.

Aurora experienced an outbreak of Civil War antagonisms. It seemed to be a gathering place for southern sympathizers who assembled at clandestine meetings. The Union men organized two military companies, the cavalry Esmeralda Rangers and the Hooker Rifles, unmounted.

The Dixie group "made a complete pandemonium of our town and continued their hideous orgies until late on Sunday morning, cheering Jeff Davis, Stonewall Jackson and the Southern Confederacy," reported the *Esmeralda Star*, August 23, 1862.

In Aurora at the time was Lieutenant N. Noble, whose company had gone to Adobe Meadows, some fifty miles to the southeast, to quiet Indian trouble. Noble had been ill and stayed behind.

The Confederate outburst aroused his anger and the *Star* reported he was "determined to let them know that our Government and its authorities were not to be trampled upon with impunity."

Taking a squad of the local guardsmen, Noble went to the home of a rabid southern sympathizer. The *Star* tells us "though he offered resistance and clung to the house like a tick, he had to come along, although not without a good deal of trouble, and kicking Private Michael Stewart on the shin, which Mike responded to by forcible presentation of his toe in the rebel's rear, after which he made no further resistance, and was marched to the county jail."

The prisoner was escorted the next morning to a flagstaff where Lieut. Noble administered the oath of allegiance to the United States to him before a crowd composed of everybody in town. Following the ceremony the officer made a speech in which he declared that other rebels "would not get off so easily."

This apparently squelched further anti-union outbursts for a long time until news was received of Lincoln's assassination.

The events of that day have been reported in varying ways by different writers. Youngs' diary gives a succinct, but clear story of the events in his entry for April 15, 1865.

"About 10 A.M. the Telegraph brought the astounding news of the assassination & death of Pres't Lincoln & Sect'y Seward on the previous evening," he wrote on that long-ago day. "Sadness & gloom pervaded the whole Union People. Tears pushed from the eyes of young men & old. All the flags were hoisted at half-mast. Stores & business houses closed & buildings trimmed in mourning. A. G. Judy [most historians have spelled it Judeigh] a Seccessionist saying Lincoln was a tyrant & ought to have been dead long ago. Cap't Kelly was in town & on hearing of it called the Esmeralda Rangers who escorted him in making the arrest. He will be taken to Fort Churchill & put to packing sand. His wife interceded earnestly for him but to no effect."

Apparently he changed his mind during the night because of the following day's entry in Young's record reads, "A. G. Judy weakened. Took oath of allegiance & was discharged."

Undoubtedly Judy had good reason to reconsider his stubborn stand as Chalfant explained, "At the time it was no funny business to be sent to Fort Churchill. A fifty pound sack of sand would be placed on the prisoner's back, and with it he marched up and down the parade ground, with a soldier with a fixed bayonet to prod him if he lagged."

On July 8, Nevada's first Territorial Governor, James Nye, arrived in Carson City and he jumped into the boundary hassle, claiming the Esmeralda diggings for the new territory and designating it as a "council district."

The census taken that August showed 3286 residents in "the valley of the Walker River and all the territory south and east of it." Practically

Tonopah Scene After an Early Day Mountain Zephyr

all of these were in Aurora. Polling places for the territorial election in the district were set at Rissue's Bridge, Marsh's Ranch, Aurora and Monoville, all now spectral names of the past.

The Nevada territorial election was held August 31, just one year, plus six days, after Braley found the first outcrop of ore, proving that Aurora was a precocious early day municipal infant. Citizens of the Esmeralda town, especially those of Union leanings, went to the polls and elected J. W. Pugh as member of the council, the territorial senate; William E. Teall, who ran a saloon, and Youngs won seats as members of the house.

The territorial legislature met at Carson City, and on November 25 divided Nevada Territory into nine counties. The first one listed and described in the bill was Esmeralda. It was an extensive chunk of land into which several smaller divisions would have fitted with area left over.

Aurora was designated the county seat. This gave the citizens a choice of officials to deal with, as the community was already established as the seat of California's Mono County. Actually, things worked out reasonably well in the complex situation. More or less by formal agreement, the California officials handled franchises and toll roads while the Nevada officers administered mining district affairs. If anybody had any civil litigation, he took his choice between Mono's judge Baldwin or Esmeralda's Judge Turner.

The first general election created an unusual situation when officials opened two polling places. Aurorans had a field day as they voted for Nevada candidates in the Armory and then walked down the street to the police station to ballot for California office seekers.

The town's twenty-two saloons did a rushing business that election day. It was probably the only time and place in history that Americans ever had the opportunity to cast votes for candidates in a State and a Territory on the same day.

Aurora's double government continued until September 20, 1863. The boundary survey crew finally reached that far and found that the line went between Aurora and Bodie, putting the former three miles inside Nevada and the latter five miles into California. Finally convinced, Mono County officials packed their records and carried them across the line to Bodie, thence to Bridgeport which is still the county seat.

They also took along all the tax funds which had been gathered at Aurora in their two years there. The Californians left the Esmeralda officials with $20,000 of indebtedness, most of it in outstanding warrants. In memory of this merry mixup, carefully preserved in two or three historical libraries, are some copies of the Esmeralda *Star*, which started publication on May 17, 1862, with datelines reading, Aurora, Mono County, California."

Having come across the plains to Carson City with his brother, Orion, who had been appointed Territorial Secretary of State, young red-bearded Samuel Clemens had gone to Unionville in the Humboldt region in December 1861 on a hopeless search for a bonanza. In some way he obtained a few shares in the Black Warrior claim at Aurora.

In a letter to his sister on October 25, 1861, he said he planned "to go to the Esmeralda mines in the spring." He evidently left earlier for he wrote his family in February, 1862, from Aurora and mentioned that he and Bob Howland, Governor Nye's nephew, owned a portion of the Horatio and Derby and for the first time prophesied it "bids fair to be a big thing." His luck was to prove bad in this case . . . as it did in all his other endeavors at Aurora, except the letters he wrote to the *Territorial Enterprise* in Virginia signed "Josh." They were to lead him to his first newspaper job and local fame and thence to world-wide renown as one of America's favorite authors, "Mark Twain."

Hopes were high in 1862 that Aurora was destined to be the gold capital of the world. It was a shallow dream.

The Esmeralda mines, variously credited with producing as much as $30,000,000 in gold and silver, actually were grass roots operations. The deepest workings went down a mere ninety-four feet and the Wide West, in which Mark Twain almost hit his jackpot, produced its richest treasure a bare fifty feet below the ground.

Every Aurora habitation was jammed full by April 1863, with stages bringing in twenty-five or thirty newcomers daily as the town boomed lustily. Lots which had sold the previous year for a few hundred dollars were bringing from $2500 to $5000. With a population nearing four thousand, of which around two hundred were women and eighty were children, the citizens now had a complete city government. Masonic and Odd Fellow organizations had been instituted, there were two churches and twenty-two saloons—the latter much better patronized than the former—more than a score of stores and practically every other line of business and profession.

The correspondent responsible for leaving us such precise details also recorded that there were "seven hundred and sixty-one houses of which sixty-four were of brick and three hundred would compare favorably with a like number in any other mining town," according to Chalfant.

This fellow proved a meticulous census taker in other details, too, reporting, "There are only sixty-five graves—largely called into use because of sagebrush whiskey, poor doctors, some killed."

All this had happened in less than three years.

Life for a newspaperman in these rough and rugged out-of-the-way places was never calm and peaceful. The Esmeralda *Star* was run by a staunch Union man, Major E. A. Sherman. He wielded a vitriolic pen in defense of the Union and with antipathy toward the thugs who then held sway in the community. One offended ruffian delegated a gunman to assassinate the editor. Sherman was wounded, but recovered and continued to attack the iniquitous element until he later sold out to a man named Avard. The editor of the Democratic Aurora *Times* had his troubles, too, being none too popular with the Union folk. Challenged to a duel he was shot in the foot and carried a permanent limp the rest of his life.

During its few years of munificent glory, Aurora daily shipped its rich gold bars to civilization via stages. One of the most persistent legends about the "rich yield" of the Esmeralda mines, still heard occasionally from descendants of old timers, is that much of the gold that was shipped out was hauled back on the same stage, to be carried out again the next day. This increased the total output credited to some mines, substantially boosting the price of its stock. Records of the express company listed the total of Aurora bullion shipments up to 1869 at $27,000,-000. Whether that is accurate nobody ever will know.

One thing is certain, though—the remarkable treasure put temptation in the way of some of the most reckless highwaymen in the West. Stage holdups became almost a daily occurrence.

Effective action taken to end the constant depredations gave rise to an Aurora legend which has been told and embroidered through the years. A leader of one of the thug gangs was a John Daley, twenty-five year-old graduate of the Sacramento River front. Whatever else Daley had done to deserve his reputation, he was known to have killed at least two men during his Aurora period.

The final act was initiated over a horse stolen by one of his men, James Sears, from W. R. Johnson, keeper at Hoy's Station on the main road where it followed the Walker River. Johnson sent one of his men, John A. Rogers, after the thief and horse. Rogers overtook Sears and pumped two loads of buckshot into him, ending his horse stealing activities for all time.

Daley was incensed greatly when he learned about this defiance of his "authority." He was heard threatening that he would kill Johnson.

The station keeper came to Aurora with a load of vegetables on February 1, 1864, and was waylaid and slain that night. According to Chalfant, "Daley either knocked him down or shot him or both; William Buckley drew a knife across his throat, and by way of finishing touches John McDowell, *alias* 'Three-Fingered Jack,' and James Masterson, or 'Massey,' rifled his pockets and set his clothing afire."

The fiendish murder aroused the townspeople, who had grown increasingly angry at seeing twenty-seven murderers in a row go free in the courts of the thug-controlled community. About 350 of the citizens met in the Wingate Building and organized the Citizens Protective Committee. This group, suspecting some of its own officers, rounded up all of Daley's known confederates and took them into armed custody.

"Guards were placed around Jail & Town," Youngs' wrote, and noted that the "Coroner's Jury were in session to the 8th." When it brought in guilty verdicts, the committee voted to hang the four known to have participated in Johnson's killing on February 9, just a week after the crime. Banishment was voted for his other followers.

Youngs' entry for February 9, the first since February 2, shows how completely the citizens took charge of law and order in Aurora during that stirring week. He wrote, "The Sheriff being at Adobe Meadows in search for Buckley, the Deputy Sheriff & Marshall's [sic] house were guarded and they requested to keep within doors. At half-past one P.M. John Daily [sic]—William Buckley—John McDowell [*Alias* Three-Fingered Jack] and Jas. Masterson were hung. Gambling and saloons were closed last eve'g. Today all saloons, stores were closed. Mining & all business suspended. A trying day for Aurora. Gov. Nye telegraphed me there must be no violence—but the people are masters. My dispatch Telegraph to the Gov.—'All quiet and orderly. 4 men will be hung in half an hour.'"

The entire populace viewed the spectacle. Buckley had arranged payment for his coffin and told the crowd he and Daley were guilty, the other two innocent. He invited everybody to "come to my wake at Daley's cabin tonight."

Daley's final request was for all the brandy he could drink. He got it, and had to be helped to stand erect on the scaffold. Masterson died coolly. McDowell, like his boss, was drunk and also had to be held up.

Governor Nye reached Aurora two days later, accompanied by Provost Marshal Van Bokkelyn. Seeing the dangling ropes on the gibbet, he is said to have inquired, "What's that up there?"

Chalfant declares that Howland replied, "That's the Aurora hay press."

"It should have been longer to hold more," the Governor is reported to have said.

The Governor had "insisted on law and order" and Aurora had become a model of deportment, even though the result required drastic steps and mob action. Apparently satisfied, he departed three days later. Thugs never again controlled affairs, although stage robbers and others did continue to make Aurora their headquarters.

There are many other delightful tales of Aurora—such as the one about the Deluge Bucket Company of volunteer firemen and its new hand pumper.

When the first blaze broke out after the vehicle arrived in town, the men rushed to the scene and pumped vigorously. Shortly, the water supply became muddier and the pumping harder. As smoke thickened, the male pumpers dwindled away. The stream from the hoses shrunk to a trickle. It was then that the women rushed into the breach and again started the water flowing through the hoses by determinedly manning the handles.

Never afterward did the male members of the Deluge Company strut their membership, especially in the hearing of any of the fair sex.

Another little tale, for which no accurate documentation can be found, concerns the continuing feud between Aurora and Bodie. The editor of one of the Aurora papers reportedly printed a story about a little girl sadly ending her prayers. "Goodbye God, we're moving to Bodie."

The editor of the California town newspaper is declared to have replied in the next issue that the little girl had been misquoted, insisting that she had really said, "Good, by God, we're moving to Bodie."

Aurorans looked down upon those in Bodie, not only literally from their higher elevation, but in other ways. Those in the "older" settlement referred to the newer place as "that shack town," and maybe with reason since Aurora preferred to build with brick while most of Bodie was constructed with lumber.

In the long run, Bodie's ghosts had the last laugh, because much of the old California ghost town is still standing, and it is preserved as a State Park.

Aurora's best years were over before 1870. Peak population had reached around 6000. Its decline was due to several factors. First the shallowness of the veins, then an expensive and inadequate milling process which failed to extract but a small percentage of the metal from the ore, but most of all, water. Pumps available in those days couldn't cope with the flow into the shafts as underground springs were tapped and nobody had devised an easy method of extracting ore under water.

During the 'Seventies an English company bought up all the mine properties and installed expensive equipment. Milling costs kept their operation in red ink. During the early 'Eighties the British firm despondently gave up and went home.

Aurora's dawns then grew very dim, and in 1883 Hawthorne snatched the county seat and Aurora's light practically went out. In later years efforts to bring Aurora back to brightness never got much beyond the glimmer stage.

Four young men bought the dormant mines and mills around the turn of the century and brought about a brief community renaissance. During the intervening years a few old-timers had continued to live there. *The Saturday Evening Post* writer, Charles Van Loan, learned in 1915 that they were a cantankerous lot and through the years they had grown so jealous none would speak to any of the others.

One of the ambitious new young owners related the tale of the shuttered general store to Van Loan. Its old-time residents had taken only their valuables when they departed, as it was cheaper to buy new clothing and furnishings elsewhere than pay the costly freight charges. So most of the town was just as it had been left. The new owners became curiously interested in the general store, locked and closed behind

heavy iron shutters. After a search they located the owner and wrote
him a letter asking him to set a price on the store and its contents.

He answered, "For two hundred and fifty dollars the store and
everything in it is yours."

They mailed him the money and he sent back the large brass key for
the front door lock. The owners felt like youngsters at a carnival reaching for prizes in the grab bag when they entered the place. They found
a treasure right inside the front door, a large, unbroken coil of two-inch
Manila rope in perfect condition. It was worth more than the entire
store had cost them.

The stock was in excellent condition. The new owners quickly discovered that the dry, clear mountain air had preserved everything and
the tightly shuttered windows had kept out the dust and bugs.

The most valuable discovery was a cellar full of liquors and wines,
just as it had been left three decades before. The informant said that
when they told a wine connoisseur of the fine old vintages which were
consumed by the owners, he wept tears of frustration. "He told me he
would gladly have paid more for a bottle of that mellow old sherry than
the whole store had cost," the young man said.

The new owners turned over the aged whiskey supply to the one
remaining town saloon and for awhile Aurora's few returned miners enjoyed some of the tastiest bourbon ever sold in Nevada at the then current price of two drinks for a quarter.

"That whiskey, mind you, was as old as sin, as smooth as oil and as
mellow as an autumn sunset in Kentucky; but suffering Cyrus, how power-
ful!" the owner was quoted as saying.

The store was well stocked with men's and women's clothing, as good
as new, of fine material, but in the styles of the 'Seventies and before.
There were "frock coats of rich doeskin, with flaring, square-cut skirts
and lapels edged with braid; fancy vests with the entire front cut out to
show a frilled skirt; old-fashioned collars; sky-blue satin neckties; vol-
uminous peg-top trousers; queer old boots of finest leather and enough
flat-topped derby hats to supply an army of Yiddish comedians," Van
Loan wrote.

In the end the young mine owners sold out to a strong Nevada company operated by Roy Hardy, one of the state's most successful twentieth
century mining operators.

This organization installed modern equipment and economical meth-
ods and reduced production costs to such a degree that it made a good
profit from ore which couldn't be worked with the equipment available
in the 'Sixties and 'Seventies.

For a short period, while World War I raged in Europe and the demand for metal made prices high, the clanking noisy mills created a
constant roar day and night, never stopping. Then the war ended, prices
dropped, and the Esmeralda ores had been worked to their limit.

Former U. S. Senator George W. Malone, then an engineering student at the University of Nevada and the Pacific Coast Intercollegiate heavyweight boxing champion, obtained a summer job at Aurora during this period. Recently he recalled the noise, dust and excitement of that summer. "I'd heard there was a heavyweight boxer down that way who thought he was pretty good," Senator Malone said. "I needed a job to help me finish college and I figured that I'd look over this would-be white hope and maybe a bout could be arranged. I felt I was pretty good and could take him, and the arrangements were made. I beat the fellow.

"Those who bet on me made it worthwhile . . . I had more money at the end of that summer than I ever had before."

Malone was still there when the power finally was turned off and the mill stopped its day-and-night clanking for the final time.

"There was complete silence for about a half a minute," the Senator said, "Then every dog in the town began howling at the top of his lungs. Those curs had lived all their lives with the roar of those rolling heavy steel balls and the growl of ore falling to the bottom of the bins in their ears. I guess the silence must have hurt their ear drums. Anyway, they didn't stop howling for a couple of days.

The canine cantata was Aurora's final requiem.

Soon the mill was torn down and moved to Mina and for many years grazing cattle and occasional ghost town chasers were the few rare signs of life around the old brick buildings.

Now the latter are gone, too . . . only the graveyard remains to greet Aurora's rosy dawns.

Springdale, 1908-1909, Pioneer Miner Oscar Anderson in Buggy

—Las Vegas Review-Journal Photo.

NDELARIA DEPOT 1898
FRED BARNES CONDUCTOR
FRANK REGAN BRAKEMAN
ABE CHURCH ENGINEER
OHNNIE McGILLIS FIREMAN
CHAS. MEADOWS MAIL CLERK.

Candelaria Depot, 1898

Candelaria, 1898, Mineral County

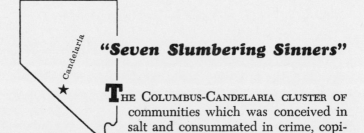

"Seven Slumbering Sinners"

THE COLUMBUS-CANDELARIA CLUSTER OF
communities which was conceived in
salt and consummated in crime, copious silver and origin of the nation's
borax industry, comprised a convivial jackpot of uninhibited early-day
Aurora offspring. This raucous septet—Columbus, Candelaria, Belleville,
Marietta, Metallic City, better known as Pickhandle Gulch, Rhodes and
Sodaville—was a crude colony of rambunctious little towns.

They were far out in a harsh, scorched country where few had ever
visited when the first discovery was made in 1864. The ancient sea-bot-
tom location is an area where saline flats formed when the waters re-
ceded aeons ago. It is a bare land, where the southeastern border of
Mineral County joins Esmeralda County. The towns lie between the
Excelsior and Monte Cristo ranges, bald, burned, igneous volcanic up-
heavals.

In common with other early-day mining camps, all boasted their full
quota of hooch and sin emporiums but in comparison with the "modern
metropoli" of the day, such as Virginia City, Aurora, Austin and Eureka,
they lacked many conveniences, and boasted few luxuries.

Nell Murbarger dubbed them "The Seven Somnolent Sisters." It just
isn't apt to tag a feminine title to the ghosts of these dusty, wild-action,
he-man communities, where murders generally were ruled to be "justified," and occurred frequently.

There was almost a complete lack of law, and no churches at all.
Wood was extremely scarce and water was worth almost as much as
bullion. This brought wisecracks from editors in lusher communities,
who quipped that this was "no hardship," since none of the residents
used it to drink nor ever washed. This was a canard, of course, because
when the White Mountain Water Company finally piped a supply from
nine miles away the price dropped to a nickel a gallon and Leo Eberle,
Candelaria barber, immediately put a sign in his window, "Baths at
Reasonable Rates   Hot Water $1.25—Cold Water 75 cents."

Oddly, these towns aren't too well known, although hundreds daily
rush past three of them and within a few miles of the others, on busy
U. S. 95 between Tonopah and Mina.

Columbus lies on the north side of the big, white flat west of Coaldale where U. S. 6 and 95 join. Rhodes and Sodaville are right beside
the road, the former six miles south of Mina, the latter halfway between
these two places. State Route 10 turns west at Rhodes and in seven
miles reaches Belleville. Marietta is nine miles farther west on a desert
road from there. On another desert road, which branches east just beyond Belleville, one comes to Candelaria. This road also leads back to

U. S. 95 halfway between Rhodes and Coaldale. In the old days a road led from Candelaria to Columbus, five miles through a canyon. Metallic City was just below Candelaria in this gulch.

Seven Mexicans found the first ore in the area on August 31, 1864, and named their claim the "Jesus Maria." Other claims also bore Spanish titles, one being "Candelaria," named for a Catholic Church, Mass Day, and the town which grew up was named the same.

Indians were on the warpath in the area, so the originators of the Columbus mining district organized at a safe distance, in Washington, a small mining town in the Toiyobe Mountains south of Austin. José Ochoa was elected president, and C. L. Benedict, recorder—although the latter's name appears on one of the Candelaria claims. Maybe he was chosen just to write the minutes—they are in English.

Samuel Youngs, hearing of the salt deposits of Columbus, where the only water was available, decided to build a mill there to grind the Candelaria ores. Hauling the equipment overland, Colonel Youngs' pack train was caught in a cloudburst in a canyon and the equipment was spread over the flats below. But he recovered enough of it to erect a four-stamp mill, with A. J. Holmes as a partner. A little later the Columbus Mill and Mining Company and Sweetwater and Hazeltine erected ten-stamp plants at Columbus.

In the meantime Candelaria had started to become a town. A fellow named John McDonald is credited with being its first white resident. As might be expected, he opened a saloon. Customers were scarce, and within a year he sold out to a Zadoc Pierce who carried some groceries as well as liquor. J. B. Hiskey surveyed a townsite, and by November 1865, the place boasted nineteen business buildings, eleven of them saloons. Within the next four years Candelaria was rated the second largest place in Esmeralda County, with a population guessed at between 900 and 1000. Later as Aurora declined it became the county's largest community.

The ore had to be good, because Youngs got $60 a ton for milling it. Considering that wood cost $15 a cord and transportation of the ore by muleback down the canyon from the mines another $8 a ton, his price wasn't exhorbitant. The plentiful salt was roasted with the silver ore to form a chloride, which was turned to metal by a process similar to photographic developing.

With its mills busily grinding away, Columbus grew into a town, such as it was, with living conditions definitely primitive. This was to be expected when those working there were just looking forward to getting enough of a stake to move onward. There were some adobe shacks and a "hotel," described by an early visitor as being fourteen by twenty feet in size, built partly of adobe and partly of rough lumber.

He said it was so poorly constructed that the constantly-blowing salty dust sifted inside most of the time, adding a gritty, abrasive condiment to the food, cooked in a lean-to at one end and served on a few crude tables. It's hardly necessary to note that the "hotel" also had a bar at one side.

Beds were scarce, and space on the floor of the mills, near the heat of the furnaces, was eagerly sought as the best place for one's blanket roll. The restaurant menus boasted no oysters or other fancy food as did those in Austin and Virginia City because Columbians were meat and bean eaters. Cattle were driven in from the feeding grounds when meat was needed, shot and slaughtered in an area just far enough away to avoid the smell. The coyotes and dogs kept the crude abbatoir scavenged.

Youngs and his partner, Holmes, got into an argument in 1869, and the latter was frozen out of the mill operations. Most of the town was on Young's side. Holmes was bitter. He vowed that he'd "make grass grow in the streets of Columbus." His threat was considered highly amusing since the heavily chemicalized soil would hardly grow spindly weeds.

Holmes almost saw his threat against Columbus materialize, though. He went to Candelaria and gained control of the area's richest producer, the Northern Belle. It poured out nearly $4 million of ore by 1878 and returned a million-and-a-half in dividends. Holmes cut off the supply of ore to the Columbus mills by erecting a twenty-stamp plant at a spot seven miles west of Candelaria. This became Belleville.

The new mill would have been enough to kill Columbus if a chemically-wise, out-of-pocket prospector hadn't arrived in 1871. He suspected that the cotton balls which blew over the surface of Columbus lake were borax. His name was William Troup, or Troop—historians spell it both ways.

He borrowed a wash tub, gathered some sagebrush wood, and boiled up enough of the cottony stuff to prove that it was practically pure borax. This brought William T. Coleman, a California financier, into the picture. Associated with him were John Ryan and Chris Zabriskie. By 1872 he was producing the first commercially refined borax in the United States.

Columbus perked up again to its greatest prosperity during the 'Seventies as silver and milling were forgotten. The new activity interested Francis Marion Smith, who had been making a living at Columbus by supplying wood which he hauled from distant hills to the mills. In 1880 it was reported to have two mills, two stores, six saloons, a blacksmith shop and livery stable, a doctor, express office and a newspaper, the *Borax Miner.*

It was while scouting out wood sources some ten miles northwest of Columbus that Smith discovered Teel's Marsh. He immediately suspected that the yellow-white crust was the same mineral that was being refined at Columbus. It was. Smith staked claims to the entire area. By 1872 he was refining borax too, under the name of "Teel's Marsh Borax

Co." That's how and where the later multimillionaire borax king got his start.

The fourth in the cluster of towns, Marietta, was born near this operation. "Borax" Smith built a general store there to pick up additional profits. Before long Smith had his eyes on bigger things. He obtained control of the Columbus operations, established the Pacific Coast Borax Company and adopted the now-famous "20-Mule Team" trademark which still remains much in evidence on grocery shelves and TV screens. He imported a thousand Chinese coolies to refine and work the salt and borax deposits. The refined borax had to be hauled 150 miles to Wadsworth by wagon, while camels grunted and sighed their way overland to Virginia City and plodded to Aurora hauling salt on their backs.

Chinese were used in the various tasks—which were "no jobs for white men." One of the constantly recurring lively incidents was the arrival in Columbus of Chinese drivers returning down the canyon with empty wagons after hauling salt to Candelaria. The little wagons had no brakes. As the vehicle crowded the horse and mule teams the animals speeded up. The Orientals always became panicky and started to scream. By the time the vehicles reached the bottom and emerged into the main street of town the teams were traveling at full speed and the scared Chinese, pigtails flying behind, were hanging on for dear life and yelling at the top of their lungs.

Naturally the Orientals had their joss houses and opium dens, even though the latter mostly were just cellar holes in adobe huts. One of the major news events of the period was a wholesale riot by the entire colony over the affections of a "China Mary." After it subsided the *Borax Miner,* started by W. W. Barnes, commented that the Comstock couldn't claim any sort of trouble "that Columbus couldn't top."

The Columbus paper had many salty tales to relate. One that struck the readers as unusual was the trial and execution of one Johnny Stewart, who went by the nickname of "Bully." All he had done was to shoot and kill a gent named Frank Durand, which certainly was not anything out of the ordinary for the neighborhood. What made this killing different was that "Bully" Stewart was tried and executed by due process of law at Aurora on April 24, 1874. A legal execution was "unusual."

Another of Columbus' incidents related by the editor concerned the activities at the New Year's Eve dance in 1873. It was quite a social event for the time and place since there actually were two real women present. One was a gal from Fish Lake, the other a Chilean lass who played the guitar in the orchestra, such as it was. Miners drew lots to see which would tie a handkerchief around his left arm to signify he was "woman" for the night.

During the festivities a Mexican named Victor Moncaga, a new arrival in camp, strenuously objected to the Chilean girl playing her guitar instead of dancing with him. He grabbed the instrument and smashed it. A respected Columbus resident, Antonio Rivera, protested. Moncaga stabbed Rivera to death and fled. He was caught by the town's "law" and locked in the Columbus "jail"—a pretty frail shanty.

Other "respected" citizens decided this wasn't good enough. Some of them spirited the officers to the other end of town on a pretext while a majority removed Moncaga from the calaboose and led him to the cattle slaughtering grounds. There he was strung up on the windlass used to hoist the beef carcasses. When both parties arrived back at the bar the officers were told what had happened. Everybody agreed nothing could be done about the matter, so all had a drink, and the dance was resumed, sans guitar.

Later a group went back to cut Moncaga down. His body gave a convulsive jerk, so they returned and said they couldn't find it in the darkness—although it was full moonlight. The following dawn the party finished its drinking and dancing and returned to the slaughter grounds. Moncaga was no longer kicking. A coroner's jury assembled on the spot, returned a verdict that the victim was "dead." Everybody then went back to the bar to celebrate this verdict. Justice had been done in Columbus.

Two days later a couple of dusty horsemen came riding into town. They were deputy sheriffs who had trailed Moncaga the hundreds of miles over desert and mountains to arrest him for two murders in San Bernardino. They announced that a $2000 reward had been posted for his capture!

At the height of the borax and salt boom, abundant deposits were discovered north of Columbus and they gave birth to the clapboard and shingle towns of Sodaville and Rhodes. Sodaville eventually became the first terminus of the Carson & Colorado Railroad out of Mound House, alleviating a long wagon haul. Subsequently, the line was extended to Belleville to haul bullion from the mills, then on to Candelaria—where the first train arrived on the same day that water began dribbling through the new pipeline from the mountains—and finally to Keeler, below Lone Pine in California.

In 1875 the borax interests moved their main operations ten miles south to Fish Lake Valley, signaling the decline of Columbus, Marietta, Rhodes and Sodaville as the crust was cleared from the flats. Some borax operations continued as late as 1890, but the cream had been skimmed by Smith and his company.

Sodaville, after slumbering a few years, emerged as a much larger and busier town early in the twentieth century when Jim Butler discovered Tonopah, and it became the railhead for the extensive shipping operations to this rich new Nye County boom.

But Columbus was deserted. The Chinese were moved en masse. White families sought richer pastures. As was the case elsewhere, the freight costs were more than furniture was worth, and the residents departed, taking only their valuables and clothing.

During the heyday of Columbus, Candelaria also boomed along and after the railroad came remained a busy producer of silver. Its reported production of bullion through the years is variously said to have totalled between $33 and $55 million.

In 1880 Thompson & West credited Candelaria with six stores, one hotel, ten saloons, three restaurants, two livery stables, a blacksmith shop, three lawyers and the same number of doctors (an unusual statistic for those early towns), and an assay office, telegraph and express office, a small one-room adobe school—but no church.

The Holmes company was a very important factor in the life and survival of the mining town, so when Holmes got into an argument with the Northern Belle operators, repeating his fight with Youngs, the matter reached the courts. He sued for more than a half-million dollars for alleged stealing of his ore. The action brought about a decline in Candelaria operations. Even though Holmes eventually won the suit, things never again boomed as feverishly as they had earlier.

About this time a promoter called "Colonel" W. J. Sutherland popped up and began promising prosperity. When he failed to pull the promised silver rabbit out of the hat and couldn't pay his many obligations Candelarians escorted him out of town. He was furious and declared he'd come back and "show them." Strangely, he did.

A couple of years later he returned from England with a couple of hundred thousand dollars he had high-graded from English backers. As usual, money talks, and upon his return with cash in his pocket, he was greeted by those who had chased him out of town, being met at the station with a band and escorted to a banquet held in his honor.

Sutherland exploited the Princess mine and was the town's "big man" for awhile. He was leader for civic betterment and to "cultivate a love of the beautiful among the people" he planted a plot of grass twenty-eight by thirty-six feet, irrigating it with the expensive and scarce water trickling through the inadequate pipeline.

But Sutherland couldn't keep up the pace. He was indicted for failing to pay a $25,000 commission. By this time he'd run through a million dollars put up by the English backers, and the Princess had failed to repay any of it. Sutherland departed suddenly for the second time from Candelaria and was last heard from cutting a gaudy path in Carson City.

As might be expected Candelaria had its full quota of killings, most of them for little reason and few ever punished. The *True Fissure* bemoaned the sudden demise of one P. S. Traver, an Esmeralda County commissioner, slain January 6, 1880 by Mike Owens. The former wanted to pay off Owens with a check, the latter demanded cash. When refused, he shot the official. Owens was acquitted. Flags flew at half mast and all the saloons were closed during the funeral—the ultimate respect Candelaria could pay to the suddenly departed.

The State Surveyor-General reported in 1886, "Candelaria is quiet, having shut down while silver is low, but there is belief that the mines will be opened shortly." It was an optimistic guess, never quite realized. The price decline caused the mine operators to slash wages to $3 a day. Miners refused to accept the cut and moved to richer fields. Candelaria's light went out.

Just down the canyon from Candelaria was its sin suburb, officially named Metallic City but known by everyone as Pickhandle Gulch, apparently because differences of opinion frequently were settled with the area's handiest weapons, the hardwood handles of miners' picks. During its heyday it boasted several prominent visitors, including fabled Lucky Baldwin, who had "pieces" of some of its mines, and the Comstock tycoon, James G. Fair, who was campaigning for U. S. Senator.

The best known Pickhandle Gulch tale is the one of "Blue Dick" Hartman's "death." This bully boy's face was stained with powder marks from a premature explosion. He brought a reputation as a tough gunman with him from the Comstock.

Blue Dick's favorite hangout was McKissick's saloon in the Gulch. A fellow called Shagnasty Joe, a habitué of the Roaring Gimlet Bar in Candelaria, was his sworn enemy. Both voiced threats to kill the other on sight—although generally they seemed to avoid a meeting.

Then one day, according to the oft-told tale, Blue Dick fell asleep on a pool table at McKissick's. Somebody thought it would be a clever trick to cover him with a canvas sheet and start the story that he had been killed by an "unknown gunman."

As one shift at the mines finished work and poured into the bistro they were surprised to hear the story. A collection was started to give Blue Dick a real funeral. Everybody contributed. Rumors traveled fast. Shagnasty Joe soon heard of Blue Dick's alleged demise and hurried to McKissick's to learn whether it was true. He lifted the sheet and saw Dick's eyes staring at the ceiling. He was satisfied. About then, another shift came in and learned the news. As they lifted the canvas shroud a friend noted Blue Dick wink an eye. He urged another collection. Shagnasty Joe was forced to contribute, but declared in a loud voice, "It's lucky somebody plugged him. If he hadn't killed the scared skunk I'd had to do it myself."

Shagnasty was just getting warmed up to telling what he would have done to Blue Dick when glancing at the pool table, he let out shriek and rushed for the door. Blue Dick had risen from the table and glaring right into his eyes, jumped at him, and started shooting around his feet.

Shagnasty Joe never was seen in those parts again. The funeral collection furnished funds for one of the wettest celebrations ever held in Pickhandle Gulch. At least that's the tale written.

The V. & T. on Trestle at Virginia City
—Courtesy Nevada State Historical Society.

Crystal Bar, Virginia City
—Courtesy of E. W. Darrah.

PART THREE

Ho! To the Humboldt!

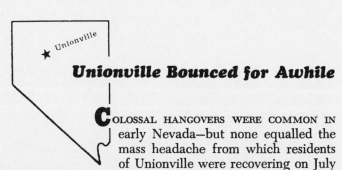

Unionville Bounced for Awhile

COLOSSAL HANGOVERS WERE COMMON IN early Nevada—but none equalled the mass headache from which residents of Unionville were recovering on July 6, 1863. The two "big" towns of the Humboldt range, Unionville and Star City, had combined in a patriotic whingding that enlivened the pages of history as the real classic of all western mining community Independence holiday celebrations. Those happy, hilarious, hopeful days are long gone—it is doubtful if there is a single holiday headache along the Humboldt range today—there aren't enough folk left to stage a very large celebration.

The current permanent population of Unionville—one of Nevada's original nine territorial county seats—is about 10! There is hardly anybody left in the rest of the once busy cluster of towns of which it was the hub. The Leonards and Ernsts still keep the home fires burning in the century-old family homesteads in pretty Buena Vista Canyon. Martha Leonard's parents and grandfather were among the first to follow the cry of "Ho! The Humboldt" when silver discoveries brought the first big rush in the summer of 1861.

Mrs. Leonard's mother went back to Illinois so her daughter could be born in "civilization" and brought the baby back across the plains to Buena Vista Canyon in 1869 when she was six months old. She has lived there since—gay, spry and happy at 90 in 1958.

Mrs. Clarence Ernst undoubtedly is the oldest living "native" of Unionville—she has lived there nearly 70 years. Her grandparents also were in the first rush of citizens who made Unionville the most important town in the whole northern section of the vast Nevada area during the 'Sixties.

And maybe it was a lucky stroke of fate that I met Neil Talcott of Lovelock when my ghost-town chasing pal, "Shorty" Darrah and I drove to deserted Star City during June of 1958. With his family he was camped along Star Creek and came over to see what we were doing shooting pictures of the ruins of the once-largest town in the Humboldts.

"My grandmother, Nellie Frenderson, lived here in the early days," remarked the pleasant blue-eyed fellow. "Our family has been around from the start—I was the last child born in Unionville, thirty years ago this week, on June 26, 1928."

The Talcott home is located just above the Leonard place in Buena Vista Canyon.

It isn't hard to understand why those who stay there love Unionville —undoubtedly it is one of the most delightful of all Nevada's playgrounds of the ghosts of the Golconda days. That is, in summer. Winters are rough.

Readers of Mark Twain's *Roughing It* find a vivid description of Unionville's first winter weather. The famed author made his initial mining effort in the canyon in 1861. Three years later it was recorded that there were all of 75 consecutive days without frost. The next twelve months were balmier; there were 87 frostless days and nights.

Yet the weather did not hinder the mining community's agricultural pursuits. In fact, home gardening threatened to upset the principal mining interest. Such was the indictment made by editor W. J. Forbes of the *Humboldt Register*.

"The warm weather takes down the volume of water in Buena Vista Creek alarmingly," he wrote in 1864. "To add to the trouble arising from this cause, men who have gardens along the banks of the creek make such trouble by surreptitiously turning the water from its course to irrigate their potatoes and cabbage. In this way the mill is frequently stopped when ore is in the batteries for crushing. [J. C.] Fall has gone below to ship an engine out; but if these gardeners have their way he could not depend upon a sufficiency of water to make the steam for an engine if he had it here. The mill has done more than any other one thing in demonstrating the richness of the Humboldt mines. It is needed —it is an absolute necessity to the county. The little potato patches are not. We like potatoes; but we can't get along without the mill. A man may do without a shirt . . . if he has plenty of whiskey. We can do without potatoes; but the mill must go on. This county was never intended by God Almighty to distinguish itself in potato growing. People who undertake to kill off, or who disregard our one vital interest, for a few paltry vegetables, will find they are kicking against the pricks. The mill must go on. An arrangement might be made under which these cabbage-headers could use the water for an hour or two after sundown, which is the only time of day water ought to be turned upon a garden."

In those uninhibited days, Editor Forbes got some replies—as might be expected from men who were accustomed to paying exhorbitant prices for vegetables in other out-of-the-way, less-fortunate mining camps. Forbes gave them little shrift. The following week he noted a letter from a correspondent, "too late for publication," upon which he commented, "Says he has been a farmer and gardener all his life and would not think of irrigating at the time we recommend. The letter is corroborative testimony of the correctness of our plan; for the writer of it is now about 60 years old, and after farming and gardening so long in his style, is today as poor as Job's turkey—owning nothing but loose wild-cat. He'd better chop."

Appropriately, the discoverers of Unionville, sick of the sagebrush-dotted alkali flats and bare hills of northern Nevada, named their find "Buena Vista," or "Good View." The date was May 12, 1861.

The overcrowded Comstock sent many intrepid wealth seekers across the arid wastes of the high basin country in search of other mineral sources. Several retraced their steps along the Humboldt trail, over which the immigrant trains still were plodding westward.

Some 150 miles to the northeast, at the northern end of the Humboldt range dominated by 9835-foot Star Peak, prospectors discovered quartz veins running parallel to a limestone reef and settled in Humboldt Canyon. Two of this group were Capt. Hugo Pfersdorff and J. C. Hannan. They became interested in some rock similar to Comstock ore brought in by a couple of friendly Paiute Indians, who offered to lead them to the site.

The setting sun was gilding the land below when the party reached the top of the ridge and looked down into the lush canyon twisting its way to a large valley lying to the east—surely a "Buena Vista." The prospectors were gratified to find abundant indications of mineral. The word spread on the wings of the wind, and soon the cry was heard across the nation "Ho! To the Humboldt!"

By July 4 of that year there were enough settlers to hold a celebration, erect a liberty pole and plat a township in the upper end of the canyon. Among the early arrivals were men who later played big parts in the building of Nevada, J. C. Fall, A. P. K. Stafford, A. W. Nightingill, W. A. Holcomb, A. W. Oliver, William H. Claggett and Sam Clemens, the immortal Mark Twain, and many others, all anxious to share in the fortunes said to be ready for the taking. The Buena Vista mining district was organized within a week after the discovery, with S. M. Carter as chairman and W. Cummings as secretary.

The *Territorial Enterprise* added impetus to the rush in an editorial effusion by its mining reporter which has become an historical classic—"I shall express an honest opinion based on a thorough examination. Humboldt county is the *richest mineral region upon God's footstool!* Each mountain range is gorged with precious ore! The other day an assay of mere outcroppings yielded $4000 to the ton! A week or two ago, an assay of just such surface development made a return of $7000 to the ton! Each day, and almost every hour, reveals new and startling evidence of the profuse and intensified wealth . . . Have no fears of the mineral resources of Humboldt county. They are incalculable."

With such press agentry it is no wonder that hopeful seekers of riches plodded out across the desert over the rutted trail to the new bonanza. And neither does one wonder that a real town grew up all along the Buena Vista Canyon, the main street becoming lined with stores, bars, billiard parlors, hotels and sundry other establishments.

Unionville was unique among Nevada's early settlements. It was the Orphan Annie of the first nine county seats. A bare six months old when the initial Territorial Assembly met at Carson City, Unionville didn't even have a representative in this legislature. When the politicians had finished dividing the more populous area along the eastern slope of the Sierra into eight counties and handing out the county seat plums "within a day's ride of each other," all of the vast northeastern territory running to the Oregon, Idaho and Utah lines was left over.

Nevada's population was concentrated in four groups during the early 1860s. First in size, of course, was the Carson-Comstock region. Aurora, and the Esmeralda district, a rough 100 miles southeast, were the most populous. Undoubtedly the most important of all outlying mining centers, was Austin, 175 miles eastward, on the well-traveled Pony Express and Overland Stage trail. Finally, there was Unionville, hidden on the east flank of the Humboldt Mountains, isolated except for the cluster of other little towns which sprung up around it after mineral was discovered.

Governor Nye's census in August placed 469 persons in the tenth district—which included all of the isolated northeastern section of the territory—and most of these were in the Unionville area. The legislature voted Unionville the county seat without argument. The county, comprising the vast northwest area, was named Humboldt, rounding out an international hodgepodge of nomenclature. The patriotic American title of Uniontown was given to the village in the Spanish-connoting Buena Vista Canyon on the east side of the Humboldt Mountains named after a German scientist.

The name Unionville had been picked in a close vote of its citizens. Civil War fever had divided the people, the Union adherents settling in the original Upper Town, while the Confederates gathered at the mouth of the canyon in a new townsite, called Lower Town or "Dixie." Finally, in the American Way, after numerous arguments and meetings, all agreed to abide by the decision of the majority.

In such an isolated spot the early residents had to find their own pleasures. They had no connection with the outer world except the stages, which ran spasmodically, and sometimes forgot to come at all. So when W. J. Forbes, already well known among the great journalists in the western camps, arrived in the spring of 1863 to establish the *Humboldt Register* the residents considered it a notable event. The consequent celebration ranks as one of Unionville's outstanding social classics.

Forbes announced his first paper would come off the press on the evening of May 3, 1863. Led by the Unionville Cornet Band, the rifle brigade lined up in three ranks before the office and fired a salute of nine blasts. A donated case of champagne from the Magnolia Saloon in Carson City added fizz to the celebration—this being augmented by more potent liquids as the affair continued far through the night, enlivened by 34 anvil salutes. Forbes and his *Register* reciprocated by tooting the big two-day Independence Week celebration a month later.

Those early pioneers didn't do things half way, and this outstanding event of Unionville history was one Forbes, a staunch Union man, said "would be remembered." It was. Tickets for the Grand Military and Civic Ball sold for $8. It kicked off the event, being held at Unionville on the evening of July 3 and continuing throughout the night, lubricated by adequate supplies of liquid refreshment.

The following day, with hardly anybody bothering to get any sleep, Unionville moved en masse nine miles north to booming Star City. There the celebration roared forward with parades, orations, anvil salutes, and much gun shooting in the air. Rousing martial tunes were played continuously by the Cornet Band (except during frequent refreshment breaks), and the night was climaxed by another, possibly even damper, all-night ball.

Everybody was still celebrating when the sun climbed over the east Humboldts and across Buena Vista Valley on the morning of July 5. Unionville's contingent straggled back home and to bed after a few more for "Honest Abe," "the Union" and "the Humboldt."

Despite its momentary effervescence Unionville was a rather quiet mining town. By 1864 it had only nine saloons. Among them were the Oneida Exchange at the corner of Main and Congress Streets. Reavis & Usher's New Saloon, nearly opposite the courthouse, advertised in the *Humboldt Register:* "What will You Drink? . . . tell us. Largest saloon in the county. Best wines and liquors—most of them. Talented barkeeps."

Probably one of the most enticing advertisements of the era appeared later in the year for this same bistro when it was bought by W. F. Sommercamp. His claim in the *Register* was headed, What? Ah, What?"

"What is so enlivening when a man is arousing from the lethean embrace of balmy sleep, and girding himself for fresh exertions and new successes—what so cheering, then, what so wakens the appetite and the mind's faculties, as a delicious cocktail?

"What so invigorating, when the burthen of the day is heavy on you, and the weary spirit grows faint, as 'something straight' to stiffen up with?

"What so appropriate in which to pledge the health of your new-found German cousin, as a mug of foaming beer?

"What so grateful when dinner's over, and we wish to lounge away a half-hour, as the fleecy clouds of odorous smoke, curling up from two ends of a prime Havana?

"What so soothing, when the labors of the day are ended, and you are about betaking yourself to your virtuous sheets, as a generous draught of something hot? And what so agreeable and natural after the draught as another?"

Sommercamp also noted that he proposed "ministering to the appetite of whosoever thirsteth and hath cash."

One of the largest structures in town was the brewery. It always was one of the first business enterprises in any mining town worth its salt in those days—the price of beer would have been too prohibitive if

Nevada's Oldest School, Unionville

—*Courtesy of E. W. Darrah.*

hauled by wagon for a couple of hundred miles across mountains and desert. It was much more economical to transport the ingredients.

Forbes commented at the time, "The brewery has removed to the new store building up the road. There is no lead pipe, yet, connecting it with this office." A little later in the year Forbes noted that business had been so good that a second story had been added to the building. At this period there were ten stores, six hotels, two express offices, two drug stores, four livery stables, a watchmaker's shop and numerous other commercial establishments, including the "Sutterly Brothers" who advertised, "Have just arrived at this place for the purpose of taking pictures in all the latest styles of the art."

The M. Clayburgh & Co. and Ewing & Washburn seemed to be the leading department stores—in both Unionville and Dun Glen. The former advertised "clothing, dry goods, boots & shoes, groceries, liquors, cigars, etc., etc." and claimed "the largest and best assorted stock of goods in Humboldt county." The other firm extended its advertised list a bit further, to include, "California blankets, coal oil and coal oil lamps, California meats, cheese and butter, mining tools, powder, fuse—And a large stock of California flour and grain, all of which we will sell cheap for CASH at our new fireproof store, Second and Main Streets."

The two leading hotels, at least as far as the *Register's* ads reveal, were the Exchange and the Pioneer. The former was in Lower Unionville and proclaimed that it offered "Excellent rooms, suited for single lodgers or families. The table always will be supplied with such substantials and delicacies as can be found in the market, artistically and genteelly served . . ." The Pioneer was in Upper Unionville and the owner promised to "render those comfortable who may favor him with their patronage" and also assured that "The table will always be supplied with every delicacy the market affords."

Masthead of the "Humbolt Register," Unionville

—*Courtesy Nevada State Historical Society.*

Actually one can get a fair picture of community life by reading through the age-browned pages of the *Humboldt Register*. Forbes was a brilliant reporter whose hand-set little items seemed to cover the entire scene. Here are some plucked at random:

"Freight teams over the Honey Lake route begin to file in bringing lumber, 'shakes,' potatoes and bacon."

"Shipped by Wells, Fargo & Co., Monday's stage, 290 ounces bullion . . . from the Gem."

"Express to Boise—Cutler, of Star City, is putting stock on the route to run express between the Humboldt towns and Jordan Creek and Boise mines. Cutler has his eyes about him. This is the shortest route for all California and the Territory; and has an abundance of grass and water almost the entire distance."

"On Way to Boise—Hundreds of people, with all sorts of rigs, are continually passing up the river to Jordan Creek and Boise . . . There will be a great recoil in this flood of emigration. Disappointments await the bulk of this tide of fortune seekers. In about three months, they will be thronging back."

"Suicide—Ah Sing, A China-woman, tired of life, rashly importunate, and so forth, bought a dose of some useful drug, Wednesday, and gobbled it down; and made no sign, but died . . ."

"That Leap Year Dance, given at the schoolhouse, Monday evening, by the ladies, is described as the greatest treat of the season; and the masculines are willing to be trotted out again, any time it may suit the convenience of their fair patrons."

"The State of Nevada—Again—In this issue we give the Governor's proclamation, calling an election for another constitutional convention . . . Congress seems disposed to press this thing. Let it. We can vote it down again . . . we'll never tire of rejecting the offer—till the good time shall have come when we can know that the property and the business in the territory are sufficient to respectably support a State government."

(Forbes opposed statehood, and Humboldt County followed his lead Yes 320, No 544, being the only one in the territory to vote against the proposition the following September. The Union ticket swept to victory in Humboldt County, 944 votes being cast.)

"HURRAH FOR THE TELEGRAPH—Next week [Sept. 1864] the telegraph wires will reach Unionville. Though surrounded by deserts, we will no longer be an isolated community. The electric fluid, leaping across the deserts on this iron hoofed steed, will unite us to the rest of the world; we will share the strife in business, and the contest of politics and arms with the more favored communities."

"The telegraph to Virginia is again in working order [Dec. 1864] but eastwardly the line has been greatly injured by the storm, and the Virginia papers keep outrunners along the roads, to gather items of news from the teamsters."

"Sommercamp is preparing for a long summer and a thirsty public. The recent cold nights have found his vats at the ice house . . . full of clear ice, which Sommercamp stores away for next summer's cobblers and smashes."

Far from the mad maelstrom of the Comstock, Unionville never was a very naughty town. There are only three violent crimes in the Buena Vista county seat recorded in the long list of several hundred Nevada slayings noted by the Thompson & West *History*.

The first listed killing occurred on Christmas, 1862, when one R. T. "Butcher Bob" Ferris shot and killed M. Brown during an argument in Unionville's Pioneer Hotel. Butcher Bob was put under bond of $2500, but according to history "was never tried," which seemed to be the common conclusion of most personal killings in those days.

George Ward was shot and killed on August 22, 1863, by a Mexican named "Jose" over a gambling argument. Nothing was done about the slaying, apparently the victim had been considered in the wrong.

The third slaying listed in Thompson and West occurred in October, 1863, when "Richard Snowden was fatally stabbed . . . by a teamster. He was somewhat noted as a politician and had formerly lived at Auburn, Calif."

Human life wasn't regarded as the most important asset of those days—Forbes, the voice of the peaceful Humboldt area, urged that the first state legislature pass a bill specifying that "death shall never in this state be inflicted as a legal penalty for crime."

The most amusing shooting in Unionville might be dubbed in today's press "The Eloping Wife Case." Initial chapter of the tale appeared in the *Register*, July 2, 1864.

"The first elopement in the Humboldt, we believe," Forbes wrote, "was made from Dun Glen last Tuesday night. Before daylight of Wednesday Chamberlain, who had been keeping a wife and hotel at that place, was over here on the swift wings of outraged innocence, looking for his truant wife and some son-of-a-gun who had helped her to outrage this poor man's feelings and so forth. He found her not!"

The climax appeared in the *Register* two weeks later. Here is the way Forbes printed it:

"A single shot was fired Tuesday morning into the wall of the bar room of the Exchange Hotel. No damage done. We had an item two weeks ago about the elopement of Mrs. Chamberlain of Dun Glen. That's it. She arrived in the hotel last week, and her former husband came soon after . . . Chamberlain tried to induce the woman to return with him to Dun Glen. She wouldn't. He suspected Bob Campbell of having got off some of his pretty talk to her, and heard of an arrangement for Campbell and the madam to start for Red Bluff. Chamberlain was excited. He got his pistol set and watched for Bob. Bob was at the wash stand, his head bowed washing. Chamberlain drew and fired a single solid shot over Bob's bow, and hit the side of the bar room . . . showing by what a slender thread hangs our eternal doom. Bob grappled with him and a fierce tussle ensued, each grappling at the scattered munitions of war. Bob got C. down and had him much as Kale Davis had the hen. Jim Vance interfered and the row was stopped. The woman, with her children rode off in a wagon to the river. No meeting between the belligerents since."

Forbes brushed off a shooting, in which one fellow was plunked twice, in one paragraph . . . "A shooting affray took place . . . Sunday, between Slavan and Williams. Two shots exchanged. Both balls fired from Williams' pistol were caught in Slavan's arm, which he held as a ward in front of his breast. No woman in this case. It grew out of a dog fight."

The Buena Vista district gave ample sign of slipping as early as Sept. 10, 1864—even before Nevada was a state. Forbes, always optimistic, hinted in that day's paper that everything in the Humboldts was not exactly rosy.

He wrote, "Humboldt is Not Dead, But Sleepeth—Already the gay streaks of morning are shooting up into the dark night that has enveloped us for the last year. Our morning of prosperity is at hand! Watch it a little longer. It will be seen elsewhere in this number that Wells Fargo and Co.'s Express shipped yesterday morning, over $11,000 worth of bullion from this county. This is the largest amount ever shipped at one time from Humboldt . . . Capital and enterprise is all that we want to make this one of the richest mineral producing countries in the world. . . . Glory Hallelujah! Humboldt is marching on. Don't go yet boys—the good, looked and hoped for, is coming . . ."

But this was whistling in the dark—the *Register* was showing signs of the pinch, too. Its columns were filled with mining company assessment notices and patent medicine advertising. These latter ballyhoos were masterpieces of fraudulent advertising, which filled entire columns, claiming to cure everything—including "weaknesses arising from excesses, habits of dissipation, early indiscretion or abuse"—"insanity and consumption"—"Females, Females, Females, Old or Young, Single, Married, or contemplating marriage"—"Secret diseases"—"Schirrus, Cancer, Tumors, enlargement, ulceration, Caries, dispepsia, heart disease, fits, epilepsy, melancholy, neuralgia, rheumatism, gout" and almost everything under the sun.

Unionville might have prospered if the Central Pacific had constructed its main line up the east side of the Humboldt as the residents expected it to do. But when the tracks were laid along the river up the west side of the range the town was doomed.

Forbes may have foreseen this—or maybe he was sharp enough to see that Unionville's budding promise had withered. He sold the *Register* on Feb. 2, 1867, to G. G. Berry, H. C. Street and M. S. Bonnifield. The paper foundered and suspended May 29, 1869. Unionville's shining editorial sun had set. The paper's equipment was taken to the new railroad town of Elko, where it was used by E. D. Kelly to print the first issues of that town's famed, and still running, *Independent*.

J. C. Fall, operator of the canyon's only good mine, the Arizona, closed his general store in 1880. It was the last of the business establishments which had catered to rugged early citizens by the thousands. He said they had spent nearly $3,000,000 in Unionville—all from the Arizona.

A few hung on, always expecting the Buena Vista mines to open up and spill forth their long promised bonanza. They never did. The Leonard and Ernst families were the only citizens remaining when Uncle Sam administered the fatal final blow by closing the post office.

Today the Leonards and the Ernsts are the remnant rulers of Buena Vista, where the old schoolhouse, the crumbling walls of the brewery, and a few homes, are all that remain of the once-glorious original county seat of Humboldt.

New Arrivals, Goldfield
—*George Storks Photo, courtesy Las Vegas Review-Journal.*

Ore Packing by Burro Back, Early Nevada

—*Las Vegas Review-Journal Photo.*

Freight Team, Early Nevada

—*Courtesy of E. W. Darrah.*

★ Star City

Star City Gleamed

LONG-GONE STAR CITY IS THE UNKNOWN mining satellite of the early Nevada days. It glittered for less than a decade far out in the Humboldt galaxy, but was hardly noticed behind the glare of the Comstock, Esmeralda and Reese River fireworks. Outside of occasional passing mentions, it has been almost completely ignored by historians and is practically unknown today by Nevadans, although during its brightest period it was as large or larger than its romantic county-seat neighbor, Unionville, ten miles south. One can't help but wonder why a mining town which attracted such notables of later years as George Hearst and James G. Fair, among many others, could be overlooked. Search through all the State's histories and you'll find scarcely a mention of the place. It's time to do something about this century-long omission.

Star Peak, an unusual and rugged 9835-foot rocky formation dominates the Humboldt range. It is assumed that it was named because it consists of five precipitous escarpments which sprawl across the top of the range roughly in the shape of a star. Straight down from it on the east side of the range in a steep, sharp canyon, was Star City, a bustling town during the early 1860s. It was discovered and settled shortly after Unionville, probably in the autumn of 1860. By 1864 it was at its peak—and by 1869 it was practically dead—and has been that way ever since.

The 1881 Thompson and West *History* is about the only place you'll find Star City mentioned. Since this invaluable pioneer history was compiled during the decade after the Humboldt town flourished, it might be expected to contain a rather complete story. It doesn't. This is all that it has to say about it:

"Star City was the principal town of the Star district . . . it has an altitude of 3700 feet, and is situated in a deep canyon, with Star Peak, a lofty mountain which is landmark for all the region south of the Humboldt, only two miles distant. In 1864-65 it had a population of 1200, which began leaving during the panic of the following years, until now [1881], but four persons keep guard over the place. It has a Crane concentrating mill capable of reducing 40 tons of ore in 24 hours. The value of all the taxable property in the place is estimated at $10,000. In consequence of the almost utter desertion of the place it has been next to impossible to gather anything of its early history . . . That 1200 active men should ever have assembled at any point and remained there three or four years without making materials for an interesting history would be absurd, impossible. The abandoned shafts and tunnels, the half-ruined chimneys, and the hundreds of trails ramifying in every direction through the canyon, are all that remain to speak of the busy 1200 who once hoped to achieve fortunes which should have made them respected and happy."

One of the best ways to visualize an old-time town is to read the ads of its merchants, their addresses furnish an index to the size of the community and their offerings provide a record of what their customers demanded. Let's look at some of the Star City ads.

Among its citizens, Isaac Miller was a civic pillar. He ran the Miller Hotel on "Main Street. Above the Plaza"—nearly everything in Star City appeared to circulate around the Plaza.

He claimed in his advertisement, "This fine, new Hotel, just completed, and furnished regardless of expense, claims merit as second to none this side of San Francisco." That was taking in considerable area, even for those days, because among other places "this side" of the Bay city were Sacramento, Virginia City and Carson City—not to mention Unionville with its two hotels.

In addition to setting a table "furnished at all times with the best the market affords," and maintaining "a supply of the finest liquors and choicest brands of cigars," Isaac also was an optimist. His ad asserted that "The proprietor, an old stand-by of the country, has erected this hotel, not so much for Star as it is, which would not justify the outlay, as for the city it soon is to be; and he respectfully informs the public, and all whom it may concern that MILLER'S HOTEL is, and is going to be THE hotel of the place ALL THE TIME."

He also advised that there were "excellent stabling accommodations immediately adjoining." The Sonoma Livery and Feed Stable advertised that it was "next door to the best hotel in town" and also that it "runs the stage line to Dun Glen, starting from the hotel next door."

It was this same Isaac Miller who was the leading man in a most delightfully graphic newspaper society item:

"Isaac Miller, proprietor of the Miller Hotel, was married Sunday evening last, by the Rev. James Lassiter, a large and respectable audience witnessing the ceremony. Miller has been so infernally happy ever since that he neglected to inform us of the former name of the unfortunate [that's what it says] Mrs. M. There was much congratulating, and kissing, and other nonsense, and we doubt if poor Isaac didn't forget his own maiden name—things were so mixed."

The mystery of the bride's name was cleared up the following week with the publication of the official wedding notice—it was Miss Ann Robrickt of Windsor, California.

It's possible that the ubiquitous W. J. Forbes, publisher of the paper, attended the wedding because there are quite a few Star items in the June 4 issue. He comments in his locals that "The Bank Exchange, Star, is the most handsomely arranged and furnished brandy-and-watering place in the country."

That's high praise, indeed, since Forbes seemed to be a connoisseur of such establishments. The Bank Exchange was operated by Alexander Wise, whose advertisement displays a highly-developed and sly sense of humor, whether written by him or Forbes, it furnishes an amusing picture of one phase of early life.

"If you are athirst give us a call—our liquors are the best to be got in San Francisco, and in full variety; gay bar-keeps, too—talented fellows with high foreheads!

"Or if you don't drink, perhaps you smoke—some do. A prime Havana is a great luxury—when a man's tired; or just been to dinner; so soothing, when it's been bought with the last quarter, and a fellow's busted. Come and Try One.

"Marble-Bed Billiard Tables—Two of Phelan's famous combination cushioned tables. Billiards is allowed to be one of the most refined games to be found. Employs the mind, while the interest on your loaned money keeps counting up. Exercises your legs, by sending you around the table to get your ball out of the pocket. Gives you grace to the body, by introducing that elegant posture, one leg in the air, hat for a bridge, and cue harpoon style. Exercises the lungs, by the large amount of whistling after bad shots.

"Come and see us, anyhow. If you don't want to buy, sit down in the shade and chew your tobacco, just as if it was paid for. Somebody might treat."

In the August 6, 1864, issue of the *Register,* Forbes announced that "George A. Vanvolkenburg has leased the Bank Exchange at Star City and is running it in the same attractive style as formerly . . ."

Wise wasn't gone though. In the same issue he was back with a new ad for the "Telegraph Saloon, Star City, N. T.," in which he used the following poetic quotation at the top—

"Man being reasonable, must get drunk:
The goal of life is but intoxication;
Glory, the grape, love, gold—in these are sunk
The hopes of all men and of every nation."

The ad continued in typical Wise prose which would shock today's Madison Avenue advertising hucksters, proclaiming, "Alex Wise hereby gives notice to whom these presents may come, that he has taken the above named establishment of Foster and Otherwise, and put it in a state of fix to meet the views of his fastidious customers.

"It isn't every man who knows how to keep a saloon; and therefore the undersigned, having discovered what's the matter with him, has determined to resist all overtures of an infatuated and too generous public, and accept no office. All statements to the contrary may be put down as malicious electioneering lies, put in circulation by my particular friends.

"Two bits a single chance; three dollars to insure." [That line baffles; does it mean 25 cents a drink and an assured souse for three bucks?]

Star City wasn't all saloons and hotels—there had to be other businesses. Here are some more of the classic examples of advertising, circa 1864:

McDonald & Thorne's New Drug Store emphasized the "newness" of the place by repetition . . .

"At the New Drug Store will be found a large assortment of fresh Drugs, Medicines and Chemicals.

"At the New Drug Store will be found a large stock of Patent Medicines, Pills and Sarsaparillas . . .

"At the New Drug Store will be found a large stock of Brushes, Paints, Oils, Varnish and Window Glass.

The New Drug Store's competitor, L. R. Stover, wasn't the blatant type. His conservative ad merely announced, "Dealer in Drugs and Medicines, and everything pertaining to the drug trade.—Prescriptions accurately prepared, from pure chemicals, at all hours of the day and night."

Question: who wrote these prescriptions?—In the entire file of *Humboldt Registers* there is only one doctor mentioned, Dr. C. W. Shaug, who resided in Humboldt City, far around the northwest side of the range.

Doctors advertised in those days, and Dr. Shaug proclaimed that he "Keeps a private medical office in Humboldt City, N. T., for the treatment of diseases—especially those of women and children. Can cure barrenness, or mitigate the reverse; also diseases of the eye, and every form of secret disease. Dr. Shaug will engage to perform all surgical operations, in a speedy, neat and successful manner, for reasonable charges. Consultation hours at 7 o'clock a.m. and 6 p.m. each day except when absent on professional duty."

There were three general stores in Star City in '64:

"Levy and Co., Fire-Proof Building, on Plaza, Star City, N. T." offered customers "Groceries, Provisions, Wines, Liquors, Clothing and Dry Goods, Tin and Hardware, Saddlery, Crockery and a general assortment of goods suitable to this market."

And, "A. Martin, West Side of Plaza (Below Miller Hotel)" offered the same stock and "in consideration of the dull times," declared he would "dispose of portions of this excellent stock for cash."

Luff and McColley, also on the "'West Side of the Plaza," had a similar stock but specialized in miners' needs, advertising "The Largest and Best Selected Stock of Goods ever offered in this market."

Then, there was the "Star Furniture Store!—H. T. Maclean—Next door to Trinity Hotel [Ah, Miller had competition, you see] has a good assortment of household and office furniture, which is offered at low prices FOR CASH.—Barroom, Office, Parlor and Kitchen Chairs, Rocking Chairs, Bedsteads, Crockery, Washstands, Glassware, etc.—Furniture Made and Repaired—Matrasses [sic] Made To Order."

Star City provided a stepping stone for one of the greatest fortunes ever wrested from the mines of this state. James G. Fair made his debut on the Nevada scene via the Sheba Gold and Silver Mining Co., which was the major operator of the Star district. The ubiquitous George Hearst, who was there, too, seemed to stay out of the maelstrom of the Comstock to pick up the rich prizes on the outskirts. Eldorado, in Clark County, Cortez, some of the Toiyabe mines and the Sheba, of which he was president, all contributed to the gilded foundation of the Hearst fortune.

Fair, a young Irishman in his early thirties, was sent to Star City from California in 1863 to build the Sheba's 40-ton a day mill. It was 1865 before he moved to Virginia City where he became a Croesus of the Comstock and later United States senator.

A story about an ore mill could be very dull reading—but since the Sheba mill was Jim Fair's initial effort in Nevada and made Star City a real booming town, here's one that isn't. Remember, Star was located in an obscure mountain canyon 250 miles across a hot, dry desert from its nearest shipping point, and Fair's accomplishment indicates one of the reasons why he became the engineering and mining genius of the Comstock Big Four.

On April 23, 1864, there was a small note in the *Humboldt Register* saying that "Fifty tons of machinery for the Sheba mill are at Red Bluff awaiting teams. A contract has been made for the required lumber." Then on May 21 the information appears that "The Sheba mill has been forwarded from Red Bluff at 11 cents a pound—50 tons. Mr. Fair has selected the site for the erection of the mill, at the lower end of Star Canyon, and the work of erecting the building has commenced."

The engines and machinery were on the ground by June 25 and Forbes commented a week later that "Mr. Fair is putting this establishment in shape much more rapidly than we thought." It was a 40-horsepower steam mill "with two staunch iron batteries of five stamps each, six Wheeler pans and two settlers." The editor also noted that Fair had contracted "for a large amount of wood, which is brought from the East Range, for $10 a cord."

Disclosing that he was a pretty bright young engineer, the paper reported on August 6 that "Fair . . . made the discovery that the adobes in common use for building material . . . are excellent fire brick . . . Heat has no effect on them, except to harden them. He has made use of thousands in constructing the roasting furnaces at the mill . . . by this discovery he saved a good many dollars to the company and got better bricks than those of English manufacture so largely imported."

Then on August 20 the *Register* noted that "Rock is being hauled to the mill, which is now at work crushing . . . The furnaces are completed . . . The president of the company [Hearst] is here . . ."

Previously the Sheba had published an ad, signed by Hearst, similar to those of many other mining companies in the Humboldt, listing shares upon which assessments had not been paid and noting they would be sold at auction. After Fair commenced building the mill, the Sheba didn't have any more such ads, indicating it was in good financial shape and stock owners were paying their assessments.

Forbes reported August 27—two months after arrival of equipment—that "The Sheba mill commenced full operations with stamps and pans all going and roasting furnaces fired . . ."

Fair's modern mill was the subject of a full column description by Forbes a week later—"the engines consume nearly four cords of wood daily . . . if anyone wants to build a mill . . . it costs about $40,000 . . . It is found, by assaying the tailings, that this mill works ore closer than they pretend to anywhere else in the territory . . . the tailings assay but $11 the ton . . ."

The Sheba ores were considered the most complicated in the area, being a hard, black laminated slate which required roasting before reduction. Proof that Fair had done a good job with his mill is recorded in the Sept. 19, 1864, *Register* when Forbes reported the success of the first mill run . . .

> "SHEBA BULLION—Over $10,000 worth of bullion was shipped yesterday, being the result of a five days' run of the Sheba mill, with three pans. In consequence of the non-arrival of the quicksilver ordered, the mill has only been running with half its capacity. The above result, which for Sheba rock—considered the most intractable of the Humboldt ores—is a pretty fair criterion of what this county will prove on development. The past week's run, under many disadvantages, has proved that the Sheba rock can be worked to within seven percent of the fire assay, while 20 is considered good work in Virginia . . . Mr. Fair, under whose direction the mill was erected, and Mr. McDonald, the superintendent, are entitled to great praise for the very able manner in which the various departments of the work have been managed, and the citizens of Humboldt county owe them much for proving, in so short a time, that the great bugbear of the impossibility of reducing the Humboldt ores existed only in the imagination or wishes of those antagonistic to our interests.

"As soon as the mill can be run to its full capacity they can ship weekly from the product of their own mine $25,000, which will compare favorably with any of the best mills in the Territory."

This indicates that Star City shined brightly in the earlier days of Nevada—until the veins played out. The Sheba was just one of the many mines in Star Canyon. Probably the next heaviest producer was the De Soto, with other rich mines including the Mammoth Lodes, the Mauch Chunk, Maston, the Almira and Yankee Claims and numerous others.

No story of Star City can overlook "The Ganders." This seemed to be the exclusive social club of the community, composed as you might guess from the name, of lively—maybe lonesome—bachelors.

The Ganders seemed to hold their meetings after midnight, with plenty of food, frivolity and liquid refreshments. Hardly an issue of the *Register* appeared that didn't carry some item about them, veiled in mystery generally. For instance, this one on April 30, 1864 . . . "A committee is out collecting oyster cans from which to get material for the manufacture of a medal . . ."

A little later "Capt. Prescott [later sheriff] was arraigned for unganderly conduct" and "banished from Star City for a period of one week." Maybe he took out a girl. Report of initiation of a new member reveals the group's motto . . . "The badge of the order, containing their motto ('Be Happy') was placed in his possession, and a basket of champagne was then broached: after which the grand procession was formed and at 1:20 moved through the principal streets, with appropriate music."

Star, being nearer the main trail from Chico and Red Bluff, became the traffic center of the area instead of Unionville. Freights and passengers from the California road, unless they came via Virginia City, reached Star first. Consequently it became the jumping off place for the mining strikes on Jordan Creek and around Boise that led to the later establishment of that area as a new territory, and a state.

The first item regarding this "rush" appeared in the *Register* on April 30, 1864. It noted that "Hundreds of people, with all sorts of rigs, are continually passing up the river to Jordan Creek and Boise . . . they are coming in a constant stream." It was reported that "This is the shortest route, with the easiest grade . . . plenty of grass, water, and wood along the route." (This was the forerunner of U. S. 95 north from the Humboldt through McDermitt and across Idaho to the Canadian border.) Editor Forbes commented "There will be a great recoil in this flood of emigration . . . disappointments await the bulk of this tide of fortune hunters."

Such a horde of travelers was too much of a temptation to the Bannock Indians of northern Humboldt County, and they attacked and killed a party of Idaho prospectors. A group of volunteers immediately organized in Humboldt County and rode forth "to avenge this atrocity and chastise the Indians."

There were sixteen Star citizens, including Captain Prescott who was elected leader, and future Senator Hutchins who rode out with this volunteer force to chase the Indians. The other towns of the area, Unionville, Dun Glen, Humboldt, and Paradise Valley all contributed to this "Indian Army."

The avengers rode off, and a couple of weeks later were back. Two of the men had been injured—by the accidental discharge of one of their own guns, and one man was killed in a brush with the Bannocks. They had "sacked and burned the rancheries of the Indians from which they fled precipitately on our approach. We found many trifling articles belonging to Dodge and the men murdered with him . . . sufficient to convince us . . . of the participancy of these Indians in the outrage. Several pounds of ammunition, some deer-hides and the usual amount of Indian trinkets were likewise part of our booty. A squaw and papoose were captured . . . but afterwards released."

When the "army" returned to Star, the scribe reported, "We were made 'happy,' for we became the honored guests of the virtuous Ganders."

The Christmas ball of 1864 at Miller's Hotel was the biggest event since the July 4 celebration in 1863—and maybe the last big county-wide event at Star City. It was the social event of the year for the whole Humboldt region. Said Forbes on the day of the event, "The ball at Star has occasioned great hurrying and bustling among the bucks. Such as did not go submitted to requisitions upon their wardrobe by those who went. Boots found strange feet and vests showing any part white were drawn or let out, as occasion demanded 'for this trip only'." According to reports afterwards in the *Register*, it was just about the fanciest shindig yet held in the entire northeastern country.

It was a farewell of sorts to Star City. That winter terrific storms blew in and ripped down many Star homes and buildings, causing a correspondent to report, "The recent wind here also played some curious freaks. A lumber pile at the upper end of the Plaza was struck by a whirlwind and a plank 20 feet long and two inches thick carried 50 yards and thrown through the upper sash of a saloon window—striking and almost demolishing the counter . . . The oldest inhabitant says that the high winds are over for this winter."

Maybe they were—but they were the first death wail of the Star Canyon town. The *Register* began to report a continuous stream of citizens leaving for other parts, leaving a legacy of legal unpaid mine stock assessments, foreclosures and unpaid notes.

The story of overlooked Star City should include its unknown and completely ignored suburb, Santa Clara. It's not mentioned in any of the histories—not even vaguely. Its mining district is not listed in the state records. Actually, the only place it appears is on the 1876 Rand-McNally map—and by then it had been deserted for nearly a decade. Yet it was a gay, lively little town of around a couple of hundred persons during the 1860s. Its monument is a couple of square blocks of excellent rock ruins of buildings.

Outside of a business card, which appeared every issue on the front page for "C. B. Simmons. Federal Licensed Auctioneer, Office, Santa Clara, Humboldt Co., N. T." there is little mention of the town in the early issues of the *Register*. On May 17, 1864, a notice calling a "Union County Convention" to nominate delegates to the State Constitutional Convention appeared. It furnishes a figure by which Santa Clara's approximate population may be estimated—Star City was apportioned 10 delegates, Unionville 9 and Santa Clara 2. At the time Star had about 1,200 persons and Unionville around 1,000, so it appears Santa Clara had approximately 200, probably a few less.

About the time E. Lobenstein established his pony express shuttle run from Star City to Humboldt City, an ad appeared announcing that he "Would run a semi-weekly express from Star City, on arrival of the Humboldt stage from Virginia, to Humboldt City, passing through Santa Clara and Port Royal [a small settlement north of Santa Clara]. All orders, letters and parcels left at the above named places to be forwarded in his care, will meet with prompt attention." This shows that Santa Clara wasn't entirely isolated, it had twice-a-week mail.

Editor Forbes has a comment to make in his May 28, 1864 issue, saying "Santa Clara—Work still progresses in the tunnels of the 'Little Giant,' 'Magna Charta' and 'Butte' companies—workmen on day and night. Contractors have completed their work in the 'Miami' and 'Wyoming' claims, and new contracts soon will be let. The Santa Clara boys pride themselves on doing more work than an equal number of rich men in any other part of the world; and say they'll by and by have the 'stuffing' to show for it."

On June 8 the *Register* carried a curious, somewhat vague dispatch, signed simple "M," from which an idea of the mores and manners of Santa Clara may be gleaned:

"Santa Clara, June 8, 1864—This is a high old place to live in; richest town in the country, for items; too rich in fact; can't pile em up rightly. Two varieties of the genus homo vegetate here, respectively styled 'Santa Clara Roughs' and 'Amazon Maids.' Roughs invite leap year proposals from the Amazons, stating time, terms &c.; which invitations are indignantly repelled—repellants stating as cause, lack of thoroughbred blood in Santa Clara, and Amazons don't mate with scrubs; going to send to Unionville, the town where the *Register* is printed, for the right sort.

The two parties have settos . . . now and then. Amazons generally get the best of it; can talk louder, roll their sleeves higher without injury to muscle, spread themselves to better advantage, slam around more promiscuously, and in fact are more generally on the rampage anyhow.

"Amusements are varied here by the occasional introduction of the 'tinpandemonium'—a regular institution here, though unknown elsewhere. All the juveniles in town come out on an average about three times a week, armed with milk pans and sticks, and beat the devil's tattoo with infernal gusto, around any member of the Roughs who has been 'caught napping' by the Amazons.

"These afflictions, and others of a worse description that loom up in the dreamy future, have nearly mashed the Roughs out. Some of them have gone clear daft already, and others are going fast. We expect the next meeting of the honorable Board of County Commissioners will result in a large appropriation of county funds to defray the expenses of hauling some wagon loads of addle brains from this place . . .

"All these things are not sufficient to stop work here, though—for the boys are on that, too—as is daily evidenced —by the noise and powder-smoke issuing from the Butte, Little Giant, Kentucky, Miami and St. Louis tunnels. Lots of muscle daily squandered making gardens here, too; while among the institutions of the town is a fine dairy, where the prices of milk, butter, and eggs are governed by Grant's success or defeat in Virginia. If Grant wins a few battles, and Richmond falls, Madame who runs the dairy, who is heavy on the Union, will give aforementioned articles of merchandise away, while if Lee wins, Richmond prices will prevail."

Evidently one of the Roughs soon was caught napping, as this paragraph appeared in the Star City items on July 9: "An elopement took place in Santa Clara last week. Nobody hurt; and the happy couple is on its way to Paradise."

First signs that all ore wasn't rich in Santa Clara's hills was a notice of sale of stocks for delinquent payments of assessments by the Union Tunneling Company on July 16, 1864. The assessments in the long list averaged about $20, so the Union couldn't have been too high-priced a prospect. And about the same time another notice appeared that the Original Magna Charta was being reorganized and that those who hadn't paid assessments had only until July 28 to do so or have stock auctioned. Shortly the Little Giant and Kentucky had similar notices in print.

The 1864 Nevada election—the first for State officers—stirred the political pot to boiling in Humboldt County. Actually the whole county was strongly Union against a few Democrats. Santa Clara was solidly Union—not a single Democratic vote being cast there in '64 balloting, or at least not one was counted or reported, and Santa Clara had no delegates at the Democratic county convention.

The Union Party convention was held at Star City on August 13 with W. B. Simmons and J. H. Maxwell as delegates from Santa Clara. Simmons was one of four nominated as a candidate for one of the two members of the Legislature. He lost out on the second ballot, but subsequently ran for and was elected Justice of Peace at Santa Clara in the September election. S. H. Lamson was elected constable and T. V. Julien road supervisor.

It is probable Santa Clara succumbed about the same time that Star City flickered out, around 1868. Its weathered, undesecrated ruins and these meager news notes are all that it bequeathed in nostalgia for later generations.

Dance Hall Girls, Goldfield

Courtesy Las Vegas Review-Journal.

Moving a House, East Rochester, Pershing County

—Courtesy E. W. Darrah and Nevada State Historical Society.

Old Humboldt House, Pershing County

—Courtesy Nevada State Historical Society.

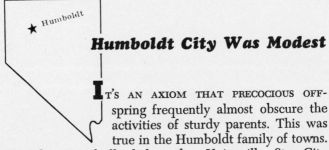

Humboldt City Was Modest

IT'S AN AXIOM THAT PRECOCIOUS OFF-spring frequently almost obscure the activities of sturdy parents. This was true in the Humboldt family of towns. Humboldt City was the sire of all of them, but Unionville, Star City and others quickly pushed it into the background, and then a second-generation upstart, Winnemucca, sprang up and took the spotlight away from them all.

Humboldt City was the place where the initial group of hopeful prospectors settled in 1860 after traipsing eastward from the Comstock. And it was out of Humboldt Canyon that Capt. Hugo Pfersdorff and J. C. Hannan climbed with their two-pack burros, guided by four Paiutes, on that May day of 1861, to discover Buena Vista canyon and inaugurate the Humboldt boom.

In a very short time Humboldt City had slipped into the background and quietly dropped into obscurity after a few years—which may be a good thing since it hasn't been completely ruined by tourist and commercial ghouls. It still has far more ruins than many of the century-old communities of the State, including two saw mills, an old Wells-Fargo office and about 30 other buildings.

The community thrived in a canyon on the northwest shoulder of the Humboldt mountains, only two gravel-road miles off present-day U. S. 40.

Our curious newspaper editor of those days, W. J. Forbes, paid Humboldt City a visit and left us a description of it in the *Register* on May 2, 1863. He described it as "A picturesque and beautiful village containing some 200 well-built houses, some of which are handsome edifices, and many beautiful gardens that attest the taste and industry of the inhabitants. A beautiful, crystal stream of water diverted from its natural course, runs, a little babbling stream, through every street."

Forbes continued the description, "Humboldt City contains two hotels, kept in good style, one the Coulter House, by Mr. and Mrs. Bailey Nichols, the other, the Iowa House, by Mr. and Mrs. Wilson; two saloons, one by Messrs. Sylvester and Helmer, gentlemen ready to argue or fight for their politics, or deal out red-eye to their numerous thirsty customers, the other by Wilson and Coulter; one blacksmith's shop by Daniels and Cooper, who will at any moment stop shoeing a refractory horse to spin a yarn; two stores with large and well selected stocks of goods; four families (five or six more are on the road for the place) and children, chickens, pigs, and dogs enough to give the place a lively appearance."

The first settler was one Louis Barbeau, who must be given credit for being the discoverer of minerals in Humboldt County. Right behind him came other disappointed seekers of riches who had left the Comstock, when they learned Barbeau had found mineral in Humboldt Canyon. First of these were A. Pryor, John Coulter, F. J. Daniels, Colerick Brothers, George W. Meacham, Thomas McKinzie, Charles Lewis, Tony Martin and John Sylvester.

The State Mineralogist reported in the '60s that there was a strong vein or reef of limestone, as high as 70 feet in spots, which was the principal geological feature of the district. Several quartz veins ran parallel to it. Below the reef were located the Reveille, Franklin, Santa Cruz and Monte Cristo veins, while above it were the Calaveras, Sigel, Adriatic, Winnemucca, Washington and St. Bernard, all in quartzite formations. Nine of the mines were reported to have been opened to depths of 50 feet or more and "tunnels were driven into the mines at great expense, but no large bodies of ore were found."

In the May 14, 1864 issue of the *Register*—a year after Forbes had paid his visit—a correspondent brought Humboldt activities up to date. "Under the able supervision of Mr. Montgomery the Calaveras Co. is having a large double-track tunnel run night and day," he reported. "They obtained astonishing assays of from $500 to $4000 per ton."

"Near to and running parallel with this claim is the Starlight—working two shifts of men day and night, with a large double-track tunnel," and "near these is the Sigel," worked day and night . . . by working process it goes $240 to the ton; assays $2300." He continues with a similar report on the other mines in the district.

Then he gives an insight into the activities of an early mining town doctor. Previous reference has been made to Dr. C. W. Shaug—the only medico in the area—who advertised that he would "perform all surgical operations in a speedy, neat and successful manner, for reasonable charges." Evidently he was kept busy, the Humboldt correspondent wrote . . .

Seven or eight very serious casualties have occurred in the last few months on this side of the mountain from premature blasts. At least they would have been serious, had it not been for the timely and skilful treatment extended to them. Mr. Smith, of Prince Royal [the little town between Humboldt and Santa Clara], badly burned, it was feared would lose his sight—but has now recovered and is at work. Mr. Lacey, of Echo [another small hamlet on the west side of the mountains], right arm broken in two places and left thigh broken, now well again. Davis, Cole and Morehouse, badly injured, but recovering. But the most serious case, the Doctor now has under treatment: Mr. Jacob Keller, while working in the Starlight tunnel, a hale and robust worker, in an instant was hurled back, the bleeding, torn, helpless invalid; his arm broken in three places, and his left hand so horribly mutilated that it seemed one mass of broken bones, torn and mangled flesh. The Doctor performed a very skilful operation upon him a few days ago, amputating several of his fingers and cutting away a portion of the hand; and if he now succeeds in saving the arm, he will do what we are all inclined to think he will.

The Atlantic and Pacific Gold and Silver Company was Humboldt City's major mining operator after March of 1864. It was a stock outfit organized in New York and "a large majority of its members are residents of that city and men of large capital." This firm bought up five major claims for a total of 8100 feet along the main lode. The company hired one of the early Humboldt mining veterans, E. L. Montgomery, from whom they had purchased some of the locations, as superintendent.

The *Register* reported, "The A and P Co. has been peculiarly fortunate in securing the services of one so well qualified . . . They recently purchased in Humboldt City a commodious dwelling, with offices etc., elegantly furnished, and have on hand a large amount of supplies . . . The stock is full paid and not assessable, and held by parties who will not sell at any price."

Activity became very slow in Humboldt City in the fall of 1864, as elsewhere in the Humboldt region. Forbes, who had slipped away to California to be married, returned and wrote a full column lamenting the situation . . . "Silver mines are the most permanent and profitable investment we have . . . then why this depression? We have been reckless, extravagant and in many cases dishonest . . . one year ago scarcely a dollar had been shipped from Humboldt County, and now about $20,000 per week is taken from the Sheba mill alone."

Even a depression couldn't keep down the spirits when Nevada held its first election campaign. W. H. "Billie" Claggett—who first arrived at Unionville with Mark Twain, but stayed longer—and William Stewart, the firebrand attorney who became the State's famed first senior U.S. Senator, came to the Humboldt to campaign for the Union party.

Forbes referred to Claggett—who was elected a state Senator from Storey County in November—by writing, "He is well known to the Humboldt people and well liked. Like a gray shirt he wears well." At the first meeting in Unionville the *Register* reported, "The meeting adjourned with three cheers for Claggett, three for 'Bill' Stewart and a repeater for Lincoln and Johnson and the Union."

The next night, accompanied by a brass band, and a wagon load of Union adherents, the rally moved to Star City and the third night to Dun Glen, then closed in Humboldt City.

It is interesting to note the differing reports on the Humboldt City meeting as written by the *Register* correspondents there and at Star City. The Humboldt man reported, "Large and enthusiastic audiences were out . . . Sunday night to hear Stewart and Claggett. The meeting at Humboldt is described as the best in the whole series in the county. The audience was composed of men from all parts of the surrounding country—from the river, the mountains beyond, and the valleys above. The speeches were better, too, and everything seemed right."

From that it would seem that things were just dandy in Humboldt City—but the record shows that the Atlantic & Pacific Company had slacked down on explorations, and little work had been done in the mines during recent previous months. At any rate, the Star City correspondent reported it in considerably different light. He wrote—in the same issue as the above report—"From Dun Glen the boys went to Humboldt City—but they took all the enthusiasm there with them, as they say they found none there. One of our Star boys, on his return, swore there were but 25 men in Humboldt City, and 28 of them copperheads."

The Star reporter was wrong about the community's loyalty. When the election was held, the vote in Humboldt City was cast for the Union party. B. H. Nichols of Humboldt City received the largest vote for the State Assembly, winning by a majority of 151, while D. B. Brown of Unionville, with a majority of 143, and J. Angus Dun, of Dun Glen, with 142, were the others elected.

The whole county was slipping—the *Register* had less and less countywide news in succeeding issues.

Thompson & West's *History,* published in 1881, writes off the county's first town as completely dead, stating "During the panic of 1865 all work was suspended, though the claims were not quite abandoned, sufficient work being done to hold possession. In 1871 work was partly resumed on the Starlight and Madia, which, however are not worked at present.

"The town seems to be utterly prostrated. The nearest place is Humboldt House, two miles away. The place seems capable of being useful, and in the hurly-burly of mining may again wake to life . . . Humboldt City may be said to be the best illustration of the celebrated 'places that were' that is known."

Between the Humboldt crest on the east, still snow-capped as late as the month of June, and the triple-peaked Trinity range across the river to the west, U. S. 40 traces an historic path by old Oreana, Torreyville and Etna or Aetnaville, and swings past the dim old roads still visible to Trinity, Arabia and a host of other little mining towns of mid-century bonanza days.

They were satellites of Unionville, taking their place in northwest Nevada's mineral galaxy after the founding of the Eastern Star Mine at Trinity in 1863.

The ubiquitous Forbes, editor of the *Register*, must have owned a few "feet" of the mine, for there was scarcely an issue of his paper during 1864 that failed to mention the lonesome diggings in the foot-hills of the Trinity range.

Through the spring and summer of 1864 Forbes carried notes of progress at this mine. On May 7, the Evening Star was down 65 feet, and "ore was taken from which a splendid result was obtained at the mill—three bricks, 948 ounces of bullion worth $1,000.28; the result of 2½ tons of ore was worked at Fall's Mill." Then the editor commented, $400 a ton will do, if the Star should get better as they go down."

Forbes made the 35-mile trip to visit the mine in August and gave his readers a full column report on it. He noted that "The town is quiet, like all the others. Some building, and some prospecting; and two com-panies at work."

From this report it is learned that the ledge "was first discovered in a bowlder [sic] cropping from the surface." It had been worked out and the ledge followed down for 130 feet, "running regularly as far as traced."

At the same time he reported that "a boarding house is to be put up at once and arrangements perfected for a regular employment of a large force of workmen." And at the dump, Forbes "saw some of the handsomest silver ore we ever laid eyes on—plenty of it coated with horn silver." Also it is learned that unlike the complex Humboldt min-erals, "These Trinity ores are simple, requiring no roasting" and there was plentiful water and "wood in abundance at half the Virginia price."

This is pertinent when it is considered that of all the enthusiasm on the east side of the Humboldts, only the Sheba at Star City actually had shown rich promise. It also reveals the genesis of this pre-railroad mine boom near the river.

Forbes had another piece of important news for his Buena Vista Valley readers—a mill was to be built at Trinity. At the time the only others in the entire area was the one at Star City, built by Fair for the Sheba and Fall's little mill at Unionville.

The editor reported that "Joseph Voshay, one of the largest owners in this mine, has just returned from San Francisco, in company with George Webber, late of Mendocino county. Mr. Webber and Nathaniel Page . . . have shipped a 40-horsepower steam mill of 10-ton stamps— from the same shop and patterns which turned out the Sheba mill. Web-ber contracted in Chico for delivery of machinery within 30 days. He has employed the men who put up the Sheba mill, is going straight about putting the mill in order."

This was a highly important development for the Trinity district since it obviated the necessity of shipping the ore all the way to Unionville. On October 6 "fires were lit in the furnaces, and the engine works beauti-fully." By October 15 the *Register* reported that "The mill is all ready now, except that some stamp heads have failed to arrive from San Fran-cisco." And by November 12 it could be reported that the mill "not only does credit to those who constructed it, but will prove profitable to its owners." At the time it had only five stamps "but the power of the engine and the framework of the battery are adapted to the putting in of five more stamps, which will probably soon be added."

That marked the start of Trinity, which grew to a sizeable little town which boasted the customary saloons, stores, and other businesses, and a hotel owned by George Lovelock, pioneer of the Humboldt region who settled in the area where the Pershing County seat continues to bear his name.

Trinity was a long way from the seat of law and order and it was to be expected that matters would be settled forcibly at times—and they were.

An election for a "Recorder of Trinity" was held on July 19, 1864, which Forbes apparently delighted in setting into type this way:

> "Wiley J. Fox (Deep Red) and D. H. Williams were the candidates—both recognized as 'copperhead.' Fox was elected by a majority of two votes. A fight occurred between Williams and B. F. Smith. Williams fired one shot from a Deringer [*sic*]. Took a finger off a bystander who interfered. Smith then lit in, and times were very lively for a few minutes, and Williams emerged looking much like a badly beaten candidate. This, we believe, is his third performance with weapons within the past few weeks; though we are not prepared to state in how many of these instances he has been blameworthy. Chapman says 'he thought it would be just like the damn fool to shoot and now he is satisfied.' We are indebted to Andy Houghtaling, and Parkinson for information in the above matters. 'The Meadows' fellows were out in force at the election and everybody went to bed so drunk they didn't know who was elected till the next morning, when Houghtaling decided that Williams had been beaten."

But wait—in the very next issue is printed a letter addressed to the editor, reading:

> "I notice in your last issue some remarks in regard to a fight at Trinity, between D. H. Williams and some other party, in which you bring up my name without any knowledge of mine. In which statement you say that I said, 'It would be just like the damn fool to shoot.' I have known this Williams for some time, and always was satisfied he would shoot; having had some difficulty with him once, and tried his pluck. Yet, I will say for myself that I made him retreat in good order. But by your connecting my name with an affair that does not concern me, may bring on another quarrel,

and one or the other of us might not get to retreat in good order—but be left to be buried on the field. By giving the above a place in your paper, you will confer a favor on, Yours truly, W. H. Chapman."

By 1865 the mill was grinding out Evening Star ore, and life was never dull in Trinity, a lone habited area with no neighbor within miles.

Two major factors, in the middle 1860s, changed the placid life along the Humboldt. The rich Montezuma Mine near Trinity was discovered, and the Central Pacific picked a route along the river as the site for the railroad. This left the main towns on the east of the Humboldt Mountains isolated and resulted in a surge of life and the sprouting of new towns along the route of the railroad.

The Montezuma was a true bonanza, and the busy town of Arabia grew up near it. The Humboldt County Assessor, J. Q. Dryden, in 1868, expressed the opinion that "a mile square within which the Arabia mines are located would produce more bullion than any other ever known."

Today it is realized that this was a mite too optimistic; nevertheless the Montezuma poured out some very rich ore. It is reported that every ton of ore produced half a ton of metal, consisting of antimony, lead and silver, the vein being solid, containing no rock.

By 1875 the mine had spewed forth a treasure of 7000 tons of ore, which yielded 3150 tons of lead and $455,000 in silver, according to the State Mineralogist.

The upsurge of the Montezuma resulted in increased production in the other mines of the Trinity district—the Evening Star continuing to produce and mill its $65 a ton silver ore, producing a total of $100,000 before water halted operations, the chloride assaying mineral as rich as $1200 a ton.

With such rich ore, a larger mill was needed. The Montezuma firm constructed a large one on the railroad at Oreana, near the river where plenty of water was available. At the time it was reported to be the largest and most complete in the State and was declared by George Lovelock to have cost $250,000 to construct.

It was in charge of A. W. Nason, and is claimed to have been the first mill in the United States to ship lead to the commercial market. Lead previously had been produced at other spots, but was used locally, such as the ore from the Potosi mine near Las Vegas, which was melted by the Indians for bullets.

The huge Oreana mill had five big stacks from which smoke poured. They were fueled by charcoal, hauled long distances as the mountains were denuded. Some historians report that bleached cattle bones left by early pioneers were gathered along the trail and burned to furnish steam.

The big mill gave birth to a sizeable town around it. Oreana was the busiest and largest town along the Humboldt at the time, larger than either Lovelock or Winnemucca.

It not only had all of the ordinary business houses, saloons, gaming parlors and a prostitution district, it possessed its own jockey club which held regular races where the miners could bet their hard earned wages—or that portion left after the saloons, girls and games had first grab. Lovelock operated a large hotel at Oreana.

Further up the river toward Humboldt City, a couple of smaller towns grew up, Torreyville and Aetnaville, which handled the shipping of ores on the railroad from mines in the Humboldt canyons and acted as receiving points for supplies for these isolated diggings. It would be pretty hard to find either of them today along the shores of the lake behind the Rye Patch Dam.

The Oreana mill was estimated to be producing $45,000 worth of ore annually and continued to operate until the place burned near the end of the 1870s. During its later years, figures show that the mill was processing annually more than 30,000 tons of ore, paying from $30 to $700 a ton.

After the mill burned, the ores were shipped to Salt Lake City until the rich veins ran out, but loss of the town's major industry caused the decline of population and business. Oreana perked up in later years when the Rochester and Spring Valley booms hit, and even was the terminus of one of the State's many long-gone railroads, the Nevada Shortline.

Today, new Oreana along U.S. 40, is a filling station with some relics of the old days around it, but the pioneer towns are gone. Autoists whiz past, anglers fish, and water sports are enjoyed on the lake. The ghosts of the old-timers probably look on and wonder "What's this world coming to?"

A Portion of East Rochester, Pershing County

—*Courtesy E. W. Darrah and Nevada State Historical Society.*

★ Mill City

It Was a Lovely Dream

JUST A SHORT DISTANCE FROM HUMBOLDT City was Mill City, a misnamed maverick of the bonanza days which has managed to survive for nearly a century in spite of the fact that it has been battered by enough mistakes and bad luck to sink a dozen bigger towns.

It was conceived in a grandiose dream, almost as amazing as the Sutro tunnel, which collapsed in a welter of unpaid assessments, and has been knocked flat time after time only to bounce back and keep going. Its history can be traced in definite phases.

Mill City was located on the Humboldt River, athwart the old immigrant trail where thousands of covered wagon pioneers forded the stream, some 28 miles below present Winnemucca.

When the Humboldt mines began to boom in the early 1860s it was picked as the site for a mill town to grind the Humboldt ores—the water power to be furnished through a fifty-mile canal from Golconda.

When this idea went down the gopher holes, along with the 1865 collapse, Mill City was dormant until 1868, when the Central Pacific built through it. Rail shipments from Unionville, Star City, Humboldt City and Dun Glen brought it to life again. When the shipping ceased, Mill City drowsed along through the years until the tungsten discoveries again revived it.

In recent years, since diesels were put on the railroad, it even ceased being a rail stop and lost its post office, but kept alive through the largess of occasional tourists who halt while zooming across U. S. 40 to buy gas or liquids for human consumption.

Its grandiose conception was the dream of Joseph A. Ginacca, who with J. A. Algauer, had been one of the very first settlers at Frenchman's Ford—later to become Winnemucca. The Unionville, Star Canyon, Humboldt Canyon and Dun Glen mines were being exploited as the "richest spot on God's footstool."

Water power in the canyons fluctuated and was scarcely strong enough to operate a large mill, although Unionville had J. C. Fall's plant, and Star City was proud of the Sheba mill built by Fair. The sluggish Humboldt didn't offer enough steady flow to furnish sufficient power, so Ginacca conceived the idea of digging a canal from Preble, on the river near the site of present Golconda, to Mill City and nearby Lancaster.

The latter was a small community at the river crossing on the Red Bluff-Chico road where Charles Adams, in 1864, advertised in the *Register* that "The undersigned has just established a lumber yard at Lancaster, on the Humboldt River, and is now prepared to furnish the people of Humboldt County with lumber, at the yard, or delivered at the shortest notice. Also 20,000 shakes." Nothing at all remains of Lancaster, although it predated Mill City.

Ginacca could visualize gigantic developments at Mill City if the proper power was available. After plodding over the terrain and surveying the possibilities, he interested his friends, the Lay brothers, at Golconda. Planning went on for nearly a year, during which time the Lays raised some capital in France and the project generally was called the "French Canal." The Humboldt Canal Company was formed with offices at 804 Montgomery Street in San Francisco, and with Edward A. Breed as secretary. In those halcyon days of Nevada's silver glory, stock in almost any project was eagerly bought by folks who expected to get rich quickly. The canal stock was no exception. Plenty of it was sold all over the country, and actual digging was started in late 1862. The ditch was to be fifteen feet wide and three feet deep. It was figured that this would supply a sufficient flow of water, not only to run "40 mills of 20 stamps each," but also to irrigate land along the way.

Ginacca employed hordes of Indian laborers using ox-powered metal-faced wooden scrapers. Due note of the important project was taken by Forbes in the *Register*. At that time the future had a very rosy glow for everybody in the Humboldts. It was natural that some of the bright fellows in the mining towns would figure a way to cash in on Ginacca's canal—and they did.

The Indians hardly had scraped out the beginning of the ditch nearly 50 miles away, when the Mill City and Water Company popped into being. President of this promotional project was Dr. Shaug, the busy medico, with J. A. Algauer listed as secretary. To gain an insight on the promotional wiles of the day, it is enlightening to glance at the company's advertising in the *Register*.

The first notice that Mill City was destined to take its place on the Nevada map is noted in correspondence from Humboldt City in the May 14, 1864, issue which read, "Mill City is progressing rapidly—more than 20 lots have recently been disposed of, a portion of the contract being that purchasers bind themselves to erect substantial buildings thereon before the first day of January next." Since Shaug was the principal promoter, one is inclined to believe he wrote the Humboldt City correspondence.

Then on May 21, 1864, in the following issue, the first advertisement for the townsite appeared. As a piece of history, it is reprinted here in full . . .

"A RICH STRIKE! WHO WILL BUY A CHANCE?—The Mill City and Water Company have duly incorporated and laid out a town, and named it Mill City. It is located at the terminus of the great Humboldt Canal in Humboldt county N.T. and where 40 or 80 mills will be located.

The water afforded by the canal will all be used at, and within the limits of Mill City. The company has already procured the purest soft water in abundance, within the city limits, for culinary and other purposes.

"For a full and perfect description of Mill City, its advantages for location, health, beauty and future prospects, the reader is especially referred to the prospectus and map, a copy of which will be found with each of the following agents, to-wit: O. R. Leonard, of Star, in the Star District; Thomas A. Freeman, Unionville, Buena Vista District; E. W. Councilman, Dun Glen, Sierra District; and L. E. Ritter of San Francisco, Calif.

"C. W. Shaug and J. A. Algauer, agents for Humboldt County, N.T.

"Said company are [sic] now ready to sell lots on terms so favorable, that a rapid growth in population and wealth must ensue. C. W. Shaug will be at the company's office in Mill City on Monday of each week, where all persons desiring to purchase an interest in said town can do so; and also examine the city, the water, and other advantages, that no other point possesses. 200 No. 2 corner lots can be drawn at lottery, at $20 a lot, and 200 inside lots can be drawn at $10 per lot, by all that wish to engage in such an enterprise, for luck. All said lots will be equally selected, in point of value and location, or others can select the choice for higher figures.

"P.S.—Reader, don't forget to carefully examine our Mill City Prospectus."

The first fading of the rosy glow surrounding the French Canal construction began to appear in the winter of 1864. This is obvious by references made in the article by Forbes in the *Register* of Jan. 21, 1865:

"THE HUMBOLDT CANAL—This mammoth enterprise feels the pressure of the times, but yet the work progresses. Contractors have not been able to work advantageously, of late, but keep doing what they can. Thirty miles of the canal have been completed. This completed portion is not connected; but it is nowhere interrupted to any considerable extent of unfinished work.

"Some wiseacres have prophesied, that on account of the large amount of sand in the soil, the canal would not hold enough water to flow. Engineers knew better, and the falsity of that position has had a remarkable illustration since the completing of a section comprising some 25 consecutive miles. A small ditch was cut at one place to drain the water from a warm springs into the canal. The water where it entered the canal amounted by measurement to eight inches. It ran, on the easy grade of the canal, eleven miles down. At different times the water has been turned in through the headgate, to drown out gophers and other animals burrowing in the work. Water was let in to fill the banks 18 inches on the sides. The water flowed through the entire length of the finished portion, and very little diminution of quantity could be perceived—although no 'puddling' had ever been done.

"The work, as far as completed, fully justifies all calculations of the projectors. All that is wanted is the demand for water power for mills. Work can be done much more rapidly, if the proprietors of the canal are made to see that mill power is wanted. At the present rate of work, Mr. Ginacca tells us, he will have the water to Grass Valley, a point 40 miles from the head of the canal, about the last of April."

There were other clouds on the horizon. Every week's issue contained a notice of payments due on assessments of the stock of the canal company. They were being levied at $3 a share every month. By November, the eleventh assessment was being called. Stockholders were having to pay heavily for their investment in Ginacca's dream.

The editor popped up with a bright idea for using the canal during the dull dead winter days of 1865, suggesting the possibility of cutting the vast areas of sagebrush along the route, "Bailing it like hay, and shipping it down the canal for use as fuel in the mining towns and mills."

This item was picked up by the *Mining Press* in San Francisco, which missed the point and added the thought that "large portions of the sagebrush can be culled out and piled up after the ordinary manner of cord wood."

Since the brush in the area wasn't much thicker than a man's thumb, Forbes couldn't help but crack back, "We imagine we see fellows trimming and cording 'the larger portions of sagebrush.'"

Then in the March 11, 1865, *Register* appeared this item: "GINACCA'S BRIDGE—The ground on the line of the Humboldt Canal was frozen so deep, during the late cold spell, that work had to be for the time suspended. Ginacca, unwilling to let the time pass unimproved, has employed it in hauling timbers for a bridge . . . He expects to have the work complete in about 15 days . . . The bridge will be a great convenience to the public, being on the road to Idaho . . ." This may have been the first bridge across the Humboldt in the Winnemucca region.

Even after all indications made it apparent that the Humboldt mines were not of bonanza richness, many clung to the idea that Ginacca's canal would be finished and Mill City would become a metropolis of mills. The April 1, 1865, issue of the Humboldt *Register* reported that "Mill City begins to loom in the premonitory shadowings of a town to be." Then later it notes that "Dickinson, of the Aetna mine in Prince Royal, is having a 20-stamp mill built in San Francisco, to be put up at Mill City." It is possible it was built and run with water piped from the river, because of the forty mills planned for the place only one small one ever actually operated.

It is evident that Ginacca hadn't actually decided to stop digging during that frigid spring of 1865—or, if so, hadn't made it known. Naturally, he wouldn't with $100,000 worth of hopeful buyer's cash already used up and purchasers being dunned for more and more assessments.

When Forbes read in his exchanges that Los Angeles County was building a ditch "11 miles in length, tapping the San Gabriel . . . and fertilizing 40,000 acres of land previously useless" he couldn't help but make a typical Forbes reply in his Humboldt *Register*. It read, "Passable! Passable! but it wouldn't make much of a show beside the Humboldt Canal—54 miles long, and a capacity to carry all the water of the Humboldt River."

It was about that time, too, that many were figuring on shipping agricultural supplies from Paradise Valley by boat down the canal when it was finished.

Thompson & West's 1881 *History* tells us ". . . the canal never reached that point [Mill City], stopping at Winnemucca, 28 miles from the place where water was taken out. For some reason it was not found profitable and the work was abandoned, no water having been through the canal for 10 years. About $100,000 were expended in constructing the canal to Winnemucca . . . " The end of canal work and the depression concluded Mill City's first era.

Today the completed portion of the canal is overgrown with low sagebrush and weeds, an obscure monument to a doughty pioneer with a big dream, across the face of the Humboldt plain.

The late Adell "Casey" Jones of Fallon, Nevada, visited Mill City in 1909 with her father, and lived there for some time in 1951 when she found innumerable valuable old-time documents in the ruins of the Organ hotel and store, adding bits of historical lore on the place. "Uncle' Joseph Organ, as everybody called him, and his wife, 'Aunt' Patty, lived on the Starr Creek Ranch, after closing out their store in Star City, but sent son Peter down to manage the new store at Mill City," Mrs. Jones recalled.

"Of course the Humboldt Canal 'died aborning' but Mill City survived for the simple reason that it was the closest point on the railroad to the mines at Unionville, Star City, Dun Glen, etc., when the Central Pacific came along. There was a small mill there at one time—when we lived there in 1951 you could still see the old waterwheel, foundations of the mill and follow the old pipe line which brought water [for power] up from the river.

"Mill City was not a ghost town until the 1940s. Its population was never over a few hundred, but it had a post office, railroad station, telegraph operator, section foreman and crew. I think the development of the Nevada Massachusetts Tungsten mine in the 1920s and '30s probably gave Mill City a huge 'shot in the arm.' They were still shipping tungsten from there in 1951—but I guess it's dead now. [The tungsten operations closed down completely in 1958.]

"The Organs, besides the hotel and store, kept a livery stable, blacksmith shop, had freighting contracts, interests in mining, and he served as school trustee, etc.

"The only thing I could never find at Mill City was a cemetery."

The last statement of Mrs. Jones is highly interesting, because the Thompson & West *History,* published in 1881, concludes its report on Mill City, "The town claims to be the healthiest in the world, having so far no necessity for starting a cemetery."

Other enlightening information gleaned by "Casey" Jones is contained in a newspaper article she wrote in 1954: "Ten men are listed in the voters directory for 1868, with Anthony Gintz as agent; there are 26 in 1870 and 38 in 1872. Out of the lot, only one man had to use his X mark, which is rather remarkable for that day and age.

"I delight in poring over the Old Mill City ledgers from the Organ store, comparing prices quoted in them with those of today. Sixty pounds of beef for $4.80. Two meals and a bed (Organ's Hotel) for $1. A roll of butter for 25 cents, 10 pounds of potatoes for 30 cents. Wages were low, too. A lot of the store bills were settled by labor in freighting or haying on the Star Creek ranch, and a dollar a day seems to have been the going wage for the 1880s.

"On one page of the old ledger is a recipe for liniment: 'one ounce of oil of origamum [*sic*], one ounce oil of cedar, one ounce oil of camphor—add to one pint of alcohol.' It sounds as though it could have cured more than Mill City's aches and pains."

Mill City, as it was at the start of the 1880s, is reported in the Thompson & West *History* as follows: "The present population is about 50. It has a store for general merchandise, one hotel, saloon, livery stable, blacksmith shop, and foundry; also telegraph, express and post office. It is supplied by water by the Mill City Water Works."

The little town enjoyed another period of "prosperity" during recent years, with many families connected with the tungsten mine living there—but with its closing they, too, moved away, and things looked black again. Only the stopping of an occasional tourist in the whizzing throng on U. S. 40 brought some gasoline and refreshment business.

"Casey" Jones reported that the town's only old mill was torn down a few years ago and the lumber used to build one of the gas stations (plus bar) on the highway. *Sic gloria transit.*

It was inevitable in the mad scramble for riches in Nevada during the 1860s that there would be some Scotchmen in the melting pot of mineral chasers—John W. Mackay of the Comstock Big Four was the most famous. But it was another, J. Angus Dun, whose name was given to a lively, bustling little Humboldt early mining town, which had the typical highland title of Dun Glen.

A further flavor of Scotch was added by the fact that it was located on the north flank of 7430-foot high Auld Lang Syne peak, the highest in the East Humboldt Range. Records don't tell whether Dun Glen or the mountain was named first—maybe Dun christened both of them, undoubtedly he did the town.

Dun Glen was the rowdiest of the Humboldt circle of towns, being farther away from the county seat at Unionville than most of the others. It was nine miles northeast of Mill City, about 25 miles by road from Star City and several miles farther to Unionville. To reach the town required a long dry trip, broken only by an oasis in the middle of the valley called Jacob's Well. This is one spectral spot which has completely disappeared into the ethereal mists. But it existed, because a correspondent wrote in the September 24, 1864, *Humboldt Register*, "At Jacob's Well, in the valley, we halted for water and refreshments. This place is considerably embellished with notices and poetry stuck up in conspicuous places about the house; two of them as near as I can recollect, read as follows:

" 'Travelers MUST patronize the bar, or pay 12½ cents apiece for water for their animals.'

> 'To Jacob's Well the traveler comes,
> His dropping heart to cheer:
> We've whiskey, brandy, gin and rum,
> Likewise good lager beer.' "

Maybe that was Nevada's first singing commercial.

Discovery of mineral high up on the alluvial fan of the East range is credited to D. P. Crook in 1862. It is evident that he spread the word or told some of his friends because early in 1863 he came back with J. Angus Dun, D. McLarkey, J. Slade, A. J. Elsey, R. Monroe, Thomas Ewing and James A. Banks.

What happened to Crook and the others is unrecorded, but it is quite evident that Dun, with a Scotch eye to business, must have laid out a townsite because an advertisement in the *Humboldt Register* read, "GREAT AUCTION SALE ON REAL ESTATE in the town of Dun Glen, Humboldt County, N.T.—The undersigned will sell at public auction to the highest bidder, for cash, April 30th, 1864, at 1 o'clock p.m., in the town of Dun Glen, 50 choice business lots. Persons wishing to purchase will do well to improve this opportunity, as these are the only remaining lots unsold." It was signed by J. Angus Dun.

The Thompson and West *History* describes its location thus: "The hamlet is surrounded by high mountains, partially covered with stunted cedar trees, which furnish the wood for the settlement."

Its peak population is undetermined, but the old history says, "At this time [1863] and for two or three years after, the population reached 250, but since then has dwindled down to about 50. Nearly the whole industrial interest is stock-raising." Since this was written in 1881, the latter statements indicate that the Auld Lang Syne mines, like so many in the area, had proved less fruitful than expected.

The mining district was named "Sierra"—Dun missing the boat here as it could fittingly have been called "Highland" in keeping with the other Scotch nomenclature—and was highly regarded during its first years. The county assessor, M. H. Haviland, in 1868, reported that the Neptune series of ledges, on which the Tallulah, Empire, and Essex mines were located, "were well charged with various kinds of silver ores, the rock assaying as high as $6000 a ton." But it was the Gem which was the top mine of the area—and proved to be the major producer of the district according to mining records. The assessor declared that its ores assayed "as high as $16,000 to the ton."

A new ledge was struck in the Gem early in May 1864, which had "an abundance of metal," according to the *Register*. At the same time it was noted that "Seven tuns [*sic*] ore taken over this week to the Auld Lang Syne mill." This latter reference establishes the fact that Dun Glen must have had a mill by this time—although knowledge of how large it was has not yet turned up.

Later in the same month, Forbes took a trip across the sage flats and visited Dun Glen for the purpose of viewing a new mine, the Croesus, "about two miles above Dun Glen." Evidently he was impressed, writing half a column about it and aiding in the sale of stock by reporting that "in much of it gold is readily seen with the unaided eye, and it is rich in silver chlorides."

A bit of information regarding the type of housing in Dun Glen is afforded by Forbes' report on the superintendent's [E. X. Field's] home: "Field has an excellent town residence in Dun Glen, with sleeping apartments, kitchen, dining room, office, store-house for barley and bathing accommodations, admirably arranged."

Strange as it may seem, Dun Glen miners apparently didn't work on Sundays, a practice not followed in most other early Nevada mining towns, where the only holiday observed was July 4. The *Register* noted on June 18, 1864, that "Dun Glen is enlivened Sundays by a large working force, resting from its labors in the Gem, Tallulah, Lang Syne, Croesus, Badger and other mines."

Possibly it was this free time for social events which led to the first sensational murder reported in Dun Glen—although there may have been other shootings which weren't important enough to note.

It happened at a Saturday night dance on August 6. Since the *Register's* story is a perfect example of life as lived in the far outland mining towns, it is offered here in full.

"HOMICIDE IN DUN GLEN—An altercation took place at a ball in Dun Glen about 12 o'clock Saturday night which resulted in the death of Louis Stonehill, a merchant in that place. We give, as nearly as we could make it, a correct and impartial account of the circumstances. W. D. Jackson and Louis Stonehill were dancing in opposite ends of the room; Stonehill calling for the quadrille. J. complained that S. did not call loud enough. After getting through with the supper dance, Jackson went to the chief musician and told him to play and call, and he didn't want any more of Stonehill's calling; that a Chinaman could do better.

"S. called him to account, and threatened violence, if any more such remarks were made. Afterwards, the quarrel was kept up in the saloon. Others interfered and got the parties to put off the subject till the next day. This was agreed to. S., afterwards in the saloon, asked a party to drink. Granger got into a quarrel with him, and the quarrel between S. and J. was renewed—bystanders thinking Granger in the fault at this juncture. We are told, too, that about this time G. furnished Jackson the six-shooter he afterwards used.

"After some further words, Stonehill went out, and Jackson went out soon after; and S. hearing some remark to Granger, replied to it. Some words exchanged and Jackson fired. The crowd gathered, and another shot went off, passing through a bystander's coat, through Stonehill's leg and hitting another bystander's boot heel. Stonehill ran through the saloon, back to nearly where he was standing when first shot; then began to stagger. He was assisted, and walked across to his store, where he fell, and in a few minutes was dead.

"It was then discovered that the first shot had pinned his left arm, and passed into the chest and into or near the heart.

"Jackson made his escape, and kept concealed for awhile. After learning of the death of Stonehill, he came out and surrendered himself to the law, and the examination was in progress at our last accounts.

"It is claimed on behalf of Jackson that Stonehill had his hand behind him for some time, while talking; as if resting the hand on a pistol; that he withdrew his hand during the heat of the quarrel, raising and lowering, as if bringing a pistol to bear; that he had no pistol, but that maneuvering was such as might and did lead J. to think a pistol was held on him. Granger was afterwards arrested for complicity in the affair."

The following issue of the *Register* reported what happened to Jackson as follows:

"THE DUN GLEN HOMICIDE—W. D. Jackson, arrested for killing Louis Stonehill, last week, was, after protracted examination, acquitted as having acted in self-defense."

The miners of the '60s were looking for lodes and were not particularly interested in placer gold, although it turned up in nearly all the canyons during the early workings. It could be expected that sooner or later the Chinese railroad workers, who were left stranded on the high desert when the tracks were finished, would discover these latent deposits of gold dust and nuggets—and they did.

Just as they moved in at Tuscarora, in Spring Valley, Rochester and throughout the area wherever there was placer, the Chinese spread across Dun Glen canyon and into every ravine around Auld Lang Syne peak. During the 1880s and '90s nobody knows how much gold they retrieved but it had to be considerable according to unofficial reports of old-timers in the area.

However, the Thompson and West *History* reports that, by 1880, the town's population had "dwindled down to about 50" and that "the whole industrial interest is stock raising."

Dun Glen held on against steadily declining business until September 23, 1887, when the postoffice closed. During that winter somebody must have rounded up some cash and re-started mine operations because the office re-opened March 13, 1888, and survived this time until 1894, when the mineral ennui caught up with it. There wasn't another Dun Glen postal cancellation until March 4, 1911, when the placer town three miles up the canyon, Chafey, went under and the old Dun Glen office was re-opened because it was nearer the activities in Baxter Canyon and several other Auld Lang Syne mountain placer diggings. But it was short-lived, closing on April 15, 1913, and never since has any postal clerk had to wonder where to route a letter addressed to the little East Range town.

Visitors won't find a whole lot left at Dun Glen. It has been long gone.

A home in Dun Glen during its livelier period. The baby is the present Mrs. Dorothy (Riley) Hapgood, of Winnemucca. Fred Braito, a friend of the family, is doing the baby-sitting for the picture.

—*Courtesy of E. W. Darrah.*

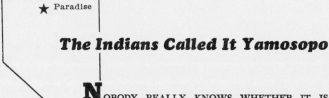

The Indians Called It Yamosopo

NOBODY REALLY KNOWS WHETHER IT IS true, but the historians report that W. B. Huff climbed his way from the head of Rebel Creek to the top of a pass on the north side of 9600-foot Santa Rosa Peak on a June day in 1863, gazed at the lush, widespread valley lying along the Little Humboldt River and its many tributaries, and exclaimed, "What a paradise!" And this is how this rich agricultural wonderland between the Santa Rosa and Volcanic ranges, some forty miles north-northeast of Winnemucca supposedly got its name. Three other fellows could have said it, if anybody did, because Huff was with R. D. Carr, J. D. Whitmore and W. C. Gregg when they gazed upon the valley while making a prospecting trip from Star City. All knew good, rich farming land and immediately they forgot their search for minerals as they staked out homesteads along the creek meadows. They weren't the first white men in Paradise, though. Peter Skene Ogden had crossed the range from the Quinn River in 1831 and traveled down the Humboldt on his famed expedition. Paradise still is a prosperous valley and it abounds in some of Nevada's outstanding ghosts.

A month after the four men staked out their claims, Gregg was back in the valley with fourteen head of stock, a mower and hay baler, and wagons. During the 1863 season he cut and baled 250 tons of wild hay, for which he received high prices at Star City. He had found something richer than the low grade ore which had brought hopeful hundreds to the Humboldt.

By the next spring, 1864, others, who had left their farms in the east and mid-west to answer the siren call of western gold only to find disappointment, joined the rush to Paradise. The wave of farmer immigrants that year included Richard Brenchley, Charles A. Nichols, William Stock, M. W. Haviland, Thomas Byrnes, A. Denio—remember these fellows, they all show up later in this saga—M. Maylen, P. H. Scott, E. Lyng, George H. Carrol, J. B. Carrol, W. C. Hinkey, George A. Middleton, John Stockham, R. H. Scott and Joseph Hufferd. The latter's wife was the first white woman to enter Paradise Valley. Haviland also brought his family.

Soddies and wattled willow huts were the first houses, followed later by fine ranch spreads and tight log houses. Brenchley and Nichols ploughed the first furrows and planted the first grain in the valley on March 12, 1864. They later threshed one thousand bushels of wheat from a planting of 45 acres, for which they received $9,000—a high price for grain in those days, but remember this was the first local supply availible in those mad Comstock days when freight had to be hauled hundreds of miles in wagons. The settlers also planted large vegetable gardens which grew lustily.

While all this was going on the Paiutes and the Bannocks were watching carefully, and were far from happy about the situation. The whites had moved in on their lands, destroyed their piñon pines and despoiled their hunting grounds. What was now known as Paradise Valley long had been a grazing ground for large herds of game animals. From its two flanking ranges, the Santa Rosas and Volcanics, the valley furnished much of the Indian food supply, and naturally the redskins were peeved about the invasion; mighty peeved. They called it "Yamosopo," which meant "Half-moon Valley."

The situation set the stage for a parade of Indian battles which would delight the soul of any TV or movie writer—and which, to a large degree have been passed over lightly as history dwelt upon the Pyramid Lake fights.

The first outbreak occurred in March 1864—the same month the second group moved into Paradise—when three prospectors, Dr. H. Smeathman, W. F. White and Frank Thompson, were attacked farther north. Dr. Smeathman was wounded and fell from his horse, crying for help. His companions fled, leaving him to his fate, and two days later reached Rabbit Holes and then continued on to Humboldt City.

Two months after this another party of four was attacked along the Quinn River, north of the Santa Rosas. G. W. Dodge was killed, and a man named Noble was wounded. The latter and his remaining companions made their way to Star City and reported the outbreak. This was the attack which led to the formation of the Humboldt "Indian Army," whose adventures we have already seen.

These two 1864 killings raised the curtain on three or four years of attacks and harassments which led to the establishment of Fort McDermit on the Quinn River near the present Idaho line, and Fort Winfield Scott in Paradise Valley, portions of which still may be seen there.

Trouble really broke out in the spring of 1865. Black Rock Tom, a strong Paiute chief, went on the warpath against the whites. On March 14, E. F. Dunne, of Humboldt County, sent a telegram to Governor H. G. Blaisdel, telling him that the redskins had killed Lucius Arcularius, the Wall Spring station keeper on the Honey Lake road—main supply line to the Humboldts—and two men at the Granite Creek Station.

On March 17 the Indians were reported gathering at a war camp on the Humboldt near the head of the Mill City canal—close to present Golconda. M. W. Haviland arrived at Star City on March 20 asking that help be sent to Paradise Valley to protect the settlers from the anticipated attacks.

Two friendly Indians came to the home of Aaron Denio (for whom the town of Denio, at the state line in Oregon, north of the Black Rock desert, is named) on Martin Creek on the morning of April 4, 1865, and warned him that in "two sleeps" the warriors would attack, kill all the Paradise settlers and steal their stock. All residents were warned as rapidly as possible, and plans were made to move to a safer spot.

T. J. Fine, one of the farmers, was in bed with "inflammatory rheumatism" and a cart was made for him from the hind portion of a wagon. A storm delayed the start until the next day when the party set out for Willow Point, several miles down the Little Humboldt.

Progress was slow. Cottonwood and Martin Creeks were running bank full, and the trail was deep in mud. After finally getting the cart across the streams, Denio and a man named Rembreaux loaded the children aboard it with the ill man and dragged it toward Hamblin's corral, three miles farther—the others remaining behind to get the rest of their goods and themselves across the flooded creeks and follow along.

It was expected that Christopher Fearbourne, and two others named Barber and Collins would join them with an ox-wagon. But these three awoke in the morning to find their house surrounded by Paiutes, who made no hostile moves until the men started to leave with the loaded wagon. Then Barber went to the corral, saddled a horse, told the Indians he was going after a beef to bring in food for all, and was allowed to leave. He notified three other men who hadn't yet departed—two of them returned with Barber to aid the besieged pair while A. and T. J. Bryant, with twelve-year-old Robert Denio went south to join the party headed for Willow Point. This group succeeded in evading a band of warriors which attempted to cut it off.

The other trio, Barber, Byrnes and Lackey returned to find that the Indians had fired the cabin in which Fearbourne and Collins had taken refuge. A party of twenty-two mounted Indians attacked the rescuers, but they managed to get away and join the group at Hamblin's corral, which brought the party to ten men, one boy, three women and four children, armed with an assortment of guns—three rifles, one musket, two double-barreled shotguns and six small revolvers. The Indians attacked and kept up a fire at long range. Aaron Denio, by general agreement, was in command.

Then, in the best traditions of TV tales, a youth named Thomas Byrnes volunteered to ride through the lines of the attackers to Willow Point and get help for the besieged. And, shades of all those celluloid chase epics, he did just that, mounting the fastest horse in the shed, dashed daringly right at and through the attackers and out-racing the pack of of screaming Paiutes who gave chase and fired frantically at his fleeing form. It was the real life prototype of all those hundreds of similar chases which have been made through the live oaks and around the rocks of moviedom's favorite locale at Newhall, California during the last four decades.

I doubt if any script writer could have done it more justice than did the now unknown author who penned the description of this ride in the

1881 Thompson and West *History of Nevada*—"The fleet-footed horse flew over the plain to the south with the rider apparently unharmed, and soon passed from the sight of those anxious watchers at the little fort. It was a race for life. If overtaken by a stray bullet, or the mounted savages, the lives of all at the corral would have paid the penalty, and, seemingly inspired with the terrible emergency, the noble animal flew like a winged Pegasus out of sight from the pursuers."

Young Byrnes arrived about three in the afternoon and found thirteen men at Willow Point, all anxious to hurry to the rescue—but there were only twelve horses. This brought about a sturdy bit of pioneer heroics which I don't recall having ever before read or seen in movie westerns.

According to the Thompson and West story of the event—written only fifteen years after it happened—the fellow doomed to remain behind because of the lack of an extra horse was the eldest of the party, a white-bearded old veteran named Givens.

When the others were mounted, according to the *History*, "he seized a rifle in one hand, and laying hold of the pommel of a saddle with the other . . . kept pace with the relief party over that thirteen miles, refusing to get on a horse, and every little while shouting, 'heave ahead, boys, heave ahead, the women and children must be saved!'"

The party of armed horsemen and Givens made that thirteen miles in fast time, arriving before dark. When the Indians saw the approaching horsemen they withdrew.

The members of the besieged party quickly loaded up and plodded through the dark to the safety of Willow Point, arriving at three a.m. And what do you think they found there? Lieut. Joseph Wolverton and a troop of twenty-five men, who had come in answer to Haviland's warning at Star City a couple of weeks before, but just a few hours too late to help this time.

The next day the soldiers and the settlers rode forth after the Indians. They were gone. At the cabin where Fearbourne and Collins had remained, they found the charred bodies of the two men.

The Indian wars continued all that summer of 1865, and Paradise promised to be the scene of much more frontier trouble with the savages.

Although troops had arrived in Paradise Valley to protect settlers during the Spring of 1865, many of those who had taken up homesteads departed for safer climes. Nevada was a vast area and the wily Indians had no intention of allowing the whites to take over their former happy hunting grounds without fighting for their rights. They killed some travelers on the Honey Lake Road near the Humboldt River on May 20, and in July word was rushed to Unionville for a physician and aid when a large band attacked an Idaho-bound party near the Quinn River, killed P. W. Jackson of Virginia City and seriously wounded three others. The Paradise folk split into two parties to raise a crop of grain during the summer of 1865—keeping wary guards on the lookout at all times.

One of the parties on Martin Creek, making headquarters at the R. H. Scott cabin, found plenty of Indian signs. Scott went to seek military aid. Unexpectedly he stumbled upon a night camp of Col. McDermit, who had come north to put down inflamed Humboldt tribes. The officer detailed a Sergeant Thomas, Company D, California Volunteers, with sixteen men to return with Scott to Paradise.

A party of six of these men under a corporal ran into a large body of Indians, variously reported as from 27 to 50 about four miles from the camp. Although the Indians made no attack, their attitude was far from friendly and the corporal sent a man back to Sergeant Thomas for assistance.

As the sergeant with his crew rode in, a battle started. The fight spread through the brush, every man for himself as the Indians hid themselves and attacked separately. Paradise Valley residents jumped into the affray to help conquer the redskins and when they saw five Indians go into a cabin they set fire to it and shot the Paiutes as they rushed out of the burning building. When the shooting was finished, 23 Indians had been killed, the balance escaping.

Col. McDermit wrote from Quinn River on August 1, "We have killed 32 Indians since I took the field, and have had one wounded, and one man killed." Seven days later this outstanding officer was shot from ambush by an Indian and killed as he rode along a trail near his camp on Quinn River. A short time later Fort McDermit was established near the spot—and today the Oregon border town of McDermit, on U.S. Highway 95, is located there—although the name has been corrupted on some maps by the addition of an extra "t" to the colonel's name.

Late in August some friendly Paiutes came into Paradise Valley and told Col. Bryan, who had arrived to lead the military, that they could guide him to the camp of hostile Shoshones. He sent Lt. Penwell and twenty soldiers with the Paiutes to their Table Mountain hideout. Editor Forbes duly reported the event in his *Humboldt Register* this way,

> "The Pah-Ute guides led the party upon the camp at daybreak this morning, so cautiously that the entire gang was taken in, and ticketed for the happy hunting grounds before they knew what was the matter. Seven bucks bit the dust, and one or two squaws were killed by accident."

A few days later, on September 13, Capt. Payne attacked an Indian Camp on Willow Creek, just over the hills from Paradise. The fight lasted three hours, 31 Indians being killed and a white man wounded.

Such sporadic fights went on through the next year, but in the meantime Gov. Blaisdel had taken an interest in the situation, showing an understanding of the Indians' side of the argument for which he deserves credit at this late date.

In his message to the legislature in January 1866, Gov. Blaisdel reported, "Lack of time forbids detailing the incidents of my visits among the various tribes; suffice it to say, some of their arguments were unanswerable. They said, through their interpreter, 'the white men cut down our pine trees, their cattle eat our grass, we have no pine nuts, no grass seed, and we are hungry.' I found them, in several instances, with nothing to subsist upon but rabbits, mice, grasshoppers, ants and other insects."

Possibly the visit of Gov. Blaisdel to the tribes calmed down things for a brief spell as nothing worse than a few scares interrupted the summer of 1866 in Paradise Valley. During that summer the Army moved in and constructed Fort Winfield Scott at the north end of the green valley, at the same time erecting Fort McDermit further north on the Quinn River.

The building of the fort caused some of the settlers to move farther north and settle. The site of Paradise City grew up around the C. A. Nichols home, which was built that year. However, the forts seemed to stir the Indians to renewed activity and the following winter the soldiers were kept busy as the redskins moved in to the attack again.

The development of Paradise Valley into the fine cattle and agricultural community it is today actually began in 1866, after Fort Winfield Scott was built. Having soldiers on the spot held the disgruntled Indians back for awhile. The first store in the valley was opened by George A. Middleton. Thompson & West noted in the 1881 *History of Nevada* that he sold his whiskey at 50 cents a shot, "though regular customers got it at reduced rates." Coffee was $1 a pound, bacon 50 cents, beans 30 cents, flour and sugar 50 and tea $1.50. That seems pretty expensive for those days, but remember everything had to be freighted by wagon from Chico and Red Bluff, over the Sierra and across the dreaded Black Rock desert.

More and more houses and business places began to grow up during the summer of 'Sixty-six around the area where the C. A. Nichols family had settled in the spring. Among the other arrivals who later became highly important to the early days of Paradise, was Charles Kemler. He first freighted goods to the valley, then moved there and opened the first store in the actual townsite—conducting a hotel in connection with it. In 1873 he built one of the flour mills in Paradise.

For a time the Indians did not bother the settlers, and they were able to get in good crops and build better homes. On December 12, 1866, Company A of the U.S. Cavalry, commanded by Capt. Murry Davis, with Lt. John Lafferty assisting, occupied Fort Winfield. Exactly one month later Lafferty, on a patrol, ran into a band of Indians on the upper Little Humboldt. The cavalrymen killed several of them and destroyed their camp. In February the same officer drove another band out of a camp on the south fork of the same river, the Indians escaping into the deep snows of the Santa Rosas. In this same month Capt. Davis was transferred and Lafferty took command at Ft. Scott. More than any other single officer he made Paradise Valley secure for the white settlers—although it required some bitter fighting to convince the Paiutes they couldn't recover their pet valley.

When the redskins ran off stock belonging to Charles Gagg on March 13, 1867, Lafferty took fourteen troopers and rode in pursuit, in the middle of a fierce storm which obliterated tracks. On the ninth day he found the Indian camp, killed six of them, captured their arms and regained the stolen stock.

This one action gained him the respect of the braves—they realized apparently that Lafferty was an officer who never gave up. Consequently the Indians stayed away from Paradise most of the summer, although they still sought to gain revenge by killing when they found the opportunity.

Such an opportunity came on August 1. The Hon. J. A. Banks, of Dun Glen, who will be remembered as Humboldt's "pious" delegate to the State constitutional convention and speaker of the house at the second legislature, made a trip to Paradise with a Rev. Mr. Temple, a visitor to the area from New York City.

With Lt. Lafferty as host, Banks and the pastor went fishing on Cottonwood Creek. Banks wandered upstream by himself. Later the officer and the Rev. Temple returned to the fort, expecting the legislator to follow when he had caught as many fish as he wished. When he failed to appear after several hours, a search was made, and Banks' mutilated body was found along the stream. Soldiers sent in pursuit of the killers never caught up with them. Banks was buried in the fort cemetery with the Rev. Temple conducting services and Lafferty, angered at the incident, took his command and rode forth on a foray of retribution. He killed a number of Indians wherever he found them. It put a fear of the army into the Paiutes, but was Lafferty's last Nevada action. Lt. Joseph Karge arrived at Fort Scott with reinforcements to relieve him.

The Indians quickly put the new officer to a test, raiding the eastern part of the valley and running off all the stock in that area on November 19, 1867. Karge went in pursuit but, unaccustomed to Indian fighting, moved too closely in the deep snow and the marauders escaped with their booty.

It was a bitter winter, and the settlers had to subsist on their stores of supplies, wheat ground in coffee mills furnishing the bulk of their subsistence. The Indians, pleased over the success of their previous raid, repeated the operation as soon as spring gave an opportunity, running off all of M. W. Haviland's stock. The act was executed by a band under the guidance of a notorious renegade named Big Foot.

Lafferty, who still remained at the post in a subordinate position, begged Karge to give him command of the pursuing group, but the latter

was irked at the former commander because of pointed remarks he had
made about the handling of the November chase, and instead ordered a
young lieutenant named Hunter to go after the raiders.

When the commander gave the untried officer a detail consisting only
of Sergeant John Kelly, Corporal Thomas Reed and one private, Lafferty
—who knew his Humboldt Indians—protested that Karge was "committing
murder." The small detail was joined by a Paradise citizen named John
Rogers, who had lost a favorite horse.

The party picked up the trail at the mouth of Deep Canyon, a few
miles north, and the inexperienced officer recklessly led his men on a
dash up the canyon. The Indians met them with fire from ambush, the
officer, his sergeant and the one private being brought down with bullets.
The corporal and Rogers, only nicked by gunfire, lost their horses but
managed to gain the shelter of rocks.

Rogers volunteered to go for help, Corporal Reed staying to hold the
Indians away from the wounded men. The citizen managed to escape the
redskins and reach the fort. By the time the rescuers arrived, Big Foot
and his band had slipped away. Corporal Reed later received a medal
for his one-man stand against the band of braves.

What might have happened if Lafferty had still been in command at
the time is merely a matter of speculation. He soon was transferred to
Arizona, gained distinction in a number of fights with Cochise's Apaches,
lost part of his jaw and was disabled for life on October 20, 1869, and retired with high commendation from his commanding colonel.

However, Big Foot's raid was the last big one in Paradise, and during
the next two years only occasional small forays were made by little strag-
gling bands. These, too, ceased after the winter of 1869 and Paradise
settled down to peaceful expansion.

From then on until today Paradise Valley has been a true showplace
for Nevada. It's an easy one-hour drive from Winnemucca on paved
highways, and produces many thousands of the State's livestock. From
its early Basque, German, Italian and French settlers have stemmed
some of Nevada's best known and leading families.

The winter of 1866-67 was the last one during which pioneers had to
grind wheat in coffee mills as A. C. Adams erected the Silver State Flour
Mill in 1867. It still stands in good running condition. Battiste Recanzone
purchased the mill in the early 1880s and Paradise folk still boast that
its products took several first prizes at the St. Louis World Fair.

In addition to the Kempler store and hotel other businesses grew
in substantial buildings, many of which remain. According to Adell
"Casey" Jones, who lived there many years, Alfonso Pasquale, who delighted in fast horses and fancy dress, was the builder of many of the
structures which still remain in tree-shaded antiquity. Most of them are
still being used—the Fritz Buckingham family occupies the old Kempler
home. Fires have destroyed the Pasquale store, the Kempler store with

its dance floor mounted on springs, the three-story Auditorium Hotel and other buildings.

The old residence of William Stock still stands, however. Remember— he was one of that first group to arrive in 1864. Above the entrance gate hangs the ox yoke that Stock used when he hauled into the valley. It is the home of the Fred Stewart family—Mrs. Stewart was a daughter of Stock. Of course, much of Fort Winfield Scott is gone, but several of its buildings remain, used as the home and barns of the Buckingham family.

In 1880, the Thompson and West *History* reports "Paradise City now contains over 100 inhabitants, three hotels, two public halls, three stores for general merchandise, one drug store, one brewery, four saloons, one cabinet shop, two blacksmith shops, one physician, a barber, a harness-maker, carpenter, butcher and one school house." It also had its own newspaper, *The Paradise Record*, a 24-column four-sheet weekly.

At that time only three homicides had occurred—not counting deaths in Indian battles. On May 5, 1867, Cyrus Able met Joshua Morford on the road. The latter said, "We can't both live in the same valley" and commenced shooting. Able returned the fire with better aim, and Morford fell, mortally wounded. John McKinsey resisted arrest on September 24, 1869, and was shot dead by a member of the Sheriff's posse named Rafferty. On May 4, 1879, Charles W. Hymer shot and killed J. K. West. He was tried and executed, proving that Paradise, aside from the Indians, wasn't a lawless outpost.

Even the mad outbursts of its mining sector, when fairly rich ore was discovered in the Mt. Rose district in 1871, failed to upset its decorum. The strike brought on a rush of miners and rough characters during the mid-'70s, but they apparently confined their fireworks to the mining towns, Spring City, twelve miles from Paradise, Queen City, halfway between, and two smaller suburbs with the unusual names of Hard-scrabble and Gouge Eye.

Spring City burst into activity in 1871 as a real wild-eyed mining town. It never grew into the full flavor of its name, to become "a city," even in mining terms, probably never having more than 200 residents at the most. But it had seven saloons to slake the the thirst of its inhabitants. It had its own brewery, too. Spring City boasted two general stores, two hotels and one restaurant and, of all things, a book store—if you take the word of the Thompson and West *History*.

You don't find too much in the history books on Spring City's ac-tivities. Apparently, however, it was the opposite of its neighbor Paradise Valley in the matter of morals and peace.

One indication of its toughness is the fact that a suburb with the in-triguing name of Gouge Eye existed close by. It would be interesting to know the reason for this unusual mining camp moniker but so far it hasn't been discovered. Another later nearby mining town also had probably a very appropriate name—Hardscrabble. It was a title which would have suited a great many other mining towns which bore much more optimistic names.

It was because of Spring City, its neighbors, and Queen City which grew up on Martin's Creek about six miles from both the mining town and Paradise, that the whole region gained an undeserved wild reputation during the '70s.

Drury, in his delightful *Editor on the Comstock Lode* refers to a visit of one of the miners from the district to Virginia City. Drury wrote, "I can recall when an ornery stranger reeled into a C street saloon, and pounding on the bar with his six-shooter until the glasses danced, announced: 'I'm a roarin' ripsnorter from a hoorah camp, an' I can't be stepped on. I'm an angel from Paradise Valley and when I flap my wings there's a tornado loose. I'm a tough customer to clean up after. Give me some of your meanest whiskey, a whole lot of it, that tastes like bumble-bee stings pickled in vitriol. I swallered a cyclone for breakfast, a powder-mill for lunch, and haven't begin to cough yet. Don't crowd me.'

"The visitor having delivered himself of this gasconade, the bartender busied himself hunting for some fusel oil, while rubbing the glass with red pepper. One by one the loungers near the stove quietly slid out of the side door, and when the bad man turned around, the place was empty."

Queen City was so isolated in a canyon along Martin's Creek that it never had a chance to rival Paradise or Spring City in size or activity. Actually, it was a name given to the settlement which grew up around the Paradise Quartz Mill when it was built in 1874. This originally was a little 10-stamper with a roasting furnace—about like the plant Fair constructed for the Sheba at Star City. It was located along a creek with plentiful water supply, to handle ores from the surrounding mines.

But Queen City wasn't destined to reign long on its canyon throne. A population count in 1879 showed 100 residents, but in the following year there were only 18 and there were no stores open. It probably wasn't much later that these, too, were gone and Queen City began disintegrating into the few dumps and ruins which mark the spot today. During its life the mill, according to the records, produced a total amount of bullion estimated at $235,000.

The Paradise Mining District, originally called the Mt. Rose District, produced a total of $1,545,362 in silver and gold between 1879 and 1912, according to the University of Nevada bulletin on mineral resources. The figure evidently does not include the Spring City-Queen City output in the earlier years. Practically all of the total came from the Paradise Valley Mining Company shafts at Spring City.

Recently some of the Paradise Valley residents have been fostering efforts to revive mining interest in the region—though, one wonders why, when it is one of the largest beef producing sections in the state and an agricultural paradise still.

Of all the places in Nevada where visitors may find "Old Nevada" in its finest glory, there are none more easily reached, more hospitable, or having as much history in sight, as Paradise Valley. It's worth a visit anytime—but spring and early fall are the best times to make the trip to the Paiute's beloved "Yamosopo," which that first party of wandering prospectors so appropriately rechristened "Paradise Valley."

Interior of Blacksmith Shop of William Luke,
Virginia City, 1860-61

—Courtesy Nevada State Historical Society.

PART FOUR

The Rambunctious Reese River Rush

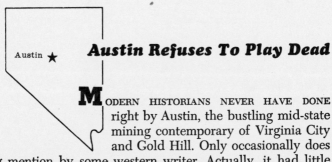

Austin Refuses To Play Dead

MODERN HISTORIANS NEVER HAVE DONE right by Austin, the bustling mid-state mining contemporary of Virginia City and Gold Hill. Only occasionally does it get a passing mention by some western writer. Actually, it had little or no connection with the Comstock Lode—economically, geographically, or in any other way. It was a modern "metropolis" on its own account and was discovered separately, nearly two hundred miles east of the Comstock by a Pony Express rider. It spawned far more mineral strikes than Virginia Citians dreamed existed and probably peddled more phony stock than any other nineteenth century western mining town.

It is located almost in the geographical center of Nevada, astride the old Pony-Express-Overland Stage route, which transcontinental U.S. 50 follows closely today, and it still refuses to play dead.

Just a few years ago its couple of hundred residents fought Battle Mountain to a standstill when the larger community on the railroad attempted to gain the county seat. Austin doesn't even attempt to lure tourist dollars by claiming to be a ghost town.

It is located 6147 feet high in a canyon on a pass through the towering Toiyabe range, and is about as far away from Nevada population centers as a town can get. Yet the handful of citizens remaining from the more than 10,000 which once was there now receive distant television programs via a translator and in 1950 finally got sixty-cycle power so they could use ordinary electrical appliances.

While Virginia City was cutting a wide swath during the bonanza days, Austin was the hub of a vast kingdom of satellite towns which developed from mineral discoveries over a widespread, unexplored district. Altogether, Austin spawned at least four other county seats—seven if you count its "grandchildren."

The fact that Virginia City has received practically all of the publicity about Nevada through the years never bothered Austin's citizens. When Oscar Lewis wrote the only book about the Reese River City a few years ago the citizens weren't even annoyed when he titled it *The Town That Died Laughing*. One old-timer reflected the attitude of the residents, "It's a good title even if we aren't all dead yet."

Austin was independent from the Comstock right from the start. Its hidden treasure of silver was discovered by William M. Talcott, a Pony Express rider stationed at isolated Jacobs Station just west of the Reese River—not by some disappointed prospector who failed to stake a location on the Comstock. The unusual part of Talcott's find was that he wasn't even looking for ore, he was on a wood-cutting chore and picked up a couple of pieces of outcropping, wondering what it was.

Talcott gathered his samples on May 2, 1862, and gave them to a friend named O'Neil, who had a ranch in Washoe Valley. The latter turned them over later to another fellow named Vanderbosch, and asked him to have them assayed. They proved to be fairly rich, so O'Neill and Vanderbosch headed for Jacobs Station and told Talcott what they had learned.

These three, with two others, John and "Wash" Jacobs, went to the spot, made locations and organized the Reese River Mining District—which embraced more territory than any before, extending more than one hundred miles in every direction. One of the claims the party located, the Oregon, later yielded ore running as high as $7000 to the ton.

Accidental discoveries of golcondas are legend in history, but it is improbable that any were more unintentional than the Reese River strike, because Pony Express riders were in too big a hurry and too busy dodging Indians along the way to stop and do any prospecting. The route, laid out first in 1855 by Major Howard Egan, and later by Major Simpson, led right through Pony Canyon where Talcott picked up his samples. He named his discovery location "The Pony."

When word spread about the new strike—and such information in some uncanny manner seemed to travel with the speed of lightning in those days of slow communications—the rush to the new district was soon in full swing. Very quickly a collection of tents, shacks and dugouts sheltered five hundred men at the foot of the canyon. The town which sprung up was called Clifton. When the population became too crowded it was suggested that the townsite be moved to a better location in exchange for work on the road from Clifton to the site.

David E. Buel, who was to become one of the civic and business leaders of the community, and who had arrived among the first, was from Texas and suggested that the new site be named after the founder and hero of his home state, Stephen F. Austin. It was.

Less than six months after Talcott's discovery there were so many people in the district that they requested the legislature to create a new county named after Colonel Frederick W. Lander, the Paiute war hero who had been in charge of building the wagon road across Nevada—the highway that became the Overland Stage Route.

The legislature obliged, slicing large portions from the original Churchill and Humboldt counties to create Lander County which at the time took in practically all of the southeastern half of the territory.

Jacobs Station, which had been named for George Washington Jacobs, agent of the Overland Mail Company, was designated as temporary county seat, with the provision that voters could choose the permanent site at the next general election. Busy, booming Austin easily won the seat when the 'Sixty-three election was held.

Some idea of the rapidity with which Austin grew is indicated by the fact that lots, which a year before had sold for a song, or could be obtained by two or three days' work on the road, were going in the fall of 1863 for as high as $8000. By this time the International Hotel had been built and there were 366 houses, reported the ever-present tabulator who popped up in every new mining town. Population was optimistically guessed at more than 10,000, six mills had been erected and were grinding away, and Reese River stocks were being sold on the San Francisco exchange. A school had been opened in a tent, a volunteer fire department organized and, strange as it may seem, a Young Men's Christian Association organized—the only place such a group is found in early Nevada history.

With every square inch of ground located for miles in every direction, Austin became the gathering place and focus for some of the greatest swindles of mining history. Within three years, more than six thousand Reese River mining and milling companies had been incorporated. Easterners and investors in foreign countries, especially England, were suckers for anything bearing a Nevada label, so in addition to silver corporations, stocks were peddled for freight companies, irrigation, farming and stock raising projects and waterworks.

Probably the topper in all these swindles was the Reese River Navigation Co., which proposed, in a gaudy prospectus, to return huge dividends by loading the ore aboard "barges and towing them down the Reese River" to the railroad at Battle Mountain. Thousands bought stock in this ephemeral phony. A major portion of the year the stream bearing John Reese's name would hardly float a canoe, let alone a barge. There is an old, old story which goes this way: "What was that?" asked a passenger when the stage hit a rut and made a tiny splash. The driver answered wryly, "Gents, don't be alarmed, we just crossed the Reese River."

Another delightful phony promotion was noted by the late Senator James Scrugham in his *History of Nevada*. A prospectus, published in London to promote a wildcat mine, described the property as "being within half a mile of a railway"—although the Central Pacific was just being built one hundred miles north—and claimed the mine was in the "immediate vicinity of some of the famous properties at Virginia City and Gold Hill," which were two hundred miles away.

The gullibility of those in other parts of the country was well displayed in Austin's never-forgotten Methodist fund-raising campaign to build a church. When the deacons received a great many mining shares as donations they decided to organize the Methodist Mining Company and sell the stocks in the east. Some sources say that "more than a million dollars worth" was purchased by good church members. It is very probable the faith of many of these investing devout Wesleyans was shaken to the foundations when they discovered that many of the donated stock certificates were worthless scraps of paper. However, Austin Methodists were able to say with great pride for many years that they had the "handsomest church in Nevada."

With money flowing in plentifully, Austin was a fun-loving place, with men willing to pay for a chuckle. One of the first fund-raising gimmicks of many, culminating in the famous Gridley sack of flour, was the Buel shoe auction. Dave Buel, the man who named the town, had immense feet. In 1864 when the women campaigned to raise funds for a school, Buel donated a pair of his boots to be auctioned. The crowd loved the idea, and amidst a flood of hilarious wisecracks the oversized brogans were sold over and over to those in a crowd which gathered on Main Street, netting $106—which was a mighty good price for a pair of shoes even in those days.

Austin's history is probably more complete than that of any other pioneer Nevada town because of the *Reese River Reveille*. It was established by a William C. Phillips on May 16, 1863—barely more than a year after Talcott found his first out-croppings. Right off the reel it proved a success, even at fifty cents a copy. Phillips didn't stay long, selling the *Reveille* in September to O. L. C. and J. D. Fairchild, who made it a tri-weekly. They brought in Adair Wilson and Myron Angel, two noted bonanza days members of Nevada's great newspaper clan, as editors. It shortly became a daily. Angel later edited the invaluable Thompson and West *History of Nevada, 1881*—the only reliable book of early information on Nevada outside of the Comstock Lode area.

Since Austin was on the transcontinental telegraph line, news was one thing the residents didn't have to depend upon San Francisco to ship across the mountains and desert. The *Reveille* boasted that it printed "hot" news two days before papers bearing the same items could be received from the coast or Virginia City.

The *Reveille* tooted a loud horn, sounding Austin's glories through booms and busts and has never since halted publication come fire, flood, or decline of population. Complete files of this great pioneer newspaper fortunately have been preserved—one of the very few of the early papers of which this can be said.

In 1933 William M. Thatcher, then a seventy-year-old attorney, took over as editor and lived on the job, keeping the *Reveille* going until his retirement in 1949. He was the recognized oracle for Central Nevada through these years.

Jock Taylor, another veteran newsman succeeded him, and keeps the *Reveille* a gay, snappy weekly still. He was elected president of the Nevada Newspaper Publishers in 1957. Jock can wield just as virile a pen as his predecessors when the occasion warrants. One thing he won't stand for is the frequent claim by Lucius Beebe and Charles Clegg that their revived Virginia City *Territorial Enterprise* is the "oldest newspaper in the state."

He editorialized in 1957, ". . . In recent months the *Enterprise* has been sniffing around a new telephone pole, getting closer and closer until finally it ventured to lean up and lift its—voice . . . The *Territorial En-*

terprise was established in Genoa in 1858, later moved to Carson City and finally to Virginia City . . . it continued publication for a long time rather feebly, up to the early part of this century . . . and died entirely. It remained dead for thirty-six years—and a thing that is dead cannot grow older . . . let the *Enterprise* call itself the first newspaper in Nevada —but never the oldest one."

A rather sad note was appended to the *Reveille's* long, long history in January 1957, when Taylor announced on the front page that the paper's most lengthy subscription had been terminated by death. This uninterrupted subscription to the paper was taken out by Joseph Moss, one of the early pioneers, a couple of days before the first issue in May 1863. Upon his death it had been continued without a break by his son, Joseph Jr. When the latter died in December, 1956, the ninety-three-and-a-half year subscription ended.

The *Reveille* recorded Austin's first death, a Tennessean who succumbed to lung fever, in June 1863, and the first birth, a son born to Mr. and Mrs. W. M. Middleton, about the same time.

Violent crime was a common occurrence in most of the early mining towns and caused little excitement. But Austin had a crazy one-man crime wave on the night of July 18, 1863, which seems outstanding. The perpetrator was a fellow named William Cornell, recently arrived from Illinois. For some unexplained reason he had developed a delusion that everybody was trying to kill him.

Cornell's carnage commenced when his partner, William Meligan, stuck his head through their tent flap about nine o'clock that night to see if he was there. Cornell clouted Meligan with an ax, inflicting an ugly gash over his eye and knocking him to the ground. The madman then rushed across the street to Dunham's saloon, swinging right and left at everybody present. All managed to duck his blows—one shot was fired, but missed the wild ax wielder, who ran into the street.

He took a slash at a passerby, John Capron, cutting all the tendons above his left elbow, chased a group of men into a store and clopped a fellow from Dayton known as "Frenchy" in the head, inflicting a deep slash from the top of the scalp to the neck. It is a noteworthy example of the toughness of those old boys, to record that Frenchy walked to the nearest saloon, a bit groggy from the blow, gulped down a stiff drink, mounted his horse and rode down the hill to Clifton to get his wound dressed. In the meantime, Cornell clouted E. Anderson, another newcomer from Sweetland, California, and gashed his head above the left ear, carved the next man he met, Charlie Ludlow, in the same way and ran down the street until he met Billy Mills, of Clifton, who had the whole right side of his scalp raised by a wild swing of the sharp weapon.

Cornell continued his carnage as he raced down the hill. A barber named Hammersmith saved his head by flinging up his right arm, getting it and his hand cut, a fellow named Powell received a gash in the back and Charlie Trueman, falling sidewise to escape an ax blow, suffered only the loss of the breast pocket of his coat.

At this point, for some unknown reason, Cornell reversed his weapon and commenced hitting his victims with the handle, knocking several almost senseless, but causing no further serious damage. He ran through Clifton and headed across the valley toward Jacobsville. A hastily organized posse, which was pursuing him, was kept so busy picking up the wounded that they lost his trail in the darkness.

The following morning his body was found about a mile west of Clifton. A gash had been made on the back of his head by the ax, and his throat was cut from ear to ear. It was always assumed that he made the fatal wounds himself, nobody being found who had seen him after he raced as fast as he could run into the dark from Clifton.

Austin rode high, wide and free, and was full of gay life and doings. Its streets were busy places at all times. Main Street in its early days featured one sight to which residents never became quite accustomed—a string of camels plodding up the road, carrying heavy loads of salt for use in the mills. The humped desert animals never were a success on Nevada's rock deserts because the sharp stones cut their feet severely. Hauling salt more than one hundred miles over the rough trails with sore feet didn't make them any happier.

During their layover they were kept tied to a hitching rail next to Charlie Holbrook's store, where they sighed, grunted, snapped and spat at all who came close. When a nearer salt supply was found, in Great Smoky Valley, the camels passed from Austin's scene.

The *Reveille's* editor loved to gloat about Austin's weather: "Cool and pleasant as can be. People living on the Humboldt, Truckee and Carson rivers have our unconditional sympathy. There they doze in hot air, and sweat and scratch and fan themselves and fight bedbugs, mosquitoes, fleas and tarantulas; drink ice water until cholera infantum, etc., comes and then gulp pain killer till it kills them. Yea, verily, sympathy."

This sounds delightful until compared with another item which appeared in a March issue, which recorded the fact that "the heaviest snowfall of the season occurred last night." It was sixteen inches deep. This wasn't unusual; owners of buildings considered long tin troughs, slanting from the roofs across the sidewalks, a standard necessity to chute the heavy snow from the tops of their buildings to the street. Many of these tin "tongues sticking out" are still in place, and elicit constant inquiries by tourists passing through on the Lincoln Highway.

Lander County weather wasn't always delightful, and sometimes it caused real problems. The *Reveille* was happy to report three weeks after the "big snowstorm" that "The mule schooners which have been in the mud of the Reese River Valley during the last three weeks, are now daily drifting into port and discharging their cargoes in front of the anxious merchants of town. Quite a number of the staple articles are getting painfully scarce and discouragingly high in price. If fair weather continues, it is likely that needles and pins, sardines, nutmegs, matches, cigarettes, pills, etc., will be cheaper than they have been for some time past. High freights are a great burden to a community."

The brittle pages of old issues of the *Reveille* present as clear a picture of early-day Austin as any movie studio could ever devise. Those old-time editors duly noted almost everything that happened—everything. Researching among the *Reveille's* pages is a gay frolic, not a task.

This item for instance: "ARRESTED—A gentle bibulous damsel, recently from the base range (meaning the Toiyabes), who was not conducting herself with becoming propriety and decorum, was arrested in one of the saloons of the city and locked in the corporation hotel (the jail) about noon today."

Those editors missed nothing—"Mrs. Pringle has received a supply of Dolly Varden hats and the exquisite flowers and lovely trimming to suit."

They didn't lack appreciation either—"THANKS—We are under obligation to John King and George Watts for a fine mess of sheepherders oysters, fresh from the shell." And this, "SUCCESSFUL TRIP—Mr. W. B. Wilson, accompanied by some lady friends, returned from a successful and pleasant fishing excursion to the headwaters of the Reese River last night. The party . . . caught 379 fish while gone. Of these Mr. Wilson caught all but 373 . . . We fell heir to a couple of dozen or so last evening which we disposed of with much relish."

Neither did the editor neglect to note the doings and sayings of the children with such tidbits as this one—"LITERALLY CORRECT—In our public school the geography exercises are elaborated by questions and answers relative to the form of government of the different countries described. Yesterday the teacher propounded the question—'Who elects the President of the United States?'—when a bright little shaver about the size of a vinegar cruet, the son of a prominent Democrat of this city, immediately shouted out, 'the black Republicans.' He was sent to the head."

Politics were a major subject of argument with the Civil War raging in the east. Reuel Gridley, a grocer in upper Austin, supported David Buel, the Texas Democrat who had named the town, in the race for mayor against a young Republican merchant named Charles Holbrook. Dr. R. C. Herrick was a backer of the latter. The pair arranged a wager which called for the loser to carry a sack of flour the mile and a quarter from Clifton, at the bottom of the canyon, to upper Austin.

The Gridley sack of flour became one of Nevada's greatest historical treasures. On April 21, 1864—two days after election, with flags and a band, Gridley having lost the wager, hoisted the sack on his shoulder, marched to Clifton, where all in the parade stopped for refreshment at the Bank Exchange Saloon, then retraced the march back uphill to the front of Grimes and Gibson's saloon, where a stand had been erected.

There the sack was auctioned and sold over and over until a total of $4349 had been realized for the Sanitary Fund.

Towns in the Comstock heard about the sack of flour and Mark Twain, an old friend in Iowa, urged Gridley to bring it there and sell it for the fund. He did and continued to San Francisco for the same purpose, then to the east. He ended his journey at the St. Louis World's Fair. The Gridley sack of flour had become nationally famous and had raised a total for the fund variously estimated from $100,000 to $275,000.

The Sanitary Fund was the forerunner of the American Red Cross. Gridley's flour-selling stunt may have been the very first of those national fund campaigns for altruistic organizations which now plague the public continuously.

The aftermath was sad. Gridley returned home from St. Louis heavily in debt from his altruistic journey, his health broken, and his business slackened to such a degree that his partners withdrew. Gridley left Austin two years later, in 1866, and opened a store in Paradise, California. He died there on November 24, 1870. It wasn't until 1882, when the Grand Army of the Republic, realizing his unselfish contribution to the relief of suffering among the war wounded, raised funds for the erection of a marble marker over his grave. It was dedicated on September 9, 1887.

The old Gridley store building still stands unused in upper Austin. Recently steps have been taken to preserve it as a historical attraction.

Culture came earlier to Austin than to most mining towns. The principal reason for this was the community's location, right on the shorter "southern" stage route to the west. The Lander County seat was the first "big town" reached by westbound pioneers—they were still coming in a stream during the 'Sixties—after leaving Salt Lake City.

The excitement of the Reese River rush and the booming growth of the town caused many families to decide on settling there instead of going on to California. That brought a great many women and children into the town's population earlier than in many of the others. Where there are women and their offspring, churches and Sunday schools become an immediate necessity. They did in Austin.

Gridley, the grocer, organized a Methodist Sunday School in July 1863, the first formal religious group in town. This pleased the Nevada bishop of this faith and he made the trip two hundred miles across desert and mountains to conduct the town's first religious service in August of that year.

Bishop Joseph Cruickshank Talbot, of the Protestant Episcopal Church, realized that among the fast growing population of Austin there was certain to be a large number of persons from the long-settled Atlantic Coast section, stronghold of that faith. He visited Austin early in the fall of 1863 and held services. A lot was donated at the corner of Paul and Pine Streets for a church building. Until a minister could arrive, D. N. Goodwin brought the Episcopalians together in the courthouse for regular services, which he conducted as a layman. It wasn't until 1878 that St. George's Church was built. It is still being used.

In the meantime, the Roman Catholic diocese had taken early cognizance of the large number of its faithful residents in the new town and conducted services there, too, with the beautiful St. Augustine's Church being built in 1866. Services have been held regularly in this venerable building ever since.

This influx of church goers didn't stop the rougher element from pursuing their playfully lethal pastimes. The *Reveille* on November 29, 1863 noted succinctly that two murders and "one shooting (probably fatal)" had occurred during the last twenty-four hours. The editor "deplored" the too-frequent use of firearms for "trivial provocation" and declared that as long as ruffians insisted on making arsenals of themselves that "peaceful citizens are compelled to carry weapons in self-defense." The editor also expressed himself strongly against celebrators "giving vent to their exuberance with wild shooting." But roaring guns couldn't halt the march of "culture" in this isolated island of humanity. The town's first "Grand Ball" was held at the International Hotel in Thanksgiving in 1863 to inaugurate the town's lively future social life.

The *Reveille* editorialized in favor of planting flowers and trees, cleaning sidewalks, and "eliminating some of the cur dogs which roam the streets." This was to be a continuing campaign through the years.

Rather sarcastically, the editor headed an item "GOOD GIRL!" I read, "Josephine Helen Mansfield is going to lecture on women's rights." During the nineteenth century lecturers were the rage, and in the 'Sixties one of the most popular was Artemus Ward. They didn't have any Hooper rating system as they do in radio and television today, but if there had been Ward would have been right at the top. In 1864 he made a trip west and stopped in Austin.

There was no hall in the town but Ward was prevailed upon to give a lecture in an unroofed, partially completed store building. A large crowd gathered as the noted entertainer walked up the street from his hotel carrying a lantern to light the way.

Miners at Big Creek, fourteen miles south in the mountains, urged him to come to their town and give a lecture. Ward's manager was dubious, pointing out that there had been considerable Indian trouble on the outlying roads, but they made the trip. Ward lectured before one hundred and fifty miners, who paid two dollars apiece to sit on kegs, boxes and the floor in the town's largest establishment, the brush-roofed Young America Saloon.

On the way home Ward and his manager were waylaid by a "band of Indians." Both were dragged from their buggy and forced to their knees. One brave asked the humorist his name, and when he replied, "Artemus Ward," the Indian said, "Uh, talkee man!" Holding a knife threateningly the brave ordered, "Talkee now!"

Teeth chattering, Ward commenced one of his lectures, the "Indians" interrupting with howls of glee. As they yelled louder Ward had to shout to make himself heard. He put his best efforts into the talk in a strenuous attempt to pacify the redskins. When he reached the climax one turned disgustedly away and said, "Oh, bosh."

Then Ward realized it was all a joke—some of his new friends in Austin had masqueraded and ridden out to have a little fun with the "tenderfoot" from the east. The party returned to Austin, joking and laughing—but it is reported that it took Ward some time to appreciate the full humor of the prank.

In 1865 Austin received another boost to its aesthetic program. The new Odd Fellows Hall was completed, giving the town a place to stage theatrical performances. It was opened by a husband and wife team named Chapman, who offered such dramas as *Black Eyed Susan* and *Reveille*. Other traveling theatrical troupes crossing Nevada made Austin a regular stop. Among prominent stars of the period who appeared in the Odd Fellow's Hall were such well known thespians as Charles Pope, Walter Laman, Virginia Howard and many others. They all drew capacity houses.

The brightest flower to bud in this isolated silver-producing mountain town was a little girl who grew up there. Her name was Emma Wixom, who had been born the daughter of a physician at Alphia Diggings in California on February 7, 1859.

She arrived in Austin with her family around her fifth birthday, in the spring of 1864. Bystanders watching the Gridley Sack of Flour parade applauded her as she marched in that historic event singing *John Brown's Body*. Her father served as one of the auctioneers of the sack of flour.

The *Reveille* took enthusiastic notice of her vocal ability on December 27, 1870. As a girl of ten she had sung on the same program in the Methodist Church with Baron von Netzer, a vocalist of international fame. The editor of the *Reveille* wrote, "Considering the extreme youthfulness of the gifted cantatrice and the few opportunities afforded to train her voice, it really was a rich treat to listen to her almost pure soprano executed with a finish truly astonishing in one so young, and not often met with outside professional circles."

This proved to be more than hometown enthusiasm, as the future proved. Emma's mother died a couple of years later, and Dr. Wixom sent the girl to Mills College in Oakland to further her education. In 1877 she went to Europe with a group from the school and studied under Madame Marchesi in Vienna, who described her voice as "wonderful."

Her father followed her to Europe to handle his daughter's affairs when her success seemed assured. Shortly, she made her first concert tour, becoming an instant success, acclaimed everywhere.

Fond of her home state and never forgetting her childhood pleasure in pony rides on the desert amid the wild flowers, she adopted the professional name of "Emma Nevada," instead of an Italian or French pseudonym as was the style in those days.

She was highly popular throughout the world in operatic and musical circles and returned in triumph to the United States in 1885. It was almost impossible for her to meet the demands of those who wished to hear her concerts. Tickets sold at a premium.

She returned to the scene of her childhood on December 4, 1885, twenty-one years after she had first arrived in the Lander County seat— on a special train. She was met at the station by the whole population and rode in a decorated carriage up the street from Clifton over a route well remembered by her, the Lander band leading the way, playing *Home, Sweet Home.*

That night, amidst a flood of floral tributes, Austin's own "little girl" sang a concert in the Methodist Church, the whole town attending, those unable to get inside crowding around the windows to listen in awe.

Austin was justly proud of its "little Emma" and stories of her triumphs were blazoned across many later front pages of the *Reveille.* She returned to Europe, married Dr. Raymond Palmer, a resident of Paris, and was chosen to sing at the coronation of King George. Through her life she probably was Nevada's greatest ambassador of goodwill in Europe, repeatedly telling her friends of the beauties of her home state. She died in Liverpool on June 26, 1940 at eighty-one years of age.

With all its culture, everything in Austin wasn't a continuous parade of sweetness and light.

Rufus B. Anderson, an eighteen-year old youth, gained a slight niche in Austin history by killing Noble T. Slocum on May 5, 1868. Anderson was "hung" on October 30, after being convicted. It was the execution that put his name into history. The noose was improperly adjusted the first time and the youth landed on his feet below the gallows. The same thing happened the second time and the crowd began to demand that he be spared. But the third attempt was successful, the noose held, and he strangled his way to the hereafter. Most Austinites were disgusted over such a bungled exhibition.

Bars and parlors of Pony Canyon had another tidbit to discuss in August of 1868 when a gent named Vance blew into town proclaiming he was a bad-bad-boy—as many with inferiority complexes were wont to do in those days. He strutted around bars, until finally he spotted a "victim," a tough little Hibernian known as "Irish Tom" Carberry, quiet when sober but with a reputation for coming out on top in shooting scrapes at Aurora, before he moved to Austin.

When Vance challenged him, Carberry, being sober, announced that he wasn't carrying a gun. The badman told him to get one and "Come back shooting."

Irish Tom, never one to back away from a braggart, obliged—obtaining his pistol and sauntering back up the street. The "hot gun" was watching for him and opened fire immediately, missing five shots as Irish Tom steadily advanced until within close range, when he laid his gun across his arm, aimed and steadily drilled Vance through the heart. By this time law and order had come to Austin. Tom was arrested—but it took a jury only a few minutes to acquit him.

The Lander County metropolis wasn't neglected on stage robberies. The *Reveille* reported June 27, 1872—"On the morning of the 26th the Eureka stage was again stopped near Mineral Hill and robbed. One man did the job. He stepped from the roadside and said 'Stop.' He had a six-shooter. The highwayman said 'Pass out the box.' The driver 'passed' as directed . . . That was all there was of it. The operation caused no confusion and but a few seconds delay. The passengers inside hadn't time to get scared."

On August 3 of the same year the Battle Mountain stage was held up about halfway between the towns. The *Reveille* reported, "The road agents . . . ordered the passengers to alight and obliged them to stand in a row by the side of the road with their hands pointed toward the firmament while one of their number 'went through' the party to the tune of about one thousand dollars in coin and watches. The treasure box was broken open . . . nothing of consequence was found in it. The robbers then broke open and examined all the baggage on the stage, even broaching a box of eggs in their search of concealed treasure, without, however, finding anything to pay them for their trouble."

Floods were one of the town's recurrent major problems. Austin is located in a canyon considerably downhill from the ridge and sudden thaws send deluges funneling down, filling business houses with mud and damaging property. Two years in a row, in 1868 and 1869, the town suffered severe flood damage. Merchants became accustomed to piling sandbags in front of their places to divert the rushing waters.

A cloudburst broke over the higher levels on August 13, 1878, and all the previous floods seemed trickles in comparison. Water, ranging from three to ten feet deep roared down Main Street, sweeping sidewalks, awnings, merchandise, cows, wagons and buildings with it. Main Street was gutted, and buildings and houses were three and four feet deep in mud. The *Reese River Reveille* building was completely destroyed, its type and equipment washed away and buried in mud. But in less than a week the paper continued publication—you couldn't keep the *Reveille* from tooting regularly.

A couple of years later Austin, solidly built from the start, had its first fire—a common scourge in most mining towns. It started in mid-morning on August 9, 1881, in a watchmaker's shop, and swept Main Street with a wind blowing up the canyon. The *Reveille* listed as destroyed the Odd Fellow's and Masonic Halls, telegraph office, Elrod

Block, post office, Wright's Drug Store, Parrett and McGamb's Blacksmith Shop, a livery stable, photo gallery, two barber shops and five saloons.

This aided in increasing the speed of tobogganing silver prices and a general business decline. Many of the silver towns in the Toiyabes had proven worthless, and many others were simply the result of promotion schemes. John Muir reported in 1878, "In one canyon of the Toiyabes range near Austin, I found no less than five dead towns without a single inhabitant. The streets and blocks of 'real estate' graded on the hillsides are rapidly falling back into the wilderness."

During the lush days more than $50,000,000 worth of minerals had been shipped out by wagon from the Reese River district over the long, rough trip to the Central Pacific at Battle Mountain.

So, is the saga of the Nevada Northern Railway one of frustration, near-failure and final futility. State Senator M. J. Farrell was the major power behind its construction, which he believed would re-establish withering Austin as a mining center. He pushed the 1875 legislature into passing a bill [over the veto of Gov. "Broadhorns" Bradley, who opposed all railroad subsidies] encouraging its construction and permitting Lander County to issue $200,000 worth of bonds to finance the project.

Various delays prevented construction, but Farrell continued to urge the project, until it became generally known as "Farrell's Folly." His persistence finally prevailed and the Nevada Central Railroad Company was organized on September 2, 1879. The clinching argument for building the road was the acquisition of most of Lander properties by the Manhattan Silver Mining Co., headed by the famed Stokes brothers, Anson and J. W., of Philadelphia.

Construction from the Battle Mountain end of the line, where the three-foot wide narrow gauge road would connect with the Central Pacific, commenced immediately. Only about five months remained—all of it in winter—to build nearly one hundred miles of roadbed before the expiration date in the bill.

The construction crews fought blizzards, frozen ground and other obstacles to complete the line. With only a day left before the deadline the rails were still several miles north of Austin. Workers struggled day and night to "reach the Austin city limits" under the time allotted. Otherwise the money from the bonds could not be used to help pay for the construction.

When all seemed doomed, a special meeting of the Austin City Council assembled on the final evening before the midnight deadline to seek a solution. Everybody felt that a railroad would save the Lander county seat from the creeping state of desuetude into which it had sunk. Some nimble mind suggested a solution, which eagerly was adopted and rapidly made into law—the City Council unanimously passed an emergency measure annexing a strip of uninhabited land northward far enough to meet the point the tracks would reach by twelve o'clock.

Then the Council adjourned and led a large and a hastily assembled delegation of citizens several miles north on the Battle Mountain road to the edge of the newly-stretched city limits. Shortly, it greeted the arrival of the tracks to the "City of Austin," with fireworks and no doubt, firewater, with only minutes to spare. The race against time was won only because of the council's last hour emergency action—whether it was legal or not. A couple of days later the railroad actually reached its terminus at Clifton, which long since had been absorbed into the limits of growing Austin.

The mining company discovered that the cream had been skimmed long before in the mines, and actual shipping on the new railroad never did reach the volume Farrell and its backers had expected. When the Stokes Company ceased operations in 1887, the trains chugged less frequently and more sporadically between Austin and Battle Mountain until the franchise expired in 1938, when the final toot of an engine whistle was heard along the Reese River. Two or three years afterward the rails were pulled out to become steel in Uncle Sam's war machines. Many old timers insist that it was no misnomer to call the Nevada Central "Farrell's Folly." The fact that only $250,000 worth of minerals came out of the Lander County mines during the first 20 years of this century are strong indication that they probably were correct.

Austin still boasts one of the state's most unusual early-day relics in the Stokes Castle, which stands like an abandoned lighthouse in lonely grandeur amidst the junipers and piñons atop a hill a mile west of Austin.

It ranks as one of Nevada's boom-time enigmas. Nobody has learned exactly why the Stokes brothers chose this lonesome crest for the location of their costly fifty foot-square cut-stone aerie back in 1897. Austin and its surrounding silver towns still were active, and the Stokes had heavy interests in them and other properties in the area.

First they had to cut a road up the canyon to the site, then haul all the supplies and materials in by wagon. The castle was the wonder of the area—and still is a highly unusual ghostly memento of the bonanza days when folks did unusual things.

With unlimited land to spread over, the Stokes restricted their palace to a small ground area and went up three stories. The kitchen and dining room were on the ground level. The second floor was an immense living room and bath. The third story contained the bedrooms and another bath. The roof could be used as a lofty porch. The windows were built deep and narrow, and originally had balconies.

The Stokes used the castle briefly for a residence until production declined and they, like so many others, went away, leaving their strange edifice to the winds and weather.

One of the favorite legends for the location and design of the castle is that the Stokes brothers suspected one of their foremen of high-grading large quantities of rich ore and built where and how they did to watch shipping operations. No basis for this belief has ever been uncovered.

Being close to U.S. 50 the castle has been an attraction to tourists who, through the years, have believed strange tales about its past, or conceived some of their own, until today it's difficult to sort fact from fiction.

Austin happily still lives. It never did die, laughing or otherwise. And it's still the county seat, regardless of repeated attempts of Battle Mountain, now the big town of the county, to wrest the prized honor from it.

Austin's importance in the early development of this state never did receive the credit it deserved. Actually, some of the incidents told here have reached print credited to its gaudier and more raucous Comstock contemporary.

Any town which can sire three-score offspring, not to mention second and third generation bonanzas such as Tonopah and Goldfield, deserves its place in the sun. It was a mighty good town—and still is, even though it is only a shadow of what it once was.

Raiding of a High-Grader's Cache, Goldfield
—Courtesy of E. W. Darrah.

Ione, in 1897

Hamilton ★

A Prolific Municipal Clan

FAMILY TREES GENERALLY ARE A BORE. Maybe that's why all the historians and writers seen to have skipped the largest and one of the most important in Nevada, the copious genealogy of the Reese River municipal clan. Its short-lived sire was the Pony Express station of Jacobsville but the real fountainhead was its precocious offspring, Austin. It spawned three score or more of bustling, busy mining and mill towns hundreds of miles in all directions.

Some were puny infants, as might be expected in the raucous mining excitement of the 1860s, and died early in life. Others did themselves proud, becoming populous and rich. Four, like their "daddy," became county seats.

In Old Testament style, one example could be written in this manner —Jacobsville begat Austin, Austin begat Ione, Ione begat Belmont, Belmont begat Tonopah, and Tonopah begat Goldfield. Other county seats Austin sired were Eureka and Hamilton, which was succeeded by Ely. All of these were fountainheads of considerable families themselves and produced many municipal descendants, so you find Austin's apparitional offspring all over the mid-state map of early-day Nevada. Go any direction from the Lander County seat and you will discover them in various stages of somber decay. Many of the spooky, tumbling remains were solid brick and stone structures which now are skeletons or piles of rubble. Others were of a more transitory nature and evidences of their existence are more gossamery and vague. All, regardless of how illusory or immaterial their physical remains may be, are shadowy evidence that a lusty life prevailed in this vast, isolated area during the middle part of the nineteenth century.

Hardly anywhere, except in the brittle pages of old newpaper files in dusty storerooms of Nevada's county recorders, will be found on-the-spot descriptions of that century-ago mad, merry scramble for nature's riches which was as uncontrolled as a prairie fire

One who did leave us a clear word picture of the scene was John Muir in his *Steep Trails*. He wrote in 1878 this delightful, but apparently little known, comment on the phenomena which was the Nevada silver rush.

"The dead mining excitements of Nevada were far more intense and destructive in their action than those of California, because the prizes at stake were greater, while more skill was required to gain them. . . .

"Mining discoveries and progress, retrogression and decay, seem to have crowded more closely against each other here than in any other portion of the globe. Some one of the band of adventurous prospectors . . .

would discover some rich ore—how much or how little mattered not at first. These specimens fell among excited seekers after wealth like sparks in gunpowder, and in a few days the wilderness was disturbed with the noisy clang of miners and builders. A little town would then spring up, and before anything like a careful survey of any particular lode would be made, a company would be formed, and expensive mills built. Then after all the machinery was ready for the ore, perhaps little, or none at all, was to be found.

"Meanwhile another discovery was reported, and the young town was abandoned as completely as a camp made for a single night; and so on, until some really valuable lode was found, such as those at Eureka, Austin, Virginia, etc. which formed the substantial ground-work for a thousand other excitements."

Among Austin's more affluent offspring were Eureka, Hamilton, Belmont, Cortez, Tuscarora and a flock of others. Out of this far-spreading ore-seeking "family" undoubtedly came a very large share of the State's vast mineral contribution to the world. This Reese River clan deserves a larger place in history than it ever has received..

Many refused to die—or, at least, stay permanently in their graves. Just recently Ione shed its shroud and began mining cinnabar, while Big Creek found that its sparse silver-gold ore was full of something more valuable—uranium.

Let's take a look at some of the first generation.

Shortly after the strike which made Austin the booming mid-state city in the early 'Sixties, prospectors, following their age-old way of life, loaded their burros with beans, bacon and tools and plodded away in every direction, optimistically searching for a hidden treasure of their own.

Down the west side of the Toiyabes sprung up Canyon City, Big Creek, Lander City, Washington, Ione, Grantsville, Berlin and Union. A few miles west, across a valley, Ellsworth and Weston were born.

Of the western slope towns, short-lived Big Creek's enthusiasm is shown elsewhere in the yarn about the visit by Artemus Ward to address the miners in the Little America saloon. Its ore was discovered shortly after Austin's. It boasted a mill, a couple of stores, a school, justice court and even a branch telegraph line connecting with the overland circuit at the Lander County seat. It became dormant in 1867 and just recently has revived through uranium operations.

Canyon City was only seven miles south of Austin. "A glorious future" was predicted for it by the *Reese River Reveille* in 1863, when it boasted a hotel, two restaurants, three saloons and a butcher shop. It also had a post office from August 19, 1863 to October 14, 1867.

At the mouth of Big Creek, favorite picnic area for Austinites, on the bank of Reese River, David E. Buel, early-day Austin civic leader, built Lander City. It was twelve miles from Austin and enjoyed quite a lively life as long as Big Creek lasted, then it dwindled and soon was quiescent.

The distinction of having the first billiard table in Nye County is one of the few that the community of Washington boasted. It was farther down the range, in a high canyon, and at its peak achieved "three-saloon" size. It rated a post office from July 29, 1870 until August 27, 1872 during its short life. It also was where the Columbus mining district was organized in 1864.

Among the prospectors who set off from Austin early in 1863 to seek riches was P. A. Havens. He pecked away at every promising outcrop along the west side of the Toiyabes and over into the Shoshones.

High on these rocky slopes around the 7000-foot level near the bottom of Shamrock Canyon he discovered some rich gold, silver, lead and copper ores. It didn't take long for the grapevine telegraph to spread the word, and miners flocked into the Shoshones, establishing the town, like so many others of those days, along the bottom and sides of the canyon. It was called Ione, and is hemmed in on the south by 9081-foot Mt. Berlin, on the north by the southern 10,072-foot twin of the Shoshone Peaks, with the road leading to the Reese River Valley and Austin, fifty-five miles away, over the pass between these snow-covered domes.

Hundreds of younger mining communities have bloomed and died since the little Shoshone mountain town was christened in the Spring of 1863. For almost a century Ione has been left to die a dozen times, but just refuses to stay under a shroud. Author Nell Murbarger aptly dubs her "The Little Ghost That Won't Lie Down." Today it is one of the very few active mining districts in Nevada. Maybe it's the mountain air, but whatever the reason, Nye County's earliest community, and first county seat, always has hung on when other more flamboyant boomers faded and died all around it.

A constant stream of ox-wagons hauled in equipment and supplies during the summer and fall of 1863, and by winter the main street was lined with saloons, stores, restaurants, rooming houses and all the other common early mining town commercial accoutrements, including a line of bawdy houses. She was a precocious youngster far out in the unknown hinterland of the vast new Nevada territory where county lines had never been surveyed.

There was considerable argument among the citizens whether Ione was in Lander County or in Esmeralda County of which, Aurora, one hundred miles to the west, was the county seat.

Daily reports of new discoveries in the various canyons spreading down the flanks of the mountains, Sheep, Knickerbocker, Buffalo, Berlin, Union and Grantsville, were the talk of the saloons. It wasn't long until the need of a nearer seat of government was felt and some of the community leaders began to lay plans. Accordingly, when the Territorial legislature met in January 1864, it received a petition from the rapidly developing Shoshone region for a new county.

The legislators, enthused over the riches pouring from the Comstock, Reese River and Humboldt mines, agreeably accepted the claims that this was another strike that would surpass all others. New lines were drawn on the territorial map, lopping off huge portions of Esmeralda and Lander counties to establish a vast new county named after Territorial Governor James W. Nye. The legislators had refused to be swayed by an opposing petition signed by Lander County citizens.

Ione was designated as the county seat, funds appropriated to build a courthouse, and the new government formally was established April 26, 1864, when the county commissioners and other officers appointed by Governor Nye met for the first time.

These officials were recipients of a piece of Governor Nye's political pie—hardly any of them being previous residents of the new county. The rough and ready Shoshone miners didn't cotton to most of them, and only Sheriff Ed Irwin, who was well liked, survived the first county election the following autumn.

However, it does seem that the appointive first officers deserve one bit of belated credit—they did show rare prudence and economy, unlike more optimistic new county heads in other places, by setting a tax rate of a mere eighty cents per $100 valuation and deeming $800 enough for a courthouse. Many claim an old log cabin still standing is the original courthouse—but there is no proof that it is.

Ione boomed rapidly, as a county seat, boasting a population in excess of six hundred by 1865, with local news clarioned in the area's first weekly paper, the Nye County News.

The new county had scarcely begun to function, though, when the rug was pulled from beneath Ione's dreams by the discovery of another "richest strike" at Belmont, fifty miles eastward on the far side of the Toquima range. The biggest part of Ione's population packed up and pulled out to get in early on this latest bonanza.

But Ione fought to keep the county seat, even though Belmont boomed and grew to be a great deal larger than the Shoshone town ever had been. Money talked then as it still does, and the legislature handed Ione and its district the first lethal blow when it moved the county seat in 1867 to booming Belmont with its 1500 residents and three big mills.

During Ione's first splurge other settlements had sprouted in the various canyons. Berlin, five miles south; Union, over the hill from Berlin and now the site of the Nevada State Ichthyosaur Park, and Grantsville, three miles southeast of Union, where Havens had made new ore finds.

Two mills were installed to treat the ores, the Pioneer, a five-stamper on the outskirts of Ione, and the Knickerbocker, a mile south of the town. The latter was an ambitious project with twenty stamps and six roasting furnaces. It was built to handle the Grantsville ores. The latter boomed quickly into a larger town than the county seat with its rich ores and some of the State's early mining leaders.

The district's mines showed gross production of only $10,506 in 1866 and $33,552 in 1867, while Belmont was shipping out ore valued at $153,189 and $702,713 in the same years.

It was enough to subdue most mining towns when the ore had begun to run thin, but not Ione and its neighbors for awhile. Production even increased during 1868, but it began to fade off for the next few years.

However, the final blow of losing the county seat and much of its population didn't cause Ione to lie down and die. Steve Roberts, one of the town's first pioneers and Nye County assessor, was reported by the *Reese River Reveille* in February, 1872, as saying that the Ellsworth mill ten miles west in the Mammoth Range had "infused new life" into Ione, as it was the principal source of ore in the section. The *Reveille* commented at the time Ione was "an old camp and has passed through many vicissitudes. It has had many ups and downs, at one time promising to be a leading district, and anon all but deserted . . . There are good mines there . . . The little town is looking quite lively; it has two saloons, two billiard tables, one store, one restaurant, one livery stable, all doing good business, and it only rests with themselves to make it as prosperous as it was in 1864 and '65."

During 1869 the towns had a "Pony Express" connection with Austin, that won a place in history—not because the rider carried the mail though Indians and every sort of weather six days every week, but because he was the ever-dependable "errand boy" for a vast isolated area.

The *Reveille* paid him tribute on April 15, 1869, stating that "The rider is named Barnes . . . a small sinewy fellow, as tough as a hickory sapling. He is so hardy and free that he disdains a coat and rides in his shirt sleeves, heedless of frost or gales. Besides the mail he is the common carrier for the people along the route. Three times a week he distributes from ten to twenty parcels of nameless little, but imperative wants, to the people in the valley. He receives the orders on his homeward trip, fills them in this city and distributes them on his outward trip. He carries the mail; buys tobacco for the 'Old Man's' pipe, and medicine for his rheumatiz; picks up all sorts of notions for the 'old woman', Lubin and hoop skirts for the girls, gimcracks for the boys, and soothing syrup and rubber dolls for the baby; everything indeed, from sole leather to hair pins.

"But do not think of the bottom of this mail rider! He rides seventy miles six times a week, 1820 miles a month or at the rate of 21,840 miles a year. He does all this, yet appears to think he has done nothing.

"Pony Express men are proverbially brave and hardy fellows, but we do not know of one whose feats excel those of little Barnes, the modest mail rider of Reese River."

Then in 1877, the Alexander Company became interested through Manuel San Pedro, in the Grantsville diggings, and that town rocketed to a population of more than one thousand. In 1880 it contained ten stores, two drug stores, a hardware store, furniture store, five restaurants, two bakeries, five saloons, two barber shops, one jewelry store, two blacksmith shops, two meat markets, two livery stables, a brewery, bank, express office, newspaper (*The Grantsville Sun*), a foundry, and assorted bagnios.

One of the most unique features about these faraway Shoshone mountain towns is that they seemed to enjoy a great paucity of violence. Either their citizens were peace loving or the places were so isolated that the outside world didn't hear about any killings which might have occurred there.

The Thompson and West *History* contains a listing of hundreds of violent killings all over early Nevada, but has none for Ione, Berlin or Union, and only two in Grantsville.

The first of these occurred August 10, 1880, when Thomas Mack was bulletted to death while he slept, by Thomas Burns. The pair had been drinking all night, separated in the morning and then Burns returned about noon and shot Mack when he was asleep. The report does not say what happened to Burns.

But, on March 29, 1881, Mattias Salmon, declared to be a member of the notorious Vasquez gang, was hung from a windmill by vigilantes with a card labeled "329" pinned to his shirt. Salmon had shot and killed S. E. Merrill, a well known Grantsville resident, for no known reason.

Shipments from the district averaged around $300,000 a year through 1881—then the bottom dropped out again. This time it appeared as if Ione's goose was cooked; so few were left there that the post office which had served the district since September 2, 1865, was closed on April 3, 1882. Mail in the area went to Grantsville, where the post office had opened on February 3, 1879.

But always there were a few living in Ione. In 1882 there were twenty-five residents recorded, and one store, a saloon, a livery stable and a blacksmith shop still operated. Not much, but enough to keep the place alive.

Then in the last decades of the century the Berlin mines received a surge of life. The Nevada Company, of New York, headed by J. G. Phelps Stokes, then residing in Austin, bought them and resumed operations. This boomed Berlin, and again reawoke Ione as the mill there was reactivated. Now it was Berlin's turn to have the post office, which was opened July 10, 1900. At the same period, Grantsville's office, which had continued all through the district's slumbering years, was closed forever.

After this little flurry, quietness descended, with always a few staying around Ione. It paid off for them in 1907 when J. L. Workman discovered mercury a couple of miles up Shamrock Canyon. Ione boomed again for this flurry, and got its post office back on July 16, 1912—only to close it on April 30, 1914. But once more, on the momentum caused by the demand for mercury and lead during World War I, the post office was re-opened, for the third time, on December 18, 1918, and has continued since.

Mineral reports of the Union district, if charted, would show a repeated series of peaks and dips to almost zero, but never once during nearly a century has Ione ever been entirely deserted.

While the Reese River rush was at fever pitch almost any sort of mineral showing, anywhere in the region, or even none at all if a stock promoter was on hand, caused a new town to spring up. Amador, seven miles north of Austin, had 1500 citizens and pretensions of grandeur in 1863 when it sought to obtain the county seat from Jacobsville. It lost the election and languished. By 1869 it was deserted.

Yankee Blade was only four miles north of Austin, and its life was like a bouncing ball, up and down. The *Reese River Reveille* commented on March 3, 1872 that the Yankee Blade mines "are now yielding ore of a very high grade and preparations are being made to work them more extensively than heretofore . . . all the miners, who have worked there the past year have done well, some so much that they talk of retiring to the States." But that condition didn't last long and soon Yankee Blade became very dull, and stayed that way.

Several of the towns down the east side of the Toiyabes actually were larger and more lively, some producing well, others being little more than sites for the widespread sales of promotional mine stocks.

Charles C. Breyfogle, who was to bequeath Nevada its most famous and mysterious "lost mine," quit his post as assessor of Alameda County, California, to found the town of Geneva, ten miles south of Austin. He made some money in the promotion, but when ore showings proved meager, he sold out and went prospecting to the southward on what became his fateful historic "lost mine" journey, which is told in many books. By 1864 there were five hundred persons living in Geneva. A short time later they were gone—so was the town.

A sawmill was the major reason for the existence of Globe, seventeen miles down the mountains. Its ruins are almost impossible to locate today. Guadalajara, a mile farther south, was the scene of a silver discovery by Mexicans in the early 'Sixties. It never was very large. However, its Mexican founders built their cabins of stone, and some of these walls remain.

But, Kingston, a couple of miles farther over a canyon range, was a bustling milling "metropolis." It had two water-powered twenty-stamp mills grinding away at its low grade ore by 1867, and eight years later boasted four amalgamating mills. George Hearst, the California mining tycoon, optioned the property at one time, but got into a row with the owners and pulled out, taking his money to South Dakota, where he bought the Homestead Mine, which contributed so much to the future Hearst fortune. You can find the shell of one of the mills and the foundations and ruins of other structures in the delightful mountain canyon yet.

Millett, forty-two miles down Smoky Valley, became the freighting center for the Toiyabe and Toquima mines. It had its saloons, general store, post office, "Lakeview Hotel," and wagon shops. Today some of its remaining buildings are used as the headquarters of a large cattle ranch. The rock walls of what apparently was the large general store still stand—and afford a setting for the extramundane re-creation of the gay days of yore when teamsters and miners gathered in this Smoky Valley outpost of civilization.

Just four miles west of Millett, at the mouth of Park Canyon, the La Plata Company built a mill, and the *Reveille* reported that a "sprightly little town" grew up there. It was named Park Canyon, and still provides interesting ruins of the stone mill and other buildings. There is a legend that a deposed Hawaiian monarch owned mining properties and resided at Park Canyon for awhile.

Only a few miles from Millett and Park Canyon, silver values were discovered in Ophir Canyon in 1863. The Murphy Mine, which was to produce nearly $1,000,000, was located there the following year and its rich ores resulted in one of the busiest places in this entire area. It had all of the accoutrements of a larger community—school, church, various lodges, and, of course, several saloons—although its population never exceeded a thousand.

The *Reveille* in 1872 reported "We were shown yesterday a fine specimen of ore which was taken from the fourth north level (of the Murphy Mine) which was thickly studded with native silver and would probably work far up into the thousands. Present indications warrant the belief that the Murphy Mine will soon rank among the most permanent and best paying mines in eastern Nevada." This time the *Reveille* wasn't far wrong; the Murphy was worked profitably until 1890. The mill ruins and those of stone and log cabins are still visited annually by scores of deer hunters who trek through this area after the plentiful but wily Toiyabe bucks.

Pueblo, in another canyon forty-five miles south of Austin, led a brief but merry life as a placer town. Following the 1863 mineral discovery the townsite was laid out across two streams which met there. It wasn't a big town, and its veins proved shallow and short. So did Pueblo's life.

There is a sequel to the Pueblo saga, though. The Goldfield strike in the early 1900s spread prospectors far and wide again, and there is an oft-told legendary tale about one of them finding a panful of dirt there beside a skeleton. When the dirt was panned, its contents proved rich in value. The prospector searched out the source and discovered a three-foot wide ledge which ran $5000 to the ton. So Pueblo came to life again for a brief while, but its resurgence was completely obscured by the much richer diggings of those later days at Goldfield, Tonopah, Round Mountain and Manhattan.

The Great Smoky Valley is less than a score of miles across and bounded on the east by the Toquima range where the snow-capped peaks above the 10,000-foot mark are strung north and south, capping the timber line like glistening pearl beads. Prospectors clambered up their slopes, too, looking for ore showings. They didn't find as much, though, as they had in the Toiyabes and towns were fewer. They found a rich lode on the flank of one peak.

The name given the community which had sprung up indicates that it was founded by one of the many "Cousin Jack" miners who flocked to the Nevada rush from Great Britain. It was called Northumberland— and lived a great deal longer than most of its brothers, hitting a peak in 1879, and then almost evaporating in 1881. One mill continued to grind away sporadically there until 1941.

But it was Jefferson, which lies six miles east of present-day Smoky Valley mining town of Round Mountain, which was the "big" community of the upper Toquimas. If ghosts could only talk, maybe the wraiths of this early-day town, high on the southern flank of Mt. Jefferson in the Toquimas, could tell who first found mineral there and named the diggings. Searching for the forgotten discoverer in the tomes of latter-day historians is profitless, for they all disagree.

But it is pretty certain that quite a town had grown up by 1874, because the Jefferson post office opened for business on October 22 of that year, and even in those days government officials didn't grant offices unless there was population to warrant it. Then, too, the 1876 election records show that more than six hundred votes were cast in Jefferson and that yardstick indicates there must have been somewhere around one thousand or more folk habiting the district at the time.

As usual, that ubiquitous early-day prototype of today's census bureau inquisitors left a list of business establishments, which affords a flashback to the way the canyon town residents lived. It was seventy-six miles to the "big town," Austin, and freight between those points cost thirty dollars a ton.

Jefferson had a post office, two general stores, three eating houses or restaurants, two bakeries, a butcher shop, livery stables, a lumber yard, and even its own justice of peace. It also had its own brewery—as did most isolated old Nevada mining towns. (An odd commentary on the growth of fast transportation is that Nevada, one of the top states in the nation for beer consumption, does not have a single operating brewery today.) The tabulator didn't list any hurdy houses or ruby-light establishments, but you can bet they were there.

During the early 'Seventies it boasted two mills, one on the Prussian Mine, the other on the South Prussian (or Jefferson). The latter was a ten-stamper, the other slightly smaller.

The South Prussian was the jackpot mine of the six in the district, reporting for tax purposes (which could be only a small fraction of the total) a gross yield of $401,120 during its operations in the 'Seventies before it ran out and and closed the mill in 1878. Most of the production was chloride of silver, containing a small percentage of gold. Nobody can sneer at production like that—especially when the bulk of it—$363,000 —was produced in the two years of 1875-76. It was rich ore too, some of it yielding as high as $20,000 to the ton.

During the boom, altogether 120 locations were recorded. Most of them turned out to be just granite. Only a few rich-paying veins were found in layers of porphyry and slate imbedded in the principal rock.

It is probable that underground water halted the prosperity parade. Only thirty-seven tons of ore were reported during the years 1877-1882. Thompson and West states that "only four miners" were working at Jefferson in 1881. The government closed the post office January 29, 1879. Over the next decade sporadic attempts, largely in vain, were made to re-open the mines on a paying basis.

Then the Charles H. Stoneham interests (sports fans will remember he long owned the New York Giants) bought the Kanrohat, or Sierra Nevada, in 1917, during the short-lived metal demand brought on by World War I. This outfit purchased a flotation plant and employed Jay A. Carpenter—for years now the director of the Mackay School of Mines at the University of Nevada—as superintendent of the modernized operation. Carpenter checked the workings diligently and honestly, as is his nature, and reported to his employers that the only sulphide ore he could locate was in a winze in the lower adit. He resigned. However, the Stoneham interests went ahead with their plans, erected the mill, but soon gave up because of low-grade ore.

A decade later an outfit named the Elsa Mining Co. spent considerable money rehabilitating the property and the mill, installing up-to-date equipment in the latter. Elsa didn't linger long.

Today thousands of tourists annually zoom past still active Round Mountain, some of them commenting, "I wish I could see a real ghost town," without ever realizing that Jefferson is up a canyon just a short distance east.

The recent private owners of the property have kept its stone buildings in better repair than in most old communities. Jefferson, according to history, was a "right good little town" back there in the 1870s.

Farther south in 1866 hopeful prospectors headed up a gulch and discovered some surface veins of gold. Manhattan's first short span of life was the result. Its real days of glory though came in the 1900s. Others went on through the gulch and over the pass and made the rich strikes which boomed Belmont on the southeast slopes of the Toquimas.

Belmont Was A Bumptious Baby

BELMONT WAS ONE OF THE REESE RIVER family's booming and bumptious new county seat triplets along with Eureka and Hamilton. It became the focal point of south-central Nevada's mineral production of the late 'Sixties and in turn begat a boisterous bevy of mining towns of its own. By far the most outstanding of its progeny, born very late in Belmont's life, was tumultuous Tonopah.

The discovery date of Belmont's silver—gold—mercury ore is somewhat shrouded in the muddled past. It is generally believed to be in 1864 during the frantic scramble by prospectors in every direction from Austin. In any event, by 1865 the town had a burgeoning population and two years later had become the brightest star in a galaxy of mining centers south of Austin.

The State Legislature, disregarding the anguished cries of almost deserted three-year-old Ione, voted in 1867 to move the county seat to the bustling Monitor Valley "metropolis." With the customary optimism of an unlimited future, Belmont's new county commissioners appropriated $3400—more than four times as much as Ione got—for a new courthouse.

It was nearly seven years later before the fancy new two-story structure, built from bricks and lime fired at Belmont, was constructed. The building still stands today, empty and forlorn, on the hillside overlooking what's left of the once-bustling mining town. It served as the county seat, although only a handful of residents remained in the town, when Jim Butler—an uneducated farmer who had been elected county district attorney—stumbled across the rich Tonopah lode. Three years later Belmont's last reason for existence faded away when the county government was moved to the new boom town.

While Belmont was booming it was a wild one. Files of its old newspapers, the *Silver Bend Weekly Reporter*, the *Mountain Champion* and best of all, the Belmont *Courier*, never lacked for lively news happenings to fill its columns.

Life as it was lived in 1867 is well illustrated in a tale about the feud between the Irish and Cornish miners. A major part of the population was composed of these divergent European racial groups who had carried their age-old animosity with them across the Atlantic and into the Nevada wilds.

The Irish were in the majority and when it was announced that orders had been received from the New York offices to close down the Silver Bend Company operation, trouble began. There were no indications that the ore bodies were petering out. The rumor started that the owners planned to hire the cheaper "Cousin Jacks" and re-open shortly.

The Irish drowned their anger with red-eye and decided to punish the mine superintendent, a man named Canfield. They grabbed him and mounted him astride a rail, borne by some of the burly Irishmen, the rest gathering around as they paraded down Main Street. The mob grew rougher, but decided to stop at the Highbridge Saloon to re-prime. They allowed Canfield to dismount, continuing to heckle him. As they prepared to continue the march, a soft-spoken, unobtrusive bystander, spoke to the victim and told him, "If you do not choose to get on that rail, you need not do so." The intruder was Lewis M. Bodrow, former city marshal in Austin, who had just arrived from the Reese River town.

Such opposition offended Pat Dignon, one of the mob leaders, and he punched Bodrow in the jaw. At about the same time another of the inflamed miners stepped out of the saloon door and fired his pistol. The shot started a wholesale shooting fray, in which a score or more shots echoed through the noise of the melee.

When the sudden brawl ended, Bodrow was face down on the board walk, his body riddled with bullet wounds and two deep knife stabs. Two bullets from his pistol had stretched out Dignon, a few feet away. Dignon was dead, too.

During all the excitement Canfield had been helped to escape by some of his friends. The more solid Belmont citizens raised a fund of $2000 to spur the search for the mob leaders. Two of them subsequently were captured and imprisoned.

Probably Belmont's most famous bit of violence—at least it has received more publicity and been the subject of wild legends—was the lynching in 1874 of a couple of lads named Charlie McIntyre and Jack Walker, miners recently arrived from Pennsylvania.

An argument between the pair and a gent named H. H. Sutherland resulted, as most arguments then did, in a shooting affray. Sutherland was wounded by Walker, while a stray bullet buried itself in the leg of Bill Doran, an innocent bystander. The newcomers promptly were clapped into the jail, located in the basement of one of Main Street's business houses. Walker was bound over to await Grand Jury action—law and order having come to Belmont with all its trappings—while McIntyre was handed an eighty day sentence "for drawing a weapon in an angry manner."

A report on the action that followed was dug out of the old Belmont newspaper files by Nell Murbarger for her *Ghosts of the Glory Trail*. According to these accounts, the two men escaped the impromptu calaboose but were found two days later by Sheriff Jim Caldwell, hiding in an abandoned mine. He returned them to jail, and attached leg irons chained to the floor.

The escape of the men aroused new interest in the pair, and the idea of lynching was fanned by constant potions of sagebrush liquor. Around midnight the crowd decided to take action, descended on the jail office, where they tied up Sheriff Caldwell and his deputy, and went down to the jail. Later when the Sheriff was released by the night watchman, he went below and found Walker and McIntyre hanging from the joists, both very dead.

According to Belmont papers that was all that happened.

But the Belmont correspondent of the *San Francisco Chronicle* added a few gruesome touches, telling his readers that the mob had riddled the bodies with bullets, and that the floor and ceiling were splashed with blood of the victims!

When this report reached Belmont, Sheriff Caldwell denied it immediately, declaring there were no marks of violence or bullet holes in either body. Nevertheless, the blood-spot story had been planted. And it grew and remained alive until finally, Lee Brotherton, who owned the building for years, splashed the ceiling with red paint to give tourists what they wanted.

"When I told them that the story wasn't so—that there were no blood stains, they acted as if I was just too mean and cantankerous to show them the spots," he admitted. "So, in self-defense I spattered some 'blood' on the ceiling, and everybody has been happy since."

Belmont's mines produced $15,000,000 in gold and silver, and 11,000 flasks of mercury, by 1885. Thereafter, production declined, and for several years there were very few residents. Belmont couldn't help but come up with one more ripple of amazing excitement long after its heyday, however. During the 1890s Nye County's politicos decided to inject a bit of humor in a campaign. They nominated a character named Andy Johnson for district attorney of the depopulated county. Johnson's qualifications were almost negative—he was uneducated, never bathed, and operated a mule ranch. The whole thing was considered a joke—but Andy managed to get elected.

He hadn't the slightest idea what his office entailed, but he was wise enough to get the only lawyer around, William Granger, to take care of the legal details, and the few cases which came up were handled by the latter. Andy decided he had a lifetime job and was mightily irked when the next election rolled around and old Jim Butler, a Monitor Valley hay rancher, decided to run against him for the office. Butler, as uneducated as Johnson, was a mite cleaner because he was married. Butler won the election.

Andy claimed fraud and demanded a recount. When it was time for the new official to take over, he refused to relinquish the office. He stayed right at his desk for nine full days and nights, refusing to open the office doors to anybody but friends bringing him food and liquor. Finally he gave up and went back to his mule ranch.

Butler turned over the duties of his office to a young attorney named Tasker L. Oddie. When Old Jim discovered Tonopah in 1900, he brought in his young assistant as a partner—and Oddie rode the crest of the Tonopah bonanza and became Governor of Nevada and later United States Senator, which was a long jump from assistant district attorney of almost-forgotten Nye County of the 1890s.

In after years a few flurries of activity brought Belmont back to struggling life. Discovery of turquoise in 1909 enlivened things for a while, and some overlooked ore pockets discovered in 1914 resulted in construction of a ten-stamp, one-hundred ton flotation mill.

During recent years population has been almost non-existent but Belmont, a little off the beaten track of tourist travel, still is one of the best preserved of Nevada's great galaxy of ghost towns.

When Belmont burgeoned back in the 'Sixties, prospectors had a new base from which they and their packed burros could plod' off into the wide, wild blue yonder to ferret out more of Fortune's fabulous hidden mineral caches—and they found them.

Morey was one of the first. Silver was located there in 1865 and soon there was a saloon, a post office, boarding house, express office and a blacksmith shop. But the ore was not plentiful and it wasn't too long until Morey was no more.

A ten-stamp mill was built in 1873 but it ran for only a month. Then in 1880, another mining surge caused Morey operators to ship their ore to the Tybo mill for seven months. The Morey mines have continued to operate sporadically, and figures show that through the years to 1948 a total of $475,117 had been produced there.

Danville, was located near the head of Danville Canyon, on the east slope of the Monitors, by P. W. Mansfield in 1866. Unquestionably he must have been an ambitious example of those wide-ranging prospectors of the early days, because his discovery was high on the mountains, around the 7500-foot level.

Hotcreek, south of Morey, was promising enough to rate a post office by 1867, and a year later boasted a population of three hundred, two stamp mills, the regular stores, saloons and other business houses. Hotcreek is one of the fortunate sprites of the 'Sixties which can boast that some of its first buildings are still useable. The Hot Creek Ranch Company which acquired the property, has kept the structures in better repair than those in other towns left as neglected prey to the elements.

After the first big flurry in the 'Sixties, when population exceeded three hundred, Hotcreek's production cooled off and by 1881 only twenty-five residents could be counted.

The "metropolis" of all this eastern desert country was Tybo. It has been booming up and down with occasional revivals since an Indian led a prospector to its ore in 1866 and showed him a lode running $2000 to the ton. The Belmont *Courier* proclaimed on August 1, 1874, that a sample of pulp from the Slavonian Chief "assayed $20,786.01" to the ton. That's figuring down to a fine, but highly lucrative, point. The same paper, less than a year later, reported a find by John Grevich and Tom Meretvich in which the poorest ore in a vein "twelve to sixteen inches in width," carried values of $3000 to the ton.

Probably the most colorful figure of early Tybo history was Dr. J. W. Galley, who brought his family west for his health and found popularity and a fair share of fortune. When Tybo became too rough even for its most rugged citizens, Dr. Galley was elected justice of peace. One of the better tales of Nevada mining day lore concerns his first case. The town bully, one Newton, had pulled a gun on Alex McKay, a rancher. Newton was hailed before Judge Galley and continued his swaggering ways in court, cursing McKay and threatening him.

The quiet medico produced a cocked double-barreled shotgun, pointed it at the defendant, and demanded order. He got it, and held Newton to answer under $1000 bail. The bully yelled, "Bail be damned —come to Belmont and get me."

Judge Galley again pointed his gun at Newton's midriff and asserted, "You'll stay here 'till hell freezes over or your friends furnish bail."

Newton discovered his friends had faded away—he stayed. Doc Galley's future verdicts were established.

Tybo, like the others in the area, has gone through periodic revivals. The Louisiana Consolidated Mining Co. put in a flotation mill in 1917 and ran it three years. The Treadwell-Yukon Company took over extensive holdings in the area in 1925, constructed a three-hundred-and-fifty-ton flotation concentrator, and took out $6,781,405 between 1929 and 1937. Total production for the Tybo-Hotcreek area between 1874 and 1944 totalled $9,789,281.

Troy, thirty miles south of Currant, on U.S. 6, was founded some fifty miles east of Tybo in 1869 following a silver strike in the Quinn Canyon Mountains. It had a twenty-stamp mill built by an English company in 1870 and the customary stores and other business places which supplied the wants of the miners. But its ore cupboard soon was exhausted, and by 1873 it was deserted. Few of its ruins remain. However, it has a monument which may be seen for miles in every direction, 11,268-foot Mt. Troy at the north end of the Quinn Range.

The great popularity of the Austin newspaper was evidenced in 1866 when a rich horn-silver discovery turned up in a desert valley fifty miles south of Tybo. The finders called the mine and the subsequent town, Reveille. It became quite a sustained bugle toot.

The ore was twelve miles from the nearest water so that a mill was too expensive a luxury at first and the owners freighted thousands of tons of their rich ore by ox wagon the 140 miles to Austin. It provided sufficient profit to build a mill at the water supply in 1869. More than

Mary Mine in Silver Peak, Nye County

—*Courtesy Nevada State Historical Society.*

$4,000,000 was realized from ore hauled the twelve miles to this mill before the veins ran out in the 'Seventies. Soon afterwards far-away Reveille was heard from no more.

About seventy miles straight west of Reveille was Montezuma. It's about a dozen miles west of present Goldfield. Quite a few miles south of Montezuma were Gold Mountain and Old Camp. It is odd that Old Camp, later dubbed Oriental, where the original strike was made by a Thomas Shaw in 1866, is located on Gold Mountain, while Gold Mountain, later renamed Stateline, is eight miles across Oriental Wash on the south flank of Slate Ridge. Several mines in this faraway spot on the edge of Death Valley produced well, and activity has continued there sporadically through the years. Still farther south, on the Spanish and Mormon Trail, was the agricultural settlement of Pahrump.

San Antonio was the major stage station on the main route between Belmont to Ione during the boom days of the 'Sixties. It was in the pass between the south end of the Toiyabes and the north end of the San Antonio mountains. The latter is the range which extends northward from Tonopah. The ruins of San Antonio are about thirty-five miles north of Tonopah and thirty-six miles southeast of Belmont.

Undoubtedly Fremont camped or, at least stopped briefly, for water and rest at San Antonio on his 1845 westward trek across the midstate. That trip has been traced down through Smoky Valley on the east side of the Toiyabes, around their south end, and thence across country to Walker Lake where he, Kit Carson and the rest of his party of fifteen men, rejoined the other half of the group headed by Theodore Talbot, and guided by that venerable cross-country traveler Joe Walker, for whom Fremont named the lake and river.

San Antonio—always called "San Antone" by Nevadans—blossomed around its ample water supply in 1864-65 when prospectors found rich silver ore in the Liberty and Potomac mines some dozen miles southward. An optimistic ten-stamp mill was built at San Antone in 1865—the same year the rush got started to Belmont—and brought a stream of traffic through the place. Salt was hauled from Rhodes and Sodaville by one of the camel trains then commonly used.

The mines failed to produce enough ore to make the operation worthwhile, however, and after a year the mill was dismantled and hauled across the valley to Belmont, where business was bigger and better. A year later a four-stamp mill was erected to handle the output—but in the meantime, San Antone had grown into a "tourist town."

It was the road junction for travel southward to Silver Peak, Gold Mountain, Old Camp, Pahrump, Death Valley and other far outlying early mining camps in the remote areas of the new mining state.

The place boasted a two-story combination stage station and hotel. There were, of course, saloons where travelers could slake their thirst

Belmont Court House (in 1947)

—E. W. Darrah Photo.

and lose their money gambling; bawdy houses and necessary stores to meet the needs of the inhabitants and travelers.

There were plenty of roughs and rowdies around San Antonio—as might be expected in an early-day out-of-the-way stage station town where travelers loaded with gold passed frequently.

Then, too, there were taxes as always.

Those two facts were the major ingredients of one of the liveliest tales about one of the most colorful gents in Nevada history. His name was Aaron Winters. The story has been told many times of the manner in which he and his California Spanish wife, Rosie, discovered the vast borax deposits of Death Valley. But, little has ever been written about what happened to the couple later.

They sold their Death Valley claims to William Coleman, the early-day borax king, for $20,000 and "retired" to a ranch in Pahrump Valley, in the southern tip of vast Nye County. Occasional travelers stopped with them for a meal or supplies, and one day during 1886 a visitor left a copy of the Belmont *Courier*.

When he read a notice that taxes were due and payable in gold at the county seat, Aaron being an honest man, decided he would have to make the 250-mile trip to Belmont and perform his civic duty. He packed some food, left Rosie to run the ranch, and departed northward in a buckboard drawn by his best team of horses, his sack of gold pieces in the jockey box.

The old prospector was a wily old-timer and wise to the ways of the wayward lads who waited for unsuspecting suckers. Before he left, he oiled and loaded his Navy revolver and slid it beneath the seat where it would be conveniently at hand. On the dashboard he hung a holster containing a rusty, broken old gun.

Aaron visited along the way with old friends and saw no sign of road agents. This didn't make him careless, and he kept warily alert when he arrived at San Antone, his last overnight stop on the way.

He took the sack of gold with him when he went to his room. The following morning he was up early, hitched the team, and drove up town, where he openly took the sack of gold from his shirt front and tossed it in the jockey box. Naturally, the fact that the old prospector who had "struck it rich" on Death Valley borax was in town, was known to everybody.

Leaving the gold, he walked into a restaurant for breakfast, keeping one eye on his vehicle. Shortly he spotted a couple of men approaching the buckboard, and when one reached into the jockey box, Aaron cat-footed to the door, blasted with his Navy gun and dropped him. The other ran, but was collared by the marshal. Before Winters could get out of town the jailed man escaped.

That didn't delay tough old Aaron. He departed for the county seat bent on getting the taxes paid and returning to Rosie. Nothing happened until he was within a short distance of Belmont, when two armed men stepped from behind a rock on a turn in a steep place on the road. Winters recognized one as the escaped San Antone robber, the other was a young stranger. The older man did all the talking, and snatched the rusty gun from the holster on the dash.

When he saw that it was broken and couldn't be shot he began to laugh, showing it to his companion as he guffawed. This gave Winters the chance he wanted, and he snatched the good gun from beneath his leg and killed the bandit with one shot. The youth immediately dropped his gun and held up his hands.

Aaron chuckled as he made the young man roll the dead bandit from the road. Then he forced the captured robber to walk ahead of the team while he held his gun on him and completed the trip to Belmont. The odd parade created considerable interest as Winters herded his captive down the street to the office of the sheriff, an old friend, and turned him in.

After the duty of paying the taxes was completed, Aaron returned to complete his business with the sheriff. The latter told him that the jailed boy was a midwestern farm kid, who had been working in the mines, and had been misled into the robbery caper by the smooth talk of the dead bandit, who had a price on his head. Aaron was entitled to the reward, which was far more than the taxes had cost. That cheerful news made him feel considerably mellower about the holdup. He talked to the youngster, who told him that he hated mining and was homesick for farm work. His story tickled the fancy of old Aaron and he offered to give the boy a job on his Pahrump place.

So far, this tale is substantially factual. The sequel is delightful but has never been verified.

The legend is that Aaron returned to Rosie and the Pahrump ranch with his new hand, who ever after was faithful and devoted to his rescuer for the rest of Aaron's life. When the old-timer was about to pass away, several years after frail Rosie had died of tuberculosis, he is said to have called for his "foster son" and told him, "Everything is yours, take good care of the ranch, and promise me one thing—always pay your taxes when they're due."

Today San Antonio, one of the very few towns in Nevada bearing the name of a saint, slumbers peacefully in the sunshine of midstate Nevada, its tranquility, like that of Belmont disturbed only by the occasional stops of prospectors, hunters or wandering cowmen, most of whom know nothing about its romantic history of those early days.

Cortez Was A Loner

CORTEZ, AT THE NORTHERN EDGE OF THE Toiyabes some sixty-four miles away, was one of Austin's earliest precocious offspring. It was located on the slopes of Mt. Tenabo. The Cortez district attracted wide interest because of immense lodes, and the distances they could be traced, when it was discovered in May 1863 by Dr. I. Hatch and some prospecting friends from Austin.

Among one of the first to invest heavily in Cortez locations was the ubiquitous George Hearst, who ranged throughout Nevada gobbling up likely strikes to help snowball his holdings into an immense fortune.

The *Reese River Reveille* waxed enthusiastic about Cortez on January 4, 1867, reporting, "Of the vein there is little exact knowledge, but it stands out upon the mountain face, a large palpable fact. It will probably be developed, and when that day arrives we believe the Nevada Giant will be regarded as one of the remarkable veins of the world."

The Nevada Giant was considered the most promising of the early mines but it turned into a pigmy when other larger strikes were made. It soon was gobbled up in one of the numerous consolidations which were formed.

At first probably profits from sales of stocks proved more highly profitable than returns from the plentiful ore, since tax on production for the entire area never exceeded $45,000 annually until 1873, when it reached $75,674. The Cortez operated almost continuously until a few years ago. Better than a quarter-million gross yield was reported as late as 1939. That is one of the reasons it is fairly well preserved.

The strike in 1864, when silver fever was at its highest, quickly attracted a rush of hopefuls. A mill was built in 1865, and very rapidly a town of more than one-hundred residents spread out over the slopes of Mt. Tenabo.

The first mill and a steam hoist to work the Garrison, which eventually turned out to be the greatest producer of the district, required water which wasn't available. Because of the desire to go deeper in the mine the owners imported a string of burros to haul water in barrels from a spring three miles away. No record of how many jackasses were used is left us, but there must have been a pretty long parade of them continually on the go, because a sixteen-stamp mill and a steam engine hoisting ore will use plenty of water.

The Cortez company invested $100,000 in another sixteen-stamp mill, locating it about eight miles around the mountain by wagon road and four miles from the mines by trail, where there was wood and water. Once again the burros were brought into action, the patient beasts carrying the ore over this mountain trail from mine head to mills. During this period most of the mining work underground was done by the Chinese, the Mexicans working on top and at the mill.

Evidently the big investment didn't pay off—unless the company got it back on stock sales—because Samuel Wenban bought the entire mining operations in 1869 for $6,000.

This actually marked the real turning point in Cortez early fortunes as production began to increase from 1871 onward. Altogether, through the years, the mines have paid taxes on a gross yield of $6,375,839, a respectable return for any little mountain district.

Cortez, like so many other early-day Nevada mining towns, had a copious Chinese graveyard—but it was only a temporary burial place for the Orientals who succumbed to overdoses of opium, malnutrition, hatchets or stilettos. When mineral streaks became so barren that even the Chinese could glean no further return, they dug up the bones of their compatriots and moved onward. Sooner or later the remains were shipped back to China to be interred with those of their ancestors. So, today you won't find a mound to mark the spot where several hundred Chinese lived at Cortez, but you'll see a pleasant cemetery containing those of other nationalities who died there.

Isolated from the niceties of civilization, it attracted large numbers of rowdies, and during its early days there were frequent killings. Hardly a night passed without the popping of guns.

One poker game shooting left a legendary story which I have never found verified. but which continues to pop up frequently in Nevada "historical" volumes. It is the tale about a fellow named Bill Broadwater who played reckless poker and soon lost his entire poke to one John Llewelyn. Then he wagered his six-gun—and lost. He had nothing left but his Henry rifle. He held a losing hand again. This was too much for him, and he snatched up the gun, pulled the trigger and drilled the winner through the heart.

Broadwater, surrounded by men who had witnessed the unprovoked attack, surrendered. Two deputies, Glassford and Maguire, were delegated to take the prisoner to Austin on horseback. Several miles out, Glassford alighted to tighten his cinch. Broadwater, seeing his opportunity, reached over, snatched the rifle from the saddle scabbard and covered his two guards. He disarmed them and rode down the trail to freedom.

Cortez residents were pretty peeved about it—but there wasn't much they could do except offer a reward. Several months later the sheriff of Trinity County, California, recognized the wanted man—he had obtained a job sorting potatoes. The sheriff captured him, unarmed, among the spuds. Broadwater, according to the story, was brought back to Austin, tried, convicted and sentenced to twenty years in the Carson City prison.

When Simeon "Sam" Wenban bought out his partner, George Hearst, in 1867, and acquired sole ownership of the Cortez Mill, he started a twenty-eight-year reign as the kingpin of the community. Although the ore proved less valuable than at first believed, Wenban pushed operations to the limit. He kept two hundred woodcutters busy denuding the hills of pinion pine and juniper and roasting the wood into charcoal to keep the wheels of the mill constantly turning.

Weban wrested a fortune from the Tenabo veins during the next thirty years through hard work and continued faith in his mines. His biggest golconda was a rich streak he ran into in the Garrison mine, which he had acquired along with the others.

In 1889 Weban sold out to the Bewish-Moreing syndicate, a British-owned firm, which operated under the name of the Cortez Mines Ltd., until 1891, when its explorations failed to prove out and it transferred the operations back to Wenban. The old-timer still had faith in his mines and spent large amounts in new exploratory shafts and tunnels.

He died in 1895 and, with nobody around to carry on, Cortez went into a decline. Numerous leasers made sporadic attempts, but none ever proved successful, until 1919. The Consolidated Cortez Silver Mines, Inc. was formed with 2,000,000 shares at one dollar each, built a one-hundred-ton concentration and cyanide mill and began to turn out silver in paying quantities. During this period approximately 150 men were employed, and Cortez boomed along for several years, then again production halted, and it began to return to the spectral world with so many of Nevada's other famed early mining towns.

If you visit Cortez, pronounce it like Nevadans do for some unknown reason—"Cort-us." Not as the Spanish do, "Cortezz."

There were dozens more of Austin's mining offspring tucked away in the mountains and hills north and northwest of the Lander County metropolis. The busiest of them was a small group—Copper Basin, Copper Canyon and Galena—a dozen miles southwest of Battle Mountain, the Reese River district's railroad shipping point on the Central Pacific.

The origin of the Battle Mountain name is a tidbit of history to be noted. It got its designation in 1857. John Kirk, of Placerville, California, leading a wagon train, decided to veer southwestward from the churned-up, constantly-dusty Humboldt trail at the bottom of the river's southern loop, and seek out a short cut.

Some eight or ten miles from the main route, in what since has been known as Copper Basin, where a spring offered good water and there was plenty of grass to replenish the half-starved stock, the party camped. It was the group's final resting place. Just before dawn, Indian raiders swept down the hill, massacred the party, burned its wagons, stole the stock and departed.

News of the massacre quickly spread, and soon the curious were visiting "Battle Mountain"—and some of them found the first out-croppings of the true fissure veins which ran for miles through the hills. The first settlement to spring up was called Copper Basin.

It was a natural thing for the initial settlers to refer to the small range, which was about twenty miles long and ten miles wide—as "the Battle Mountains." Today's maps label them as the Galena Range, or show them as the northern arm of the Fish Creek Mountains.

The heavy silver-lead ores which were found along Duck Creek quickly attracted the attention of British capitalists, who had been drawn to the region by the Reese River boom. So, when a town was planned in 1869 by the English company, it didn't just grow willy-nilly like Copper Basin and most other early day mining camps, it was platted with typical British thoroughness, and named with the Latin word for the area's predominant lead ore, Galena. The company laid out wide streets, a public square, parks, a city water system, a rather lavish hotel, a public hall and substantial business buildings.

The production pouring out of the small Galena smelter attracted attention, and diggings in Copper Canyon, three miles south, proved that the galena ores found in the quartzite formations had changed to copper. Another English company rapidly acquired the properties and installed a concentrating mill, the product of which was shipped to Liverpool, England.

The mill at Galena was separating the silver from the lead and the latter also was being sent overseas to Swansea, Wales. Most of the ores ran quite heavy, Thompson's and West's 1881 *Nevada History* listing the values as averaging, on the whole, from $150 to $500 a ton.

From 1871 to 1883, ore value ran from a low of $36,000 to a high of $114,485—pretty rich pickings in those days when isolated mining operators regarded it as poor business to pay taxes on more than a fraction of the actual values.

Then activities apparently ceased for a couple of decades—Galena, Copper Canyon and Copper Basin passed into a coma. Buildings were moved to Battle Mountain, mills were dismantled, weeds grew up on streets, and only the ghosts—and maybe a couple of never-give-up old timers—inhabited the places. The Galena post office closed its window May 27, 1887.

The district was revived during the Tonopah-Goldfield flurry at the start of this century, but today the Copper Basin output isn't all metallic, it is turquoise. The district has proven to be one of the finest anywhere for this distinctly western gem.

Which proves you never know what's inside a Nevada rock.

PART FIVE

Off Into the Northeast

Eureka ★

"Eureka!"

EARLY DAY JACKASS PROSPECTORS DIDN'T use road maps—they just headed wherever their fancy, or their lead burro, took them. So Austin also was the progenitor of booming bonanza towns far to the east and north. One of the greatest of these was Eureka, seventy miles east on U.S. 50, which still clings to life as a county seat. The 1960 census counted only 754 persons in all of Eureka County.

If you prefer your golconda ghosts straight and undiluted without tourist trappings and phony makeup, you'll like Eureka. It was one of the greatest of Nevada's early communities, yet today there are far more inhabitants in its nine cemeteries than there are on the streets. For seventy-five years efforts have been made to inter what once was Nevada's second largest city, but nobody has ever quite succeeded in getting Eureka to sit down and hold hands with the coroner. It is very doubtful that anybody ever will. Two examples of the never-say-die spirit of its citizens stand out.

The first, a beacon of pride for the community, is the fact that in 1933, when President Roosevelt closed the banks in this country, the Eureka bank was one of the very few allowed to remain open. It was so solidly solvent that federal bank officials made an exception in its case.

The second is a six-page red, green and white folder which tells the history of Eureka County in pleasant, simple language and invites tourists to stop and enjoy "the old mining camp atmosphere, beautiful sunsets and the Saturday night dance." It was printed in 1957. The pamphlet is no pitch for curio stores selling "authentic" souvenirs made in a New Jersey factory, it is just a nice little invitation to come and visit and take potluck.

It's not surprising, because Eurekans are like that—real, regular western folk who love their hometown, regardless of the fact that the mines with all their bullion and excitement and all but a few score of its former citizens are long gone.

Peter Merialdo is an excellent example of a Eurekan. He was a county official there for three decades before being elected the Nevada State Controller in 1950. He polled the highest vote on the Nevada ballot when he ran for re-election in 1954. He lived in Carson City during these years but anytime he was asked where his home was he proudly replied, "Eureka."

Then take Judge Albert Henderson of the Clark County District Court. Judge Henderson's folks were among the early pioneers of the Fish Creek Range community and Eureka is still "home" to the jurist, although he has lived in Tonopah and Las Vegas for the last forty years.

Eurekans are particularly proud of their pioneer families, such as the Skillmans, Hjuls, Wittenbergs, Miolettis, Franks and many others who came to the district in the early days. They stayed, and raised families which helped keep Eureka a very lively near-ghost like its sire, Austin.

There is no documentation for the fact, but many historians blithely assert that the town was named because one of the five prospectors who found the first ore in 1864 yelled "Eureka!" which means "I have found it." Maybe one of this little party which had left Austin a few days previously did just that because "Eureka" had become a common American idiom in the west after Marshall found his first gold flakes at Coloma.

The ore baffled those first fortune chasers. It was heavy, and unlike anything they'd seen at any other diggings. They decided to try some of it in their camp fire. A flow of white metal resulted. Maybe that is when somebody said, "Eureka!"

When they cooled off the button, the five prospectors still were puzzled. Some claimed the ore was silver, while the others insisted that it was too soft. These said it was lead. But it was too hard to be lead. Both sides were correct—it was a combination of the two metals which were to make Eureka the second largest Nevada producer in mineral values and the world's greatest lead center in the nineteenth century.

In view of this fact it seems a little strange that the discovery didn't result in any immediate rush. One reason may have been from the fact that efforts to separate the ore proved unsuccessful. Another, perhaps, was that the Comstock and Austin were at their peak booms, capturing the popular attention; Eureka was far away in the unknown wilderness.

In 1869 the problem of separating the metals was solved by the erection of draft and blast furnaces and Eureka bounced into frenzied activity. Very shortly foreign capital became interested. The Ruby Hill mines were purchased by Eureka Consolidated Mining Company, and an English outfit, the Richmond Mining Company, bought up adjoining claims and with characteristic British thoroughness organized them on a complete operating basis. Eureka Consolidated's big plant and furnaces were erected at the bottom end of Main Street, the Richmond plant arose at the upper end.

In 1875 the romantically-famed Eureka & Palisade Railroad, "The Slim Princess," puffed into life, linking the eastern Nevada metropolis with the main line of the transcontinental Central Pacific 90 miles away, and Eureka became the queen city of the area—probably to the disgust of already fading Hamilton and ambitious Pioche farther southeast.

Before this, in 1873, Eureka already had growing-pain ambitions and had lobbied a new county through the state legislature with the same old argument of "being too far away" from Austin. The fine brick courthouse erected in 1879 is still being used.

Main Street today has the bare remains of the once-busy smelters and refineries as outposts at both ends. Many of the old buildings house the desultory business establishments required to meet the needs of the remaining population and the passing tourists. Still in business are the first churches. The eldest was the stone Episcopal structure, followed closely by the Catholic edifice.

But Main Street today is no longer the scene of lethal gun and bowie knife battles. No better commentary on the great change in its life could be found than in the fact that during December, 1956, Eureka had its first jury murder trial since 1934. The case grew out of a quarrel between two men in a Eureka hotel in which it was charged the accused had used an electrician's knife on his antagonist.

The times and the weapons were different than in the old days but the verdict of the jury was reminiscent of pioneer times. After deliberating less than an hour, the panel returned a verdict of "not guilty."

In the seventies Eureka refused to take a back seat for any town, including its sire, Austin, or pompous Virginia City. Population was surging right around the five-figure mark, between 8,000 and 10,000. It boasted three newspapers. One of them, the Eureka *Sentinel*, founded in the early days by the Skillman family, is still being published.

Along Main Street and its intersecting roads there were 125 saloons, notes the ever-present tabulator, 25 gambling houses, 15 tent shows, volunteer fire companies—the "Hooks" and the "Knicks"—and all the other necessary establishments to fill needs of the population. Plus nine cemeteries!

Such a town was bound to attract the plentiful freebooting citizenry which delighted in relieving Wells-Fargo stages of their heavy loads of bullion. The cry of "Pass down the box" was commonly repeated in the neighborhood.

Probably the most notorious case of bullion hijacking was the one which wrote finis to the story of A. J. "Big Jack" Davis. He had been one of the gang which perpetrated the first train holdup at Verdi in 1870 and served a reasonable length of time in the calaboose for that caper. After getting out of jail, Davis couldn't resist the opportunity held out by the booming eastern section. His stage holdups were as well organized as some of today's master-minded criminal exploits.

One of the key features of a Davis holdup included a signalling system to outwit the express company. Wells-Fargo didn't take kindly to losing bullion, the value of which it had to make good, and had taken to sometimes putting two shotgun guards aboard, one generally riding out of sight inside the coach.

Davis realized that this could result in sudden death unless the second hidden guard was anticipated. To meet this problem he had his spotters signal with small fires from previously established peaks—one fire meant a single guard, two meant a pair.

When Davis learned that the southbound Tybo stage was to carry a rich load of coin for the mine payroll, he planned to acquire the treasure. He delegated Tom Laurie as fire tender for the holdup, and with two assistants rode to Willow Springs, where they surprised and tied up the station tender and a visiting rancher.

A guard named Eugene Blair, who had never lost a gunfight with bandits, was riding as messenger. With him as a second guard was Johnny Brown.

Brown had noticed a beautiful red star which appeared to be just over the top of Pancake Peak and had mentioned it to Blair, remarking it "almost looks double." Davis and two pals, waiting at Willow Springs, saw it, too—it looked to them like a single blaze.

When the stage rolled into Willow Springs Davis called out, "Blair, surrender." Blair jumped down and ran toward the barn. Two shots followed, but missed him. Johnny Brown had jumped out and one of the bullets hit him in the leg. Blair stumbled and Davis jumped him. As they stood up Brown could distinguish them and he promptly poured a load of lead into the bandit.

Davis' confederates, realizing that they had mistaken Laurie's fires, which had been built too close together, mounted their horses and departed. Brown's blast had ended the career of "Big Jack" Davis. A few days later Laurie and the other two bandits were nabbed.

Today's citizens of Eureka are full-fledged practitioners of the mind-over-matter theory. To a man, they hold the optimistic belief that the Fish Creek Mountain mines, which produced in excess of $60 million in gold and silver and controlled the world lead market with an output of 225,000 tons of that metal, will boom again. Modern diamond drilling methods recently have been used to probe the Ruby Hill and Diamond workings for lost lodes displaced in ancient geologic upheavals. Then, too, in recent years there has been a real bustle occasioned by explorations for oil—with the discovery of Nevada's first producing well—just a few miles away.

Eurekans are proud of their historic town. Charles E. Van Loan, the noted *Saturday Evening Post* writer, discovered this 'way back in 1915. During his visit a traveling salesman stopped there briefly and told him, "The place is dead, but they don't know it . . . At that, I got to hand it to them—they're the greatest boosters in the world!" Today's Eurekans are still the same.

Ghost town? Not on your life. In fact its residents are inclined to sneer derisively at the extensive "ghost town" advertising and publicity campaign which has been carried on by its larger and more raucous contemporary, Virginia City.

Eureka invites visitors by simply telling them "There's much to see" . . . the historic Colonnade Hotel; the famed Jackson House (now the Brown Hotel); the Opera House, where famous stars appeared and where entertainment still is offered, although on a movie screen; the *Sentinel* office, housing one of Nevada's oldest newspapers; the two-story brick courthouse; the sandstone Episcopal and Catholic churches; the huge slag dumps; the cemeteries "where its inhabitants far outnumber the living;" the "mountain scenery, the old mining camp atmosphere" and "the beautiful sunsets unequalled anywhere."

Nothing ever daunted Eurekans. Through the years the community suffered every type of calamity—fire, flood, decline in metal prices, ore turning to borrasca and bank failures.

They always dug in and looked ahead to another great day coming. One indication of this optimism was the name of one of its later, but now-departed newspapers. It was called the *Eureka County Resuscitant.*

Its editor was the complete optimist. Here's an example: "Since Eureka County became an integral part of the state her years have been as changeful as the changeful moon that each night varies. Adversity and prosperity have alternately filled her cup, and her citizens have ever drunk the draught of bitterness with complaisance, patience and gracious submission, believing, without doubt in their hearts, that the treasures of her mountains will sooner or later give them plenty, happiness and contentment, even unto satiety."

Eureka always did impress visitors. Back in July 1872, the then-editor of the *Reese River Reveille*, that ubiquitous mid-state newspaper, visited the youngest of Austin's booming offspring and penned an enthusiastic description of the community.

"A person visiting Eureka after an absence of eight months, cannot fail to be impressed by the wonderful improvements which have been made in that length of time," he wrote in his issue of July 10, 1872. "Several furnaces have been erected, fifteen-stamp mills built, besides a large number of elegant and substantial business houses and residences. Main Street, from below the old McCoy furnace nearly to the Jackson smelting works—is completely lined with buildings, many of which for elegance [those old-time editors certainly liked that word] and desirability cannot be surpassed by any town in the state. Nor are the improvements confined to Main Street alone, for the cross and back streets, have been built up in a proportionate degree and a large number of buildings are in process of erection, besides others which have been contracted for and will be built as soon as the necessary lumber can be had, the scarcity of which material has proved a serious drawback upon the prosperity of the camp, by retarding improvements which otherwise would have been made.

"The streets look lively—business men appear cheerful and perfectly satisfied with the present condition of affairs and confident in regard to the future . . . the prospects of the town and the district were never more encouraging than at present and appearances certainly indicate that but a short time will elapse when Eureka will occupy a most prominent if not a foremost position among the mining towns of the Pacific Coast."

No editor any place ever wrote a truer prediction than that. Within a few years Eureka was a name known around the world. Its production poured out to world markets while Austin, Virginia City, Hamilton and Pioche were beginning their downhill toboggan rides.

In 1876 or 1877 John Muir, the noted naturalist, after visiting Hamilton and the declining towns wrote, "In marked contrast . . . is the orderly deliberation into which miners settle in developing a truly valuable mine . . . We were kindly led through the treasure chambers of the Richmond and Eureka Consolidated, our guides leisurely . . . calling attention to the precious ore masses which the workmen were slowly breaking to pieces with their picks . . . while down in the bullion works the bars of bullion were handled with less eager haste than the farmer shows in gathering his sheaves."

The history of most early-day mining towns may be gleaned from a study of the graveyards, the saloons and the amount of activity by the vigilantes. There are three phases of Eureka's history in the cemeteries. The first marks the early days before it was realized that the booming camp would grow into a city. The graves of this period are mostly anonymous and hard to find, being marked by mounds of rock, or here and there an occasional faded, weathered and eroded wooden slab. Realize that in the early days mounds of rock atop a grave were considered a necessity to protect the bodies from wandering and hungry hordes of coyotes and other animals.

The second era is marked by marble slabs and shafts, ornamental iron fences and other evidences of prosperity when cash was plentiful and funerals were civic events. There are many family plots evidencing the fact that Eureka was a family town from shortly after it started. One is struck by the number of graves of young men, women and children. It makes you realize that the pioneers of these early days were young folk—not bearded old pioneers as we are wont to picture them.

The latter begin to predominate in the third phase of the cemetery history because when the riches faded out and the town began to decline it always was the young who departed and the older ones who stayed on, expecting a return to boom days. Among the graves of the older ones in the third phase of the cemetery story you notice the fact that many of those who remained apparently didn't have families living there. Otherwise, there wouldn't be so many dates and places of birth missing from the pine slab markers which replaced the marble used in the flush days. It is these faded slabs which record the memories of those old boys who had real faith in the comeback of the town, but who slipped away before their dreams could materialize.

Back in 1916 Charles E. Van Loan, the author, visited Eureka and told his findings in the *Saturday Evening Post*. Among those he talked

with was an old-timer who knew quite a bit about old Eureka. He told
the author:

"It wasn't that this was such an unhealthy camp . . . and it wasn't such
a bad place for killings, either. We had some, of course, off and on, but
not done by folks who made a business of it, you bet! The first man
killed here was George Mills, a member of the Nevada Assembly in the
'Sixties. Cornelius Buckley did it. Then Buffalo Bill Maize was plugged
by the Flying Dutchman. Bulldog Kate was shot and killed by Hog-
Eyed Mary. Jack Brannan was killed by Gus Botto and a little while
after that Botto was killed by Jesse Bigelow. But, these, you understand
were just killings in the natural run of events.

"Somewhere I've got the statistics on Nevada homicides in the early
days and more than half of them were for trivial causes and some for
no cause at all. Right from the start we aimed to discourage the desperado element and get rid of the men who killed for the fun of the thing.

"Pioche now—that was the place to get your through-ticket to Kingdom Come! They can all say what they like, I claim that Pioche, for
her size, was the worst man-for-breakfast camp in the world . . . they
had a lot of mix-ups in their mining claims and the miners would get
to fighting underground and what they couldn't settle with picks and
shovels they would settle with guns when they got to the top. They used
to say that in Pioche you could hire a man killed for a $10 note, but
that was stretching it some. The usual price was $25; Indians and China-
men cheaper and Mexicans free.

"We came near having some real excitement along in the 'Seventies on
account of Virginia City getting hit by a moral wave. Ever since the
early 'Sixties Storey County was the hangout of all the bad men in
Nevada and they just naturally wore out their welcome by staying too
long. . . . They formed what they called the Committee of 601, blamed
if I can remember what the 601 stood for, but one thing is sure, it didn't
stand for any foolishness . . . Naturally a lot of thugs headed for Eureka,
it was the newest camp in the state and next to Virginia the biggest
and the richest. The first thing we knew they were trying to run the
town. More through good luck than good management, they didn't
manage to kill any of our prominent citizens but there was no guaranty
that they wouldn't . . . the boys saw what was coming and held a
secret meeting . . . we decided to give them a dose of the 601 and that
night the steering committee called on the gentle strangers. Usually the
conversation ran something like this:

" 'You're going under the name of Three-Fingered Johnson, ain't
you?'

" 'Well, what if I am?'

" '. . . Oh, nothing much, but your name is on the list. You'd better
leave town by noon tomorrow.'

" 'Who says so?'

Eureka in 1870

The Eureka Mill, Sixty-stamp Capacity

Eureka, about 1870
—*Courtesy Nevada State Historical Society.*

Eureka, about 1880
—*Courtesy Nevada State Historical Society.*

" 'The local committee of the 601.'

" 'Holy Moses! Have they got one of them over here too?'

"Well, sir, it worked like a charm—all you had to do was say 601 in those days. I hope they went to Pioche, because there was a town that didn't have to import any bad men, she had plenty of her own."

During the earlier days, as in most mining camps, the saloons generally were the first and largest buildings available for public meetings. It is frequently noted that many Sunday church services were held in the stale-beer atmosphere of these boom town bistros.

Some of them, especially in the larger, richer towns, were quite elaborate affairs. Wells Drury, in his *Editor on the Comstock Lode*, tells about "The Tiger," one of Eureka's leading refreshment emporiums operated by Joe Mendez. Drury, quoting an advertisement of the place, remarks "I don't know if it says the truth—I never was in it myself."

The advertisement describes a place which some of our modern barkeepers might well consider. It read: This saloon has been fitted up with a view to comfort, unsurpassed by any similar establishment in Nevada. To a stranger it is a perfect mystery. Upstairs and down, turn as you will, you always find yourself before a bar, supplied with the choicest brands of wines, liquors and cigars. Experienced and attentive barkeepers are always on hand to serve patrons of the house. San Jose Fredericksburg beer constantly on draught. Also English Porter, German wine, St. Louis beer, Milwaukee and the celebrated Culmbach beer on tap."

But, 601 and other law and order to the contrary, Eureka was a long way from being a dull town. Life had its variety—witness this group of items taken at random from the 1880 volume of the venerable Eureka *Sentinel*:

> Jan. 1—The Hooks and the Knicks (the volunteer fire departments) disbanded and immediately reorganized. It was a move to get rid of the stiffs.
>
> Jan. 17—George Cooper took a shot at the late Charlie Lynn in Lautenschlager's billiard hall.
>
> April 1—Miss Lottie Hasty suicides.
>
> April 6—Old Adam, the Shoshone Indian, buried alive.
>
> May 6—Miss Lizzie Maymer on her bicycle—and off again.
>
> June 16—Col. Reilly laid a monster egg in the *Sentinel* office—it is still here.
>
> June 26—First grand Parade in Eureka of the Union Guard Brass Band.
>
> Nov. 18—Patsy Green fills a Chinaman with birdshot on Rudy Hill.
>
> Nov. 23—The cold wave. Mrs. Higley and Benny Small married.

Nov. 24—A Pole partially eats a Frenchman in the Truckee saloon.

Nov. 24—A Paradise reporter turns up his toes.

One can't help but wonder about some of the details of these stories—but the old-timers forgot such trivia. They only recalled the building of the Eureka & Paradise Railroad, the fires and the floods, when the furnaces shut down finally and other major events.

Eureka was the hub of a mining district that included Ruby Hill, a major suburb, and some eight or ten miles south, Pinto City and Vanderbilt City. To the north the largest towns spawned in Eureka's orbit were Diamond City, Mineral Hill and Newark. Diamond City had been a Pony Express station which grew into a mining center following discovery of the Fish Creek Mountain ores.

It seems hardly believable that a busy town in a mining district which was active for thirty consecutive years and produced $6,000,000 worth of ore could be completely forgotten and unknown. But Mineral Hill comes mighty close to being in that category. Outside of the folks in its neighborhood, and some mining men, it is doubtful if many Nevadans ever heard of the once-busy place. Yet, it probably holds a distinction no other Nevada town ever had—it was responsible for a couple of civil suits in the British courts of law.

This town with the unimaginative name, was a contemporary of Eureka. Rich leads were discovered in 1867 by prospectors who seem to have been ignored by history. It is located on the west slopes of the northern section of the Sulphur Springs Range and is just inside the northeastern shoulder of Eureka County. Until 1873, when boundary lines were readjusted, it was in the southwestern corner of Elko County so, like many other Nevada mining towns, it has paid taxes in two counties and its history has to be dug out from two courthouses far apart.

Discovery date is generally given as 1869 in the few places Mineral Hill is mentioned, but the Nevada Bureau of Mines' mineral bulletin credits it with the production of seven tons of ore, netting $5,048 in 1867, so somebody's wrong on the date.

It is known that a big rush followed, which isn't surprising because nearby Eureka and the rich White Pine diggings were in the first flush of their booms at the same time. Mineral Hill was forty-five miles north of Eureka and only thirty-five miles from the Central Pacific at Palisade. This probably accounts for the fact that the town was built mostly of sawed and dressed lumber instead of the logs and stones used for construction in places farther away from a railhead.

Two hotels, the same number of lodging houses, four saloons, two stores, a couple of blacksmith shops, a pair of restaurants, a meat market, bakery, Wells Fargo office and a brickyard were serving the populace by 1870. A year later a fifteen-stamp mill, a three-story hotel, named "The Grand," and a school house were built.

Its ores, mostly silver, but containing small amounts of lead, gold, copper and zinc, were fairly rich—much of it running about $200 to the ton—but the operation never became very spectacular and this may account for Mineral Hill being pretty much forgotten by history.

Actually the Bureau of Mines report shows a steady annual production from the start, through 1887, when it dwindled off every year until 1897, at which time only three tons were reported. There was another brief upsurge for three years, starting in 1912—then nothing more.

The report, based on bullion taxes paid, credits the district with an output of only $1,714,037 through these years—but then, it is generally conceded that nearly everybody paid a token tax on full production. Since the State couldn't possibly have afforded enough deputies to make certain of getting its full share, the actual figures vary with the real returns, depending upon the honesty of the producers. Other sources credit Mineral Hill with a total of more than $6,000,000 profit, so take your choice. In common with other mining strikes, it didn't take the promoting sharpshooters long to discover Mineral Hill. In this case, the genius of the plot was one Asbury Harpending. He was later to become notorious in the west for some infamous promotions—the best publicized being the noted "diamond hoax" in the Uinta Mountains of Utah, which fleeced come of the top New York financiers. A later stock-selling scheme was the Havilah mining boom in the Kern River section of California.

In Mineral Hill's case though, the ore may have fooled even Harpending. He entered the scene in 1871, apparently for an agent named Ike Bateman. He sailed to England as an agent for the owners of the mines. Here the plot begins to thicken.

He contacted one F. Doulton, who introduced him to a financier named Albert Grant. Harpending sold Grant with a flowery sales pitch, representing the ore as "so rich that there is a million dollars worth lying on top of the ground."

Undoubtedly Grant was gullible, as he swallowed Harpending's report—but he was shrewd, too. He formed the California Mining Company, with a capital of $5,000,000, all of the shareholders being his employees. They elected the officers and directors of the company, which was registered in England on May 14, 1871, and agreement was made between it and Harpending for the purchase of the Mineral Hills mines for $1,500,000.

Certainly this was cheap enough, considering that there "was a million" in ore "on top of the ground." The contract of sale was pre-dated to February 20, according to Lester Mills, the Elko County historian in his *A Sagebrush Saga.*

Grant then formed a second corporation, the Mineral Hill Silver Mining Company. It purchased the property of the aforesaid California Mining Company on June 21, for $2,500,000 half in cash, the remainder in "paid up" shares in the new company.

Grant sold stock easily on his claim that mining engineers had been sent from England and upon inspection, "reported the mines exceedingly rich." It was fancy finagling, 1871 style, and it didn't take long for the new company to sell more than enough stock to pay off the entire cost to Grant's closed original company.

Here, though, according to Mills, a new issue popped up, which somewhat obscured the big promotion. Doulton, in Harpending's original contract, had been promised a fee for his part in the affair. He, in turn, had made another side deal with one Thomas Smith—evidently the direct contact to Grant—to pay him one-half of whatever he received in excess of $20,000.

Grant initially paid Doulton $25,000, then later $15,000 more, according to Mills, plus 1000 shares of Mineral Hill Mining Company stock. In the interim Doulton and Smith had had an argument over their deal. Smith notified Grant that he was entitled to half of any more payments after the first $25,000, but the financier ignored his ultimatum and paid Doulton direct. In midst of this fuss Doulton died.

That's when the first suit got into the British courts. Smith sued Grant for his share of the fee promised by Doulton. The case went before the Vice-Chancellory, where the above transactions were aired under oath, and Smith was awarded $8,750, plus interest at four per cent.

The trial attracted wide attention in England, where there was great interest in Nevada mines at the time. British financing was prominent in Austin, Eureka, Cortez and other producing regions of that period.

One editor, Mills reports, wrote, "The point which is worthy of attention is the peculiar manner in which financing such as this is done. To buy a worthless piece of property for $1,500,000 and sell it again for $2,500,000 within five weeks is no bad thing, except for the buyers."

Sure, it was a fine deal for Grant's gang—but it was no different than promoters were accustomed to doing in San Francisco, New York and elsewhere. Some of the Virginia City and Austin deals made this one smell like a rose.

The odd thing about the Mineral Hill promotion was that it really wasn't as bad as painted, if Grant and his company had known how to operate profitably with the complex Nevada ores.

The Mineral Hill Silver Mining Company came in and built a twenty-stamp mill and a costly roasting furnace, which ate up profits. The English company plodded along in typically slow British fashion until 1880 when, unable to meet demands of creditors, it was thrown for the second time into the High Court of England.

Eureka Court House

—Las Vegas Review-Journal Photo.

Old Eureka Theatre

—Photo by Cliff Segerblom, courtesy Las Vegas Review-Journal.

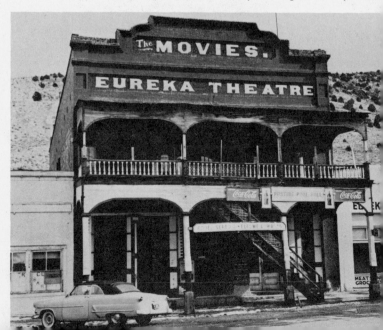

That was the end for Grant and his financial house of cards—the court ordered the mines sold.

The Austin and Spencer Company, an American group which had also been operating mines in Mineral Hill on a smaller scale, obtained the properties with the highest bid.

Mineral Hill slowed down during this period. In 1880, while the English litigation was going on, many residents left the town. By the end of the year only eighteen miners and two families were living there, according to the Thompson and West *History*. Only 113 tons were produced, according to the mineral record, during 1880-82, this by the reorganized firm of Spencer and Barker.

The new company evidently came up with working capital, and production again boomed through 1883 to 1887, and then slowly dwindled off until operations ceased after 1897, when only three tons of ore was reported. The next surge was in 1912 and the subsequent three years, falling off to 106 tons production, netting $3,338 in 1915.

Apparently this was the final gasp, and since then Mineral Hill has just been lying in the summer sun and under winter snow and slowly eroding, falling apart or being vandalized by junkmen and others.

There seems to be no printed record of any shootings, holdups or even social events of the place. Neither is it known whether it had the customary redlight district, being under British control—but it must have had, every mining town considered this enterprise a necessity.

It certainly deserves more than just bare passing mention and a marking on old-time maps—today's maps don't even show a road to it, but one exists—and maybe this notice will let the ghosts of Mineral Hill know that they haven't been forgotten entirely.

Newark, about twelve miles northeast of Eureka, was discovered in 1866 by Stephen and John Beard, who sold out to the Centenary Silver Company. The Beards then went north and placered around Tuscarora, getting in on the discovery of that big-timer. The Newark owners moved a twenty-stamp mill all the way from Kingston, but the workings proved shallow and only about $100,000 was taken out. There are crumbled foundations, and in the mid-1950s, the brick mill chimney was standing—it still may be.

Eureka, through the years, has kept bouncing back. A resurgence occurred in 1909, when eastern capital came in and bought up the old workings, installed pumps to remove water, and planned to go deep for the ore and ship it to the smelter at Salt Lake City.

Tragedy hit in the form of a cloudburst. It dropped on the high hills, a flood came roaring down the canyon, destroying everything in its path. The worst tragedy of all was that the water picked up the roadbed of the "Slim Princess," upon which the life of the town depended, and spread it all over the country under two feet of mud. In a twinkle Eureka was back to the mule wagon days for a connection with the outside world. Then to add a final touch, the bank failed and took most of the local fortunes with it.

However, Eureka went serenely and happily on its way for years, until the mines completely played out—and then continued to exist as county seat and center of an agricultural valley. It always was and still is a town Nevadans can point to with pride. It's a nice place, whose residents mostly always have been friendly folk.

176 Mine, New York Canyon, Near Eureka

—*Courtesy Nevada State Historical Society.*

Life Popped in Palisade

SURE AS SHOOTIN' A LOT OF OLD NEVADANS
are going to say that "Palisade ain't
no ghost town."

"What is a ghost town?"

If you want to take the TV and movie version it's a place where all
the buildings remain, filled with furniture, clothes—even food on the
tables. I contend that any old historical community which once had
hundreds or thousands of active, busy citizens and lived through a period
of lush, rollicking days which now has dwindled to a skeleton existence
where only a few hardy citizens keep it alive deserves historical consideration. It may not be a specter itself, but it's the home of a multitude
of happy wraiths.

Such a place is Palisade—once highly important and very active. Today
it isn't even on the main highway, but it's still perkily alive. The post office
which opened May 2, 1870 never has been closed.

The sepulchral horns of the diesel locomotives on the Southern
Pacific and Western Pacific trains, as they zoom through this Humboldt
River town, are constant reminders of this streamlined age. 'Twasn't always thus. Palisade's hills first echoed the high-pitched toots of the little
funnel-stacked wood-burning Central Pacific's "Leviathan" and "Antelope" in 1868.

So, Palisade, sitting beside the famed Humboldt, thirty-nine miles by
road southwest of Elko, has watched nearly a century of railroad progress,
from spark-spewing little tea-pot engines pulling loads of Chinese track
builders, to today's sleek streamliners that whiz through in a swirl of dust.

But in the old days all trains stopped there—for a variety of reasons—
and this fact caused one of the most delightful legends in all Nevada's
history.

Nobody knows who first dreamed up the idea—probably some of the
rough and ready railroad workers and freight teamsters hoisting a few
dust-laying draughts of brew in the Junction Saloon. There were plenty
of teamsters around in the early 'Seventies. W. L. "Nick of the Woods"
Pritchard, had more than 500 wagons and 2000 animals hauling supplies
to Eureka and other southern mining centers and bringing back ore for
transhipment on the railroad before the Eureka & Palisade was built.

Whoever started the ham-acting drama, it daily became a hilarious
relief from the humdrum life of local citizens. It was such a well-kept
secret that Palisade gained a nationwide reputation for being the
"toughest place in the west." Undoubtedly, there are hundreds of descendants of travelers on early day emigrant trains who cherish the
stories told by their ancestors of the "gun battle and Indian attack" they
witnessed during a stop of the Overland Limited at the little Humboldt
River junction town.

When the train rolled out of the west end of the twelve-mile canyon, commonly known as "the Palisades," it came to a stop so passengers could stretch their legs, pick up sandwiches at the station lunchroom or rush across the street for a couple of quick snorts in one of the saloons. The train always made quite a lengthy halt while the engine was watered and refueled.

Every trainload of tenderfeet climbed down to find the station platform and yards full of scowling-faced rough characters, all armed. When the last passenger alighted it was the signal for the fun to start. Shooting commenced in all directions, "victims" falling everywhere—all of them quickly surrounded by "pools of blood," the "props" being buckets of blood brought down daily from the town slaughter house. Passengers screamed with terror and ran for safe spots, diving under the train and finding protection wherever they could.

Strangely, the only "victims" were the home folks—not a single tenderfoot or member of the train crew ever seemed to be hit by the hail of bullets. None of the passengers seemingly ever noticed that the victims quickly were carried across the street to the Junction Saloon, where they could watch the last act.

The Shoshones, who had lived at this bend of the Humboldt for centuries, got a kick out of the "bang-bang" drama, so they got into the act, too. When the limited "whistled-in" her rear-brakeman, the howling, painted savages suddenly burst upon the scene, and commenced stabbing and scalping victims with enthusiastic abandon.

White-lipped passengers scurried aboard the cars, and the train chuffed away along the Humboldt, with all of them thankful to be alive —impatient to write letters to friends, relatives and newspapers about the killings they had seen. In the meantime Palisadeans laughed merrily over their drinks and thought up ways to improve their "community production."

The coming of the Central Pacific, followed by the rush to the White Pine mines and the subsequent developments at Mineral Hill and Eureka made Palisade a prominent railhead.

Business boomed. Saloons, hurdy houses, hotels and other establishments sprung up to meet the need of the ever-growing traffic through town.

Railroads were beginning to be planned all over Nevada. One of the most logical to be proposed was the Eureka & Palisade, to run ninety miles between the big mining boom town to the south and the Central Pacific main line. Capitalized at $1,000,000, it was organized in November, 1873, by Erastus Woodruff, William H. Enor, Monroe Salisbury, John T. Gilmer, C. H. Hempstead and J. R. Withington.

But things didn't get moving until the following year, when the franchise was transferred to Edgar and D. O. Mills, the eastern railroad tycoons. They found ready financing and buyers for half of the stock in

William Sharon, the famed Comstock financier (whose application for a Palisade, Eureka and Pioche Railroad had been vetoed a couple of years previously by Governor L. R. "Broadhorn" Bradley), A. K. P. Harmon, John Shaw, Isaac L. Requa and Thomas Bell, all prominent in Nevada history.

Lucius Beebe may write all he pleases about the V. & T., and other authors can rumble on as much as they wish about the Central Pacific, but for sheer, unadulterated excitement, the· Eureka & Palisade contributed as much as any narrow-gauge line that ever ambled through the sagebrush.

Of course, Palisade had gained its small place in the sun on the transcontinental line before ore even was discovered at Eureka. But, when the great deposits in the Fish Creek Range began to produce, Palisade's importance grew. It became the railhead for shipments of the ore to smelters and of supplies for the mining camps to the southward, including Hamilton and Pioche.

Consequently it grew into an important anchor spot for a large part of eastern Nevada's development.

"Nick of the Woods" Pritchard had, as they say today, "a real good thing going" with his five-hundred wagons continually churning up dust on the road both ways. Mining operators paid him $20 per ton to haul their ore to Palisade. But, the real jackpot came from the return trip of the wagons. The demand for supplies and materials was very great. Pritchard's ore wagons returned from the railhead filled to their brims. He charged $40 per ton—twice as much as for ore—to carry these foodstuffs and supplies.

It was rumored strongly that Darius Ogden Mills was backing the original incorporators of the proposed railroad in 1873. The route had been pretty well surveyed by Pritchard's ox teams, which had worked out the most feasible grades and stretches during their many trips.

Pritchard wrangled the job of building the railroad line, and started immediately with a crew of fifty-eight white men and more than one-hundred Chinamen. In 1874 the Mills brothers took actual control. Pritchard stayed on. Two years later the roadbed had reached Alpha, thirty-eight miles from Eureka. Then Pritchard suspended the work, as he explained, "for the winter." But the rumor immediately became widespread that the wagon-freight king intended to build the rails no nearer to the mines. Real credence was given this rumor when he began to lay out a town, building a large depot, railroad shops, and a hotel large enough for seventy-five guests at Alpha.

The big mining interests took stock in the rumors and complained to D. O. Mills, demanding that work go ahead on the railroad. He sent his brother, Edward, to the scene and the latter took charge, ordering resumption of construction. Pritchard realized he was "finished," sold his freight and stage lines, and "retired" from the Nevada scene.

The track was completed into Eureka on October 22, 1875, and the first locomotive chuffed into town and was greeted by the howling cheers of 10,000 residents who lined the hills to witness the historic event.

Palisade was the headquarters of the road, with the shops located there. D. O. Mills had installed his brother as president of the line and ordered the finest rolling stock ever built for a narrow gauge, including four locomotives, fifty-eight assorted freight cars and three passenger coaches—all painted canary yellow.

One of the parlor cars, seven feet wide, had scarlet and green plush seats and a capacity of thirty-six passengers. Freight charges were vastly reduced over the wagon rates—$10.50 per ton for base metal between Eureka and Palisade. Flour and hay at $16 per ton bore the highest rates. At these charges the Eureka & Palisade became the major transportation link, through connections with teams at Eureka, for such other boom towns such as Belmont, Tybo, Morey, Hot Creek, Tempiute, Pioche, Hamilton, Mineral City, Ward and Osceola. The railroad ran a wagon line from Eureka to Pioche, and intermediate points, employing around 400 mules in this sideline.

Through the years the sleek little trains chugged forth from Eureka past Diamond, Garden Pass, Old Fourth, Horse Shoe, Oak, Alpha (where Pritchard's big dream died almost before it got started), Blackburn's and Bradley's and through Pine Valley to Palisade, and connected with the Central Pacific. Fare from Palisade to Eureka was $8.40. (Readers might be interested in some of the through fares from Eureka in those days . . . to San Francisco $45.75, Reno $29 and Ogden $31.)

The road paid its original cost back to Mills in the first year of operation and continued to increase his wealth at the same rate for several years. It hauled as much as 35,000,000 pounds of base metal ingots annually during the years when Eureka was the bright star in the mining world.

Palisade, too, boomed ahead in keeping with its new status as a busy railroad terminal. Thompson and West's 1881 *History* describes the town following the E. & P.'s arrival as consisting of "two hotels, two saloons, a barber shop, a boot and shoe shop, two stores, a post-office . . . the shops of the Eureka and Palisade Railroad Company, and various railroad buildings. At these shops are manufactured all the box and flat cars required by the company. Large piles of base bullion bars are usually to be seen stacked up at the freight house waiting shipment. During 1878, 31,038,884 pounds of base bullion were brought by rail from Eureka. The water supply is brought from a huge tank located on the mountain side to the northward at a height of three-hundred feet. This, in turn, is supplied from never-failing mountain springs. The recent census (1880) gives the population . . . white and blacks 165, Chinese 48, Indians 40; total 253."

The little railroad town had become a permanent fixture on Nevada maps, even though its fortunes ebbed and flowed with booms and busts of various mining sections.

Life in Palisade and Eureka, in fact, all along the weed-grown right-of-way of the Eureka & Palisade, had grown dull and desultory during the dead decades of the late nineteenth century. The Tonopah-Goldfield booms at the start of the 1900s were like a stiff jolt of adrenalin to all the state's old mine towns. Eureka perked right up when U.S. Smelting obtained control of the mines and started shipping low grade ore to its mills at Salt Lake City. Ogden Mills, who had succeeded his father, D. O., as the head of the railroad empire, picked John Sexton, who had been a favorite of the elder Mills, to put the little narrow gauge back on its feet so it could handle the suddenly-booming traffic.

The new E. & P. manager was 55 when he swung down from the mainliner at Palisade. He was just under medium height, square jawed, slightly bald, with wide-apart, deep-set bright eyes and a pleasant but quizzical expression on his face.

H. A. Lemmon, of Reno, in a speech about Sexton in the early 1920s, declared that he "still lives in a past age and cannot seem to adapt himself to the simplicity of today, who labors under the delusion that his railroad property is his own and who is obsessed with the amusing old-fashioned notion that he will run it as he sees fit and that if the state and government don't like it they can, jointly and severally go plum to blazes."

I'll wager Sexton used stronger language than that. He didn't like attorneys either, and never employed one while he ran the E. & P. He quickly put the road and its rolling stock in top condition—and showed an immediate profit, something the little narrow gauge hadn't recorded for many years.

His first publicized battle was with the all-powerful Southern Pacific, which long before had taken over the original C. P. The big company's mainliners habitually roared through Palisade at full speed.

The E. & P. tracks crossed those of the S. P. right in the heart of town. One day the eastbound Overland Limited came rolling out of the tunnel and spread one of the E. & P.'s handcars, and an Italian section hand, far and wide.

Sexton wrote a letter to Julius Krutschnitt, president of the S.P., suggesting that he instruct his train crews to use a little caution when zooming through Palisade. The S.P. president brushed off the E. & P. official's complaint sarcastically, by pointing out that the S.P. carried the traffic of an empire while Sexton only operated two trains weekly.

That did it! The next S.P. train that came rolling into Palisade had to burn brakes and wheels for a sudden stop, and was held up four hours. By odd chance, an E. & P. train, loaded with rusty old steel rails, was stranded with a broken truck right across the main line. Sexton was "desolated" over the fast train's delay, and expressed even more sympathy

Palisade, Eureka County, about 1870
—Courtesy Nevada State Historical Society.

Boarding House at Cortez, Eureka County
—Courtesy Las Vegas Review-Journal.

bcause his entire section crew and the E. & P. wrecking derrick "were at the other end of the line."

A few days later, one of Sexton's trainmen "failed" to make a flying switch and a car jumped the tracks—again, strangely across the main line, where it again held up traffic. Southern Pacific officials screamed dire threats—but the accidents continued until the S.P. agreed to bring all its trains to a complete stop before crossing the light rails of the little E. & P.

So, for a great many years afterward, every S.P. mainline engineer respectfully saluted the narrow-gauge rails of the E. & P. with five whistle toots before starting up again to roll on his way.

Sexton's next famed battle was with the State officials at Carson City. The State Tax Commission was composed of the Governor, attorney-general and the three members of the Public Utility Commission. This group also constituted the State Railroad Commission. This fact afforded Sexton quite a problem.

When he appeared before the group, sitting as the Public Utility Commission, he had to establish his valuations at a top figure to justify high rates. Then, a few weeks later he would have to appear before the same men acting as the Tax Commission, and try to persuade them that the property wasn't worth half as much as he had said before in order to keep tax assessments reasonable.

The Tax Commission sent him a citation to appear and show cause why valuations of the road shouldn't be increased considerably for tax purposes. Sexton didn't even acknowledge it. The commission obtained a writ from the Supreme Court. When the Eureka County Sheriff attempted to serve it he found that there wasn't a train running on the E. & P. and all its offices had been closed . . . to all appearances the railroad was out of business.

Sexton remarked that the Tax Commission could establish its assessments on the basis of the value of the property "as junk." The State Railroad Commission, composed of the same members, ordered Sexton to start running his trains. He stood pat.

The State officials tried every sort of legal remedy. None worked. Eureka residents were boiling, and demanding that the officials do something since they otherwise wouldn't be able to lay in supplies for the winter. The Nevada politicians even pleaded with Ogden Mills to repudiate Sexton's action.

The railroad tycoon expressed sympathy and showed them a contract with Sexton giving him full power to act. The document still had three years to go—but some of the officials later declared that the ink was fresh on it, although it was dated two years previously. Then the State tried to compromise. Sexton wasn't having any.

The State officials finally gave in and trains started running again—but commission members were out to "get" Sexton.

The U.S. Smelting people had enjoyed a ridiculous rate of a quarter-cent a ton per ton-mile on its ore from Eureka to Palisade. This tariff had been set before Sexton took over, so he promptly, without bothering to get commission approval, raised it to one cent.

The smelter officials ran screaming to the commission, which issued an order commanding Sexton to appear. The latter jumped a mainliner, went to San Francisco, visited S.P. officials and in a few days a joint tariff was issued by the Southern Pacific and Eureka & Palisade covering the through shipment of ore from Eureka to the company's smelter at Salt Lake City in Utah. This action removed Sexton from the authority of the Nevada Commission. The latter and the smelter company appealed to the Interstate Commerce Commission, which set a date for. a hearing. Sexton then cancelled the through rate and the federal body disclaimed jurisdiction. This put the battle back in the State's Commission's hands, and its members gleefully set a date immediately for a hearing. Those who were watching this cat-and-mouse game wondered what Sexton possibly could do next.

The shipping point for the smelting company was at the Ruby Hill mines, several miles from Eureka. A few days later the mining company frantically telegraphed the railroad commission that Sexton crews were tearing up the track on this mine branch.

The commission immediately obtained a federal court injunction commanding the E. & P. officers and employes to cease destroying the track. A federal marshal was dispatched on the next eastbound S.P. limited to serve the writ. When he arrived at Palisade there was nobody there upon whom to serve it—there wasn't a single official or employe of the E. & P. in town, the ticket office was closed, and there was no way to telegraph to Eureka. He wired Carson City for instructions and was told to get to Eureka in any way possible and serve the order. He hired a rig. Two days later, when he arrived in Eureka, he found that the entire twelve miles of track to the mines had been removed.

The commission capitulated. The smelter company agreed to the one cent rate, and also to pay for replacing the rails. Everybody else laughed, probably including the federal judge who issued the writ, and said, "Old John whipped 'em again." Magnanimously, Sexton invited the members of the state commission to join him for a hunting trip. They didn't accept.

Succeeding commissions occasionally took a flyer at Sexton, but more as a diversion from routine than anything else. None of these affairs ever went far because the officials knew they couldn't whip the E. & P. boss in the end.

But back in Washington there were some, notably Postmaster General Burleson, who unwittingly stumbled pompously upon Sexton's spear. For several years mail had been carried by stage to Eureka for $8,000 a year—but when snows blocked the passes, the schedule was sporadic.

The postal department sent an inspector from Washington, who offered the contract to the E. & P. at $16,000 annually if and when the usual formalities were completed and a bond posted guaranteeing regular delivery.

Sexton snorted. He informed Burleson's minion that there would be no bond, no formalities and no fines for delays. On that basis he was willing to haul the mail at the old rate of $8,000, but only as he pleased. The inspector threw up his hands in frustration and entrained for Washington.

It was a heavy winter. Mails from the overland trains began to pile up at Palisade. More inspectors came to plead with Sexton. Wires kept sizzling back and forth between Washington and Palisade. The federal officials insisted that Sexton was operating "an alleged railroad and couldn't refuse to transport the mail."

Sexton promptly informed them that his railroad had its rights, too, and would carry the mail only in the same manner that he transported other commodities—and that was without bond, contract or fines.

Two Washington inspectors received orders to proceed to Eureka and investigate matters at that end of the line. They did—Sexton even gave them passes. When they went to pick up their tickets at Eureka for the return trip the agent was sorry, but all trains had been cancelled—he didn't know "when there would be another."

The inspectors fumed and fussed and telegraphed Washington. Finally they were advised to hire a sleigh and make the return trip to Palisade. The passes were full of snow. The road had been little used for many years, so it took the inspectors and their driver six days to make the ninety-mile trip.

They were weary, cold and disgruntled as they came over the hill out of Pine Valley and looked down into Palisade, but they probably turned the air blue when they saw an E. & P. train pulling in from Eureka.

When that story got into the nation's newspapers Postmaster General Burleson's dignity was deflated dangerously. He called for help from his colleague, the Attorney-General. This dignitary came up with a regulation which put Sexton's railroad into a class which could be forced by the government to carry its mails on all regular passenger trains.

The E. & P. had two such regular passenger trains scheduled in its printed timetable every week. Burleson and his boys figured they had that pesky fellow out in the sagebrush hooked at last. The postal department sent a bevy of fairly important dignitaries, bolstered by a gentleman from the Attorney-General's office, to impress Sexton with the might of government and his necessary compliance with the regulation.

In the meantime more and more mail for Eureka piled up mountain-high at Palisade—all because the postal department insisted that the E. & P. put up a bond and comply with its red-tap regulations.

The party from Washington was happy to see an E. & P. train made up, a passenger coach at the rear and steam in the locomotive, when the group alighted from the limited. They walked over to Sexton's office and he greeted them pleasantly. He drew the attention of the group to signs posted prominently announcing that "All regularly scheduled trains are indefinitely annulled," and that only special trains would be run "hereafter." It was dated that day.

The spokesman for the federal party protested that the train on the tracks apparently was slated to leave on schedule, and demanded that the pile of mail be put aboard.

"That's a special—you'd better read the sign on it," Sexton chuckled.

The party adjourned to the platform and found a large canvas banner stretched along the side of the passenger car. It read, "Special Train, This Car for Japanese and Dogs Only."

By this time everybody in the nation was interested in reading about the running battle between the Postmaster General and Sexton—and most of them, since the public is prone to pull for the underdog, were backing Sexton.

The "Japanese-Dog" banner hit national headlines—and further, was put on the.overseas news wires. At this period, the Japanese were a sensitive race, and Nippon's newspapers screamed loudly at such an "insult." The Japanese foreign minister protested to Washington. This brought the matter to the State Department—the third Washington agency to get mixed up in the Eureka mail mess.

A search of the laws, that fitted the case, availed none—nothing prohibited Sexton from running special trains for anybody or any group. The State Department asked Senator Newlands of Nevada, and Senator McMillen of Alabama, to hurry to Palisade on a "diplomatic mission" and tactfully explain to the irascible Sexton that he was causing the nation considerable pain and humiliation.

The E. & P. boss was at his genial best, having known Senator Newlands for many years and taking an immediate liking to Senator McMillen. He listened, and then said, "Gentlemen, any dealings with the Government is bound to cause pain to someone." Then he suggested that he had prime old stock which he kept for such an occasion, although he didn't partake himself, he felt certain the Senators would appreciate it. .

Secretary of State Lansing was busy cabling apologies to Japan and wiring the Senators to take action quickly. The Senators took the next limited back to Washington, mellowly influenced by their genial host and his fine private stock, and pushed an immediate bill through Congress which gave the Postmaster General special authority in negotiating certain mail contracts, and he immediately wrote one the way Sexton had wanted it all the time.

The regular schedule of the E. & P. resumed, this time carrying the mails without benefit of bond, red-tape contracts or other folderol. It continued to haul the mail on that basis until the line ceased operation a few years ago.

Once, during World War I, a high official mentioned to Sexton that he couldn't run a special train except on government order and a permit of the State Railroad Commission. Apparently this gentleman had never heard of the above case—or many others similar—and Sexton's reply probably sums up the man's attitude as well as anything he ever said.

He told the official, "Well, by God, the Government and the Nevada Railroad Commission aren't running this railroad, and they aren't going to. I am doing that little job myself."

He did it, too—even William Gibbs McAdoo, when he became federal administrator of railroads during the war period, was wise enough not to order Sexton to do anything with the E. & P.—although he may have suggested an item or two.

The Sexton saga could string out with many such instances of this colorful character's antagonism of orders and red-tape, but one more should suffice to show the sheer joy he got out of living.

Because of the man's magnetic way of handling people to get things done he was made chairman of Eureka County's Council of Defense during the first World War.

He had just accepted the position when the Second Liberty Loan drive was announced. He wired the state chairman early on the first day of the drive, "Eureka quota of $176,000 subscribed. I am taking entire amount."

And he did just that—subsequently distributing the bonds to his neighbors so thoroughly that every third person in Eureka County had purchased one of them. That's the way Sexton got things done without following the normal routine.

Then, too, one story still lingers on among the few old-timers left in the county. Ask any one of them about Sexton's knitting bee, then sit back and listen. The Red Cross issued a nationwide plea for people to knit sweaters and socks for the soldiers—any World War I vet will remember them.

Nobody knows how Sexton accomplished it, but Eureka County residents believe they held the national per capita championship knitting honors at that time. Lemmon, in his speech, recalled that "one of the most pleasing sights I ever saw was on a visit to the Palisade school where every teacher and pupil was busily knitting . . . but more inspiring still was when I stepped into the town's one saloon and found the usual crowd of hangers-on with chairs tilted back against the wall, and every mother's son of them manipulating knitting needles and a ball of yarn, even including the bartender. Sexton did all sorts of things—one wonders how."

But he still wanted no truck with federal red-tape. Somewhere there still may be an old retired regular army officer who remembers when Sexton refused government vouchers to haul drafted men from Eureka to Palisade.

"When I do business with the government I have to pay cash," Sexton told the flabbergasted Major. "But when the government does business with me I have to wait and wait and sign a million papers. I have decided that from now on it will have to pay cash for anything I have to sell it."

He stuck by it, too, and Uncle Sam's national army draftees from Eureka had to ride to Palisade in wagons the government rented from somebody willing to take the vouchers.

Yet, Sexton liked and helped Service men—no man in uniform, who was not on government business, ever had to have a ticket to ride E. & P. trains as long as Sexton ran the road.

He hated anything or anybody anti-American as did the rest of the Palisadeans. So when a fiery-throated I.W.W. member stopped off and made a speech defaming the President and American soldiers, a mob quickly grabbed him, stripped off his clothes, added a suit of tar and feathers, and sent him headed down the mainline toward Dunphy, the next station sixteen miles away.

The head of the State Defense Council demanded of Sexton why, he, as county chairman, didn't halt the men. The letter was answered immediately. Sexton recited how incensed the Palisade residents had become at the treasonable utterances of the visitor and said that he had gently remonstrated with the speaker, seeking to show him that he was in error. Failing, Sexton said that the citizens had quietly escorted the I.W.W. to the outskirts of the town, "gently removed his clothing, which they laid in a neat pile," and that then some citizens "whose identity I could not establish" carefully warmed some tar to an agreeable temperature, selected only the softest and best grade of goose feathers from a pillow someone had found, and then applied the tar and feathers with "delicacy and tenderness."

The county chairman continued that he had personally and vigorously protested such "villainous" acts and had "struggled with his neighbors" (whom he couldn't identify) but had been rudely seized and "forcibly compelled to witness this violation of the laws, both federal and state."

He closed the missive with an explanation which the State Committee found "eminently adequate and satisfactory." Sexton explained, "after the tar and feathers had been applied, this unruly and illegal mob said to the innocent victim of their inflamed passions, 'Now, you blankety-blank son of a blank, if you ever show your head again in this community, we will lynch you.'"

Then he concluded the missive with, "By God, we'll do it, too."

No, Palisade, with its constant stream of moaning streamliners, is no ghost town—but, oh man, what a happy gang of wraiths it has sitting around in its ectoplasmic sphere recalling to each other the gay times of the past when its now long-gone spectral railroad was a busy little narrow gauge which took no guff from the big lines and made more money than some of them ever dreamed of making.

It's a sure bet that one of the top ringleaders of this phantom clan is twinkling-eyed John Sexton. Why, it's a sure-shot wager that even the ghost of old "Nick of the Woods" Pritchard quiets down whenever Sexton's specter flits into the crowd.

Remains of Como Stamp Mill

—*Las Vegas Review-Journal Photo.*

Early View of Tuscarora

—Courtesy of E. W. Darrah.

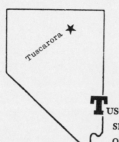

Tuscarora Tooted

TUSCARORA WAS A ROOTIN'-TOOTIN' RIP-
snorter of a town. More than most
others of Nevada's early mining camps
it came the closest to being the pro-
totype of a movie writer's dreams. It had gold, silver, miners, prostitutes,
leading citizens, shoot-'em-up buckaroos, fraternal bodies, Indians, stage
robbers, 6000 Chinese, traveling opera troupes, gun fights, stamp mills,
isolation—being snowed in sometimes for months—and an unusual historical name. In fact, it had just about everything!

Why it missed a shining place in Nevada historical lore is hard to understand. It is mentioned here and there, but until recently nothing ever
seems to have been done to uncover one of the richest treasure troves in
Nevada's bonanza history. Credit for digging it out of the musty, brittle
files of the Elko *Free Press* and the Elko *Independent* goes to Lester W.
Mills, long-time Elko high school teacher. These facts are included in an
Elko County history, published under the title *A Sagebrush Saga.*

Among the hundreds of prospectors who flocked to the Reese River
strike and then branched out in all directions seeking mineral were John
and Steve Beard. They found and sold their claims at Newark. Then they
heard rumors of rich ore to the northward and plodded off in that
direction.

They moved on and on until they got into the Goose Creek country
around two hundred miles northeast of Austin. There on a hill at the
6200-foot elevation, they found placer gold in 1867.

Placer deposits in Nevada's dry high desert were different than
those in the streams of California. Most of that state's mineral strikes
came from the finding of outcrops. A few colors from the ground-up
pieces of these would cause an old-time prospector to grow excited. But,
much of Nevada's gold didn't appear in out-crops. In many cases the
ledge had eroded away from millions of years of exposure to weather
and spread the gold through the surrounding ground. Tuscarora was
such a discovery—as were others in this northern region, Cornucopia,
Gold Creek, Cope, now Mountain City, and many others.

Although some sources give the discovery date as 1868, it must have
been a year previously because a mining district was organized there
on July 10, 1867. Present were the Beard brothers, plus Ham McCann,
William Heath, C. M. Benson, Jake Madeira, Charles Gardner, A. M.
Berry and John Hovenden, old-time prospectors who undoubtedly were
the first to follow in the footsteps of the Beards to the new strike.

When the question of naming the new district was brought up, Benson
suggested Tuscarora. He explained that when he was young he had been
a sailor on the U.S. gunboat *Tuscarora,* and always liked the name. The

others agreed that a warship's name would make a good mining district title.

Nearby hills and canyons soon were prospected by the increasing horde, which appropriately called the discovery hill Beard Mountain—a title it still bears. Water was brought to the diggings in a ditch from McCann Canyon, and by 1871 Tuscarora was known throughout the west for its surface placer gold which was yielding the locators anywhere from $4 to $20 a day per man.

It was W. O. Weed, seeking richer ground that year, who ran across a silver ledge a couple of miles northeast of the original camp. The Beard Mountain miners moved en masse to the new strike, seeking other ledges. Among them were the Beard brothers. They staked a location which later was to become the Navajo, one of the richest producers in the district. However, as so many others who made rich discoveries, they sold the Navajo a short time later for $10,000. It went on to produce $3,000,000 and the Beards, following a common pattern, were in poor financial circumstances in their last years. Steve, however, achieved a distinction uncommon among most prospectors—he was elected to, and served a term in the 1878 state legislature.

All the new discoveries in Tuscarora also were rich in horn-silver. This soft, rich ore presaged a bounteous future for the district. However, it wasn't until 1872 that the Goose Creek community began to grow into a real town in its new location.

One Colonel DeFrees, enroute from Elko to the Cornucopia strike, was impressed with the ore he saw at Tuscarora, and went looking for some of his own. He uncovered a ledge on what became known as Porphyry Hill and soon other similar ledges were discovered, the assays showing values of as much as $600 in silver and $60 in gold to the ton.

That really started a new rush. Original Tuscarora was completely abandoned and a new town laid out on Mt. Blitzen's slopes—retaining the original Indian name, however. Stores went up, homes were built, and machinery was hauled in by ox-teams from Elko, the bustling county seat and Central Pacific town which had boomed as the railhead for the White Pine mines.

Tuscarora busted at the seams and rapidly became the rip-snorting hell-roarer of Nevada for the next fourteen years. The broad, good natured figure of hearty Smith Van Dreilen was one of the most familiar in those days. This plump Dutchman was the pioneer stage operator from Elko to Tuscarora and continued to run his fleet of horse-drawn wagons until the mines were dissipated.

Several other stage lines were soon plying the route from Elko through Taylor Canyon and up the slopes of Mt. Blitzen. "Uncle John" Gibbons was the best known and liked among the stage drivers who wheeled their vehicles through rain, snow, slush and wind, keeping difficult schedules between the two points.

Probably every difficulty known to staging occurred on the Tuscarora run. Snow often piled up eight or nine feet on much of the high-altitude trail, and drifted as deep as twelve feet in the Taylor Canyon section. During this period runners replaced the wheels and when travel became impossible, even in this manner, drivers, who had no passengers, frequently unhitched their horses and allowed them to use their instinct to go to safety. During the alternately thawing and freezing spring months it was necessary to make frequent changes from wheels to runners to traverse the varied snow-covered and muddy sections of the road.

Flooded streams were another hazard. Driver Joe Mattos barely escaped with his life fording the raging Rocky Creek in 1882. The horses and wagon were swept downstream, the animals drowning, and the vehicle being demolished. The driver escaped by grabbing an overhanging limb and pulling himself to shore.

Some idea of the rapid growth and extent of Tuscarora business may be gleaned from a report in an Elko paper on August 26, 1877, which said that twenty-eight railroad carloads of freight had arrived for Tuscarora. It listed the cargo as including six cars of general merchandise, three carloads of salt, five of lumber and the others machinery and other equipment.

This vast bulk of feight had to be hauled the fifty-two miles over rough desert road by wagon. The perishables and lighter articles went by horse drawn "fast freight," the rate being three cents a pound, fifty per cent higher than the two-cent charge for "regular freight" by slower ox-drawn wagons. It took two days one way for "fast freight," a week for "regular freight."

The usual freight team consisted of sixteen oxen, weighing around 1600 pounds each and much stronger than any horse or mule string pulling a train of four huge loaded wagons. On steep hills it became necessary sometimes to split the train and haul the wagons to the top two at a time.

Old Elko newspapers reported as high as seventy-five outfits on the road at one time during Tuscarora's busiest days—that means three-hundred or four-hundred wagons.

One thing hasn't changed much during the last century in Nevada—activity still goes on twenty-four-hours a day, especially in the casinos and bars. Early-day Tuscarora, like all the other booming mining towns of that time, never dreamed of any such thing as a two-day workless weekend, a three-day holiday, or in fact, any holiday except Independence Day. The constant chase for riches continued every day, including Christmas, Thanksgiving and Sundays. Determined pressure by church folk finally brought about the Sunday closing of stores in 1876—but it was 1889 before merchants agreed to close on Thanksgiving.

Tuscarora's 3000 miners worked hard—but they played just as hard. In the traditional American pattern, Saturday nights were times for fun. The first stops always were made in the town's many saloons where everybody fueled up for the evening's frolic. The favorite drink through-out Nevada was whiskey straight and few were the citizens who ever stopped after two or three shots—they'd have been considered a weakling.

Anyway, whiskey was considered a needed tonic in those early out-of-the-way boom towns. An advertisement which appeared in the Elko *Independent* in 1879 is an illustration. It read, "100,000 cases—Great Remedy—Strongly recommended by the Medical Faculty for all cases of: Nervousness, Debility, Indigestion, Fever, Weakness, Dyspepsia, Chills, Etc.—SIMOND'S NABOB WHISKEY. This is pure barley and wheat spirit, remarkable in fragrant ehers, which imports a delicate aroma. The solid residue contains a large amount of tannin, derived from storing in oak casks, which imparts to fine old whiskey one of its individual qualities.—B. Reinhart and Co."

After priming their pumps, Tuscarorans fared forth on Saturday nights for a variety of fun. A fight or two, or a fire, a visit to a social club, an opera or theatrical performance, an oyster supper and certainly a visit to the miners' real social center, the redlight district. Tuscarora may have been isolated, but it was never dull—nor lacking in any of the pleasures enjoyed in more metropolitan centers.

The annual Fourth-of-July celebration was more of the same, with added flourishes. It always started off with an anvil salute—the customary number being twenty, though in some of the larger places the blasts sometimes tallied as high as forty. Mills notes that Tuscarora's miners opened one Fourth with a twenty-nine anvil salute—but nobody has discovered why this number was selected, possibly because the noise-happy miners managed to round up fifty-eight anvils.

It took two anvils to make such an explosion. The chisel hole of the lower one was filled with black powder, the second placed upside down over it. When the powder was ignited, by a blaze on the end of a pole, the blast blew the top anvil skyward with a tremendous noise.

The day always featured various contests, races of all sorts, nail-driving events for the women and others in which skill or speed could be matched. Tuscarorans particularly liked weight-throwing events in which they could pit their muscular skills.

A story in the Elko *Free Press* records the fact that W. A. McDougal, a burly Scot, flung a sixteen-pound miner's sledge a distance of seventy feet, eleven inches on July 4, 1888. It was a new record—and as far as known still stands. Today's hammer throwers, using an iron ball on a cable, spin rapidly and toss the same weight thrice that distance—but how far could they throw a cumbersome miner's sledge?

Plunkett's Hall was the town's major social center, according to files of the Tuscarora *Times-Review* (rates "Invariably in Advance, fifty cents a month by carrier"). Virginia City's Opera House had railroad car springs supporting the floor—Tuscarora's Plunkett's Hall topped this. It had a tilting floor—used on the flat for dances and such events, tipped down at one end for theatrical affairs.

Some of the finest touring opera and theatrical companies made the hard, long trip to Tuscarora and found appreciative audiences which made the rough journey worthwhile. The Goose Creek miners liked their theatricals. Take the case of the Nellie Boyd troupe. At Elko, its efforts in presenting *Franchon the Cricket, East Lynne* and *A Case for Divorce* were too sophisticated for the local audiences, which critically commented in loud and emphatic voice throughout the productions. After three nights, Nellie cut off her Elko appearances and hauled her props and troupe to Tuscarora, which then was the largest city in the county.

There the company's performances were liked so well that it was requested to remain a second week. This caused the editor of the Elko *Independent* to chide his own townsfolk by writing "Nellie Boyd's troupe is to play another week in Tuscarora. They are appreciated there." Probably what the Elko editor failed to realize was that the miners on Mt. Blitzen were more intrigued with the appearance of fluffy femininity than they were critical of the players' acting abilities.

That may do an injustice to the Tuscarorans. Certainly they had a hankering for some of the niceties of life, as records show that the town boasted two skating rinks, a ballet dancing school and an elocution teacher, as well as an early established regular school with classes through the first ten grades. The Goose Creek town also boasted the customary mercantile establishments and churches and two booming lumber companies, one of which covered a larger area and carried a bigger stock than can be found anywhere in Elko County today.

It was natural in such a fast-growing district that claim jumping would become common. The notorious incident occurred when "Long Tom" Smith moved in on a piece of ground which had been set aside as an alley in the Tuscarora business district. When business men remonstrated, "Long Tom" chased them off with a pistol. Two, John Howerton and W. W. Bobier, suffered clouts on the head for their efforts. They were so mad that they demanded the local deputy sheriff oust Smith from the area. This worthy took a long look at "Long Tom's" ready forty-four and decided to retire to the brewery to map out a strategical plan. Smith, emphasizing his determination, blasted a couple of shots into a nearby store, narrowly missing the proprietor and proclaimed profanely that no so-and-so was going to chase him from his claim.

Sheriff Ed Seitz was summoned by telegraph from Elko. Being of sterner stuff than his deputy, he moved in and took "Long Tom" into custody, ending Tuscarora's downtown claim "war."

This event, however, caused Tuscarorans to demand that Elko County officials give them suitable police protection befitting the largest community in the county. A Justice of Peace was appointed but he proved no solution since he spent practically all of his time as a patron of his fav-

orite saloons. Claim jumping continued and there was talk of riding the
soused Justice, suitably bedecked in feathers, out of town on a rail. He
finally resigned when the citizens threatened to organize a "601."

This brought out the establishment of real law and order. However,
Tuscarora continued to be one of Nevada's real early-day hell-raisers.
One of the best known tales of an amusing town character is about a lad
with the strangely spelled name of Rockafellow, who was considered the
champion loud-mouthed user of vile language in public. His favorite target, for some now-lost reason, was a Major John Dennis.

Establishment of law and order soon brought him before the bar of
justice charged with making public threats against the Major. Dennis
immediately bailed him out, informing the Judge that he was doing so
for "the pleasure of beating hell out of him."

The tale has a twist. History records that Dennis received the beating
of his life, after which Rockafellow left town and the Major's bail money
was forfeited.

When the wind was right you could smell Tuscarora for miles. The
Goose Creek mining boom hit just at the right time to absorb a great
many of the 10,000 Chinese whom Charlie Crocker had imported to build
his Central Pacific. When the rails were finished they were turned loose
in a strange land and these Orientals sought any means of livelihood. The
call of gold was as strong in their hearts as it was in the white man's.
When the miners deserted the worked-over placers around old Tuscarora
the Chinese moved in. Soon the constantly burning incense in their joss
houses tainted the clear mountain air and the foreign scent became an
accustomed odor on the slopes of Mt. Blitzen.

One of the classic legends of Tuscarora's old Chinatown is about a
covetous miner who determined to get back some of the gold he had lost
in an Oriental gambling house. He filled a paper bag with black pepper
and sulphur, climbed to the roof of the casino on a cold night when
the fire in the stove was blazing furiously, dropped the bag down the flue
and awaited results.

A coughing pandemonium quickly broke out in the gambling house,
everybody rushing out the front door. While they sputtered outside the
man broke in the rear door, holding his breath, and scooped up several
thousand in gold from the tables. For once somebody "had beaten the
Chinks at gambling."

The sequel was what might have been expected—within a few days he
lost all his loot back to the Chinese gamblers.

The Orientals were indefatigable workers, and retrieved gold from
gravel which had been tossed aside by the white placer miners. They
built water ditches around the mountain—traces of which may still be
seen—and washed out the flakes. In their first year, 1871, reworking the old
diggings, they retrieved $500,000 worth of gold. They rigged up a hy-

draulic machine in Eagle Ravine, and other sluice operations in Gardner, Half Moon and Canton Canyons.

Finally around 1884 they had stripped the sands so thoroughly that hardly a single flake of gold was left. They had picked up better than $1,000,000 worth. Holes and gravel piles are about all that mark the spot today. They moved to richer diggings in other parts of the state and before long the odor of Chinese incense was no longer sniffed in Tuscarora.

Chinatown had only been a sidelight to the big doings going on further up the mountain. Many new mines were located, and machinery was shipped across the mountains to work the ore. Some of the better mines included the Grand Prize, Navajo, Belle Isle, Independence, Dexter, Argenta and Commonwealth.

The strikes in Tuscarora were rich—one of the most fruitful finds in the entire west was in the Hornet. Miners broke into a small underground vein which was almost pure silver.

Grand Prize muckers cracked open a three-foot wide mass of hornsilver at the forty-foot level. Two months later the Grand Prize hit another bonanza. The owners incorporated for $10,000,000, and bought up most of the other paying mines.

The Grand Prize quickly became the major producer. The first months after the mill went into operation it shipped $80,000 in silver through Elko. The first year's report showed shipment of 740 bars, averaging $1880 each, for a total of $1,390,561.58, and paying dividends of $400,000.

Later veins pinched out, and the stock prices dropped, only to bounce up again when a new mass was uncovered. In December 1877, Grand Prize stock was quoted at $940 a share, two months later it skidded to $160, rallied in March with a new find to $450. It bounced up and down, and finally stayed down. Stock was quoted in January 1879 at $5.25 a share. Two years later you could pick up Grand Prize certificates for five cents. The property was sold at a sheriff's sale to the Argenta Mining Company.

Nine years later, a new vein was uncovered. It assayed $35.16 gold, $1411 silver to the ton, and the old Grand Prize bounced upward again. Then it flooded, and it was too costly to pump the water. It has been dead since, but old timers insist it still is full of rich ore.

The roaring town had its full share of mine explosions, knifings, shootings and other violence. A great many of the miners were Cornishmen, who flocked from England to Nevada during the early days. The "Cousin Jacks" were rough and tough and prone to settle arguments with knife duels, no holds barred. The site of these gory affairs generally was in a convenient place—the cemetery.

Those who watch television today probably believe that it was customary for cowboys to infest every early-day town. Certainly this wasn't true in Nevada. Actually the old towns in the northeastern part of the state—Elko and White Pine counties—were the only ones which fitted at all into this picture. Then, as now, this was the "cattle country" of Nevada. Tuscarora probably had more excitement from high-spirited steer herders than any of the other small towns.

This resulted from the arrival of the Altube brothers, Bernard and Pedro—the latter known to all as "Palo Alto." They drove a large herd from California in 1872 and located in the wide valley between the Tuscarora and Independence mountains—the latter being the next eastward toward Elko. They purchased thousands of acres in Independence Valley, their properties running across the entire valley and up the sides of the slopes and extending miles north and south.

Palo Alto was the boss—and dressed befitting a Spanish grandee, huge sombrero, gay-colored serape around his immense shoulders and soft-leather, high-heeled boots. Most of his many buckaroos were Mexicans, hand-picked by Palo Alto to ride his wide ranges and tend his thousands of cattle. They could ride, shoot and toss a lariat with the best. In other words, they were everything a modern script writer could dream. Too, Palo Alto was a paternal and good-natured boss who believed that his men were entitled to occasional sprees for doing their work well and diligently.

When pay days came he'd hand the vaqueros their wages in hard yellow gold coins and tell them to take the day off. The three dozen or more men would mount their mustangs and ride pell-mell for Tuscarora. It was their custom to sweep into town at full gallop, yelling as they blazed away with two six-shooters apiece, letting loose the exuberance which had been bottled up for weeks as they rode the range.

The group would come to a sliding stop before its favorite saloon and pile inside. Then, citizens would emerge from safe hiding places where they had ducked when the familiar sound of the arriving buckaroos had been heard. Danger was past for a moment until the men fully slaked their long-built-up thirsts.

When that point was reached, time came for mothers to herd their children inside and prudent men to hunt cover, because the Altube cowboys continued to relieve their monotony. Lights were shot out, bottles and glasses on the back bars made fine pistol targets and an unwary pedestrian was in for a scary time as the fun-loving cowmen peppered the walk around his feet with shots.

Generally, a few of the buckaroos were tossed into the bastille to cool off. Strangely, as wild as these occasions may sound, records indicate that nobody ever was injured. Tuscarorans became accustomed to the Altube ranch pay day celebrations—and truth be known, probably looked forward to them as a break in the routine monotony.

When the cowboys mounted and swept out of town at conclusion of the periodic celebrations, saloon keepers and others figured up the amount of damage done and sent bills to the ranch. A few days later either Palo Alto, or one of his foremen, would quietly ride in and make the rounds paying for the damage committed.

But today Altube ranch is a mere shadow of its once great immensity, comprising only 45,000 acres, the rest having been broken up and sold to numerous others. The headquarters is known today as the Spanish Ranch and is located on Palo Alto's old stamping grounds.

Her mines having filled with water and her veins having pinched out, Tuscarora like scores of her contemporaries, slowly faded. The constant string of freight wagons plying back and forth to Elko became fewer. In 1885 the head office of the telegraph company in San Francisco, evidently peeved at the cost of maintaining an unprofitable line, sent a message to its Tuscarora agent declaring that if teamsters didn't cease using the poles along the way for fuel that the line would be discontinued.

Today glory holes, filled with water, show that the mines were flooded, not worked out. Wide meadows surround the once-wild town where thirteen big mills ground out ore, and only the stack of Union Mill remains, as a memorial shaft for all the others.

There always is a coterie of old-timers around, ready to yarn about the good old days and waiting for the time when somebody will come in with modern pumps, empty the shafts and bring the old town back to glorious activity again. Maybe that day will come.

Pioneer Bakery at Hornsilver, Nevada

—Las Vegas Review-Journal Photo.

Off to the Mines

—*Walt Averett Photo, courtesy of Las Vegas Review-Journal.*

Some Northeastern Mavericks

CORNUCOPIA, FIFTEEN MILES NORTHWEST of Tuscarora, was a small horn of plenty and ran out its supply of riches in a few short years. Although it was one of the liveliest northeastern Nevada boom towns of the 1870s its total production of gold and silver amounted to only about a $1,000,000. It was a whizzer while it lasted, but its lively ghosts are pretty generally undisturbed by curious visitors these days for the simple reason that it is just about as isolated as it was back in 1868 when Matt Durfee first found colors there.

There is but one way to reach it, via State Route 11 to Deep Creek—sixty-eight miles north of Elko—then up eight miles of mountain goat trail southeastward in the Bull Run Mountains. Unless you're traveling by jeep or jackass don't try to get there.

Matt Durfee was a determined old desert rat who hadn't found anything worthwhile in the Bull Run district around Columbia, another early town a dozen miles north of Deep Creek. He had wandered off into the Bull Run Mountains, pecking at all likely-looking ledges. When any of his samples panned colors he'd bring them back to an old friend in Columbia named Jack Coffman to have them assayed. Time after time Durfee's samples ran too low-grade to be worthwhile, and he went back looking for richer rock. He sampled every ledge in the area and they all showed ore—but not much.

He had camped for three seasons right on a mass of rotten quartz and, like others of those days, paid no attention to it as he prospected ledges. Finally, in desperation, grunting, "Don't look like it'd run a dime to the ton," he picked up a handful of the barren-looking rock and panned it. He refused to believe what his eyes showed him. As he was headed for Elko to get more supplies, he filled a sample sack with the stuff and took it along. An Elko assayer ran the sample and blinked—the campground gravel ran $500 silver to the ton. Durfee at long last had proved to himself that there was rich ore among those Bull Run ledges.

He didn't leak the news, but headed back northward and staked his claims. Then he went on to the Bull Run settlement and told his old friend Coffman what he had found and urged him to go back and stake some claims of his own. The latter refused, saying, "All you got is some loose flakes in gravel, I'll stay here where I know there's gold."

The sequel to this little discovery tale is that soon the secret got out, the rush to Cornucopia quickly brought Matt Durfee a lot of company and a town began to spring up. It soon had its own saloons and other business houses and then the enthusiastic influx grew so large that a two-story hotel was built, the first "skyscraper" in the Bull Runs.

By 1873 the town boasted better than one-thousand residents and records show it had more than four-hundred voters. Among them was Jack Coffman, who could have profited a great deal more if he had gone with Matt Durfee when the latter urged him to come with him and stake original locations.

The stage line was extended from Elko through Tuscarora to the new camp. In 1875 Woodruff and Ennor, who operated the largest transportation system in the state to the busy boom areas off the railroad, inaugurated a competing route from the Carlin railhead to Cornucopia, advertising, "Making fast time. Fare $2.50."

As the development holes went into the hills, more and more ore was uncovered and it wasn't long until almost a continuous pall of dust, churned up by the three-wagon train freight loads pulled by multi-yoked teams of plodding oxen, marked the trail to the shipping railhead at Elko.

Isolated Cornucopia didn't have too much room for fun aside from its drinking and gambling houses and the ever-present bagnios which peddled their brief moments of feminine company to the bearded miners. Occasionally some made the trip to Tuscarora to let off extra steam, especially when the latter community was staging one of its frequent series of horse races.

But like other mineral communities—none of them could hide too far away for the promoters and others of their ilk. Soon Matt Durfee's strike attracted business and professional men anxious to get their major share of the riches.

A few brought their families. This fact resulted in one of the romantically delightful tales of Cornucopia's early days—one which almost seems to have been lifted from the pages of mythology. It was the tidbit of Cornucopia gossip in the autumn of 1874.

The town's baker had a pretty daughter whose company was sought by all the younger men. Competition for her hand was good-naturedly keen. Finally the choice was narrowed down to two of the suitors, a Cornucopia lad and a "city slicker" from Elko, who seemed to have the favor of the father.

Since foot racing was considered proof of a young man's physical ability in those olden days, somebody suggested that the two should compete in a running contest for the young woman's hand. She was agreeable, saying she would marry the winner. Wagers were made. Judges and other officials were selected. The course was laid out. The two men lined up. The starting gun went off. The Cornucopia man, who had the financial and moral backing of most of the home-town folk, streaked down the course to an easy victory.

True to the agreement, the young woman married the winner at a nuptial event which was attended by everybody in the area—and legend, of course, says they lived happily ever after. Probably they did, since rumor whispers that the girl in the case was aware of the fact the Cornucopia lad had been quite some shakes as a foot racer in his old home town before coming west and landing at the Bull Run diggings.

Cornucopia was about as isolated as the Arctic during the long, bitter winters. And like the others of the time, it had its outstanding tragic incident. Lester W. Mills tells about it in his *A Sagebrush Saga.*

In the bitter December of 1873, a deputy sheriff named Ellis was sent to Cornucopia to arrest a badly-wanted man. When he arrived the subject had managed to make his escape and the officers started the sixty-five mile trek homeward.

A Pogonip blizzard caught him, but he plodded onward undaunted. He found a cabin, fashioned a pair of snowshoes from a couple of the boards and continued through the far-below zero weather. Along the route he encountered a stage driver who had taken refuge in a clump of willows and built a fire. The driver urged him to stay with him and continue the trip together when the storm abated. The deputy decided to go onward—the attraction of being home for Christmas appealing more to him than a small fire in a clump of brush.

The following day, the blizzard having died down, the stage driver reached Elko and was surprised to learn that the deputy had not yet appeared. A searching party was organized and combed the entire area between the stage driver's camping refuge and Elko without discovering a trace of the missing deputy.

Later in the spring members of the Elko Masonic lodge, of which Ellis had been a member, renewed the search. They found the body that May, perfectly preserved, beneath a ledge along the creek in Adobe Canyon. The deputy had lain down peacefully, with his arms beneath his head, and frozen to death. He had taken the wrong turn down the canyon while plodding through the blizzard. As happened so many times, he was just a short distance from safety—if he had continued on just a little farther he would have reached Carlin, which lies at the mouth of the canyon he followed.

In the long run, Jack Coffman's original prediction, that Matt Durfee's find was "only a few flakes on top of the ground," began to prove correct. For awhile, it looked as highly promising as cornucopias filled with fruit at a green-grocers—but when the largest, richest mineral ore chunks had been removed from a few yards down, the hungry miners found nothing more. Cornucopia collapsed. Merchants and promoters, miners and prostitutes headed down the Bull Run slopes and hied for happier pastures.

By 1878 nearly everybody had gone—and since that time few humans have intruded to upset the placid existence of Cornucopia's horde of happy ghosts. It's a dandy spectral hunting ground for chasers of Nevada's wraith communities if they travel by jeep or jackass—a helicopter would be better.

It's not unusual that there were many duplications of names in early, vast, meagerly-populated Nevada. Communications were sparse, except on main traveled roads—so duplications such as Midas, Aurora, Hot Springs, Spring Valley, Paradise Valley and such, were to be expected. Too, the westward trek of Southerners following the Civil War, explains many of the deep-south landmark labels and town titles. "Charleston" is a fine example of this Dixie influence.

Southern Nevada's highest peak, 11,910-foot Mt. Charleston, was known to Spanish Trail travelers and the first Mormon settlers as "Snow Mountain" until the southern influence retitled it after South Carolina's major city sometime in the Seventies.

And Nevada's rowdiest and most isolated early-day gold camps in the high mountains in the northern fringe of Elko County also became "Charleston," after first being known as "Alleghany's Camp" and then, more formally, "Mardis"—both in honor of its "founder."

The town of Charleston deserves more than mere passing mention—although you won't find much in print about it anywhere—because it has harbored a parade of unusual citizens from the beginning right through to the present. Among its early denizens, many were "popular" gents who had their pictures posted on walls, posts and trees over a wide area of the west. They found Charleston a haven of refuge. Its situation was ideal—if an approaching dust cloud indicated a posse, it was a simple matter for a man with a price on his head to disappear down-river or into the mountains.

The reputation of the town, which "Alleghany" Mardis fathered, is well illustrated by the report of one old-time Elko County sheriff. Returning from a long man-hunt into the northern wilds, this worthy officer declared, with a tinge of pride, "I didn't get him, but, by damn, I rode plumb through Charleston without being shot at!"

Clad in his grease-spotted buckskins and moccasins, George Washington Mardis, was one early-day character the TV western fiction writers and historians have overlooked. It's too bad, what little is known about him is on a par with "Old Virginny" Finney, the alcoholic christener of Virginia City.

"Alleghany" Mardis, was known along the board walks of Elko, Tuscarora, Cornucopia and other northern towns in the 1870s. He had "fit" Indians as an Army scout, wore his hair long around his shoulders, and one side of his face was scarred and blackened as the result of a battle with the redskins.

"Alleghany" liked to talk—especially after he had wrapped himself around a few gills of red-eye—when he was "in civilization." He fancied himself as a philosopher and a gospel spieler, his interpretations and vernacular being distinctly unusual. But, on the whole, he didn't care to stay long among folks, preferring his own company where nobody could argue with him. At times he was gone for months in the then unknown mountainous district through which the southern Idaho line runs today.

Alone, he could preach fiery sermons to his burro—named "Sampson" according to Nell Murbarger in *Ghosts of the Glory Trail*. Sampson probably twitched appreciative and patient ears and never disputed his master's forceful Old Testament interpretations.

"Alleghany" had been gone several months when he turned up in Elko in the spring of 1870, spreading the news that he had "struck it rich." This time nobody argued—the old Indian fighter had pockets full of shining raw gold nuggets.

When he returned to his strike, he was followed by a horde of gold-hungry prospectors. He led them far to the north, about seventy-five miles, to the southwest flank of 9911-foot-high Copper Mountain, where the Bruneau River sweeps northward to the Snake and thence to the Columbia and the Pacific.

There, along a tributary with the unusual name of "76 Creek," Mother Nature had eroded a rich ledge of Paleozoic sedimentary crystalline rhyolite into well rounded pebbles, among which gold nuggets were thick.

The prospectors who tagged along with "Alleghany" found that the old Injun fighter was right, the gravel ran fifty feet thick in places along "76 Creek" and on the west side of the Bruneau, and their pans yielded two and three dollars with every washing.

"Alleghany's Camp" mushroomed into a street of log cabins, stores, bawdy houses and other establishments of the sort which supplied the needs in such distant, isolated places.

Mardis prospered—and apparently didn't waste all his gold because he soon changed his old buckskins for fancy store clothes and paraded the streets as the "first citizen" of the town, which soon was dubbed Mardis in his honor. As was to be expected, the acquisition of riches changed his life. Where, in the past, women wouldn't give him a glance, he now became a "catch" and soon was led to the altar. Like all others of her sex, the new Mrs. Mardis was looking for "security," and shortly the couple purchased a ranch along the Bruneau where the old man raised fine horses.

About the same time that "Alleghany" found the gold along "76 Creek," young Jesse Cope, a giant young freighting teamster hauling supplies from Silver City, Idaho, to Elko, stopped along the east fork of the Owyhee and also found gold in the gravel. The town of Cope grew up contemporaneously with Charleston, which was some thirty-five miles southeast.

It was natural that there would be a fanning out of prospectors from Cope and Charleston. That's how in September 1873, Emanuel Penrod, C. T. Russell and W. D. Newton discovered the rich Island Mountain district just a few miles northwest of Charleston, along Gold and Meadow Creeks, north-flowing tributaries of the Bruneau. The district was named for an isolated peak which popped up by itself 1000 feet above the surrounding plain. Penrod had been one of the discoverers of the Comstock Lode—and shortly another gold-bearing creek between the two districts bore his name.

The Island Mountain district became one of the richest gold strikes in early Nevada history. The town that grew up there was named Gold Creek and was another wild one in the early days.

As happened in all Nevada placer towns of the period, hordes of Chinese, left adrift with the finish of the Central Pacific, soon moved in to re-work the ground from which the white men had hurriedly panned only the rich nuggets.

All of this resulted in the climax to the George Washington Mardis saga. The tale is a bit vague and garbled in the few sources which record it, even to the year that it happened. But, on September 11 of either 1880 or 1881, Mardis left on a trip from Charleston to Elko—apparently a pretty regular thing for him since he had become a wealthy, ranch-owning, important citizen. Somebody in Charleston asked him to deliver $250 in gold to an Elko merchant in payment of a debt. This fact apparently was known, at least to a six-toed Charleston Chinese resident.

"Alleghany's" fine team returned home pulling his empty buggy the next day and miners and cowboys—the region having developed into ranching territory during the decade since the gold discovery—went searching for him and soon found the old Indian hunter's body, riddled with bullets, the gold missing, near the bridge across Penrod Creek. (Some accounts report the gold was buried near the scene and never found. Why, they don't say.)

Near the body bare footprints were discovered. A Chinese immediately was suspected, the orientals being the only persons around hardy enough to go barefooted. The prints showed six toes on one foot. The irate posse sped to Charleston's Chinatown and forced all the orientals to display their feet until they found one with an extra toe.

While the rough Charleston men felt that this evidence was sufficiently damning, most of them had long resented the one-sided suddenness of vigilante law in the wide open west, and graciously allowed the extratoed Chinese two days to come up with an alibi.

When he failed, he quickly joined his ancestors at the end of a rope, with the entire populace, white and Chinese, as an audience. According to the records, it was one of the last lynchings in Elko County history.

After the placer gold was skimmed, both Charleston and Gold Creek and other mining regions went into a decline and virtually passed from sight for a couple of decades. During this period cattle barons such as the Altube brothers and L. R. "Broadhorns" Bradley, later governor of Nevada, became the "kings" of Elko County.

In 1889 the "great storm" killed thousands of cattle and bankrupted many of the stockmen. They were forced to seek manual labor of any sort. An old Negro made a pertinent comment which is still recalled by old-timers in the region. Noting the economic fall of those who had previously strutted down the streets of Elko, he remarked, "Lawd, Lawd, how de snow done equalize society."

Then, just before the turn of the century, miners discovered the area again and once more the cattlemen had an influx of the rough and ready clan of gold hunters in their midst. The revival started, as before, in Charleston and by January 31, 1895, its rebirth was substantial enough to regain a post office.

Gold Creek blossomed again, too. Shortly it put on airs with a ten-room, three-story hotel, including a bellhop in livery, electric lighted streets, a municipal water system and a newspaper, among other commercial establishments.

Outside interests kept things moving. Some lode mining developed and in 1907 Utah capitalists built a canal at a cost of $25,000 to bring water from "76 Creek" to work the gravels of Badger Creek. Other companies invested, and with modern methods worked out the values, but they ran into many problems, principally the lack of water, except during short periods of the spring and summer.

It was during the turn-of-the-century boom that Pete Itcaina, another fabulous character of twentieth century Elko County, followed the footsteps of "Alleghany" Mardis into the Charleston country. Pete was a fitting successor of Mardis.

Instead of buckskins, he always wore overalls, and was widely known in the entire northeastern section. He first came to Nevada as a sheepherder, starting in the Reno district. Then he branched out on his own in Elko County and built up his holdings steadily, being joined during the years by a brother and four nephews.

In May 1958, he sold his ranch—76,000 acres, including 1100 cattle and 11,000 sheep—for close to $1,000,000, getting $400,000 down payment. He moved his wife and family to their Elko home.

"Alleghany" found nuggets and Pete built a fortune on sheep and cattle—but the latter never let his fortune change him. The classic Elko County story about him concerns the time he went into the Silver Dollar Saloon in Elko and ordered a drink.

The strange bartender, looking at his dirty overalls, refused to serve him. Pete did what many others have wished they could do when they felt insulted. He went right out, bought the Silver Dollar, came back and fired the offending bartender. Pete died at his Elko home on June 4, 1959.

Today you'll find the former wild gold camps almost entirely gone—huge, modern cattle and sheep ranches occupying the country. Old-timers in the area can show you a couple of tumbled log buildings, reported to have housed saloons.

Nobody knows how much gold was taken out of those diggings—those rugged early miners just didn't think it was the State of Nevada's or anybody else's business and never reported the yield. The only recorded production was made on the Island Mountain district from 1934 to 1941 when tax was paid on 529 ounces of gold, 552 ounces of silver, 1,900 pounds of lead and 300 pounds of copper, valued at $19,039.

If this much could be obtained from well worked over diggings in that short period, it may be guessed that many, many times more was gathered in the lush, early days when every placer miner figured anything under $30 a day was poor pickings.

But Charleston's nearby contemporary, Mountain City, originally Cope—being on a busy highway is one of the most resilient towns in Nevada. Four times it has bounced back from oblivion like a yo-yo. It was born from placer gold, boomed as both a lode gold and silver ledge dandy and then after a long dormancy burst forth as a rich copper producer. Slumbering again, it's now looking for a uranium resuscitation. These didoes make it practically an outcast from this state's heavily populated spectral world where all the wiser wraiths realize it is just biding its time catering to tourists and sportsmen while watching for a chance to bust loose again. The story of this far northern community, which lies 17 miles south of the Idaho line, 83 miles north of Elko on State Route 43, has more than its share of historically romantic twists.

Practically all of the west's mineral strikes were made by tireless or lucky prospectors, aided by wandering jackasses who kicked loose the top of lodes, or friendly Indians who traded ore for hooch or grub. Mountain City's gold was found by a husky young driver of an ox-team freight wagon who was weary of plodding along, prodding the slow beasts on the long drag between Elko and Silver City, Idaho Territory. His name was Jesse Cope.

One early summer evening in 1869 as the train of freight wagons camped alongside the east fork of the Owyhee River he complained, as men always have done, about having to work so hard for a living.

"We ought to find a mine—then we could take it easy," was the tenor of his remarks. His companions agreed. New rich strikes were being reported all over the State—White Pine, Tuscarora and numerous others. During the night the idea magnified in the young driver's mind. Early in the morning, before breakfast was ready, he picked up a pan and moved to the river's edge. It was only a few minutes later when the others rushed to his side after he'd let out a yell. His pan showed a crescent of yellow around the bottom edge. That day the tired oxen grazed happily while the teamsters rushed along the river staking claims—among them the Mountain King and the Mountain Queen.

It didn't take long for a town to sprout along the Owyhee. It was called Cope, after the gold discoverer. Old timers called it that through the years, although it became Mountain City before its first autumn when lots were laid out for a townsite by an early-arrived promoter. He profited more than some of the hopeful prospectors when prices quickly multiplied from $300 to $1000 for chunks of land nobody had bothered to look at three months previously.

The evolution of place names is frequently unusual. Jesse Cope, who not only discovered the Mountain City minerals, also found the ores which resulted in the Bull Run-Columbia booms. Today he is practically unmentioned in history and actually, Mountain City, sixty years afterward, is known mostly for its rich copper output or as a prime fishing and hunting resort.

By the first midsummer of the community's boom, the miners themselves limited placer claims to 200 feet of the river front and running back 400 feet from the stream. Plans were made to bring a ditch from the river to the placer grounds. It was to cost $10,000, being paid for by assessments on each miner's ground.

But by the time the ditch was completed the miners had discovered gold-bearing quartz ledges and shifted to these rich ores. Anyway, placer returns which yielded from $5 to $20 a day—good money then— soon dwindled after the rich upper gravel had been skimmed off.

On the other hand the hard ore, full of chlorides, sulphurets and ruby silver, assayed richly. Col. Frank Denver, operator of stage lines, shipped 300 pounds of ore from his claim to San Francisco and received returns of $420 a ton. An assay from another, the Rattlesnake, showed $9820 to the ton. Ore running $150 was uncovered at ten foot levels. So it is hardly surprising that the miners turned to digging ore and ignored the placer working, saying, "Let the Chinamen have them." The Orientals rushed in, as they had done at Tuscarora and elsewhere, and patiently extracted every flake of gold along the river—some of them losing it as rapidly as they retrieved it at the town's Chinese district fan-tan parlors.

Speculation ran high in the early days when sales of "feet" along ledges were the common method of transfer. Some struck it rich, such as two Californians, Davis and Meador, who bought 827 feet of the Mountain City late in 1869 for $25 a foot. One of the luckiest speculation purchases was made in 1870 by W. H. Ramsey and J. A. Hardman, who paid $600 cash for 100 feet of the Argenta, which turned into one of the richest producers of the lot.

Political guillotining of silver ended the first days of Mountain City glory. Exhausted ore bodies helped it down the toboggan slide. By the late 'Seventies the town, which had boasted around 2500 citizens, was nearly deserted.

In the shifting fortune of time the town was revived and died and was revived again. The latest rejuvenation, after 1919, was the work of S. Frank Hunt. He had long been a miner, a geologist and a practical prospector who could visualize the rock strata below ground from outcroppings and surface indications. He was in middle-age, lame and frequently ill. Studying the area, he found an outcropping of gossan some three miles south of Mountain City. The longer he studied the layout the more deeply impressed upon his mind became the picture of a vast copper deposit lying below.

He immediately staked claims and dubbed them Rio Tinto after the vast 3000-year old Iberian mine of the same name—proving that some of the place names in Nevada make sense. Then for the next 10 years, talking his way into grubstakes and spending every cent he could raise he dug an inclined shaft to a depth of 50 feet. Since copper prices were around five or six cents a pound, Hunt became the object of tolerant amusement when he claimed his copper deposits would make Mountain City's previous returns seem like peanuts.

He did succeed in talking several promoters into visiting the location —but all turned him down until 1931, when Ogden G. Chase, of Salt Lake City, agreed to back the exploration. The Rio Tinto Mining Co., was formed and 2,000,000 shares of stock issued, half of it assessable.

The depression was on and the promoters conceived an unusual method of getting rid of the stock free. They sent it out to a vast mailing list. Many recipients threw it into wastebaskets—others politely returned it. A few agreed to string along and pay the assessments set at a maximum of five cents.

Hunt disposed of considerable of it over the store counters, bars and in the Elko redlight district. Nobody believed it was worth anything but they liked Hunt, and accepted it with a wry grin and a feeling of charity.

The initial assessment of two cents was levied and Hunt got together a crew and started to sink his shaft deeper. He predicted that the vast mass of copper was located at a depth of 250 feet. The office force in Salt Lake City and the miners, mucking in the ever-deepening hole, worked without wages, only the promise of future pay keeping things going. Hunt, who was president of the company, not only worked right beside them, he did the camp cooking. Two log cabins and a tent-house at the mine were the nucleus of the future town of Rio Tinto.

On February 23, 1932, the miners hit an ore body at the 227 foot level, closer than Hunt had predicted. The initial samples ran 40 per cent pure copper—the old geologist-prospector had read his geologic surface writings correctly.

The despised and discarded Rio Tinto shares, which had cost no one who still had them more than five cents a share, sky-rocketed to $17. International Smelting Company purchased controlling interest, and moved in complete equipment.

Shortly the big company was turning out 450 tons of ore daily and earnings exceeded $4,000,000 a year. Hunt had been right again, copper was making Mountain City's past seem pretty pale indeed.

The mining firm built a model company town at Rio Tinto. It had modern apartment buildings to attract permanent families, a hospital, an accredited high school, an elementary school, a motion picture theater, social center, newspaper and other modern facilities. A couple of miles away Patsville grew up around the Copper King mine. Both towns had drug stores, shoe shops, cafes, boarding houses and other facilities.

Mountain City zoomed back into the merriest era of its life. A two-story hotel was moved from Gold Creek, the old bank building was repaired and put in use, and other structures soon rose. Eleven saloons supplied the liquid needs of the residents of the three towns.

It took the State of Nevada until 1938 to pave the road from Dinner Station to Mountain City. During the interim most of the shipping went north over the surfaced Idaho roads 117 miles to Mountain Home.

Everything pointed to permanency—the company did its best to bring in metropolitan comforts. The apartments had central heating, the houses electricity and running water. Then one morning in 1947 the company announced that it was closing the Mountain City workings because efforts to find new ore bodies had proven unsuccessful and operations could be carried on no longer at a profit.

Another era in Mountain City's bouncing history had ended. Patsville and Rio Tinto became real specters. Only a few merchants, saloon keepers and gamblers, existing on the small pickings from passing tourists, keep the old place alive. Population slipped to less than one-hundred.

Talk to any of the old-timers in a Mountain City bar and you'll hear optimistic hopes for another resurgence—probably with uranium. One of them expressed the general feeling profoundly by remarking, "As of now, tomorrow must be for Mountain City for today is passing her by."

That easily could be the requiem for scores of other little towns spread over the northeastern corner of the state, including a whole flock of them which once were shipping places on the original route of the Central Pacific. The railroad changed its main line when it built the tracks across the Great Salt Lake, rather than going around the north shore. This left a number of towns which formerly were fairly busy railroad communities without visible means of support.

Nora Linjer Bowman attended a dance held at Tecoma, one of these places, while on a visit to a northeastern Nevada cattle ranch during her college days right after World War I. The remnants of the town's past glories impressed themselves on her mind and she left a near perfect description of one of these forgotten railroad towns in her recent book, *Only the Mountains Remain*.

She wrote: "But, of course, I had to carry on so I fell in line with the crowd going to—above all things—an old dilapidated saloon.

"This large, weather-beaten building housed three establishments. The saloon was in the center, the rooming house on one side and the restaurant on the other. The saloon was about thirty by seventy feet and was a relic of former boom days. At the rear were two enormous doors hung with equally large hand-wrought hinges forged by the local smithy . . . They said men on horseback had entered through these doors, a-roarin' and a-shootin' as they came, and that they left the doors resembling sieves. Tonight the moonlight was softly streaming through the many bullet holes. The saloon had been floored with heavy, three-inch planks of fir, now worn down by the horses' hoofs and boot heels, and some of the knots protruded as high as one or two inches, making the boards both awkward and dangerous to walk on . . . The rusty, pot-bellied stove in the center of the room leaned crazily on its three remaining legs.

"A bar of beautifully polished mahogany extended part way along one wall. On the back bar were sad-looking mirrors cracked by bullets and because of age, were plain glass in spots. The tin shades of the hanging kerosene lamps also bore marks of having served as targets for more than one drunken man's six-shooter. A few decrepit tables and chairs were scattered around, also an old gambling table. It amazed me that so isolated a place as this could have been self-supporting, but Herman claimed it had been, for men on horseback had come from as far away as two-hundred miles. They'd also had customers from the nearby mines and railroad. We stepped up to the bar, put one foot on the brass footrail, and looked at the bartender . . . Across his vest hung a heavy watch chain . . . Very deliberately he pulled out his plug of tobacco, cut off a generous chew, moistened it well, spit a few times . . . 'Ladies (emphasis on the ladies), what'll it be?' he asked. 'We have any kind of hard licker you might fancy. Just name it and we have it.'"

Old Stage Station at San Antonio

—Courtesy of E. W. Darrah

PART SIX

The White Pine Wonderland

Carson City

Three Old Stage Stations

LONG BEFORE Pony rider Bill Talcott found the ore which broke open the Reese River rush and sent prospectors hunting all over Eastern Nevada, other white men had been chasing across White Pine County. Probably one of the earliest, if not the very first, was Major Howard Egan, veteran of Brigham Young's Nauvoo Legion and one of the party which accompanied him across the prairies in the van of the Mormon migration.

Egan was a busy scout and must be given chief credit for proving that the mid-state trail was a shorter and faster way between Utah and California than the Humboldt route.

He had gone with a party over the Spanish Trail to California to drive a herd of livestock back to Utah. Being anxious to find a better northern way than the dreaded Humboldt, he had returned across what now is the mid-state route, mapping in his mind the various landmarks.

It is entirely fitting that the Egan Mountains and Egan Canyon should bear his name on Nevada's maps today, although there is nothing now left of the Egan Canyon Pony Express and stage station of the 'Sixties except maybe a few scattered rocks. When the stage line was later established, Egan became superintendent of the Salt Lake division and his two sons became pony express riders and then stage drivers.

Life was merrily busy along this Indian-infested trail for the next decade, or until the construction of the railroad eliminated the overland stage line.

The stations in Nevada, as compiled in Root and Connelly's *The Overland Stage to California* began on the present Utah border at Prairie Gate, 1436 miles west from Atchison, Kansas—the starting point. The last station on the western border near Lake Tahoe was Friday's, 1843 miles west of Atchison. This made the Nevada link of the trail 407 miles long. (It is 402 miles across U. S. 50 today from the Utah border to Spooner's summit at Tahoe.)

From east to west, the stations with the mileage between them, were: Prairie Gate 18, Antelope Springs 13, Spring Valley 12, Schell Creek 12, Gold Canyon (Egan) 15, Butte 11, Mountain Spring 9, Ruby Valley 12, Jacobs Wells 12, Diamond Springs 12, Sulphur Springs 13, Roberts Creek 13, Camp Station 13, Dry Creek 10, Cape Horn 11, Simpson's Park 15, Reese River 12, Mount Airey 14, Castle Rock 12, Edwards Creek, 11, Cold Spring 10, Middle Gate 15, Fairview 13, Mountain Well 15, Still Water 14, Old River 14, Bisby's 11, Nevada 12, Carson 14, Genoa 11, and Friday's.

Some of them grew into important places—one, Carson City, became the state capital and one of the five county seats in the group. The other stations which ascended to county seat status were Jacobs Well, later Jacobsville; Stillwater, Dayton and Genoa.

Although Egan had proved his point that the route across the middle of Nevada was shorter and better, the government still insisted on doing it "officially." This resulted in Captain J. H. Simpson of the Topographical Engineers, with a party of 64 men, departing from Camp Floyd, south of Salt Lake City, on May 4, 1859, to survey the "southern," as it was dubbed, trail. He reported that his party "crossed the Great Basin in a general course south to west to Genoa and returned on August 5."

Captain Simpson, in his official report, *The Shortest Route to California*, claimed the result was the opening of a wagon road which lessened the distance to San Francisco "a trifle over two-hundred miles," considerably over-optimistic, and claimed it "immediately . . . became the postal route." Simpson also reported "emigrants to California have used it ever since." That parade, of course, diminished with the completion of the Central Pacific in 1869.

Two of the early White Pine area stations, Schell Creek and Egan Canyon, later had mining "booms" of their own. Schell Creek became a busy station after Senator Gwin of California prevailed on Russell, Majors and Waddell to extend the Overland Stage Line, already running from St. Joseph to Salt Lake City, on to the West Coast. It was an eating stop and frequently an overnight halt.

Indians were so troublesome that troops were sent out early in the 'Sixties to protect the travelers and mails. For some reason the name of the station then became Fort Schellbourne. Later, after the Indians were subdued and faded back with the encroachment of civilization, the "Fort" portion was pretty much dropped from general usage. Today you'll find it near the top of "Schellbourne" Pass in the north end of the "Schell Creek" range of mountains, about 40 miles north of Ely.

A stage trip was no picnic for the passengers with clouds of alkali dust, freezing cold in winter and stifling heat in summer. There were other problems, too. Floods at one time created a swamp three miles wide at the upper end of Steptoe Valley between Schellbourne and Egan. Water stood six inches deep over soft, sticky clay. Passengers hired Indians to carry their baggage and also to carry the women, at forty dollars apiece, in "sedan" chairs. These were constructed of cottonwood poles with a sling made of burlap sacks, four braves lugging the contraption. Some of the hoop-skirted gals got dunked when an Indian stumbled or slipped. Reports indicate that braves did this intentionally to hear the women squeal.

This wet winter created other problems, too. Bulky freight was left at Schellbourne because the stages couldn't go through the muck heavily loaded without getting stuck. One traveler reported upon arrival at Carson City that there were four-hundred bags of mail piled up at Schellbourne awaiting transportation across the bog. They were estimated to weigh around 20 tons, a pile-up that wouldn't be possible to move for several months.

Ransom Young and James Wabb were a couple of young hoodlums from the coast. They had started from San Jose for the East with a pack mule. They fell in with three men who had struck it rich in California placers, sold their claims, bought a herd of 150 horses and were returning to their homes.

The two young rowdies were hired to help herd the horses. Foolishly, the owners let it be known that in addition to the animals they were carrying a large amount of gold. Everything went along well until the day after the party camped at Schell Creek. It moved on, but three days later Indians reported the finding of the three hacked and murdered bodies of the mining men. It was a long way to law-and-order at Austin. Schell Creekers formed a posse and went after the two murderers.

They pulled a very smart detective stunt that the movies apparently haven't heard about yet. The posse hitched up an empty stage coach and went after them, riding in it instead of on horses. The pair were thus trapped unawares a couple of stations farther east and returned in the coach to Schell Creek.

Young broke down and confessed, blaming the hatchet killings on Wabb. A "trial" was held, they were led to a plank scaffold beside the graves of their victims and hung. Young made a speech full of "advice to young men" to steer clear of crime. Wabb contented himself with cursing his captors loudly until the traps were sprung.

An Irish prospector named James McMahon discovered an ore-bearing ledge in 1871 and Schellbourne immediately burst into bloom with a minor boom. W. J. Forbes, the old Humboldt editor who was running the Hamilton *Inland Empire* at the time, carted in a batch of type and a press and started a newspaper, the Schell Creek *Prospector*. It was short-lived, being published from July, 1872, to the following January.

That's about as long as the town lasted; the Cherry Creek boom drew the miners to its richer ores. Actually, most of the boom buildings which had been erected at Schellbourne were carted overland to Cherry Creek on the other side of Steptoe Valley.

The next Pony Express and stage station west of Schellbourne was Egan Canyon, called Gold Canyon in the station list as given, but re-named for Mayor Egan, who was superintendent of the stage line west of Salt Lake City.

Egan was a lonely station and isolated. A tale of an Indian attack survives the days before gold was discovered in 'Sixty-three. One morning the station keeper, Mike Holden, and "Slim" Wilson, a rider waiting for his next relay, found themselves surrounded by an armed band of Indians. The expressmen began firing but the Indians steadily advanced, finally capturing them when they ran out of ammunition. The chief demanded, "Bread!"

First, the Indians ate all that was baked, then forced the white men to build a fire and continue baking. All through the day the men turned out bread which the Indians wolfed down. Toward evening the chief ordered them grabbed and said they would be killed as the Indians now had.had enough bread. They were tied to a wagon tongue, which had been stuck in the ground, and the braves began piling dry brush around them. And then, just like in an old-fashioned melodrama, a troop of the U.S. Cavalry came riding over the hill to the rescue. In the ensuing battle eighteen Indians and three soldiers were killed and several others injured.

Key to the arrival of the troops was an eastbound express rider who saw what was happening, turned and rode back for the soldiers he had passed a few miles before. Zane Grey and other authors of western tales didn't have to dream up all their situations—some really happened.

Some historians, including B. F. Miller, old-time White Pine pioneer who wrote his memoirs for the Nevada State Historical Association in later years believed that the first gold found in Nevada was that in Egan Canyon—rather than the Gold Canyon ore. Miller asserted that Indians found gold in Egan in the early 'Fifties and used it to purchase articles from traders and emigrants on the Humboldt Trail. Maybe they did— nobody can be certain.

At any rate, Egan Canyon may have boasted the first ore mill in the territory in the very early 'Sixties. It was installed by a couple of Irishmen, O'Connor and Donohoe, and was powered by water from Egan Creek. Miller declares that gold from the Canyon "virtually financed one of the old-time banks of San Francisco, known as 'Donohoe, Kelly & Company.'"

When the Central Pacific was built, killing the stage runs, Egan Canyon sunk back to quietness until early in the 1870s when the San Francisco financial firm, which had profited from surface operations, reopened the workings with the idea that cheaper ore would be profitable with rail transportation only 100 miles away. Operating the mine and managing the newly erected mill was General William S. Rosecrans of Civil War fame. The company managed to mill out around $350,000 worth of ore before the vein pinched out around 1876, Miller asserted. He should know something about it, he was supplying fuel to the mill during its latter years.

Right after that Egan became a "one-man" town, the pioneer says, as Pat Lagon acquired its only store, one saloon, only boarding house and most of the "rooming shacks." He later sold to Charles Green and the district has since been known as Green's Ranch. The latter was active in politics, winning one seat in the Assembly on a shake of dice after he and his opponent had tied in the voting. He later defeated T. A. Comins, veteran White Pine legislator, by eight votes for the seat in the State Senate.

The next station west of Egan, up the canyon, across the desert and over the hills 35 miles, was Fort Ruby, near the south end of the Ruby Mountains. Col. E. J. Steptoe, for whom the valley was named, had left Salt Lake City September 18, 1854, to seek a shorter way to the west. During the expedition one of his party had tried panning for gold in a stream running down the slope of the mountains. He found no gold but did turn up some beautiful red stones and shouted, "Rubies!" They proved to be garnets—but the name "Ruby" was given the mountains.

"Uncle Bill" Rodgers established a trading post at Fort Ruby in 1859. It quickly became a stage and Pony Express station, later a relay station on the Overland Telegraph.

Nell Murbarger reported in an article in the *Nevada State Journal* that Mr. and Mrs. Roy Harris, owners of the Tognini Ranch, recently had to dismantle the remains of the old stage station at Fort Ruby because it had deteriorated beyond saving after nearly one hundred years. However, other old-time buildings which were standing when "Ruby was the most flourishing and popular stopping place between Salt Lake City and the Sierra Nevada"—according to the *White Pine Inland Empire*—are still preserved on the Harris home ranch.

When Taylor was in its Prime. This fine photo of Taylor from the archives of the Nevada Historical Society shows the Schell Creek Mountain town as it looked during its busiest days—about 1886. Nobody has been found who knows why the flag was flying at half mast in photo.

—Courtesy Nevada State Historical Society.

Cherry Creek, White Pine County, 1898
    —*Courtesy Nevada State Historical Society.*

Ely in 1886
    —*Courtesy Las Vegas Review-Journal.*

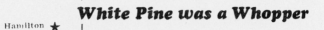

White Pine was a Whopper

HAPPY HAMILTON WAS THE HILARIOUS
queen of the White Pine district. It
was wild and woolly, rough and
ready, opulent and important—but
away off in the eastern Nevada mountains. It boasted 101 saloons, 59
general stores and the "finest and most costly hotel ever built in Nevada,"
at the height of its glory. Yet, today, Hamilton, and all its cluster of surrounding towns, long has been a gone ghost.

It was isolated near the top of a mountain—300 miles east of Virginia
City, 120 miles east and a little south of Austin, its original county seat,
and 140 miles south of Elko, its nearest railroad point. Yet, the White
Pine district attracted a total population in excess of 40,000! Hamilton
was the largest of the group of a dozen towns and had somewhere around
11,000 citizens.

Today only a few tumbled ruins remain, far from the beaten pavement
path. You can reach it two ways—turn south from U.S. 50 on a gravel road
thirty-eight miles west of Ely, or go north from Currant on U.S. 6 to
Duckwater and take the right hand road there. Located right on the
horse thief trail to Pahranagat and the south, it's a wonder the White
Pine district wasn't discovered long before it actually was.

Lying around the 7000 to 10,000 foot level where bitter winter blizzards sweep, the White Pine district became a wild galaxy of busy
bustling boom communities—Hamilton, Eberhardt, Swansea, Menken,
White Pine City, Monte Cristo, California, Mammoth City, Treasure City,
Shermantown, Greenville and Babylon among them.

In two years more than 13,000 mining claims were located. There
were 200 White Pine corporations with a total valuation close to $300,-
000,000 traded on the San Francisco stock exchange. Mills notes that "No
finer tribute to the optimism of the camp can be furnished than this for-
midable array of mining companies who waited only for the sucker—
and his money—before beginning operations. Biggest of all was the Eberhardt Milling and Mining Company, which was capitalized for $12,-
000,000. It was operated by its English owners in the slow but sure
method of British operations.

Contrasting to this was an outfit called the Munro Mutual Mining
and Tunnel Company. This was a New York corporation and apparently
was different than any other Nevada mining company. The outfit owned
several acres near the Eberhardt mine but pursued its operations as
"directed" through daily telegrams from "Madame Munro," a New York
clairvoyant. Strangely, this spiritualistic outfit was incorporated for $10,-
000,000—a third of which was set apart as a working fund. What happened to the rest is anybody's guess. At any rate, this spiritualistic method

of mining engineering didn't prove successful, and when no traces of ore were found through clairvoyancy the operation was abandoned.

Actually, the White Pine district had been so far away from everything that even the mad throng which always was ready to drop everything for a new strike, paid little attention when the newspapers reported in 1865 that Thomas J. Murphy and A. J. Leathers had discovered "paying" silver ore there.

Only a small number of miners came during the following two summers and dug around in a few places. Even these rugged pioneers didn't fancy the winter climate, described later by a German butcher who said, "Ve got ten months vinter and two months damn cold vedder."

The savory odor of a simmering pot of beans triggered the big strike two years later. Various writers have told the yarn in many ways. The one I like best—and which seems to have some basis of fact—is that the beans were cooking on the stove in the cabin occupied by Leathers and Murphy on a late December day in 1867.

Napias Jim, a Shoshone Indian, who never seemed to have enough to eat, couldn't resist the smell of those beans when it came drifting across the frigid winter air. Jim followed the delectable odor, found nobody at home and filled his stomach before departing silently. History fails to record what Leathers, Murphy and their partner, Eddie Marchand, said when they found that their supper had unexplainably disappeared.

Strangely, though, Napias Jim had a conscience—an unusual thing indeed among Nevada's hungry Indians. A few days later he sought out Leathers and confessed, offering the miner a chunk of heavy silver ore to pay for his sins and the beans. Leathers, no tenderfoot at dealing with Indians looked over the rich chunk of chloride, shook his head, probably in disbelief, and casually asked Jim where he had found it. The Shoshone, happy at getting off so easily for gulping down the beans, led the three miners over the blizzard-torn 10,000 foot high summit to the ledge on the east side of Treasure Hill.

The date was January 4, 1868. The location became the Hidden Treasure Mine—which sold less than eighteen months later for $500,000. During that brief period fabulous reports and rumors, which grew richer the further they traveled, had resulted in one of the wildest mining stampedes in all history.

Initially, the first settlement was dubbed Cave City because it was easier to build a habitation by digging a hole into the side of the mountain than it was to obtain other construction materials in this bleak area. But five months after Jim led the original miners to the Hidden Treasure, on May 16, 1868, three promoters, Ed Goben, Henry Kelley and W. H. Hamilton, laid out an optimistic townsite two miles long and one mile wide, naming it for the latter. The very first frame business building, made of rough lumber which cost $300 to $400 per thousand, was erected by June. Its occupant? The King and McIvers saloon!

From there Hamilton zoomed. A school district was set up and by July 1869, when there were already three hundred children in Hamilton, the first school was opened. By autumn of the same year a schoolhouse, costing $4000, had been erected. Action was initiated to have a new county set apart from this southeastern part of Lander. The legislature obliged in the spring of 'Sixty-nine. Hamilton became the county seat. A $55,000 courthouse was built, St. Luke's Episcopal Church rose, the J. B. Withington Hotel, constructed of dressed stone hauled from England around the horn as ballast and freighted all the way from San Francisco, was erected. It was declared to be the most expensive structure built in Nevada up to that time. The *Daily Inland Empire* and *White Pine News* broke into print. Fred Hart, one of Nevada's coterie of great pioneer newsmen, was there; so was a mining engineer named Ambrose Bierce, who had served with gallantry in the Civil War, came west and was writing some brilliant articles as a sideline. A real estate developer named W. F. Walton opened a tract containing 2000 lots, 800 of them zoned for business. The Hamilton Opera House was opened, with Miss Olivia Rand as the first star to appear on its stage. Big prices were paid for whiskey barrels and crates to use for roofs. Henry A. Comins and John C. Russell contracted for half a million shingles to be sawed in the Sierra Nevada and shipped to Hamilton at a freight cost of 13 cents a pound. The *Sacramento Union* printed a Chicago dispatch saying that 10,000 passenger tickets on the Pacific Railrad had been sold in one month to White Pine. All roads to the new district were bristling with overloaded stages and every kind of traffic, including that of the foot. Main Street was filled with business blocks for a solid mile. The town was a mile-and-a-half wide. Store buildings rented for $500 a month. Business lots brought $5,000 to $6,000. Hay sold for $250 a ton and cook stoves for $140.

People came from everywhere and from every direction. Prospectors and miners, promoters and con men, women and kids, cats and dogs, gamblers and painted "girls," Indians and Chinamen, butchers and bakers, every kind and every sort poured into the new golconda.

Yes, sir, White Pine was a whopper!

The *White Pine News*, commenting on the history of the community, was the first to say it: "White Pine . . . was a prodigy. The chloride ores of the Hidden Treasure and the Eberhardt were unknown to the North American continent, and had a parallel only in the Chanarcillo and kindred Chilean mines. Their richness running into the thousands, and their docility extending nearly to assay value, excited the greed or interest of all within hearing . . . inflamed the public to a degree unknown since the birth of California. Electrified by the prospect of interminable wealth, multitudes took their line of march for the new Mecca, and so great was the hegira, that, indifferent to sickness or climate, within the first season some 10,000 or 12,000 men had established themselves in huts and caves 9,000 feet above the sea . . ."

By July 1869 faraway newspapers had correspondents on the scene. "It's a faster camp than the Comstock . . . more men are making and losing fortunes" wrote W. W. Bishop to the *Reno Crescent*.

At the time, Hamilton was claiming 15,000 residents; Treasure City, three miles southeast, 6000; Shermantown, 7000; Eberhardt about the same number and half a dozen other towns each with more population than Carson City has today.

Water, as usual, proved a problem. An unusual feature of the White Pine strike was that snow was so valuable the first year for this needed commodity that some far-sighted miners abandoned their barren mineral claims and filed on snowbanks, "with all their dips, spurs and angles," throwing up snow walls around them to protect their water-producing claims.

The first break in the shortage came in the spring of 1869, when carts appeared to haul water from springs and retail it at eight cents per bucket. Eventually, a water company was organized. It carried better than 1,000,000 gallons a day from a large spring in the mountains through twelve-inch pipe to a reservoir above the town. From the reservoir, a system of twelve miles of pipe supplied the booming town. In 1878 the Eberhardt Mine took over the water system, the population having declined to such a degree it was no longer a feasible operation for the town alone.

The incredible Eberhardt, on top of the same mountain with the Hidden Treasure, was one of the most fabulous, unbelievable strikes in history. Its ore was so rich it was almost pure. Out of one glory hole, seventy feet by forty feet and twenty-eight feet deep at the most, 3200 tons of ore were taken that netted $3,200,000—an average of $1,000 per ton. One silver chloride boulder weighed six tons. Some of the ore ran as rich as $10 to the pound.

After this one hole was cleaned, though, there wasn't any more. Mother Nature had just pushed that lump to the top of the mountain from somewhere deep within.

That's the way it was all over that mountain. A couple of late fall arrivals built a cabin of stones they picked up on their claim. After living in it all winter they milled the stones in the walls and netted $75,000!

Likewise, some of Nevada's notorious highwaymen found the pickings good. Wells Drury in his book *An Editor on the Comstock Lode*, tells about Nickanora, the young Spanish bandit, who was getting tired of being watched and went out to the White Pine country. Soon after he got there the Shermantown mill was robbed of a sack of unretorted bullion. Nick was arrested, but he was acquitted because Judge Jesse Pitzer defended him. After that the stages were stopped nearly every week. Nick and his crowd got so they didn't care so much for big bars of bullion because they were too hard to handle. They preferred to take the stages coming in with coin.

There was no state supervision of gambling as there is now in Nevada—undoubtedly much of it was of the slick-handed variety. This gives us another amusing tale gleaned from some obscure historical book.

It tells of a rotund pedestrian plodding up the Elko road north of Antelope Springs—a long-forgotten rest station located one-and-a-half miles north of U.S. 50 at a point forty-five miles west of Ely. A considerate wagon driver pulled up and offered the plodding man a ride. The driver in relating the tale said the man threw his hat on the ground, jumped up and down on it and shouted, "No! Py golly, I valk. I learn this damfool Dutchman somet'ing . . . I learn him not to go to Hamilton and lose all his money."

Mother Nature played a strange trick. Not only the Eberhardt, but all the White Pine, proved to be just surface float and gave out a short distance underground. Sometime in the past, the earth had split it up in chunks. Returns began to diminish rapidly. The rush of traffic started going out instead of coming in.

Several financial disasters helped checker the history of the community. In the early days of the 'Seventies, shortly after the incorporation of the city, it was discovered that the Mayor, a fellow named Harper, had decamped with most of the municipal funds. Hardly had the citizens bucked up to this situation when it was learned that the county treasurer, a Lewis Cook, had managed to get away with the county's cash. These peculations bankrupted the city for a while and crippled county operations, too. Another blow came when Congress demonetized silver in 1873.

The major disaster of all resulted when Alexander Cohn, owner of a cigar store, decided that fire insurance was a better financial bet than dwindling returns from a deserting population. He started a fire in his store. He made certain the place would burn—he had turned off the valves on the city water supply. Nearly a third of the community burned to the ground. Cohn was sentenced to seven years in the Carson City prison—but that didn't bring back Hamilton, the fire had destroyed all but two business houses.

A *White Pine News* extra editorialized, "The only redeeming circumstances which will give a crumb of comfort amid the surrounding desolation is the spirit displayed by the people . . . There are so many acts of individual sacrifice of their own property, to assist others more in need, that our estimate of human nature has been considerably raised since half past five this morning . . ."

The following year fire, as it did to so many of Nevada's towns, also destroyed most of Treasure City. Wild, wealthy White Pine was withering away.

Hamilton's real death blow came in 1885, when flames again roared down the main streets through the wooden buildings. The town couldn't survive such a fire, since it was just hanging on to a bare life anyway, and it never again regained any of the affluence of its youth. It even lost the county seat to the new town of Ely after this disaster.

John Muir, the noted naturalist, had visited the area in the summer of 1877 or 1878 and wrote in the San Francisco *Evening Bulletin* on January 15, 1879, "Hamilton now has about one hundred inhabitants, most of whom are merely waiting in dreary inaction for something to turn up. Treasure City has about half as many, Shermantown has one family, and Swansea (which had 3000) none, while on the other hand the graveyards are far too full."

One of those who stayed with Hamilton was Louis Zadow. Born near Berlin, he came to the White Pine district in 1867 and opened one of the first butcher shops in Hamilton. After getting well established he returned to Germany and claimed his bride. They returned to Hamilton in 1873 as the decline set in. Zadow expanded his business to general merchandise and trained his five children in the business. For forty years he gave aid to scores of prospectors in their constant search for minerals. He was stricken and died at Hamilton on January 8, 1918 at seventy-five. The widow stayed in Hamilton until 1928, then moved to Ely.

White Pine had been a bonanza while it lasted—but it had lived too high and too fast and died while still too young.

The Hidden Treasure Mine to which Napias Jim had led the first discoverers was high on the mountains and the first settlement to spring up was Treasure City, three miles above where Hamilton sprouted a little later. At first Treasure City was the largest of the White Pine towns.

While Hamilton soon outstripped it and became the hot spot of the entire White Pine mining district, the hilltop community remained a bustling place, full of real sports, right up until the rug was pulled out from under the district's economy by exhaustion of the rich silver float.

When things were booming, some financiers worried because the rich ore from the Hidden Treasure and Eberhardt mines "threatened to glut the world monetary market." The citizens of Treasure City looked down on Hamilton, and the rest of the towns in the valley, literally and figuratively.

The first issue of the *Inland Empire* showed advertisements for forty-two business houses on the hilltop compared to thirty-one from the community down the slope.

The hilltoppers were a gay lot and spent freely, even during the dreary, snowed-in winters when they were isolated except by snowshoe, sled and horses. They paid two dollars for a handful of crackers and twenty-five cents for every bucket of water. There wasn't great demand for the latter, according to all information available, since water was used only for cooking. Whiskey was cheaper.

During at least six months of the year, the mountain-top town had no wheeled traffic at all. Four-horse sleighs made regular trips between Hamilton and Treasure City. The one-way fare for the three-mile trip, either up or down hill was three dollars—a buck a mile. Those without, walked it.

In one respect, Americans then were no different than they are today. They liked to bet on horse races. In her *Ghosts of the Glory Trail*, Nell Murbarger tells of the winter wagering at Treasure Hill. The daily mail stage at Hamilton was always awaited by messengers from Treasure City's rival express-companies, Wells-Fargo and Pacific Union. The riders would snatch their mail pouches and dash away up the three-mile climb. The male citizens of the hilltop town would frantically place bets on the result of the race.

It is described by Miss Murbarger in this manner: "As two dark specks rounded the distant shoulder of Treasure Hill, more gold pieces would make their appearance, and shouts of encouragement and derision would shake the mountain, until the snorting, foaming horses skidded to a stop and a great cry of victory resounded. Dragged from the saddle by triumphant hands, the winning rider would be borne aloft to the nearest saloon; and while hostlers threw blankets over the steaming steeds and walked them up and down Main Street to cool them, victor and vanquished joined in paying and collecting bets, post-morteming the race, and bending the elbow to Bacchus."

One of the best known stories is Fred Hart's oft-told tale of the first July 4 celebration—a joint endeavor of the first arrivals in Hamilton and Treasure City in 1868. The citizens decided they would have a "real, bang-up" Independence Day celebration. Treasure City at the time was the larger and prevailed in the matter of "site" for the program, Hamilton getting the "ball" in the evening. Hart relates that he was made chairman of the committee on "Flag, Music and Ball of the Evening."

"Place" wasn't too difficult for the committee—there was a floor for a frame building under construction. No walls were up, and there was a long drop to the ground at the rear, since everything was built on the slanting hills. They erected a railing to keep anybody from stumbling off. "Music" was taken care of in the person of one Pike, who had a fiddle. Even though it was short a string or two, he could scrape out *Arkansas Traveler* and a couple of quadrilles. The only problem confronting the committee was that Pike had a distinct fondness for the cup and a notoriously low-level of saturation, after which he became incapable of sawing out a tune. A sub-committee was appointed to ride close herd on Pike and limit him to a maximum of three drinks per hour on the eventful day. Further, the ball promised to be an assured success because there actually were two women residents—which meant that the miners wouldn't have to dance every time with each other,

Hart and his committee suddenly realized on the day before the event that the committee had failed in the part about "flag." There wasn't one in either town . . . Austin, nearest spot to procure one, was 120 miles away. The committee was agreed that an Independence Day celebration without an American flag would be a pretty flat affair. It was decided to make one. A search was started for materials. Some white canvas tenting cloth was borrowed from the store, but it had no red or blue material. The hunt went on. A quilt was located on a miner's bunk which had a red calico lining. This was confiscated.

Then the committee ran into a stone wall—there wasn't a piece of blue cloth of any kind in either community. The situation appeared hopeless when a miner rode in and reported that a Mormon family had camped below the hill. Hart and his aides made a hurried visit to them. The woman was pleased to help, but cast cold water on the committee's hopes when she said she was sure they had nothing blue. The day was saved when one of the daughters recalled a "blue veil." It was dug out of the family trunk.

Not only was the flag situation saved, but the arrival of the family increased the feminine population immensely—besides the wife, there were four daughters of youthful ages. They were invited to the celebration, particularly to the ball.

The Mormon parents said they would be happy to accept, except that the children had no shoes and couldn't dance on the rough pine floor barefooted. This impasse was solved with another sub-committee which rounded up spare brogans from miners for the the maidens to wear.

So, the next morning the parade started from Hamilton, led by the flag. Next in line, since there was no band, were two fellows who could whistle *Yankee Doodle*. The Mormon family came next, trailed in line by Pike and his body-guard and the rest of the town. The party marched up the hill the three miles to Treasure City where they were greeted by residents. The combined groups gathered in front of the town watering trough for the "literary exercises." The speaker of the day stood on the trough in lieu of a better platform.

At the finish of the exercises the group unanimously passed a resolution that the flag, waving cheerfully, if maybe a little raggedly, should be preserved permanently as part of the "archives" of the "White Pine Pioneers" which were organized at that time.

Sad to relate, the Society was a bit slipshod in its duty to posterity and wasn't too diligent in preserving its "archives," because one cold night the flag was loaned to a traveler as an extra bed cover and was never returned. Which is too bad, it would be an honored relic in the historical museum today.

History fails to tell us what happened to those Mormon girls in their brogans, nor to Pike. We know that Fred Hart went to Austin and became famous as one of the great editors of the *Reese River Reveille*, organizer of the famed "Sazerac Lying Club," and writer of some of Nevada's finest history.

We do know what happened to Treasure City, though. It just tumbled into oblivion when the White Pine district died.

Maybe the *Inland Empire* wrote the best epitaph when, as population dwindled rapidly, it conscientiously reported the demise of the surrounding suburbs. It recorded the sad happening of the one having the biblical name with the simple statement, "Babylon has fallen!"

California and Pioche in Condor Canyon
—*Las Vegas Review-Journal Photo.*

Manhattan in 1906
—*Las Vegas Review-Journal Photo.*

A Rock Drilling Contest at Goldfield
—*George Stark Photo, courtesy Las Vegas Review-Journal.*

Ely ★

No Cherries, No Creek

WHITE PINE'S BOOMS AND BUSTS OCCURRED in an orderly parade. The original Treasure Hill trove played out just as Robinson Canyon discoveries were made, to be followed one after another by strikes at Cherry Creek, Ward and Osceloa and then Taylor. Many of White Pine's early business leaders and businesses moved in succession from one golconda to another.

The travels of the *White Pine News,* still being published at Ely, are a fine example. It started publication in Treasure City in 1868, moved down the hill to larger Hamilton in 1870 and just a couple of years later picked up type, press and masthead and joined the Cherry Creek rush. When the latter faded and Taylor started to boom in the 'Eighties it joined that stampede and stayed there until 1890, when it followed the county seat to Ely. In 1923, by merger and purchase, the *News* and the *Expositor* of Ely were consolidated into the present Ely *Daily Times,* still thriving eastern Nevada modern newspaper.

One of the first districts to develop after the Hamilton-Treasure Hill area was Robinson Canyon. Mineral City was the principal community, surrounded by settlements at Ely, Lane City, Keystone, Ruth, Copper Flat, Reipetown and Pilot Knob. Mineral City, except for a few cabins, is long gone. Ely is the big town of the area now and the county seat. Ruth recently was picked up, house by house, and moved to a new site by Kennecott Copper Co. to afford room for a new copper mining development at the original townsite.

When later booms elsewhere virtually made a ghost town of the Mineral City diggings there were only three old timers who stayed on— "Uncle" John Ragsdale, A. R. "Buckskin" Watson, and a fellow named Cox.

The trio had but two eyes between them! Ragsdale lost the sight of both eyes in a mine explosion, while Watson and Cox had only one apiece. But the trio had faith in Robinson Canyon.

"We may have only two eyes between us, but we can see good prospects ahead for this camp," Watson declared. "It will be flourishing when grass grows in the streets of Ward and Taylor."

It was very prophetic—in future years the district was to produce more than half of all the mineral wealth ever dug from the ground in Nevada. For many years Kennecott's huge copper operation there has made earlier Comstock and Eureka production seem very small indeed. The huge Liberty open pit, more than a mile long, five-eighths of a mile wide and 500 feet deep, as well as the smaller Veteran and Tripp pits, where work goes on around the clock, are among major tourist attractions of Eastern Nevada. They are just up the hill from the ruins of Mineral City, where a few old cabins still are occupied. They are so vast that

even optiimistic "Buckskin" Watson never could have visualized anything like it when he made his prophetic guess.

The next strike after the Mineral City flurry was at Schellbourne, but
that one died quickly when rich ore was turned up at Cherry Creek, just
across Steptoe Valley four miles north of the old Pony Express trail into
Egan Canyon.

Naturalist John Muir left a graphic record of just how gold-hungry
prospectors deserted one diggings for another when word of a new strike
spread. Muir stopped at Schellbourne during one of his visits to Nevada.

"I asked one of the few lingering inhabitants why the town was built,"
Muir wrote.

"For the mines," he replied.

"And where are the mines?"

"On the mountains back there."

"Why were they abandoned," I asked. "Are they exhausted?"

"Oh, no," he replied, "they are not exhausted; on the contrary they
have never been worked at all . . . just as we were about ready to
open them, the Cherry Creek mines were discovered across the valley
in the Egan range, and everybody rushed off there, taking what they
could with them—houses, machinery, and all. But we are hoping that
somebody with money and speculation will come and revive us yet."

And there you have an eye-witness record of how Cherry Creek got
its start and Schellbourne its death blow. Mining records fail to show
that anybody ever did do anything about Schellbourne's low grade ore
after that first flurry.

How did Cherry Creek get its name?

Wells Drury, the old Nevada newspaperman, who should have known,
wrote in his *Editor on the Comstock Lode,* "A strike was made in 1872
at Cherry Creek . . . that soon became the leading camp in the district.
As with its namesake in Denver, one can say, 'No Cherry, no creek!' Both
streams have a satanic habit of coming to life, though, in a tearing rage."

However, most recorders credit the name to the fact that the ravines
near the town were said to be full of choke cherries. That sounds quite
logical, since this wild fruit was a cherished article of food to pioneer
housewives who made it into jam and jelly.

Cherry Creek grew rapidly as word of the strike spread. And while
historians may differ on the origin of Cherry Creek's name, they don't
argue at all that it was the real successor to the Hamilton district as
White Pine County's busiest and rip-snortingest mining town from 1872
to 1883.

Production values from its mines have been variously estimated at
between $6,000,000 and $20,000,000, experts differing again. However,
they do agree on the fact that its population exceeded 2000, many of
them emigrants from the Hamilton district.

Many of those who came to Cherry during its boom, stayed to become leading citizens of the county all of their lives. One of them was John Carlson, who was an eighteen-year-old boy straight from Sweden, who couldn't speak a word of English.

Life was bleak for him for a while, being a stranger in a strange land with few around who spoke his language. One of them got him a job driving an ox team hauling timbers to the mines. As soon as Carlson could teach his team Swedish profanity he got along fine on his new job, and soon found life brighter in his new world.

Horse-racing was a favorite sport at Cherry Creek—and one of the most amusing Cherry Creek tales is about the famous contest between the home town favorite, the Star Hill bay, and a nag named Muggins. Cherry Creek sports were ripe for a picking after the Star Hill pony had beaten every horse sent out against it. Pat Keough, a rancher who lived in Butte Valley, a dozen miles west, had seen Muggins, owned by Dan Morrison at Hamilton, beat many faster horses. Keough called on Morrison, with the result that Muggins arrived in Cherry Creek disguised as a pack animal, albeit a pretty sleek looking one. Keough and Morrison encountered little difficulty in rigging a match race with the Star Hill partisans in Cherry Creek's bars.

But Cherry Creek wasn't filled with simpletons, and some of the boys were wary of betting on such an obvious cinch without a little investigating. They quietly slipped into the livery stable and sneaked Muggins out for a midnight workout. The horse proved clumsy and slow.

Reassured by their clever stunt, the Cherry Creek folk "unloaded" on their favorite. They were a sad lot when the race was run—Muggins broke in front and ran away from the Star Hill nag.

Keough, being Irish, couldn't keep his joke. Bets had hardly been paid off when he confessed that he had figured the Cherry Creek folk would attempt just such a secret tryout and had set a trap. He had pulled one front shoe from Muggins and loaded the opposite hind hoof with a weighty pad. As a result Muggins was thrown lopsided in the midnight tryout. During the early hours before the race the horse's regular light shoes had been restored.

The story about target shooting, another favorite sport of early Cherry Creekers, shows us that juvenile delinquency was "popular" then, too. The town's boys followed their elders in the target shooting contests, going so far as to aping them by having a bottle of whiskey handy at their matches. Where did they get it? It was as much a mystery to the adults then as it is today. But they had it, and it led to a couple of tragedies. One of the ten-year-old leaders was Harvey Riley and another was Austin Cannon. One day, buoyed by their forbidden liquor, young Riley bet Austin Cannon that the latter could not shoot a hole through Riley's hat at thirty yards. The distance was spaced out. Cannon shot the hole through Riley's hat all right, but he also shot off a finger of Riley's hand which was holding the hat.

The injured boy was rushed fifty-five miles to Ely to the nearest medical help and the amputated finger soon healed. After he recovered, young Riley wanted to duplicate the feat, and he offered to put a bullet through Max Frank's hat. His shooting wasn't quite as good as Cannon's had been. He put a hole through Frank's chest, taking along part of the latter's lung. This brought about a big campaign against juvenile shooting, and it was forbidden for a long time afterwards.

Frank Crampton, old-time mining engineer, told of an interesting Cherry Creek event in his *Deep Enough*. Crampton was operating the old Exchequer and Imperial during World War I when he created a furore, especially among Cherry Creek's women, in 1920. Crampton found it almost impossible to keep a crew around to operate the mines—they were always spending three or four days going to Ely "to see the girls" and frequently getting hurt in wrecks on the bad roads.

"I had no interest or concern whatever in the morals of Cherry Creek," he wrote. "When necessary arrangements had been made for six girls to come to the Exchequer, I fixed up one of the bunk houses with rooms to rent, set up a small bar, put in a piano and had the floor polished for dancing. Soon the rooms were rented, the girls paid for their room and board and ate in the cookhouse . . . The plan worked, the men stayed home, and the mines gave up ore enough to satisfy anyone . . . the experiment was a valuable one."

Ward, Nevada, in the 1870-80 Era

—*"Casey" Fisher Photo, courtesy Las Vegas Review-Journal*

Three Later Eastern Nevada Towns

WARD WAS ONE OF THE MOST PEACEFUL places in the history of Nevada. Wandering highwaymen found no haven there. Gunmen gave it a wide berth and perambulated on south one hundred miles to Pioche, where they could shoot each other at will. Very clearly, after its start in the 'Seventies, Ward residents showed they wanted no shootings nor stage stoppings in their neighborhood. So, unlike most of the early-day mining towns, its graveyard, for the most part, was occupied by those who died natural deaths.

It is pertinent to note that the graveyard is considerably removed down hill from Ward—the reason given being that the residents had to go that far to find a place where the surface was yielding enough to dig a grave six feet deep without blasting.

Right off the reel Ward citizens showed how they felt about bold, bad boys busting loose in their midst. Two early cases established the pattern. The first one occurred in the first year when the town was shocked by the shooting to death of a respected business man named Donahue. It was reported that one of the tough characters who had moved in on the heels of the strike, a fellow named Leighton, had attempted to squeeze money out of Donahue with threats. When the business man refused to be bluffed, the bad man apparently laid in wait and gunned him as he walked down the street.

The shooting caused a considerable flurry in the community but, unlike other mining towns, there wasn't any widespread outcry for a lynching. However, the following morning when citizens awoke they found Leighton's body swinging from the limb of a tree.

The treatment worked well. Others of his ilk silently drifted away from Ward.

It wasn't until about a year later that Ward had its first stage holdup —a very common thing on the Nevada roads of those days. This seems a bit odd, too, since the town was on the busy and heavily traveled highway from Pioche to the railroad at Wells and also got traffic from Eureka, and the west, going to and from the Lincoln County boom town.

A stage was approaching Ward in the fall of 1877. Suddenly it was brought up sharply when bullets whistled past the ears of the driver and messenger, the noted Eugene Blair. The latter took aim, dropped one of the masked bandits, John Carlo, in his tracks and wounded the other, J. Crawford, as he ran away. The latter was caught later, tried, convicted and sent to prison. That ended stage holdups in the vicinity.

Another early shooting, which was the sensational news of Ward for some time, was the killing of the city marshal, Nelson Heuston, by Tim Finnigan in a dance hall flareup. The excitement started when Finnigan's gun fell from his pocket and went off. This caused some of the females in the joint, including "Shoofly, Minnie Gilmore, Big Mouth Anna and other denizens," to flee, calling upon Heuston to save them.

The latter came, demanding that Finnigan surrender his gun. When the officer raised his club, as if to strike Finnigan, and later fired and killed him.

Trial was held at Hamilton, and when testimony showed that Heuston previously had threatened to kill Finnigan if the latter "didn't quit drinking, or leave town," the jury found the slayer not guilty. But Ward's reputation was established permanently as a good place for bad men to avoid.

In recent years the area has been established as a State Park. This was done especially to save the six beehive ovens located two miles south of the townsite which still are in good state of repair. A rich strike was made there in the mid-'Seventies. The Martin White Company built two smelting furnaces and a twenty-stamp mill in the next couple of years.

Their activation brought about the founding of the town in 1876. Following the pattern of other Nevada towns, a rush of mineral-hungry miners and prospectors came. Within a year Ward claimed 1500 residents.

Located about midway on the main road between Pioche and Wells, Ward soon boasted more than the usual number of commercial establishments in most towns of the size. Like Austin, on the old stage road, it was an overnight stop for travelers, being one of the early Nevada towns to cash in on the tourist trade.

One of the favorite stops was at the Carnahan Ranch, where a Mrs. Conners was the well-liked cook whose meals had a wide reputation. Mrs. Conners, a widow, was thrifty, and during her years on the ranch she continually added to her string of cattle. In 1876 Carnahan was killed in a hay-mowing accident and Mrs. Conners moved her base of operations fifteen miles south, where she had stables, a stage station and established the main stopping place on the route between Ward and Osceola.

Naturally the place was called Conner's—and today the consolidated route of U.S. 50-93-6, running south from Ely, has to go through "Connor's Pass"—the name having been misspelled by some map makers long ago.

Ward boasted two breweries—more than a fair average per capita in a community of 1500. It also had two newspapers, the *Reflex* and the *Miner*. It listed practically all of the lodges and societies then popular in this western hinterland. .

Ward also was the nearest trading center for the gold town of Osceola, flourishing at the same time about thirty miles east on the western flank of Mt. Wheeler. And therein lies one of the most interesting of the tales about Ward, which furnished the denouement of a classic case of remorse.

A fellow named Charles Keisel was working in the Osceola placer mine owned by John Versan, J. C. Poujade and W. B. Garaghan. The latter two operated a store in Ward. One day when Keisel was working alone he found an unbelievably large nugget. Temptation proved too strong for the miner and he high-graded the big hunk of gold for himself. He skipped out to Ward and located an assayer without too many scruples, who melted down the chunk into small bricks worth $200 apiece.

Developments seem to prove that he was fundamentally honest because late one night he woke Garaghan and sobbed out the entire story, pouring a cascade of the small $200 bars out of his pockets upon the bed. The hoard totalled $4,000 in value—and Keisel said that was quite a way from the total value of the mammoth nugget, since the assayer had retained a large portion as his share in the nefarious smelting deal.

It may have been the largest single gold nugget ever found in Nevada —maybe the largest ever discovered anywhere. Nobody ever will know. Because of the persistent perfidy of man, Osceola's greatest single bid for notoriety was lost forever.

Keisel's conscience-stricken bit of belated honesty came right at a time when the partners were strapped for ready funds. They refused to prosecute, instead giving him one of the $200 gold bars. Later they gave him enough more to make the division of the big nugget equal for the three partners and the finder.

Garaghan, one of the owners, became one of White Pine's most prominent citizens, serving two terms in the legislature. He was attending the funeral of young Yatsie Briggs at neighboring Taylor in the 'Eighties where a newly-arrived preacher from the east was officiating. Following the services the sky pilot berated Nevada and proclaimed that if there were more houses of worship and fewer saloons there would be less crime.

The legislator rallied to defense of his beloved state by asserting there wasn't anywhere near as many criminals in Nevada as in the pastor's New York state—which "is full of churches."

The sky pilot had the final word, though. He retorted, "When a man commits a crime in New York he is generally sent to prison. In Nevada, I understand, he is sent to the legislature."

This wasn't the only time Garaghan came off second best in a contest of vocal quips. The Ward merchant was campaigning for county treasurer in 1888 and invited drinks for the house in the bars as he made a campaigning round. Among those who trailed him from saloon to saloon was a notorious and worthless old soak.

At one place Garaghan, during his remarks, dropped his hand on the shoulder of the tippler, saying "my good Democratic friend here." This aroused the old souse, who shook his head and said, "Oh no, you got me all wrong. I'll admit I'm dirty and ragged and worthless and look like a Democrat. I've fallen pretty low, but thank God not that low. I'm a Republican!"

It is evident that Ward was a lively, peaceable little town while the ore lasted and probably died about the time richer strikes, including the big copper find, were made in the Ely area. Then, like so many of its brethren, it just faded away.

Osceola, one of Nevada's few worthwhile placer towns, was a long-lived spot on the southwest flank of Sacramento Pass, near the eastern border of the State.

Osceola was the main supply town for the ranches of eastern Nevada for years, and its postoffice, opened March 26, 1878, continued to serve its customers until December 15, 1920. Through the years a few hopeful placer hunters have haunted its spectral remains. For years many of its old buildings remained, some being kept in repair by the few faithful who used them as habitations.

But Osceola virtually became a real ghost town later in the 1950s, when fire destroyed most of the remaining structures, leaving only one store building and a residence still standing.

It's a tenuous thread that tethers Taylor to today's actualities and keeps it from being a complete ghost. Its population for several years was "one"—Claude Gardner. It had dwindled somewhere around 1499 per cent from the 1500 citizens which made it a lively White Pine County town at the peak around the early 1880s. Gardner, who refused to "give up the ghost" grinned when he said he was the mayor, chief of police and also "dog catcher."

Gardner, who came to Nevada as a twelve-year-old in 1899 from his native Pine Valley, Utah, remembers well his visits to Taylor at the turn of the century. He recalls that they were moving many of the houses from the then-dead mining town to Ely and Lund, which were booming at that time. As a matter of fact, Taylor had a brief reincarnation during World War I. A mill was built and some ore processed, but it was short-lived. The ruins of the mill are now among the major remains of the Schell Creek range town.

The town got its name from one of the prospector discoverers, Taylor and Platt, who found galena ores carrying free milling silver and a small amount of gold in July 1872. The claims were purchased by the Martin White Company of Ward in 1875.

Along about this same time, Indian Jim Ragsdale—named after Jim Ragsdale, prominent blind citizen of Mineral City—led some prospectors to the site of the Argus. He'd seen plenty of float in the ravine leading from it and decided to cash in on the craving of the white man for mineral. The beneficiaries of his discovery gave Indian Jim $500 and a team of horses, which he proudly drove for years. W. G. Lyons, Robert Briggs and W. N. McGill found the Monitor, and others located the Hixom. The Taylor boom was on.

Actually, Joseph Carothers is given credit for its real growth. He went to Canton, Ohio, where he interested heirs of the Aultman estate which furnished money for the development of the Argus. A mill was built, at what is now known as Comins Lake. The Monitor owners built another mill at the mouth of Steptoe Creek.

When the snow melted in the spring of 1884 the first shipment from the Monitor was valued at $4,993.98—maybe they should have tossed on a couple of more pieces of ore and made it $5,000 even.

Silver was quoted at $1.29 cents. In 1885 the State Surveyor General reported, "Taylor is producing well and shows excellent prospects."

Taylor's growth was rapid. By December 1886, the Argus had shipped bullion valued at $36,000. The town had three streets, Main, Argus and June. The first newspaper, The Taylor *Reflex*—later the White Pine *Reflex*—is the source for much of the pertinent history of the town.

Like every community worth its salt, the town had a brass band—available and willing to play for any occasion.

The Fourth of July was always one of the big holidays of the year, its arrival signalled with the "firing of anvils," followed by parades, programs and "all night dancing."

Among the customary saloons, one of the most popular was the bistro conducted by Madame Minnie Gilmore, which opened in 1884. Minnie was one of those present at Ward when Finnigan killed Marshal Heuston. She furnished entertainment for her patrons—having gone to Eureka and brought back "a load of terpsichorean acrobats."

The *Reflex* carried on a continuous clean-up campaign and editorially insisted, no doubt correctly, that the probable cause of many deaths was unsanitary conditions. The paper strenuously objected to citizens allowing their pigs to roam loose through the town. When warm summer weather arrived the editor was vehement regarding the disposal of domestic sewage. Outhouses were all built on solid rock, and unless the residue was hauled away frequently the odor became "mighty thick," he ranted. The editor also constantly reminded readers to "broom out their water barrels and get rid of the wrigglers." The town water supply was hauled by Joe Lander and sold for one cent a gallon—which was pretty reasonable, compared to prices in some mining towns, or even to today's cost for domestic water.

Taylor had a school and opera house, both of which stood on the hill between Taylor and North Taylor. It also had a Chinatown, as did all the other mining towns. This one seems to have been a little more uninhibited than some, as the town children could look in windows and see opium smokers sleeping off their jags.

Prices gleaned from *Reflex* ads show that sheets cost thirty cents apiece, tablecloths, twenty-five cents; a dozen towels fifty cents, ditto a dozen pillowcases; a coal oil lamp $1; a straw tick twenty-five cents and a chamber set $1. A fresh egg was about as valuable as a piece of high grade—the price fluctuating from twenty-five cents to one dollar apiece.

Readers probably will enjoy this *Reflex* Christmas shopping advice . . . "If you live on Opera Hill walk downtown. Step into J. F. Cupid's and you'll see some very handsome Xmas presents. If they don't suit you, one door above is the Taylor Drug Store where many nice things in the gentlemen's line are on exhibition. Next comes Dave Felsenthal's where an extensive assortment of Xmas goods are on exhibit. If you haven't found what you want step into Sol Hips. Now if you live in North Taylor reverse your steps. And if you are not satisfied with Taylor's Xmas products then all we can say is, 'You should live in New York, Chicago or San Francisco.'"

The town enjoyed sporadic Indian trouble, too, like the case of Indian Sam, an impecunious beggar. Suddenly he blossomed out in a new pair of boots and quickly dropped $60 in a Chinese saloon game. Questioned, he grinned and said, "Me shoot 'um Doc Clay, shoot 'um Doc Clay's horses, mebbe so shoot 'um Doc Clay's wagon."

He was right, officers found "Doc" Clay dead by the road to Lake Valley. Indian Sam was hauled off to the county jail in Hamilton by Sheriff Morris Lyons.

A few mornings later Taylor mothers were scared, and citizens reached for their guns, when Indian war whoops awoke them. Sheriff Lyons rode out and demanded an explanation from the shouting Paiutes.

The Indian leader explained this way, "You got 'um damn poor sheriff, damn poor jail. Injun go jail, no catchum tickup. Wassa matter now?"

Investigation revealed the cause of the Indian anger. The sheriff and his guards at Hamilton, it appears, had allowed Indian Sam to roam and catch chipmunks for his own meals. He had wandered afar and back to his tribe, where he immediately killed two of his brethren. The other Indians wanted him locked up—and kept locked up.

Taylor's place in Nevada doings lasted about ten years—its post-office, which opened May 9, 1883, gave up on September 9, 1893.

But Claude Gardner was around for years and may yet be—if he's still living.

Barrel House, One of the First Houses in Tonopah

        —Photo Courtesy Las Vegas Review-Journal

"Give Me Back My Yesterdays"

DURING THE RUSH THAT SWEPT INTO EAST-
ern Nevada in the late 1860s after
Indian Napias Jim led Leathers to the
great Treasure Hill strike, around
which Hamilton, Treasure City and a dozen other towns grew up, it was
natural that hungry prospectors would hunt farther for new treasure
troves. As they searched, some of them came into old Fort Schellbourne,
the Pony Express-Overland Stage station town some fifty miles north
of present Ely, for supplies. Since prospectors were a curious breed,
some of them headed south into the then-primitive Schell Creek range,
that high bastion forming the eastern bulwark of Steptoe Valley. There
they found more ore deposits, the Muncy, the original Ruby Hill, Peer-
mont, and Aurum, in Silver Canyon on the northeast flank of the range.

Settlements grew up around all of these discoveries, but Aurum,
where an occasional sheepherder's wagon or wandering range-riding
cowboy are the only signs of population these days, emerged as the
longest-lived and principal town of the lot, even supplanting older
Schellbourne. The Aurum postoffice, which opened April 4, 1881 proves
this. It continued to serve the Spring Valley ranchers and peripatetic
prospectors long after mines had closed until May 31, 1938, when motor-
ized star routes ended its need. This was thirteen years after the Schellbourne office ceased in 1925 and a quarter of a century more than Muncy,
which shuttered its postal window on April 22, 1911. Then, too, Nevada's
Aurum mining district long ago absorbed the older Schell Creek, Ruby
Hill, Silver Canyon and Muncy districts.

Aurum, located in Silver Canyon, according to Albert Erickson, pioneer Schell Creek mining man, hale and mentally-alert in 1961 at 92 in
Milwaukee, "had been quite a camp in the 'Seventies, with a vein of free
milling quartz containing high silver values. A Dr. Brooks, the discoverer
and promoter had a ten-stamp mill built and with a two-shift force of
men drove a number of tunnels and shafts, but in time the ore bodies
pinched out. A heavy snowslide down the canyon buried and wrecked
the buildings and a number of the miners were killed. Although the
buildings were rebuilt, the mines finally were abandoned."

None of this early Schell Creek mountain mining apparently created
much stir in the state or national press, but the area did hit the headlines
as the scene of Nevada's last "Indian War" scare in 1875.

It was natural that some of those in the horde who rushed to the
Nevada strikes, only to be disappointed, would be farmers who could
visualize the great stock-raising possibilities in the lush valleys between
the mountain ranges. Spring Valley, between the Schell Creeks on the
west and the Snake Mountains along the Utah border, quickly was set-

tled with a ranch located at the lower end of nearly every mountain canyon stream.

It is a strange quirk of history, that A. J. Leathers, who was led to the Treasure Hill discovery by Napias Jim in repayment for the pot of beans he had stolen and eaten, should be the key figure in the Spring Valley Indian affair. But he was.

Spring Valley was the land of the Gosh-utes, a tribe potent enough to control the area and subjugate the Shoshones, limiting them to the number of horses they could have and restricting them to certain districts.

In September 1875 a couple of Gosh-utes came to Leathers and his partner at the time, James Tollard, and offered to show them a rich outcropping for $50. Leathers, apparently remembering Napias Jim, agreed. The Indians took them to the location in the Schell Creek range, but when the miners found the ore worthless, they refused to pay. This infuriated the Gosh-utes and they killed Tollard, Leathers escaping and reaching the A. C. Cleveland ranch—one of the best known still—in Spring Valley.

Leathers' story aroused Cleveland. Since the Gosh-utes were all camped in the nearby hills on their annual pinyon nut harvest, the rancher feared they might start a war. He captured an Indian to hold as hostage—then had to shoot him when he tried to escape. Another Indian was killed by some of Cleveland's herders when he refused to give up a rifle.

This fanned things to a fever pitch—the ranchers feared an attack and the Gosh-utes were all upset by the killing of their two tribesmen. The panic was on. Exaggerated and sensational reports spread far and wide. Volunteer troops were raised at Pioche, Eureka and elsewhere and hurried to "the front." Governor L. R. "Broadhorns" Bradley, veteran northeastern Nevada cattleman, familiar with the war potential of the Gosh-utes, telegraphed Major-General Schofield in San Francisco requesting federal troops immediately. Bradley wired that "300 Indians surround Patterson and Cave Valley and . . . appear to be on the war path. My information . . . assured me that I am not misinformed."

A Major Dennis made a forced, hasty march to Spring Valley. All he found was a tribe of peaceful, but frantic Gosh-utes, who assured the officer they just were gathering their winter's stock of pine nuts and wanted no war with the whites. The chiefs surrendered To-Ba, the Indian who had killed Tollard. He was hung. Thus ended Nevada's last "Indian War."

The post office and store at Aurum continued to operate after mining was dead, even if its customers were only the ranchers—those from the Cleveland, Bassett, Odgers, Yelland, Sampson, Cameron, McHugh and Davis spreads.

Just a week before his 90th birthday, March 25, 1959, Erickson wrote some of his memories of the camp's resurgence. He noted that he had a partner named Simon Davis "who had some mines in Silver Canyon producing manganese silver ore that assayed $400-$500 to the ton and was shipped to smelters in Salt Lake City via team to Wells.

"In 1897 Davis and I discovered some manganese outcropping which, when opened up, produced some very high grade silver ore and for two years freight teams were hauling ore to Wells and to the railroad at Oasis, Utah. These mines were sold to a mining company in Salt Lake City which shipped in machinery and a force of men to open up the property with a number of tunnels, but the vein pinched out after a year or two and the property was abandoned."

However, Erickson and Davis were there to stay, and they uncovered some other mines—both alone and together. The Davis group, which was named after Mrs. Erickson, The Clara, the Florence, Iron Duke and the Lucky Deposit, owned by Davis and Ben Sanford, who was Aurum's storekeeper and postmaster, but best of all, the Black Eagle, farther up Spring Canyon. Miners working there insisted that it was "a two-mile walk to the store for tobacco, but five miles back up to the mine."

When the Black Eagle showed real results, Davis gave his friend Erickson the key positon as foreman. "Simon Davis was a fine man," his old partner declared.

With the resurgence of Nevada mining in the first decade of the century the Schell Creek diggings boomed again, miners reopened some of the operations at Muncy, Ruby Hill and elsewhere. There were more than fifty miners working in the area, and most of them brought their families.

"Aurum was not a rowdy camp," the old-timer remembers. "It was a happy little community where the miners and ranchers had good relationships. It had the only post office and store in the area. We had service on three stages a week. Hans Anderson drove the stage and the mail route from Cherry Creek, Pat Keegan was the driver between Aurum and Osceola, and Frank Bassett was the driver of the Ibapah stage. (Ibapah, in Utah, was known as Deep Creek Station on the early Pony Express and stage route.)

The miners always were welcome at homes of ranchers, with Aurum folks always happy to host visitors from the valley when they came for mail and supplies. Consequently, what few social events that were held, brought a mingling of the residents.

"Jimmy Robinson, who lived in Snake Valley, frequently held dances at his ranch and miners and others rode forty or fifty miles to attend them. Robinson and his father-in-law, 'Old Man' Gandy, were hospitable as could be and all were welcome to stay over when they passed that way."

The families lived in log houses with dirt floors. Mrs. Paul Raddatz of Porterville, California, and her brother, Dr. Milton N. Erickson of Phoenix, were born in the Erickson cabin. She described it as follows:

Goldfield Redlight District, About 1906

—Courtesy, the Myrtle Myles Collection.

Merchant Hotel, Goldfield, Nevada

"The house and cabin consisted of two large rooms, plus smaller bedrooms. The back had the mountain for a wall. The floors were dirt and all water was dumped on the floor to keep dust from forming. It did not get muddy due to the mineral content in the dirt."

A Mrs. Cameron was the community midwife when such services were needed—the nearest doctor being at Ely around sixty miles away.

"During the thirteen years Aurum lasted, and while we lived there, he was summoned only twice," Mrs. Raddatz recalls. "Once a miner broke his leg and word was sent by a freighter for a doctor to come. The postmaster, Ben Sanford, set the leg as best he could. Three days later the physician arrived, looked over Sanford's work, pronounced it 'an excellent job,' collected his $125 fee, and departed. The second time the call was sent when a miner began to hemorrhage badly. He died before the doctor arrived, but he charged $125 anyway."

The major "gossip" item of those days was the battle for the hand of a Gosh-ute maiden named Moon Glow. She was the comely daughter of White Cloud, chief of a Gosh-ute tribe. A Paiute, who had taken the name of Charlie Murphy, after an old rancher in the district, decided that Moon Glow was the girl for him. Complications arose, Rance Ward, a miner, also wanted her. Mr. and Mrs. Erickson remember it as the "big fight" of Aurum's history. There were no holds barred, both men were badly battered, but Charlie Murphy won, and Ward went down the trail to other diggings.

Charlie and Moon Glow had six children and the Paiute would fight anybody who referred to his wife as "a squaw." He stubbornly insisted always, "She no squaw—she wife," the old-timers recall. Mrs. Raddatz also remembers that Charlie had an unusual taste for large red or black ants. "He'd catch them, drown them, pop them into his mouth and chew contentedly, saying 'Me like—all same raisins.'"

Old Bailey was another Indian Mrs. Erickson recalled with a wry smile. He was a venerable member of the Paiute tribe who had been put out to die, as was the custom. But Old Bailey didn't just give up, he built a wickiup and subsisted on berries, snared animals, and what he could beg around the camp.

One day Mrs. Erickson came in from her garden and found him standing in her doorway. She quickly gave him some scraps to get rid of him, since Old Bailey was a source of embarrassment to the women. His attire consisted of a ragged shirt and a pair of chaps, open front and rear—no pants!

One of the family's favorite characters of those days was the irascible Chinese cook they had for a while. He got tangled up in the storeroom once with a skunk, which concentrated its fire on the sack of oatmeal. The Oriental insisted on using the fragrant meal, although the men complained bitterly. The stoic reply was, "Only smell skunk, no taste."

He was the same one who refused all orders of his employers to pick over the dried apples and throw out the wormy ones. His reply was, "Me no look, me cook, skim off worms."

Altogether, through the years up to 1937, a total of $181,948 worth of ore was reported to the Nevada State Bureau of Mines—and this probably was only a small portion of the actual gross. The Black Eagle, the Davis Mines, the Lookout and Grizzly at Ruby Hill, the Grand Deposit at Muncy and the Siegel Consolidated, a couple of miles north of Aurum (discovered in 1902) were the major contributors. True, $181,000 was no great golconda, but was more than just a fragment of the State's production.

As the Erickson children reached school age it was determined that Mrs. Erickson would take them back to Wisconsin. They bought a farm, the miner returning to Aurum during the open months and spending the winters with his family until 1910, when Davis and he sold their remaining interests to a large company. Davis retired to Santa Monica, and Erickson returned to the family, where he operated the farm until he was 74.

On March 25, 1959, the old time Nevada pioneer was feted at his 90th birthday party, photographed for Milwaukee papers and appeared on television. "My wife is 87," he said, "and we have nine living children and we are all in good health and we often talk of the days of long ago when we lived in Nevada. I have lived in four states, Illinois, Wisconsin, Montana and Nevada and I claim Nevada is the most healthy state of all." Chamber of commerce, please copy.

Fortunately, Mr. and Mrs. Erickson were able to return to their beloved Spring Canyon home of a half-century before with their Aurum-born daughter, Mrs. Raddatz, in 1955. "The white-haired man sat tensely erect in the car," Mrs. Raddatz wrote. "His keen blue eyes scanned the mountain range. After forty-five years he was going back to the ghost camp of Aurum where he had mined silver for thirteen years.

"Suddenly he pointed and said sharply, 'That's it, that one with the basalt outcropping.' His wife looked closely and said slowly, 'No, I don't think so.' But the old man clung stubbornly to his decision.

"Shifting the car into low gear, it crawled slowly over a sort of jeep trail and after four miles lurched up a hummock to park at a site where a few old logs remained as mute evidence of a building having once occupied the spot.

"With an alacrity that belied his 86 years, he leaped from the car and excitedly proclaimed, 'This is it, this is the remains of the old stamp mill. See, here is part of a crucible. This is Aurum, Clary.'

"But 'Clary' continued to be skeptical. "It doesn't look right, it's too steep. Where was Anderson's house? No, but wait, show me the cemetery and I'll believe.'

"'To heck with the cemetery,' the old man said sharply, 'I know my mountain.' A bewildered look passed over his face, the look of excitement was dulled as he gazed about and said slowly, 'It's Aurum, but it's changed, our road up to the mines is overgrown, that sheepherder's wagon is sitting in what was Anderson's yard and only a little wall shows the site of the post office. It's my mountain—but the rest is truly a ghost camp.'

"His mood changed again as he gazed across the valley and the eyes brightened as he remarked, 'The red hills, Clary, they are just the same, it's just the man-made things that are gone.'

"Then in a voice deep with emotion, he looked up toward the mountain peak and said, 'Oh God, as I look at these great rock formations, the lush valley, the great pines, I can only say—Give me back my yesterdays! And, if one wish could be granted, I'd like to spend my few remaining years out in a little cabin with this mountain standing guard and listen to winds blow down the canyons and whisper lullabies to make me sleep.'"

And that could serve as benediction for these remembrances of old Nevada.

Blacksmith Bellows, Used When Nevada was Young

—Courtesy White Pine Chamber of Commerce, Ely.

Index

BOOKS OF THE WEST . . . FROM THE WEST